GRAMMAR
FOR LANGUAGE ARTS
TEACHERS

Rosemary Guruswamy

GRAMMAR FOR LANGUAGE ARTS TEACHERS

ALICE CALDERONELLO
Bowling Green State University

VIRGINIA S. MARTIN
Bowling Green State University

KRISTINE L. BLAIR
Bowling Green State University

New York San Francisco Boston
London Toronto Sydney Tokyo Singapore Madrid
Mexico City Munich Paris Cape Town Hong Kong Montreal

Senior Vice President and Publisher: Joseph Opiela
Vice President and Publisher: Eben W. Ludlow
Development Editor: Barbara Santoro
Marketing Manager: Ann Stypuloski
Senior Supplements Editor: Donna Campion
Production Manager: Ellen MacElree
Project Coordination, Text Design, and Electronic Page Makeup: Electronic Publishing
    Services Inc., N.Y.C.
Cover Design Manager: John Callahan
Cover Designer: Joe de Pinho
Publishing Services Manager: Al Dorsey
Printer and Binder: Courier
Cover Printer: Phoenix Color Corps

Library of Congress Cataloging-in-Publication Data

Calderonello, Alice.
    Grammar for language arts teachers / Alice Calderonello, Virginia Martin, Kristine Blair.
        p. cm.
    Includes bibliographical references (p.) and index.
    ISBN 0-205-32527-0
        1. English language--Grammar. 2. Language arts. I. Martin, Virginia. II. Blair,
    Kristine. III. Title.

    PE1112 .C25 2003
    428.2--dc21.   2002067122

Please visit our website at http://www.ablongman.com

ISBN 0-205-32527-0

1 2 3 4 5 6 7 8 9 10—CRW—05 04 03 02

To John, Josh, and Di—my past, present,
and future.
Alice Calderonello

To my parents, Julia and Everett Martin—
who would have been so proud.
And to David, the best of teachers.
Virginia S. Martin

To Kevin Williams and Angela Blair—the two
people who make all things possible.
Kristine Blair

BRIEF CONTENTS

DETAILED CONTENTS

CHAPTER
THREE NOUNS AND NOUN PHRASES   59

CHAPTER
FOUR MORE ABOUT VERBS   108

CHAPTER
FIVE   SIMPLE SENTENCE VARIATION   157

CHAPTER
SIX   INTRODUCING SENTENCE COMPLEXITY: ADVERBIALS, ADJECTIVALS, AND NOMINALS   208

CHAPTER
SEVEN   INTRODUCING ADVERBIALS   226

CHAPTER
EIGHT   INTRODUCING ADJECTIVALS   263

PREFACE

Our goal in writing *Grammar for Language Arts Teachers* was twofold. First, we wanted to provide students with a grammar text that explained concepts in clear, easily understandable terms so that grammar principles would be approachable and accessible. Second, we wanted to directly relate grammar concepts to the teaching of writing. In achieving these two goals, we have produced a unique textbook that provides students with a solid foundation of grammar theory as well as classroom-tested strategies for applying these grammar principles to the teaching of writing. This book is designed not only to broaden students' knowledge of English grammar but also to help students become better communicators, competent users of the English language, and more effective language arts teachers.

APPROACH

As writing instructors, we often heard negative attitudes toward English grammar expressed by our students. We also noticed that many students hadn't learned or didn't remember even the most basic information about English structure—such as how to recognize a noun, a verb, a subject, or a predicate—because they "never liked grammar." This attitude toward grammar became a wall between our students and their ability to grasp concepts that would help them understand the sentence-level difficulties they had in their writing. Recognizing the legitimacy of our students' attitudes toward grammar has not diminished our appreciation of English grammar as a subject matter or our sense of its importance for language users, especially writers. Instead, it has encouraged us to develop and refine strategies, explanations, exercises, and activities that make the grammatical concepts transparent rather than mysterious, simple rather than complicated, and useful rather than arcane.

Grammar for Language Arts Teachers therefore presents a comprehensive overview of English grammar and focuses on only the terms and concepts that can help novice learners attain a coherent understanding of the principles of grammar. To that end, this text avoids highly technical discussions of terminology and detail as well as explanations of subtle distinctions that are inappropriate for students who have no background in grammar. Such details and distinctions, we believe, overwhelm and confuse learners of English grammar by obscuring important relationships between concepts, by blurring significant conceptual distinctions, and by erasing the differences between major concepts and peripheral ones. Instead, *Grammar for Language Arts Teachers* includes subject matter, explanations, and examples that are tailored to an audience of novice learners.

ORGANIZATION

Grammar for Language Arts Teachers is divided into eleven chapters. Chapter One, "Why Study Grammar?" provides an overview of theoretical and pedagogical issues pertinent to language study and teaching. Chapter Eleven, "Grammar and the Writing Process," provides a discussion of pertinent issues related to editing and revising. The bulk of the text, Chapters Two through Ten, provides in-depth explanations of grammar concepts and how these concepts can be applied to the teaching of writing.

Many of the chapters in this text are divided into three parts: Part I—a grammar section; Part II—"Challenges for Writers"; and Part III—"Style, Choice, and Convention." This distinctive structure will benefit students and teachers alike. *Part I* of Chapters Two through Ten devotes particular attention to grammatical concepts that are especially important for English educators; *Part II* integrates the grammatical information presented in Part I with applications to actual teaching and writing situations. This section provides detailed descriptions of remediation strategies that can be used to help students eradicate the most common problems they experience with their writing. *Part III* focuses on the challenges teachers face in helping their students become not just competent but creative writers. This section (included in relevant chapters) provides detailed discussion of the sometimes conflicting relationship of grammar usage, grammar rules, and stylistic choice.

This unique three-part structure enabled us to integrate explanations of important grammatical concepts, discussions of the problems apprentice writers often experience in their writing, and descriptions of pedagogical strategies that will help students remediate such problems and improve their overall writing skills. We also chose to dedicate specific sections of each chapter to focus on these interrelated yet separate issues to give students and teachers the freedom and option of choosing those parts that are most applicable to their educational needs.

The chapters in *Grammar for Language Arts Teachers* present discussions of simple concepts before more complex topics. Where necessary, we briefly review topics treated earlier so that users of the text will not need to return to earlier chapters in order to relate information. Finally, to emphasize our belief in the importance of integrating the study of grammar with other topics and issues, we chose to begin *Grammar for Language Arts Teachers* with a chapter that explains the study of grammar in a broad, cultural context and to conclude the book with a chapter that more fully clarifies the relationship between grammar and the writing process.

FEATURES

To improve students' skills of recognizing, working with, and teaching a variety of language structures, *Grammar for Language Arts Teachers* offers the following features:

- **Streamlined Organization** As noted, to provide instructors with the utmost flexibility and students with effective grammar instruction and practical examples for classroom application, many chapters are divided into three parts: *Part I*, "Grammar Concepts," provides grammar instruction and theory; *Part II*, "Challenges for

Writers," focuses on the common problems novice writers experience with the grammar concepts discussed in Part I, as well as strategies to help eradicate these problems; and in appropriate chapters, Part III, "Style, Choice and Conventions," provides detailed discussion of the sometimes conflicting relationship of grammar usage, grammar rules, and stylistic choice to help students clarify and improve their writing. Together these sections provide complete and sound grammar instruction and useful applications to writing and teaching.

- **Straightforward and Clear Instruction** Sensitive to students' attitudes toward grammar, the text includes straightforward explanations and varied and effective examples to make grammatical concepts clear and accessible.

- **Solid Pedagogical Support** Compelling and numerous exercises conclude each part in every chapter. All chapters include "Exercises for Practice," which help students review and understand the grammar concepts presented in each chapter. Most chapters also include "Exercises for Classroom Application," which ask students to apply grammar knowledge to real classroom situations.

- **An Entire Chapter Devoted to Writing** The last chapter of the text provides thorough and effective discussions on writing as well as revising.

AUDIENCE

Grammar for Language Arts Teachers is written with language arts teachers in mind, but it would also be useful in undergraduate grammar and composition courses for English majors as well as nonmajors.

Because most college students in first-year writing classes are not far removed from high school, instructors in college or university composition programs will also find the information in *Grammar for Language Arts Teachers* both useful and relevant. And practicing teachers of writing in grades K–12, particularly those who work with middle or high school students, may be particularly interested in our reviews of important grammatical principles, our discussions of grammatical structures that cause problems for writers, and our specific pedagogical strategies to remediate those problems. We also occasionally address the challenges that particular grammatical structures pose for nonnative speakers of English. Although *Grammar for Language Arts Teachers* is not intended for current or future English as a Second Language (ESL) instructors, we mention important issues for ESL learners because it has been our experience that many teachers in both precollege and college settings may have such students in their classes.

INSTRUCTOR'S MANUAL

An instructor's manual (ISBN: 0-321-13189-4) that provides helpful suggestions on how to use this textbook, chapter-by-chapter commentary, and an Answer Key for all answers not provided in the back of this book is available for all instructors who adopt this textbook. Please contact your Longman representative to request a copy of this manual.

ACKNOWLEDGMENTS

In producing *Grammar for Language Arts Teachers* we have relied upon many peoples' kind and gracious assistance. Our English 381 students consistently provided us with ideas as we shaped and experimented with materials and approaches. We especially wish to thank Jesse McNaughton, Mary Ann Sweeney and Connie Allison for all of their help with the manuscript. We also wish to thank Bowling Green State University's Information Technology Services for their assistance with disk conversion. In addition, we thank De Winterburn and David Cooper of Helena High School in Montana for sharing stories of their teaching experiences, and especially David for his keen eye in reading some of the manuscript. And finally, we are most grateful to our reviewers for their thoughtful reading of our manuscript and for the very useful suggestions they offered: John G. Barnitz, University of New Orleans; William Eggington, Brigham Young University; Ed Eleazer, Francis Marion University; Bernie Hall, University of Houston—Clear Lake; and Judith Rodby, California State University—Chico.

Alice Calderonello
Virginia S. Martin
Kristine L. Blair

CHAPTER

ONE

WHY STUDY GRAMMAR?

Chapter Preview

Chapter 1 provides an introduction to the necessity of studying language structure. In this chapter you will learn about

- Common approaches to studying grammar and how they relate to the grammar presented in this text
- The relationship between grammar study and writing improvement
- The relationship between language and culture
- The social nature of error
- Important terms and concepts used throughout this text

Do you hate grammar? Are you afraid of it? Have you ever told someone that you are "bad at grammar"? What is it about the study of grammar that intimidates so many people? Technically, the term *grammar* refers to the structure or system of a language, which sounds simple enough. But socially, the term *grammar* can bring up images of diagramming **sentences** or memorizing rules and definitions, as well as confusion and boredom. If asked, many English teachers would explain that the underlying purpose of teaching English grammar in elementary and high school is to equip students with a knowledge of their language necessary for communicating in it easily and well. But often the relationship between **oral** and **written** communication is lost amid the myriad of grammar rules and tests, as well as the anxiety associated with them. True, it is not necessary to have a thorough knowledge of the structure of English for most people to go about their daily lives and perform their jobs. However, for you as a future language arts teacher, it is both necessary and essential. Our aim in this text, therefore, is not only to help you broaden your knowledge of English grammar but also to do so in a way that will help you understand its relationship to the teaching of writing. In this chapter we begin this project by explaining why you are about to spend a good deal of time studying the grammar of English.

Formal grammatical instruction and study—for its own sake and independent of its relationship to writing—has a long history in the Western educational tradition. Yet we don't believe that the goal of carrying on this tradition—or the argument of continuing to teach grammar because "it has always been taught"—is sufficient to justify maintaining this practice. Also, many widely held notions about grammar (for example, the idea that grammar study improves thinking ability) are difficult to prove. Nevertheless, a knowledge of grammar is necessary in order to teach both oral and written communication skills. Indeed, if we didn't believe that language arts teachers needed a solid understanding of grammatical principles as well as a knowledge of how to apply those principles to the teaching of writing, we wouldn't have written this book. To help place the content of this book in context, then, we discuss some of the myths about grammar study, briefly describe some of the benefits that knowledge about grammar can provide to both language arts teachers and their students, and explain some of the various approaches to studying and learning grammar that we use throughout this book.

THE RELATIONSHIP BETWEEN GRAMMAR STUDY AND WRITING IMPROVEMENT

Because the study of the grammar of a language is a serious undertaking that requires one to structure and retain a complex set of information, a widespread belief of long duration is that the study of grammar "disciplines the mind." This notion about grammar—that its study improves the mind's ability to understand, organize, and retain other complex subjects—is in part responsible for the fact that grammar has long been (and still is) a significant component of the K–12 language arts curriculum in the United States, despite the fact that no evidence supports this claim.

Besides the idea that grammar makes the mind more acute and agile, grammar study is thought to accomplish other goals as well. Since the mark of an "educated" person is his or her ability to speak and write using "proper" grammar, it is—and has been—widely assumed that grammar instruction helps students become more effective communicators. In particular, formal grammar instruction has long been thought to be an essential part of writing instruction. Nevertheless, the relationship of a strong knowledge of grammar to the development of writing skills may not be explicit in the curriculum. Perhaps you have experienced this in your own education.

However, despite the widespread notion that grammar study contributes to writing improvement, there is little evidence to support this assumption. For more than forty years, in fact, researchers in writing and language arts have been arguing to the contrary. Perhaps the most widely quoted statement about the relationship between grammar instruction and writing improvement appeared in a monograph published in 1963 by the National Council of Teachers of English (NCTE) titled *Research in Written Composition* (Braddock, Lloyd-Jones, and Schoer). Following an examination of previous research, the authors concluded that

> In view of the widespread agreement of research studies based upon many types of students and teachers, the conclusion can be stated in strong and unqualified terms: the teaching of formal grammar has a negligible or, because it usually displaces some instruction and practice in actual composition, even a harmful effect on the improvement of writing. (37–38)

Although Braddock and his coauthors were unambiguous and emphatic in their assessment of the role of formal grammar instruction, researchers conducted subsequent studies regarding this issue, the most ambitious of which was a three-year longitudinal New Zealand study, "The Rule of Grammar in a Secondary English Curriculum" (Elley, Barham, Lamb, and Wyllie). This study, the results of which were published in 1975, again concluded, like so many others, that isolated grammar instruction has no positive effect on writing quality.

As a consequence of the repeated failure to correlate formal grammar instruction and writing improvement, writing teachers and theorists have advocated for some time an approach to grammar instruction that is often referred to as "teaching grammar in **context**." This approach to grammar instruction suggests that although teachers need to understand English grammar, they don't need to impart all of that detailed, technical knowledge to their students. For example, we do not believe that it is necessary for students to know such terms as *gradable adjectives, deferred prepositions,* or *flat adverbs* (and we don't expect you to know such detailed terms either). Rather, it is necessary for students to know only those terms that help them directly in using the language well. Teaching grammar in context also suggests that grammar is not taught in isolated lessons as an end in itself. Rather, grammar instruction is integrated into and should serve the goals of the broader language arts curriculum. What this means, for example, is that a teacher who uses a contextual approach might not necessarily teach her students *about* the concept of (or the term for) the participial phrase (*e.g., Sitting on the hill, we watched the rocket launch*). Instead, she might help her students recognize this structure if it is causing them difficulty with **fragments** (*e.g., Sitting on the hill. We watched the rocket launch*) or with modification (*e.g., We watched the rocket launch sitting on the hill*). Or she might encourage her students to recognize this structure within different types of **discourse** and practice writing it to produce various stylistic effects within the context of a lesson on style.

APPROACHES TO GRAMMAR

As our preceding discussion suggests, when we refer to a contextual approach to grammar, we are referring to the teaching of grammar within a given context rather than to grammar instruction that takes the form of the memorization of rules without some sort of application—for example, a teacher may focus on **gerunds** (verb + -*ing* used as a noun) when students are using them in sentence fragments. In addition to the timing of the teaching of grammar and the selection of what and how much is to be taught, a teacher's own knowledge of and attitudes toward grammar also play a significant role in how students apply grammar to their writing. A common approach to teaching grammar is to present a set of rules that constitute the "right" and "wrong" use of language. This *traditional* approach to the study of grammar uses as examples language from **formal** situations (considered "the very best use of language") and applies many rules and categories from the study of Latin to the study of English. For these reasons, grammatical rules in a traditional approach are not so much based on how English is actually used but more on theories about how language *should* be used. The rules of traditional grammar are therefore *prescriptive* and result in a self-conscious and judgmental description of one's use of English as "good" or "bad." Standard English, which we discuss briefly in a subsequent section of this chapter and refer to throughout this text, is based primarily on the rules and applications of traditional grammar. When we study traditional grammar, we describe the **constituents** of a sentence as *parts of speech* and limit the range of patterns allowable under the rules of **grammaticality**. Most Americans learn traditional grammar. In this text, too, we use many of the terms and concepts associated with traditional grammar.

In contrast to traditional grammar, which is based on an ideal use of English, *structural* grammar attempts to understand and analyze the language systems and structures that produce coherent, meaningful speech. Because it seeks to understand such systems, a structural approach to grammar tends to look at how language is used and is thus more *descriptive* than a traditional approach to grammar. A structural approach also tends to focus on the systems within a language that users of that language have at their disposal when trying to engage in meaningful communication. Therefore, a structural analysis of language usually begins with the sound system (phonology), graduates to the meaningful parts of words (morphology), and then ends with the stringing of words together in a meaningful pattern (**syntax**). While traditional grammar is the result of rules of one language being imposed on another (in the case of English, the rules of Latin grammar), structural grammar seeks to formulate the rules of a grammar by describing it on its own terms. Structural grammar has been particularly useful in describing languages that do not have a written form, such as certain Native American and African languages. In this text, we apply a structuralist approach whenever we focus on how language is used rather than on how it "should be" used.

A *transformational* approach to grammar takes the ideas and descriptive nature of the structuralist approach several steps further and states that in every language user's mind are embedded the basic rules for producing and comprehending meaningful sentences in that language. These innate rules, most of which children acquire before they start attending school, comprise what transformational linguists call a person's "grammar." Every human possesses this rule set or "grammar" and uses it—without being conscious of the process—to produce and comprehend language. For example, English speakers have in their mental "grammar" the concept of a sentence as well as how a sentence is formed from a **subject** and a **verb**. They also have the rules for how subject and verb can be manifested, what variations in form they can take, what parts may be moved or manipulated or deleted, and so forth.

Because transformational linguistics considers any utterance to be grammatical if it is generated according to a person's innate set of rules, a transformational approach to teaching grammar can explain why **dialects** of a given language, though systematic and **rule-governed**, may not always adhere to standard forms of that language as described in a traditional approach to grammar. In this text, we apply the concepts of transformational grammar by occasionally using a modified form of a tree diagram, particularly in Chapter 10, to explain the relationships of parts of sentences or to illustrate sentence boundaries. We also apply concepts developed in transformational grammar when we talk about native speakers of English being able to recognize the grammaticality of a sentence.

Because we believe there is no one, true, perfect approach to the study of grammar, in this text we mix traditional, structural, and transformational approaches to grammar. Our aim is to help you understand how the various grammatical approaches can enrich or shed light on English grammar so that you can make informed decisions about the teaching and use of it.

THE RELATIONSHIP BETWEEN LANGUAGE AND CULTURE

Another important reason for studying language and grammar is to gain an understanding of the close ties between language and culture. All language varieties reflect in many ways the cultures of the people who speak them. For example, the language of a highly technological culture may have hundreds of words just to describe concepts and objects related to computing and network technology: *computer, software, Internet, ink jet printer, modem, listserv, search engine, URL, Web browser, online, BBS, domain, server, e-mail, FTP, home page, hypertext,* and so on. Likewise, an agricultural culture will have many words that describe different types of crops and livestock, particular weather conditions, tools and implements used in farming, and so forth.

The structure of language is also influenced by culture. That is, besides shaping the scope and nature of the inventory of words in a language, how a concept is perceived or how it is comprehended within the context of a particular culture also influences the structure of language. For example, most speakers of English in the United States don't perceive an apology as a complex or multifaceted concept. Thus they often use such expressions as "I'm sorry" or "I apologize" interchangeably without considering nuances of meaning such as whether or not the expression implies that the speaker accepts responsibility for what has happened (as opposed to merely expressing sorrow and regret). In some other cultures, however, the apology is a significant and complex entity with a number of different expressions to describe the circumstances precisely. As children acquire the structure of a language, they also learn the rules for its use. In other words, as children learn the appropriate structures for expressing particular meanings, they also learn when and how to use these structures appropriately within their own social and cultural context. Thus children who grow up in cultures where the art of the apology is an important social skill learn not only the various words and expressions for different kinds of apologies but also the circumstances in which each type of apology would or would not be appropriate. As the foregoing discussion suggests, then, the culture in which a language develops shapes its structure; this explains, for example, why some languages have a great many structures devoted to expressing apologies while others have relatively few.

Although every human being is born into a language community, no one actually learns to speak "just" a particular language, such as English, French, Chinese, or Arabic. Instead, each human acquires facility with a particular *variety* of his or her language, called a *dialect.* Dialects feature changes from the basic language in terms of vocabulary, pronunciation, or grammar that follow a pattern (in other words, they are *rule-governed*). In both the United States and Canada, for example, many people speak English, but they all speak slightly different varieties (or dialects) that reflect their region (e.g., northwestern British Columbia, central Ontario, western Texas, western Pennsylvania) and their social class. Regional and social dialect differences can influence vocabulary (e.g., *soda* versus *pop, grinder* versus *hoagie* versus *submarine sandwich*), pronunciation (e.g., *greasy* pronounced "greasy" versus "greazy"), grammatical forms (e.g., *I have did* versus *I have done*), and other language behaviors (e.g., cadence, pitch, speed of delivery) in such a way that persons in a particular dialect group can usually tell if someone is an "outsider" just by the way he or she speaks.

Moreover, because the **language variety** associated with educated, middle-class speakers is considered "standard" or normative, grammatical forms, pronunciations, and language variants associated with other dialects are often regarded as "bad" or substandard. Similarly, in a country where more than one language is spoken, the language used by the dominant or most powerful group also is generally considered standard and other languages are discouraged as vehicles for laws, public discourse, national literature, and so forth.

Regardless of the regional or social variety of the language that they speak, humans also learn how to adapt their language to myriad situations of use. Often referred to as *style* or ***register***, this situational variation is what occurs when a person talks one way to parents, another way to an employer, and still another way to a stranger encountered in a grocery store. Register is often described as levels of formality, ranging from informal to formal:

RANDY: *Yo, Bobbo! You going to the…thing tonight?*

BOB: *Yeah, maybe. I might hang out with you guys for a while.*

RANDY: *Later then.*

BOB: *Yup.*

RANDY: *Oh, Professor Bayard. I didn't see you there.*

PROFESSOR BAYARD: *Hello, Randy. Are you ready with your oral report?*

RANDY: *Yes, I believe I am. I hope you enjoy it; I've put in a good deal of work.*

PROFESSOR BAYARD: *Good. Well done. I'll see you shortly then.*

RANDY: *Yes, see you later, sir.*

As this conversation demonstrates, Randy knows to adapt his language forms (e.g., terms of address, length and completeness of his sentences, choice of words) according to the situation. He accommodates his language in one way to his friend, Bob, and in another way to his teacher, Professor Bayard.

Besides referring to levels of formality, register or style can also refer to other types of situational language behavior. Each of the speakers in the conversation example belongs to a number of language use groups, called ***speech communities***, whose members share a consensus regarding language structure, rules for use, and norms for interaction. Professor Bayard, for example, is a Rotarian. When he attends a Rotary Club meeting, he enters another speech community that dictates his language use in that context (specialized forms of address, ***specialized terminology***, meeting formats, etc.). And when he attends his church, where he is a deacon, he enters yet another speech community whose rules dictate how he should address the pastor, when and how to speak during a religious service, how to address parishioners with whom he interacts after the service, and so forth. Randy and Bob are also members of various speech communities. For example, they are both college students, members of the school hockey team, and biology majors.

Like most of us, Professor Bayard and Randy and Bob are also members of—or learning to be members of—a ***discourse community***, which is a type of speech community that emphasizes writing and reading. As you may imagine, an important discourse community for Professor Bayard is the community made up of his professional colleagues. Since Professor Bayard is a sociologist, his discourse community consists of other academic and professional sociologists. As students, part of what Randy and Bob are learning at college is to use language appropriately within the particular discourse communities they hope to join. Both are biology majors, and hence Randy and Bob share with other life science majors common interests in and expectations of language use, both written and oral. Language use within a discourse community is a way of maintaining the community as well as of initiating newcomers. That is, if you are a newcomer to the history discourse community, one of the jobs of your history teachers is to help initiate you into that community by teaching you the language use and other requirements particular to the form of academic communication that is appropriate in that community. As you learn these specifics, you and the teacher are maintaining the standards that apply to the type of research writing that historians do. Another example of a typical discourse community would be a community of professionals such as lawyers or engineers. When functioning professionally, members of such groups routinely practice the rules and conventions of appropriate language use within their community; failure to do so would cause their peers or clients to regard their interactions as inappropriate.

As our brief discussion should make clear, one set of language structures—including grammatical forms—is not necessarily appropriate for every situation. In our judgment, then, the most skillful language users are those who can "read" a context to determine what is appropriate and adapt their language accordingly. They may also have to learn the conventions of language use in this new context in order to adapt. For this reason, effective grammar instruction integrates examination of language structures with discussion of social contexts. That is, it looks at the standard forms and their application according to the purpose of the speaker or writer within a specific discourse or speech community. Therefore, effective grammar instruction also helps apprentice writers understand how to apply concepts to particular situations of use rather than simply to memorize rules.

THE SOCIAL NATURE OF ERROR

Have you ever had a discussion over a point of grammar? Although many language users think they share a consensus with everyone else who speaks their language regarding what does or does not constitute "proper" language use or what is or is not "good grammar," this is not at all the case. Many speakers of standard English, for example, would consider the word *their* in the sentence *Every cus-*

tomer should call now and ask for their own beeper to be perfectly satisfactory, while some would consider the use of the plural **pronoun** *their* to refer to a singular **antecedent** (*every customer*) an error. Moreover, because speakers of English are members of many different speech and discourse communities, what is considered acceptable language use in a particular context in one such community may not be appropriate in another. Consider the following conversation:

NEELA: *So, where was I…? Oh, yeah, I have chose my colors for the wedding.*

ELLIE: *Oh, great. What've you decided?*

NEELA: *I have did the craziest thing! I'm goin' with orange and pink!*

ELLIE: *No way! You're not goin' with no orange and pink. Come on!*

Clearly, within the context of this conversation about a personal topic between two friends who both speak a dialect where "nonstandard" **past participle** and **double negatives** are rule-governed options, the forms *have chose, have did,* and *not goin' with no* are acceptable. That is, in this context, the forms would not be perceived as errors by the speakers.

As you may suspect, then, what constitutes an "**error**" is more of a consensus among speakers than an actual, material fact. This may be a surprising concept to you since traditional grammar dictates that there are actual standards of language that we must adhere to. A traditional approach to grammar also does not teach that error is a social phenomenon that varies with a number of factors, the most important of which is the context in which language use occurs. The notion of context includes a variety of issues such as the medium in which the message is being conveyed (e.g., speech, writing, Internet), the purpose and **audience,** the conventions that might control language use, and the particular language community in which the communication occurs.

Generally (but not always), for example, writing is considered more formal than speech. Therefore, grammatical forms that might be considered appropriate (and not errors) in speech might not be acceptable in writing. For example, speakers might not notice (or not be bothered by) the inappropriate pronoun form *I* in the following sentence: *Between you and I, this election is a waste of time.* In a written context, however, they might consider *I* an error. Similarly, an incomplete sentence (a sentence fragment) is often considered appropriate in casual speech and in some written contexts (e.g., advertisements, fiction) but not in others. Consider the use of fragments in the following three sets of examples. Which ones would you consider errors?

Casual Speech

BETTINA: *So, are you going to buy it?*

TOMEKA: *Buy what? [This is not a complete sentence, but it is not considered an error.]*

Advertisement in a Popular Magazine

This is the car. *The car of your dreams.* Get it. *Now.* [*The car of your dreams* and *Now* are both incomplete sentences that wouldn't be considered errors.]

Laboratory Report

The precipitate was dissolved. In a 3-mole solution. [Because this is part of a formal report, the fragment *In a 3-mole solution* would be considered an error in this context.]

As we suggested earlier, besides factors such as audience, purpose, level of formality, **genre** (e.g., advertisement, fiction, report), and communication medium, the dialect of a language that is used in a particular speech or discourse community also helps determine what is or is not regarded as an error. Persons who regularly use constructions such as double negatives (e.g., *I don't want no weeds in my yard*) or nonstandard verb forms (e.g., *I have chose*) do not consider such forms errors because these constructions are rule-governed variants in the dialect of English that they speak. That is, they are not arbitrary, random, individual "errors" but a predictable, patterned variation on standard English common to a community of users of English.

One such rule-governed variety, or dialect, is **Black English Vernacular (BEV)**, also known as African American Vernacular English (AAVE) or Ebonics. According to J. L. Dillard, BEV has several characteristic language patterns that distinguish it from standard English. One particular distinction is its system of verbs. For example, present and past action may be represented by words within the sentence rather than by adding *-ed* or *-ing* to the verb (e.g., *She go yesterday*). Although we will not detail all of the features of BEV, we do want to mention some other common ones that you may recognize. For example, other distinctions of BEV include the fact that only one verb in a sequence may carry **tense** (e.g., *She took the ball and run with it and throw it.*), the omission of *be* to indicate current action (e.g., *That man talking*), and the use of *be* + verb + *-ing* to indicate a regular action (e.g., *He be smoking every night*). *Be* may also be omitted in sentences such as *She pretty* or *You late*. And in a sentence such as *My brother be sick*, the use of *be* would indicate a long-term illness or a general truth. Speakers of BEV may also drop the *-s* attached to verbs in the third **person** (e.g., *David sing*) or add it to verbs in the first and second person (e.g., *I sees, you sees*). They may also eliminate the relative pronoun (*who, which*, etc.), as in *I know the man plays piano* (as opposed to *I know the man who plays piano*), use different word order in *if* **clauses** (*I know can you stay here* instead of *I know if you can stay here*), or drop or use **prepositions** in nonstandard ways.

As you can see from this short list of distinctive features, BEV dialect has many features that are predictable and rule-governed. What is most important is that teachers recognize this dialect as a language spoken in the home and not label it as "wrong English" or "bad English." Speakers of BEV need first to be introduced to the linguistic expectations the school system has of them and then be encouraged to regard standard English as a means of communicating with a broader and more varied audience. As Dillard emphasizes in writing about one young student whose English was labeled "bad" by his teacher:

> The child was only using his own grammatical system, which is about all we can expect any child to do; and there is no *a priori* reason why we can expect him to know that the school system undervalues his system. Second, a child simply must have some rational exposition of the kind of expectations the school system has of him before he can evaluate his own performance vis-à-vis those norms, and the school system in which this child was studying did not provide such information. (55)

In some ways, working with students who speak a dialect of English is similar to working with students who speak a foreign language in that the speakers may use nonstandard patterns. But in many ways, working with speakers of different dialects is quite distinctive from working with nonnative speakers of English. The primary distinction is that the speakers of a dialect are learning the rules of another dialect of the same language, and the rules that they need to learn and the nonstandard patterns that they use may be predictable from the rules of their first dialect. By contrast, students who are learning English as a second language (ESL) are learning the entire grammar of a new language for the purpose of both speaking and writing in it. Because they are usually from a variety of language backgrounds and at various stages of acquisition, their patterns of errors may be less predictable.

Besides the many aspects of context that determine whether or not a form or construction will be perceived as an error, two other issues are particularly important with respect to writing: the role of the reader and the reader's perception of the writer. Ordinarily, the role of the reader doesn't affect his or her perception of errors within a piece of writing. That is, the usual reader is not looking for errors and therefore doesn't expect to find any. These expectations cause average readers to overlook many errors that they encounter. However, when a reader is playing a role that *predisposes* him or her to look for errors, errors become far more noticeable. For example, a person functioning as a copyeditor and looking for errors will obviously perceive them more readily than when she's reading an ordinary text for another purpose (e.g., reading a recipe in order to make chicken Marengo). English teachers, then, do not read in a "normal" manner when they read their students' papers, and it is quite likely that they perceive far more errors in their students' writing than actual members of the intended audience might.

Not only does the reader's social role affect perception, but his attitudes toward the writer do also. Consider the following construction, for example: *The drums pounded noisily. Causing my pots and pans to vibrate.* The underlined portion might or might not be considered an error, depending on who produced it. On the one hand, if the writer who created the construction is a student who has difficulty recognizing sentence boundaries (that is, what constitutes the beginning and the end of a sentence) and therefore has a tendency to produce sentence fragments and **fused sentences** (two sentences run together without appropriate punctuation), it is quite likely that it would be considered an error—particularly if the reader is an English teacher. On the other hand, if the identical construction appeared in a published work of fiction, most readers would consider it an appropriate, stylistic flourish—and therefore not an error. As this example illustrates, whether readers consider a writer to be competent and experienced influences whether and to what extent they interpret unconventional forms as errors.

Whether or not language users—including readers—perceive errors is a consequence of many factors. What this means for language arts teachers is that they need to help their students study the many contexts in which language is used if they are to become confident writers and stylists.

THE ISSUE OF CHOICE WITH RESPECT TO STYLE AND ADHERENCE TO CONVENTIONS

Because the appropriateness of language use depends on social situation and audience, a writer can select from a variety of language options. The purpose of grammar instruction is to teach students about the choices and options they have as producers of language used for communication. That is, it is most fundamental for students to understand that whenever they write, they do so for a purpose, such as to communicate ideas or information. Once they understand this, they can also understand the importance of making informed judgments regarding style and sentence structure when constructing that communication.

Rather than teaching writing as purposeful behavior and relating instruction in style and grammar to specific purposes in communication, the teaching of grammar has often focused on the memorization of rules and concepts. In a grammar class, there may be little discussion of how grammar relates to the choices students can or must make in relation to the effect they want to create in their writing. Or to express it another way, the attention can be on the *what* (grammar) rather than the *how* (style) or *why* (purpose).

There are indeed many choices writers can make. Sometimes, as we've stated, the choices are determined by the speech or discourse community a writer is in or by the genre he is writing for. For example, when writing a note (a genre) to a sister (a speech community), it may be more appropriate to use a more informal style than when writing to a parent; and when writing to a parent, a more informal style would be used than when writing to a teacher. Also, a writer's style can become prescribed by whether she is communicating with a lawyer, a banker, a specialist, a professor, and so on. Notice in the following examples how the choice of words and choice of sentence structure vary according to the intended audience:

Sister

Edie,

Are you coming over this weekend? Hope so. I really want to see you. Talk to you soon.

Love,
Zelma

Mother

Dear Mom,

I hope you will be able to visit this weekend as we had planned. I'm looking forward to seeing you. Please call me if there's any change in your travel plans. I hope to see you soon.

Love,
Zelma

Teacher

Dear Mr. Erudite,

You and I spoke recently about you visiting my home. I'm writing to ask if you will still be able to visit. Please let me know if this visit will not be possible.

Sincerely,
Zelma Jones

Lawyer

Dear Mr. Barrister,

I am writing to confirm our planned meeting on Saturday at 3:00 P.M. Unless I hear otherwise from you, I will plan my agenda accordingly.

Sincerely,
Zelma Jones

As these examples demonstrate, the style, register, and format of a letter changes according to the audience and the writer's purpose in writing (to confirm, to propose, etc.). While there are certain formalities that apply to the letter-writing form (greeting, signature, etc.), those formalities may vary according to the style of the letter and the writer's purpose. For example, it is acceptable to sign a letter "Love" when writing to a relative or a friend, but it is considered unacceptable under most circumstances to sign a letter "Love" when writing to a teacher, a lawyer, or anyone else outside one's closest circle. In fact, choosing to do so would be an inappropriate choice for the writer because it would be an inappropriate register. Writing to a lawyer or teacher requires a more formal and less personalized register.

As we've discussed, besides the genre in which one is writing, the audience for whom one is writing also affects the way in which one writes. That is, the structure and form writers produce will vary, depending on whether they are writing a love letter, a fictional story, a magazine feature article, a newspaper account of an event, an essay for a teacher, or an article for an academic journal. For example, as you saw in the letter examples, a note or short letter has a prescribed format (it contains a greeting, a signature, etc.), although the choice of words, sentence complexity, sentence types (e.g., the use of **questions**), and level of formality or register may vary according to the audience and situation. Similarly, laboratory reports and other examples of that genre (a report) would require a precise description of a process, most likely in chronological order. An article published in an academic journal describing an experiment would set out the details in a specific format.

In addition to the ways in which genre, audience, and purpose can determine the format and structure of a written text, they can also affect smaller, more localized matters such as sentence structure and word order. For example, in a children's book, the writer may use short, **simple sentences**, whereas for a research paper, the writer may choose longer, more complex sentences. A genre can also affect whether one chooses the active or the passive voice, as in a newspaper article or scientific paper, which are both often written in the passive voice; for example:

Newspaper Article

A woman *was struck* by a car while crossing Elm and Maple Streets at 3:30 Tuesday afternoon. [*Was struck* is in the passive voice.]

Scientific Paper

The chromium *will be contaminated* by the addition of phosphorus. [*Will be contaminated* is in the passive voice.]

Genre, too, can affect word choice in that the writer may express ideas using more **jargon** or genre-specific terminology when writing a research paper or a work-related report than when writing a narrative of events or a magazine article meant for the general public. That is why we can speak of "legalese," "medicalese," and the like.

Indeed, genre, audience, and purpose affect a writer's grammatical choices on every level. In particular, they can determine the level of formality, which in turn affects the grammatical forms a writer chooses to use. Very formal writing, as in a research paper, may dictate that the writer forgo using **contractions** (e.g., *It has been demonstrated* rather than *It's been demonstrated*) and take greater care with such matters as pronoun reference (e.g., *A student needs to read <u>his</u> writing* *aloud* versus *A student needs to read their writing aloud*). Genre, audience, and purpose also dictate the freedom with which a writer might creatively use fragments. For example, while it is acceptable to write a fragment in a letter or in a private diary entry, such fragments may be inappropriate in a formal paper or report.

Finally, genre, audience, and purpose can determine a writer's choice of style. For example, a writer may choose to move an **adverbial** from its typical position at the end of a sentence to the beginning of a sentence because of the nuances this creates within the whole text, as the following two sentences illustrate:

> Certainly, the foregoing data support our conclusion.
>
> The foregoing data support our conclusion, certainly.

In the first sentence, the placement of the adverb *certainly* at the beginning of the sentence makes the sentence more forceful than when it is placed at the end of the sentence. Furthermore, if writers want to create a sense of distance, formality, or objectivity, they may choose to use a variant such as the passive voice (e.g., *The following subjects will be discussed*).

Because we believe that every **apprentice writer** needs not only to learn how to use grammatical forms appropriately but also to develop a specific style, in many chapters of this text we discuss particular stylistic variations of word order, sentence length, and sentence complexity as they pertain to the specific subject of the chapter.

INTRODUCTION TO TERMS AND CONCEPTS

To help students become confident language users, it is important for language arts teachers to be aware of important grammatical concepts and terms. However, equally important is knowing which aspects of grammar are likely to produce the most problems for writers and ways in which grammatical knowledge can help students gain skill and confidence as stylists. Equipped with this information, teachers can then teach grammar within the context of writing instruction rather than as a subject unto itself. And students can learn what they need to know about grammar to become better writers and more confident language users.

To facilitate this approach to grammar instruction, our fundamental principle is the context in which language is used. Thus you will notice as you progress through this book that we do not give attention to details that are mostly of interest to grammarians or linguists (for example, we discuss the concept of adverbials in depth, but we don't focus on the concept of absolutes except in passing). We believe that detailed linguistic information and terminology are not important to an overall basic understanding of English structure. Instead, we will explore and give detailed examples of grammatical concepts and terms that

- Provide teachers with a comprehensive understanding of fundamental sentence structures

- Emphasize basic principles of how language works rather than relying on details and terminology
- Amplify concepts and terms that will aid *students* in learning to avoid errors and become confident writers
- Show the relationships between cultural contexts and how they affect language use

Throughout our text, then, we emphasize the following concepts and terms: form versus function, context, standard English, formality, grammaticality versus appropriateness, and error versus **usage**.

Form Versus Function

In our discussion, *form* refers to grammatical structures in English (noun, verb, etc.), and *function* refers to how those forms are used in a sentence (as a subject, as a direct object, etc.). What a word looks like and how it is labeled (i.e., its form) can vary greatly from how it functions in sentences, and this difference can be confusing for students. For example, most of us have been taught that *in* is a preposition, that *bank* is a noun, and that *swim* is a verb. So we might be puzzled when we come across sentences such as these:

> The ins were arguing with the outs. [*In* is acting like a noun and functioning as the subject.]
>
> You can bank on that. [*Bank* is acting like a verb.]
>
> Swimming is fun. [*Swimming* looks like a verb, but is really a gerund, which acts like a noun.]

We recognize that the difference between form and function may be a new concept for you if you are unused to distinguishing between the two. However, the distinction between form and function is significant because although forms can help us recognize the components that make up sentences, these same forms can also function in different ways in a sentence. For example, the following sentences contain different forms all functioning as subjects:

> Billy is a great jokester. [*Billy* is a noun functioning as the subject.]
>
> The old mountain goat stood at the top of the hill. [*The old mountain goat* is a noun phrase functioning as a subject.]
>
> Whenever you arrive is OK by me. [*Whenever you arrive* is a **noun clause** functioning as a subject.]
>
> Running is a popular form of exercise. [*Running* is a gerund functioning as a subject.]
>
> Running a business takes a lot of work. [*Running a business* is a **gerund phrase** functioning as a subject.]

To forgive is divine. [*To forgive* is an **infinitive** functioning as a subject.]

To travel around the world was Susie's dream. [*To travel around the world* is an **infinitive phrase** functioning as a subject.]

In these seven sentences, seven different forms all function as the subject, and many other forms may serve the same function. Language works the other way around as well: not only can different forms serve the same function, but the same form can serve different functions. Here are some examples:

David loved his dog, Circe. [*Dog* is a noun.]

The sheriff will dog the vandal's tracks. [*Dog* is a verb.]

Alice was dog tired when she returned from Las Vegas. [*Dog* is an adverb.]

As is evident from these examples, it is too simple for any student of grammar to simply look at an isolated word, such as *bank* or *dog*, and identify its form or function outside of the context of a sentence. To do so limits the word and its user. Rather words and word groups must be examined to determine how they function within a particular sentence.

Context

Context is the situation in which language is used. As we explained earlier in our discussion of genre, audience, and purpose, context can determine the choices a writer makes, particularly with respect to grammar. For **novice writers** to learn to use grammar effectively as part of developing their skills as writers, they must learn how to apply grammar to the context of their writing. They must learn that they can make choices of which grammatical structures to use, depending on factors such as the audience they may be addressing or the effect they wish to create, much as an artist chooses brushes and colors when working on a painting.

Many of us have learned to regard grammar as a set of precise rules that apply to all situations and that we must follow. This is a sensitive issue, since our society, and consequently our education system, stresses the importance of using "good grammar" as a sign of both education and social class. We are all sensitive to how we use grammar out of fear of being judged, ostracized, or mocked based on the words and grammatical forms we use. The most prevalent example of this that we've experienced is people's reaction when we tell them we are English teachers: "Oh, I'll have to watch my language" is the inevitable response—and for at least a few minutes the atmosphere may become tense and self-conscious. We are self-conscious because we don't want to be in the position of passing judgment on the speech of others, and they are self-conscious because they don't want to be judged.

While it is true that there are rules of English grammar, which rules are necessary and how they should be applied can change according to the situation. That is, the appropriateness and even the grammaticality of language can vary according to the context in which it is used. The primary function of language is to allow people to communicate. That is why, throughout this book, we present the rules of grammar with an eye toward when and how the rules are used and the problems that student writers encounter in trying to apply rules to everyday language contexts.

Standard English

Being self-conscious in front of an English teacher is a result of believing that there is only one "correct" form of English. While our text does describe the rules that apply to Modern **Standard American English**—that is, English as used by the educated middle class in the United States and represented in the media and in education—we recognize that even within these parameters, there is room for flexibility. One of the facts of every language is that there is one form that is considered a standard form but that all speakers of that language may also deviate from the standard by virtue of where they live (*regional dialect*) or the socioeconomic situations in which they live (*social dialect*). Every language has variety. Thus what constitutes the "standard" form is often determined by the context in which language is being used.

We encourage all teachers of language arts to teach the grammar presented in our text in a way that helps students recognize, honor, and build on their existing dialects, not to replace what already serves them well at home and with their friends. It is a reality that many students use language differently at home than they do at school. If students learn only to use language as it is used in school, their communication skills in other speech and discourse communities have been diminished rather than enhanced.

Formality

Besides matters such as the speech communities to which people belong or the dialects they speak, the formality of a particular situation can also determine what is or is not appropriate grammar. Throughout our text, then, we make the distinction between the formal and informal use of English. Academic writing, for example, is usually more formal than note or letter writing, and the contexts in which writing occurs are generally more formal than spoken contexts.

Grammaticality Versus Appropriateness

Throughout our text, we also make the distinction between what is *grammatical* and what is *appropriate*. When discussing *grammaticality*, we are referring to adherence to the rules that govern standard written English. When discussing *appropriateness*, we are referring to the suitable application of those rules in various contexts. For example, it is quite possible to produce a grammatical sentence that may be inappropriate in a given context. Imagine a person who asks for service in this way: "Pardon me, sir, but I wish to partake of your libations" rather than "Please give me a drink." Similarly, nonnative speakers of English may have learned rules thoroughly and may have memorized extensive vocabulary, but they may not know how to apply this knowledge to the situation they are in. And so such speakers of English may use **slang** when writing an academic paper (which is not necessarily ungrammatical but normally inappropriate) or use formal expressions such as "How do you do?" when meeting a college roommate for the first time (which may seem awkward and inappropriate in the situation). Native speakers, too, must learn the distinction between grammatical and appropriate, especially when developing their writing skills.

Error Versus Usage

Our final important distinction is the difference between error and usage. An *error* is a lapse in grammaticality according to the rules of standard written English. *Usage,* by contrast, is simply how a particular group of people uses language in a given situation or context. For example, although it is ordinarily considered an error in grammar to say "I feel well" (rather than "I feel good") because *well* is an adverb, this construction is an example of acceptable usage in many contexts.

"SIMPLE" SENTENCES

Chapter Preview

Part I presents important concepts regarding simple sentences. In it you will learn

- How to recognize a clause
- How to recognize sentence boundaries, including the differences between simple, compound, and complex sentences
- The components of a subject
- The components of a predicate, including how to recognize the types of verbs and the effect of the verb on the remainder of the sentence
- The distinctions between sentence patterns
- The form and function of words in simple sentences

Part II teaches about the challenges writers can face. In it you will learn about how writers can

- Distinguish between subjects and predicates
- Recognize sentence boundaries
- Use commas appropriately in simple sentences
- Avoid comma splices and fused sentences
- Remediate common problems in using commas

PART I   IMPORTANT CONCEPTS ABOUT
THE SIMPLE SENTENCE

THE SUBJECT AND THE PREDICATE
A Brief Introduction to the Sentence

Learned in 3rd grade

As the title suggests, this chapter is about the simple sentence. We will begin our introduction by way of telling you the components of simple sentences, which we will then explain in more depth in this and subsequent chapters. The largest component of a simple sentence is a clause. Indeed, one clause equals a simple sentence. All clauses—and therefore all simple sentences—must have a *subject* and a ***predicate***. Subjects and predicates are made up of phrases or single words. All phrases are made up of words, and most words are made up of parts of words. A diagram of this relationship, building from the smallest component to the largest, would look something like this:

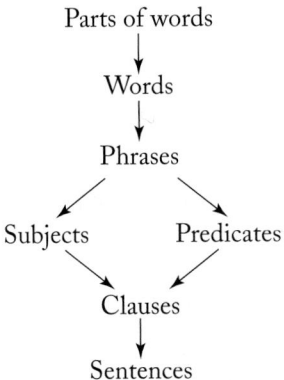

The purpose of this chapter is to familiarize you with how these components work together to create what you as an English speaker recognize as sentences.

However, you may have heard another common definition of the sentence—that it is "a complete thought." In school, you may have read this definition in a textbook or heard it from your teachers. Although sentences express meaning and are therefore related to thought, the definition "a complete thought" isn't very precise. What, exactly, is a "thought"? How do we define whether or not it is "complete"? Consider the following pair of sentences, for example:

I love spinach. But I didn't eat much.

Both *I love spinach* and *But I didn't each much* are grammatical English sentences. Let's look at each one separately for a moment. Cover *But I didn't eat much* with your hand and examine *I love spinach* by itself for a moment. *I love spinach* seems to express a "complete thought"; the sentence is straightforward and can "stand alone" to express its meaning: Someone (*I*) feels a particular way (*love*) about something (*spinach*). Now let's examine the second sentence by itself. Here it is:

But I didn't eat much.

Pretend for a moment that you saw *only* this sentence, that you hadn't read the preceding one (*I love spinach*). Would you characterize it as a complete thought? Frequently, the test for whether a group of words expresses a "complete thought" is if the word group can "stand alone" rather than being "dependent on another sentence for its meaning." Can *But I didn't eat much* stand alone? Without another sentence, how do you interpret *But*? How do you know what *much* means if you don't have more information? As this example illustrates, many grammatical English sentences don't seem to express "complete" thoughts, nor are they able to "stand alone" and not rely on other sentences to be meaningful. Therefore, we must look for another definition of the concept of "sentence," one that does not focus on meaning or content (as "a complete thought" does). When we separate ourselves from the meaning of a sentence, we see its various parts, as we described in the first paragraph of this chapter: a sentence is made up of one or more clauses, and each clause is made up of a subject and a predicate.

As you can see from this definition, we believe that it is more accurate to think of sentences as grammatical units that can be described in terms of their structural components (words, phrases, clauses, etc.) rather than as "complete thoughts." We use the terms *grammatical units* and *structural components* because sentence boundaries (i.e., what constitutes a sentence) are not determined by matters related to meaning alone. Thinking of English sentences in this way— as grammatical units—allows us to understand why *But I didn't eat much* from our example is a sentence even though its meaning depends on another sentence (*I love spinach*). It also allows us to group sentences into categories according to their structural components. All English sentences can be grouped into one of two categories: (1) sentences that are made up of one clause only (e.g., *Brad Pitt is an actor. He is married to Jennifer Aniston.*) and (2) sentences that combine two or more clauses in one sentence (e.g., *Brad Pitt, who is married to Jennifer Aniston, is an actor*).

As we mentioned at the beginning of the chapter, sentences that are made up of one clause only are called *simple sentences* and are the subject of this chapter. But before we begin our examination of them in more detail, let's look briefly at the other type of English sentence, the type of sentence that combines two or more clauses. We will be discussing these kinds of sentences extensively in Chapters 5 through 10. But for now, what's important about these sentences is that they fall into two subcategories: **compound sentences** and **com-**

plex sentences. Here is a chart that shows the categories of English sentences that we've introduced:

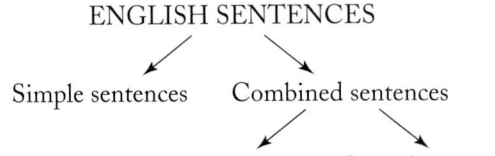

ENGLISH SENTENCES

Simple sentences   Combined sentences

Compound sentences   Complex sentences

Compound sentences are those that combine two or more complete simple sentences into a longer sentence with a connective word such as *and* or *but:*

Simple sentences:	We went to the art museum.
	We saw a Picasso exhibit.
Compound sentence:	We went to the art museum,
	complete simple sentence
	and we saw a Picasso exhibit.
	complete simple sentence
Simple sentences:	I ordered four lobsters.
	I ate all of them.
	I got violently ill.
Compound sentence:	I ordered four lobsters, and I ate all of them,
	complete simple sentence complete simpler sentence
	but I got violently ill.
	complete simple sentence

Complex sentences are similar to compound sentences in that they are made up of a combination of two or more clauses. However, they differ from compound sentences in two distinctive ways. Their first difference is the manner in which they are combined. As the examples show, in a compound sentence one or more sentences may be combined by using such connecting words as *and, but, or,* or *yet*. Complex sentences, by contrast, can be combined in a variety of ways, including making one clause a part of another or by connecting clauses using words such as *because, although,* or *if*. Here are some examples of complex sentences contrasted with compound sentences and simple sentences.

Simple sentences:	Lobsters are expensive.
	I ordered four lobsters.
	I ate all of them.
	I became violently ill.
Compound sentences:	Lobsters are expensive, but I ordered four.
	I ate all of them, and I became violently ill.

relative clause word

Complex sentences: I ordered four lobsters, <u>which are expensive</u>.
one clause as part of another

I became violently ill <u>because I ate all of them</u>.
a clause beginning with *because*

As you can see from this example, *I ordered four lobsters, which are expensive* is complex because the clause *which are expensive* is part of the other clause; it modifies (and is therefore considered part of) the noun phrase *four lobsters,* the **direct object** of the other clause. *I became violently ill because I ate all of them* is a complex sentence because it has a clause connected to another sentence with a specific type of connector, in this case, *because.*

These two sample sentences are indicators of the second distinction between compound and complex sentences. Whereas in compound sentences, separating the component sentences leaves complete sentences that are not dependent on one another to be grammatically complete, separating the sentences in a complex sentence usually leaves one sentence that is grammatically complete (e.g., *I ordered four lobsters*) and another sentence (clause) that is grammatically complete only if it is connected to the first sentence (e.g., *which are expensive, because I ate all of them*). For this reason, a clause that constitutes a simple sentence and so is grammatically complete is referred to as an ***independent clause***. A clause that must be associated with another sentence to be grammatically complete is referred to as a ***dependent clause.*** (You may also know these concepts by the names ***main clause*** and ***subordinate clause***, respectively.) In our complex sentences, *I ordered four lobsters* and *I became violently ill* are independent clauses and *which are expensive* and *because I ate all of them* are dependent clauses. We can therefore state that compound sentences are made up of a sequence of independent clauses, whereas complex sentences are made up of a sequence of independent and dependent clauses. In fact, as you may have surmised by now, all simple sentences are independent clauses. We will return to this concept of "clause" and its role within sentences in the remaining chapters of this book.

Returning to Subjects and Predicates

As you read through our brief description of different types of sentences, you probably noticed that we defined and classified them according to their *structural components*. We have defined simple sentences in this way, as well: *a simple sentence in English is a structure that must have two components or parts, a subject and a predicate.* The predicate is the part of the simple sentence that contains the verb. Let's look at some examples:

1. John / laughed.
   subject   predicate

2. The man / laughed.
   subject   predicate

3. The surprised man / laughed heartily.
   subject   predicate

4. The suddenly surprised man / laughed with his friends heartily.
   subject   predicate

5. The suddenly surprised man with the cowlick / laughed with his friends
   subject   predicate

heartily after their prank.

As these examples illustrate, every English simple sentence must have at least two parts: (1) a *subject* part that contains a subject and (2) a *predicate* part that contains a verb. The examples also demonstrate that the subjects and predicates of simple sentences can be expanded or augmented in a variety of ways and yet the sentences can still remain simple sentences. Simple sentences follow a series of recognizable patterns, which we will discuss later in this chapter. These patterns can be varied in several ways, which we will discuss in Chapter 5.

THE SUBJECT: NOUNS AND NOUN PHRASES

Although *subject* and *predicate* are terms used to describe the two primary components of a simple sentence (or any clause), a variety of forms can function as these two grammatical units. In this section we explain how **nouns** and **noun phrases** can function as subjects.

You may be familiar with the common definition of a noun as "a word that names a person, place, or thing." This is true, but nouns also name ideas and can have many functions within a sentence. Here are some examples of nouns: *potato, happiness, Oklahoma, sister, Mahatma Gandhi, number, zoo, zebra.* Noun phrases are nouns and the words related to them in the sentence (also known as **modifiers**). Here are some examples of noun phrases with modifiers: *a baked potato, intense happiness, my eldest brother, the smallest number, the suddenly surprised man with the cowlick, the apprehensive patient waiting in the other room, his younger sister's big black rabbit on the floor.* Nouns and noun phrases can appear in many forms and serve a variety of functions, which we will explore in greater depth in Chapter 3. For now, we want to focus on the function of nouns and noun phrases as subjects.

As our earlier examples of subjects and predicates showed, nouns can and do sometimes appear alone as single words when they function as subjects. Here are some examples of single-word nouns functioning as subjects; the noun subjects are underlined.

1. <u>John</u> walked to the train station.

2. <u>Tomatoes</u> are growing in the garden.

3. <u>Pennsylvania</u> was his destination.

4. <u>Love</u> is a mystery.

As you can see from these examples, single words as nouns can take many forms. In addition, nouns can name entities such as persons (*John*), things (*tomatoes*), places (*Pennsylvania*), and abstract qualities (*love*).

Not only can nouns in the subject position be single words, but they can also be noun phrases, nouns together with their related words, and other forms acting as nouns. Here are some examples of sentences with noun phrases as subjects (the noun phrases are underlined):

1. <u>The dog</u> was barking loudly.

2. <u>The big cat</u> ran faster after eating.

3. <u>The dog with the pretty brown eyes</u> looked innocent.

4. <u>Singing in the shower</u> is relaxing.

5. <u>To eat</u> is necessary.

6. <u>To eat lobster regularly</u> is extravagant.

7. <u>Behind the refrigerator</u> is where it is disgusting.

As you can see from these examples, the related words in a noun phrase can come before the noun or immediately after it. That is, in sentence 1, *the* comes before the noun *dog,* and in sentence 2, *the big* comes before the noun *cat,* but in sentence 3, *with the pretty brown eyes* comes after the noun *dog.* In addition, some of the nouns, such as *dog* and *cat,* are easily recognizable as such. However, some words functioning in the noun position, such as *singing, to eat,* or *behind the refrigerator,* appear at first glance to be forms of verbs or other structures. Thus not only nouns and noun phrases but other structures as well can act like nouns. We will be discussing the other structures that can act like nouns and how they can function as subjects (and other parts of sentences or grammatical units) in more depth in Chapters 3 and 9.

THE PREDICATE: TYPES OF VERBS AND HOW THEY INFLUENCE SENTENCES

We mentioned at the beginning of this chapter that every complete sentence has two parts, the subject and the predicate. And we have explained that the subject is made up of a noun, a noun phrase, or a group of words functioning in the ways that a noun or noun phrase normally does (e.g., as a subject). The other half of a sentence, the predicate, must always contain at least a verb; however, unlike the subject—which can (but doesn't always have to) consist of only one word (e.g., *Luther* or *potatoes*)—the number of words required in the predicate depends on the nature of the verb.

Most grammar textbooks written for K–12 students suggest that verbs in English can be divided into two categories, *action* and *linking,* and that action verbs can be further subdivided into two types, *intransitive* and *transitive.* Although explaining English verbs in terms of only these three types is something of an oversimplification, we are using these three categories for several reasons. First, they are the ones most commonly used in textbooks and other teaching materials. Second, rarely do students or their teachers in a language arts classroom encounter a situation that requires more detailed knowledge of other terms. Last, these three terms are sufficient for understanding the restrictions and requirements of most verbs and how they function in the predicate part of a sentence.

Intransitive Verbs

Let's look first at **intransitive verbs.** *Intransitive verbs can ordinarily stand alone within a predicate.* That is, they usually don't require any other words to complete the predicate part of a sentence. It is possible, therefore, that a predicate with an intransitive verb can consist of only one word, the verb itself. Here are some examples of predicates with intransitive verbs that consist of just one word:

1. She <u>runs</u>.

2. The baby <u>cried</u>.

3. The dog <u>jumps</u>.

4. The snow <u>fell</u>.

5. The bell <u>rang</u>.

We say that intransitive verbs "ordinarily" and "usually" don't require any other words to complete the predicate because there are some occasional exceptions, as there often are in English. Sometimes, certain intransitive verbs require an **adverb** (either as a single word or word group) to complete them. Consider the following set of sentences (An asterisk * before a sentence denotes that it is considered ungrammatical according to the conventions of standard English):

*1. Yesterday, the baby <u>lay</u>.

2. Yesterday, the baby <u>lay</u> *there.*

3. Yesterday, the baby <u>lay</u> *in its cradle.*

Notice that the first sentence seems odd and incomplete. That is because the intransitive verb *lay* needs an adverb, **adverb phrase**, or **adverb clause** to complete it. In the second sentence, the adverb *there* completes the predicate; in the third sentence, the adverb phrase *in its cradle* completes the predicate.

However, just because intransitive verbs don't ordinarily require additional words to complete the predicate doesn't mean that all predicates with intransitive verbs consist of only one word. Predicates often consist of elective words to add information and to expand the meaning of a sentence. For example,

She <u>ran</u>.

can be expanded to   *prep phrases*

She <u>ran</u> *up the hill.*

This simple sentence can be further expanded to

She <u>ran</u> *up the hill at a brisk pace.*

Although the predicates *ran up the hill* and *ran up the hill at a brisk pace* contain more information about the verb *ran,* in both instances the verb is still intransitive. That is, *up the hill* and *at a brisk pace*—although part of the predicates of their respective sentences—are optional: the verb *ran* can by itself complete the predicate. This is not true of the intransitive verb *lay* in sentences 1–3 about the baby.

Now that we have examined intransitive verbs, let's look at the remaining two common verb types, *transitive* and *linking.* These two types of verbs are different from intransitive verbs because they cannot stand alone. That is, transitive and **linking verbs** must take one or more words to form a complete predicate. Contrast the predicates in the following sample sentences. Note how the italicized words *the cat* and *hungry* in examples 2 and 3 work with the verbs in their respective sentences to complete the predicate.

	subject	predicate
1. Intransitive verb:	The tired, cranky children /	<u>cried</u>.
2. Transitive verb:	The tired, cranky children /	<u>petted</u> *the cat.*
3. Linking verb:	The tired, cranky children /	<u>seem</u> *hungry.*

Transitive Verbs

As sentence 2 illustrates, **transitive verbs** usually depict an action that has an effect on a person or thing. In this example, the verb *petted* implies a stroking action that is directed at an object or entity—in this case, a *cat.* Grammar books often explain that *persons or things "receive" the action expressed by a transitive verb.* Here are some additional examples of sentences with transitive verbs. Note how the underlined word or words in the predicate of each sentence seem to receive the action of or are acted on by the transitive verb:

1. Tabitha *bought* a red <u>jacket</u> for her daughter. [What did Tabitha buy? A *jacket.*]

2. The dogs in the park *ate* <u>all of the meat</u>. [What did the dogs eat? *All of the meat.*]

3. I really *love* <u>shopping for clothes</u>. [What do I love? *Shopping for clothes.*]

When the predicate contains a transitive verb, the word (or word group) that receives the action of the transitive verb is called the *direct object. Transitive verbs, then, are verbs that must take a direct object in order for the predicate to be complete.* Here are some more examples of transitive verbs and their direct objects. Again, note in each case how the direct object works with each transitive verb to complete the predicate.

1. The dog <u>bit</u> *the letter carrier.* [*Who was bitten?*]

2. The letter carrier <u>dropped</u> *her mail bag* on her foot. [*What was dropped?*]

3. The dog <u>grabbed</u> *the mail bag* between its teeth. [*What was grabbed?*]

4. The dog <u>ate</u> *two letters and an L.L.Bean catalog.* [*What was eaten?*]

As you examined the examples with transitive verbs and direct objects, you might have wondered if direct objects—which are persons, things, or ideas—are always nouns or words acting as nouns. The answer is yes. *A direct object must always be a noun, a noun phrase, or a word or group of words acting as a noun.* In the examples, *the letter carrier, the mail bag, two letters,* and *L.L.Bean catalog* are all noun phrases.

To sum this up, there are several ways you can identify a transitive verb and its direct object within a sentence: (1) you can look for an action verb that directs its action at a person, thing, or idea; (2) you can check to see if the object or thing that seems to receive the action is a noun, noun phrase, or word or group of words acting as a noun; or (3) you can try to make the sentence passive. If you can change a sentence into the passive voice, that sentence must contain a transitive verb and a direct object. [This is because to form a passive sentence, the subject and the object of the original sentence are usually reversed.] We will be talking more about the passive voice in Chapter 5, but for now, here are a few simple examples to show you how the passive test might help you determine if a sentence contains a transitive verb with a direct object:

Passive Test

Sentences That Pass the Test

These sentences can be made passive: each contains a transitive verb and a direct object.

Active	Passive
1. Evie bought a new car.	A new car was bought by Evie.
2. The girls ate too many cookies.	Too many cookies were eaten by the girls.
3. The team planted begonias.	Begonias were planted by the team.

Sentences That Fail the Test

These sentences cannot be made passive: each does not contain a transitive verb and a direct object.

Active	Not Passive
4. Jill studied all night long.	*All night long was studied by Jill.
5. Evan seems preoccupied with something.	*With something seems to be preoccupied by Evan.
6. The actors behaved badly.	*Badly was behaved by the actors.

Note: The sentences marked with an asterisk (*) in examples 4, 5, and 6 are clearly odd and ungrammatical when formed as passives; therefore, the sentences from which they were derived do not contain transitive verbs and direct objects.

TRANSITIVE VERBS THAT TAKE INDIRECT OBJECTS.   Besides requiring direct objects, transitive verbs may also require other words to complete the predicate. The most common situation of this sort is when a transitive verb requires both a direct object and an *indirect object.* Whereas the direct object of a transitive verb is the person or thing that receives the action of the verb or is acted on by the verb, *the indirect object is the person or thing to whom or for whom the action is performed.* Here are some examples of sentences with direct objects and indirect objects. In each sentence the transitive verb is in italics.

1. Bill *gave* the book to Mark. [What was given? *The book.* To whom or for
         direct object   indirect object
   whom was the book given? *Mark.*]

2. Bill *gave* Mark the book.
       indirect object   direct object

3. The teacher *bought* <u>tickets</u> for <u>her students</u>. [What was bought? *Tickets.*
direct object   indirect object

To whom or for whom were the tickets bought? *Her students.*]

4. The teacher *bought* <u>her students</u> <u>tickets</u>.
indirect object   direct object

You may have noted that like a direct object, *an indirect object must be a noun, a noun phrase, or a word or group of words acting as a noun.* You may also have noted from the examples that it is not possible to differentiate a direct object from an indirect object by word order. As these examples illustrate, the direct object can either precede or follow the indirect object. However, when the indirect object follows the direct object, it takes the form of an **object of a preposition,** as in sentences 1 and 3. Because the form an indirect object takes can vary, it is not always easy to "eyeball" a sentence that you think has both a direct and an indirect object to determine which is which. Consider this sentence, for instance:

The piano student gave Beethoven's sonatas her fullest attention.

Just looking at this sentence doesn't necessarily yield the most accurate results. It's not easy to tell at a glance if there's both a direct object and an indirect object or to identify each one properly. For this reason, we recommend that this simple test be applied to sentences that seem to contain both a direct and an indirect object. (1) To identify the direct object, once the verb has been located, ask, "What was *verbed*?" With respect to the sample sentence, you would ask, "What was *given*"? The answer is *her fullest attention* (the direct object). (2) Next, to identify the indirect object, ask, "To whom or for whom was it given?" The answer is *Beethoven's sonatas* (the indirect object). Here are some additional examples to illustrate how these two questions help identify direct objects and indirect objects.

The dancers *gave* their instructor a tongue lashing.

Question 1:   What was given? *A tongue lashing* (direct object).

Question 2:   To whom or for whom was the tongue lashing given? *Their instructor* (indirect object).

Lakeesha *bought* a book for her younger sister.

Question 1:   What was bought? *A book* (direct object).

Question 2:   To whom or for whom was the book bought? *Her younger sister* (indirect object).

TRANSITIVE VERBS THAT TAKE OBJECT COMPLEMENTS.   Although it is not common, a third distinction of transitive verbs is that the direct object can require another word or group of words to complete the predicate. This type of word is called an ***object complement.*** *Object complements complete the predicate by describing or renaming the direct object.* For example, in the sentence *Daphne considered her coworker incompetent, incompetent* is the object complement since it describes the direct object, *coworker.* Sentences with object complements arise from two separate ideas. In the case of our sample sentence, the two separate ideas are *Daphne considered her coworker* and *the coworker is incompetent.* It is the verb in the sentence that determines whether these two separate ideas are required to appear together in the predicate. Compared to other types of verbs in English, verbs that can take both direct objects and object complements are relatively few and include such verbs as *consider, name, call, elect,* and *paint.* Here are some sentences containing these verbs that illustrate how they can take both direct objects and object complements to complete the predicate.

1. Daphne *considered* her coworker incompetent.
   direct object   object complement

2. The happy couple *named* their new baby Joy.
        direct object   object complement

3. Chris *called* his friend a slob.
        direct object   object complement

4. The committee *elected* George president of the organization.
        direct object   object complement

5. We *painted* the town red.
      direct object   object complement

Notice that in some instances, as in the sentence *Daphne considered her coworker incompetent,* the verb requires an object complement in order for the sentence to be grammatical or to retain the original meaning. Consider the sentence *Chris called his friend,* for example. In this sentence, the meaning of the verb changes when the object complement is omitted (in this case, the verb implies a telephone call).

Another point to notice about object complements, as the sample sentences illustrate, is that because object complements rename or describe the direct object, *an object complement can be in the form of a noun, a noun phrase, a word or word group acting as a noun, an adjective, or a word or word group acting as an* ***adjective.*** For example, in sample sentences 2, 3, and 4, the object complements are in the form of a noun (*Joy*) and noun phrases (*a slob, president of the organization*). In sentences 1 and 5, the object complements are adjectives: *incompetent* and *red.*

Because object complements appear with a direct object, they are sometimes confused with indirect objects. However, it is usually a simple task to distinguish between the two. (1) To determine whether the word or phrase is an object complement, first look at the word order. In a simple sentence, the indirect object is either in a **prepositional phrase** (e.g., *gave the cake to me*) or placed between the verb and the direct object (e.g., *gave me the cake*). By contrast, the object complement usually follows the direct object and is not in a prepositional phrase (e.g., *painted the house red*). (2) Remember that an indirect object *never* renames or describes the same entity as the direct object; whereas an object complement *always* renames or describes the entity represented by the direct object. Then ask yourself, does the word or phrase refer to the same entity? We illustrate this procedure with a few sample sentences.

Jeanette *gave* Freddie a kiss.

> Question 1:   Does the word or phrase follow the direct object? No.
> Question 2:   Do *Freddie* and *a kiss* refer to the same entity? No.

Therefore, *Freddie* is the indirect object.

Freddie *considers* Jeanette his true love.

> Question 1:   Does the word or phrase follow the direct object ? Yes.
> Question 2:   Do *Jeanette* and *his true love* refer to the same entity? Yes.

Therefore, *his true love* is an object complement.

TRANSITIVE VERBS THAT TAKE ADVERBS OR ADVERB WORD GROUPS.   Although most transitive verbs take direct objects only, those that can take indirect objects or object complements occur with sufficient frequency to warrant discussion. We will also return to discuss this aspect of transitive verbs in Chapter 4. You may be wondering, though, if there are other kinds of special transitive verbs besides those we have discussed here. The answer is yes. There are certain transitive verbs that require both a direct object and an adverb or adverb word group (known as *adverbials*, which we will discuss in greater detail in Chapter 7) to complete the predicate. The two most common verbs of this type are *put* and *set*. Here are some examples of these types of verbs in sentences.

1. The registrar *put* <u>my name</u> <u>on the waiting list</u>.
                  direct object   adverbial

2. My mother *put* <u>the food</u> <u>there</u>.
                 direct object adverbial

3. The librarian *set* <u>the book</u> <u>on the shelf</u>.
                 direct object   adverbial

4. Jim *set* <u>the vase of flowers</u> <u>here</u>.
                 direct object   adverbial

To understand the necessity of using an adverbial with the verbs *put* and *set,* consider these same sentences without them:

1. *The registrar put my name.

2. *My mother put the food.

3. *The librarian set the book.

4. *Jim set the vase of flowers.

Notice how very odd these sentences are without the extra information provided by the adverbials we've omitted. It's quite obvious in these examples that the predicate is incomplete.

Verbs such as *put* and *set* illustrate the reality that there are always exceptions to general rules and principles in any language—including English. Depending on how you present them to your students, exceptions can be horrible obstacles or fascinating tidbits. Our preference is of course to present them as the latter!

Linking Verbs

Unlike transitive verbs, which often display action and are completed by objects of that action, *linking verbs* convey a condition or state of being. Linking verbs are commonly defined as verbs that connect or link a word or words in the predicate to the subject of the sentence. The word or word group being connected to the subject is necessary to complete the predicate and is called the **subject complement.** In the following examples, note how the linking verb (which is underlined) connects (or links) the subject to the subject complement.

1. *Eva* is a *student* now. [*Eva* (subject) = *student* (subject complement).]

2. *Maria Lopez* will remain *president.* [*Maria Lopez* (subject) = *president* (subject complement).]

3. The *children* sounded very *friendly.* [*Children* (subject) = *friendly* (subject complement).]

4. Our *puppy* looks *sad.* [*Puppy* (subject) = *sad* (subject complement).]

Because linking verbs usually convey a state of being or a condition, the verb *be* is the most common linking verb. *Be* is an **irregular verb**, which means that its forms vary (*is, am, are, was, were*). (We will discuss *be* in more detail in Chapter 4.) In fact, if *be* functions as a **main verb** in a sentence, it is always a linking verb, as the following sentences illustrate:

1. Lorna was the winner of the contest. [Links *Lorna* and *the winner of the contest.*]

2. The oldest boys were happy about the outcome. [Links *The oldest boys* and *happy.*]

3. Our dog <u>could be</u> a champion. [Links *Our dog* and *a champion.*]

4. I <u>am</u> hopeful today. [Links *I* and *hopeful.*]

5. They <u>were being</u> silly today. [Links *They* and *silly.*]

As all of the examples of sentences with linking verbs show, a variety of noun and adjective forms can function as the subject complement within a sentence (e.g., nouns, noun phrases, or adjectives). For this reason, subject complements are sometimes divided into two categories—and you may be familiar with the terms used to describe them—*noun complements* and *adjective complements. Noun complements* equal or rename the subject, as in examples 1 and 3: *Lorna = the winner; our dog = a champion.* Adjective complements, which are illustrated in sentences 2, 4, and 5, describe a state of being or condition of the subject of the sentence. How can *the oldest boys* in sentence 2 be described? As *happy.* How can *I* be described in sentence 4 and *they* in sentence 5? As *hopeful* and *silly,* respectively. Although it is important to know that several forms can function as subject complements, in the remainder of our text we do not make the distinction between noun complements and adjective complements. We prefer instead to refer to both types as *subject complements.*

Although most often linking verbs take subject complements that are nouns and adjectives, sometimes when *be* is a linking verb, it can require an adverb (single word or word group) to complete the sentence. (remember that *to complement* means to complete the sentence). Here are some examples of sentences with *be* as a linking verb; note the different types of complements (noun, adjective, adverb):

1. <u>Millagros</u> *is* still <u>my best friend</u>.
      subject   subject complement (noun)

2. <u>The small plants</u> *are* <u>beautiful</u>.
         subject   subject complement (adjective)

3. <u>The small plants</u> *are* <u>outside</u>.
         subject   complement (adverb)

    rarer

4. <u>The small plants</u> *are* <u>in the basement</u>.
         subject   complement (adverbial)

Our discussion to this point suggests that linking verbs can be identified in several ways. First, a linking verb is likely to express what is commonly referred to as state of being (rather than action); for this reason *be* is the most common linking verb. Next, linking verbs also can be recognized because they connect the subject with a word or words in the predicate, the *subject complement.* Finally, in expressing states of being, linking verbs often fall into one of several categories: perception, state of being, and change in state. Here is a representative list of verbs that often express these qualities. Note that many of the verbs in the perception category are related to the five senses.

<u>Perception</u>	<u>State of Being</u>	<u>Change in State</u>
appear	remain	become
look	weigh	get
feel	stand	grow
smell		turn
sound		
taste		
seem		

The following sentences illustrate some of the words in these categories functioning as linking verbs. In each sentence the subject and subject complement are underlined and the verb is italicized. Notice how each verb connects or *links* the subject with the subject complement in each predicate.

<u>Marcia</u> *appeared* <u>ill</u>.

<u>The young men</u> *seemed* <u>unhappy</u>.

<u>That cake</u> *smells* <u>funny</u>.

<u>My former classmate</u> *remained* <u>my good friend</u>.

<u>Evie</u> *stands* <u>five feet tall</u>.

<u>Spot</u> *weighs* <u>too much</u> in the winter.

<u>Bill</u> *grew* <u>very tall</u>.

<u>The small puppy</u> *got* <u>quite large and aggressive</u>.

<u>The five women in our group</u> *will turn* <u>fifty</u> next month.

A REVIEW OF SIMPLE SENTENCE PATTERNS

In our discussion in this chapter so far, we have described some of the forms that can function as subjects and the various combinations that can make up the predicate. In doing so, we outlined the seven basic patterns of simple sentences in English and some of the sentence variations. We would like to review those patterns here in order to make them clearer for you. We list them in the order of their appearance in the chapter and provide an example or two for each pattern. As you look at these patterns, notice how they depend on the type of verb used in the predicate.

Pattern 1: subject + intransitive verb
The sun shines.

Pattern 2: subject + transitive verb + direct object
Robbie hit the ball.

Pattern 3:   subject + transitive verb + direct object + indirect object
The teacher gave the answers to the students.
The committee gave Martin Luther King the Nobel Prize.

Pattern 4:   subject + transitive verb + direct object + object complement
The principal named him head of the department. (noun or noun phrase)
The doctor judged the prisoner competent. (adjective)

Pattern 5:   subject + *be* + subject complement
Beauty is that horse's name. (noun or noun phrase)
That horse is beautiful. (adjective)

Pattern 6:   subject + *be* + adverbial
The iron is in the cupboard.

Pattern 7:   subject + linking verb + subject complement
George became a poet. (noun or noun phrase)
Those pears look delicious. (adjective)

Although there may be idiomatic exceptions to some of these patterns and possible variations—which we will discuss in more depth throughout this text as they apply to the content of each chapter—you will see one of these patterns in every simple sentence in English.

FORM VERSUS FUNCTION AS IT PERTAINS TO NOUNS AND VERBS

So far in this chapter, we have focused on the components of simple sentences. But what about the words used in those sentences that give them meaning? You may from experience think that it is easy to give examples of the different parts of a sentence. For example, if asked for an example of a transitive verb, you might reply, "*smoke.*" In fact, as you were reading in the two preceding sections, you may have inferred that it is possible to make lists of verbs according to whether they are intransitive, transitive, or linking. Here's how such a list might look:

Intransitive	Transitive	Linking
sneeze	meet	be
laugh	sell	look
die	buy	remain
run	smoke	taste

But notice that some of the words that seem to fit so neatly in these columns can in fact be categorized differently. Examine the following examples:

1. Those chimneys *smoke* badly.

2. Some people *smoke* cigarettes.

3. Many people don't like cigarette *smoke*.

In the first sentence, *smoke* functions as an intransitive verb. In the second sentence, *smoke* functions as a transitive verb and takes a direct object (*cigarettes*). In the third sentence, *smoke* is a noun. For another example, consider these two sentences:

1. These cookies *taste* delicious.

2. Good cooks *taste* the food they make before serving it to guests.

3. This food has an odd *taste*.

In the first example, *taste* is a linking verb that connects the subject (*cookies*) to the subject complement (*delicious*). In the second example, *taste* is a transitive verb. What do good cooks *taste*? *The food they make* (the direct object). In the third example, *taste* is a noun.

The point here is that words must be examined within the context of a sentence to determine how they function. Just as many verbs can be transitive, intransitive, or linking, depending on how they are used in a sentence, we must also examine each word or phrase within the context of a sentence to see how it is functioning before we can fit it into a category. For example, notice how the words *love* and *clean* function as a different part of speech in the following sentences:

1. The kids *love* lasagna. [verb]

2. Barnaby wants *love*. [noun (direct object)]

3. The boys *clean* their room weekly. [verb]

4. After dinner, Ellen wants a *clean* kitchen. [adjective]

To further illustrate the point that words must be examined within the context of a sentence, let's consider the case of verbs that consist of two or more words. These verbs are called ***phrasal verbs***, For example, notice the italicized phrasal verb in the following sentence:

They *looked up* the word in the dictionary.

Now consider the use of *look* and *up* in these sentences:

1. She *looked*.

2. She *looked up*.

3. She *looked up the hill*.

The meanings of *look* and *up* in these three sentences differ significantly from the meaning in *She looked up the word in the dictionary*.

When you consider these examples, you might wonder *what kind of word is up?* And you have probably anticipated the answer: *it depends*. In *She looked up the word in the dictionary*, *up* is an essential part of the phrasal verb *look up*, which means "search for." In this usage, *look up* is a transitive verb, and its direct object is *the word*. (What was looked up? *The word*.) In the other three sample sentences, however, *look* is an intransitive verb, which can form a complete predicate by appearing by itself (*She looked*), by being followed by an adverbial (*She looked up*), or by being followed by a prepositional phrase (*She looked up the hill*). *Up* and *up the hill* tell *where* she looked. In this same vein, notice how *out* and *with* function differently in the following examples:

1. The girls next door *go out* <u>with</u> the strangest guys!

2. Flames always *go out* <u>with</u> a flicker.

3. The papers *go* <u>out</u> back.

In the first sentence, *go out with* is a phrasal verb that means "date." In the second sentence, *go out* is a phrasal verb that means "stop burning." It is followed by a prepositional phrase, *with a flicker*, which tells the manner in which the flames *go out*. In the third sentence, *go* is an intransitive verb followed by a prepositional phrase, *out back*. As you can see, the forms of the words *out* and *with*, like the word *up* in the previous examples, function in different ways in different contexts.

As you may have guessed, this ability to function differently according to context can be true of most words. Since we have especially talked about nouns and verbs in this chapter, we want to stress that they cannot be identified outside of a sentence. Many words may look like nouns or may be most often used as nouns, for example, but they cannot be identified with certainty until you see how they are used in a particular sentence. Think about the pairs of sentences in the following examples:

1. You can *bank* on that. [*Bank* is a verb.]
   The *bank* is located downtown. [*Bank* is a noun functioning as a subject.]

2. She likes shopping *in* that store. [*In* is a preposition.]
   The *ins* were angry with the outs. [*In* is a noun functioning as a subject.]

3. He *dogs* her every step. [*Dogs* is a verb.]
   The *dogs* ran wild. [*Dogs* is a noun functioning as a subject.]

4. *Singing* is fun. [*Singing* is a gerund acting like a noun and functioning as a subject.]
   Ernie is *singing* in tomorrow's play. [*Singing* is a verb.]

5. *Yesterday* was very stressful. [*Yesterday* is a noun functioning as a subject.]
   Susan gave me the money *yesterday*. [*Yesterday* is an adverb telling when Susan gave me the money.]

As you can see from these examples, *bank, in, dog, singing,* and *yesterday* can function in at least two different capacities, depending on their meaning in the context of the sentence. Here are more examples of some words that are used both as nouns and verbs. Can you think of some others?

1. John *starches* and presses his uniform daily. [*Starch* is a verb.]
   Lisa put *starch* in the washing machine. [*Starch* is a noun serving as a direct object.]

2. Mark will *scale* the mountain tomorrow. [*Scale* is a verb.]
   Susan used the *scale* to weigh her cat. [*Scale* is a noun serving as a direct object.]

3. Karen *addresses* Christmas cards for her mother. [*Address* is a verb.]
   The *address* is on the envelope. [*Address* is a noun serving as a subject.]

You will recall from Chapter 1 that form versus function is a crucial distinction for language arts students and teachers to understand. *Form* refers to how the words look, and *function* refers to what words do in the context of a sentence. It is worth reiterating that a word in a sentence may appear to be a noun or a verb or a preposition, but we must look at how it functions in that particular sentence to determine what it actually is. As with many other things in life, appearances can be deceiving!

EXERCISES FOR PRACTICE

A. As we've explained, recognizing the structure of simple sentences is not necessarily dependent on meaning. So that you may experience this for yourself, we have provided some nonsense sentences. Following the two examples we provide, see if you can divide the sentences into subjects and predicates. Indicate the separation with a line.

Example: Those norfous beeberhoofers / have deedered the craxflots burzently.

Example: A deezeldemp / was hartooning the crazmips.

1. The borful hugglebumps smitted a dort dragoo.

2. Pobocity crawmed the sizzleswitch ambetly.

3. A mendokit drims each zooey.

4. Cartolilly has fritchened mubbily.

5. These fappy ammosaws frowzed a zort.

6. The prexi was molling.

7. Rorori always toppols at the rilly mubi.

8. Authquills zolled labbly.

9. Three mathlos at the rilly mubment were toppolling.

10. The prexi has fritchen there.

B. The following sentences are ones you may easily recognize as simple sentences. Use a line to separate the subject from the predicate in each sentence.

> **Example:**   The ins / were angry with the outs.

> **Example:**   You / can bank on that.

1. John gave Alice a nice present.

2. The light in the refrigerator went out.

3. The trapeze artist dated the mustached woman.

4. The young lover ran up his phone bill.

5. Writing letters is an enjoyable pastime.

6. Beethoven's music belongs to the classical period.

7. The horticulturist put the vase of flowers on the table.

8. Bert smelled the dinner cooking in the oven.

9. Indecision is the key to flexibility.

10. Nostalgia isn't the same anymore.

C. Identify the subject and the predicate in each of the following quotations by dividing them with a line.

> **Example:**   The results of philosophy / are the uncovering of one or
> another piece of plain nonsense. (Ludwig Wittgenstein)

1. No snowflake ever falls in the wrong place. (Zen saying)

2. Surely joy is the condition of life. (Henry David Thoreau)

3. Ninety-eight percent of the adults in this country are decent, hardworking, honest Americans. (Lily Tomlin)

4. Comedy is simply a funny way of being serious. (Peter Ustinov)

5. All truths wait in all things. (Walt Whitman)

6. The history of the world is the record of a man in quest of his bread and butter. (Hendrik Van Loon)

7. Every book is rewritten by the reader. (Agnes Whistling Elk)

8. To look for miracles is like looking for the end of the rainbow. The rainbow is not painted; it is pervasive. (George P. Conger)

9. You can't know wisdom; you have to "be" it. (Ram Dass)

10. Love unites without casting off the diversity. (Theodosius Dobzhansky)

D.   Determine which of the following newspaper headlines are complete simple sentences (containing a subject and a predicate). Mark the complete sentences with a C. Mark the incomplete sentences with an F. In addition, if the sentence is complete, separate the subject and predicate with a line. If the sentence is incomplete, make it a complete sentence by revising it in any way necessary.

> **Example:**   Smith / cruises to a win. C
>
> Exciting games on tape for viewers. F
>
> *Revised:*   Exciting games <u>are</u> on tape for viewers.

1. Giant power plant to be built near Livingstone

2. Investigators to consider withholding evidence

3. Local reaction to weather mixed

4. Home team rallies for win

5. Setting things into perspective

6. Time to tend to the home court

7. President scolds Congress for leaks

8. Airport to resume local service

9. Army dispatching reserves

10. Congressional leaders hit with lawsuit

E. In the following sentences, identify the verb by underlining it and label it as intransitive, transitive, or linking.

Example: President Lincoln <u>signed</u> the bill. (transitive)

1. The ghost suddenly appeared in front of them.

2. The seamstress felt the softness of the material.

3. She felt sad at the news.

4. The police looked everywhere for the criminal.

5. You look lovely tonight.

6. The students in the classroom seemed serious.

7. The florist smelled the flowers.

8. The flowers smelled sweet.

9. The car sounds funny.

10. The bank teller sounded the alarm.

11. Did you taste the fudge?

12. Yes, it tasted delicious.

13. The wounded soldiers lay on stretchers.

14. He lied to me!

15. They remain friends to this very day.

16. Edna gave her studying all of her attention.

17. The political candidate stood uncontested.

18. We became good friends in high school.

19. All of her wildest dreams came true.

20. Lamar got a new car for Christmas.

21. Julie got careless with the details in her report.

22. Virginia grew tomatoes in her garden last summer.

23. She soon grew tired of eating so many tomatoes.

24. Sue runs a grocery story.

25. The unsupervised children ran wild.

26. The dog has gone crazy over that toy mouse.

27. The relationship turned sour.

28. The man turned the corner.

29. All of the schoolchildren crowded onto the small bus.

30. The crowd made a lot of noise.

F. Identify the sentence pattern of each of the following sentences.

> **Example:**   The ground is all wet.
>
> *Pattern:*   subject + *be* + subject complement

1. Fashion is an imposition. (Golda Meir)

2. She put the silverware in the top drawer.

3. Pink Floyd recorded a CD last year.

4. I'll give you my address.

5. The critics are calling Bruce Willis's latest film silly.

6. The tulips seem healthy.

7. Congress has designated January 21 a national holiday.

8. The juvenile delinquent eventually became a policeman.

9. Martin Luther King Jr. was widely admired.

10. I sent my return to the IRS last week.

G. As you know, verbs can be categorized as transitive, intransitive, and linking. Use each of the following verbs in two of these three ways.

> **Example:**   smoke   He *smokes* cigars. (transitive)
> The oil *is smoking*. (intransitive)
>
> **Example:**   appear   She *appeared* at the game. (intransitive)
> She *appeared* tired. (linking)
>
> **Example:**   feel   She *felt* the fabric. (transitive)
> She *felt* tired. (linking)

eat	ring	grow
dance	get	weigh
smell	look	
sing	remain	

H. Write two sentences for each word listed here. In the first sentence, use the word as a noun; in the second, use the word as a verb.

> **Example:**   dust   My mother hates *dust* in her house.
> (noun: direct object)
>
> Yesterday, I *dusted* the new television.
> (verb: transitive)

crowd	hate	run
bus	smell	mess
love	look	fold
leap	exit	time
jump	book	chase

PART II   CHALLENGES FOR WRITERS

RECOGNIZING SUBJECTS AND VERBS

Since it has been our aim in writing this book to present information about English grammar that is relevant to language arts teaching, you may be wondering if there is a rationale for students being able to recognize subjects and predicates—especially verbs in the predicate—and the sentence patterns they form. There are several reasons why this information is important for student learners. One is that the ability to recognize subjects and predicates is necessary for writers who wish to follow the conventions of **subject-verb agreement,** which is expected in semiformal contexts and in writing. It is also important to be able to recognize subjects and predicates—as well as sentence patterns—in order to be aware of sentence boundaries and punctuate sentences correctly. An awareness of sentence boundaries is particularly important if students have difficulty with **comma splices,** for example. (Do not be concerned if you do not know what a comma splice is; we explain them later in this chapter and return to them in other chapters of this text.)

In recognizing subjects, there are two areas of confusion for students. The first problem area is position. It has been our experience that students often assume that a word that begins a sentence is the subject. For example, in sentences such as

> *Yesterday, I talked to my mother* or *Unfortunately, the box office was closed,*

students may think that *yesterday* in the first sentence or *unfortunately* in the second is the subject simply because the word begins the sentence.

The second type of problem that students encounter when trying to identify the subject of a sentence is that nouns often resemble other parts of speech, such as verbs or adverbs. Therefore, students can often mistakenly select a word that looks like a noun, but isn't, as the subject. Students can also overlook a word that is the subject because it doesn't look like a noun. The problem that students encounter, then, is one of appearance. A common problem involving appearance is when the verb in a sentence looks like a noun, as in these sentences:

1. You can't *railroad* me.

2. Don't *crowd* the animals by the fence.

In both sentences, the verb appears in the same form as the easily recognizable nouns *railroad* and *crowd,* and so the student may too quickly assume that these words are functioning as nouns and therefore as subjects.

A related problem area for students who have difficulty recognizing subjects because of their appearance is when the word functioning as a subject looks like a verb, as in the following example:

Swimming is fun for many people.

In this sentence, *swimming* functions as the subject. However, because *swimming* was derived from a verb form, it resembles a verb, and students may therefore have difficulty recognizing it as the subject of the sentence.

Besides appearing to be a verb, a subject can also occasionally appear in the form of an adverb, adjective, or a prepositional phrase, as in these sentences:

1. *Today* is the first day of the rest of your life.

2. *"Beautiful"* is a common adjective.

3. *Across the street* is where she lives.

In each of these sentences, the form functioning as a subject may easily confuse the student: *Today* appears to be an adverb; *beautiful* appears to be an adjective; and *across the street* appears to be an adverbial phrase. Students who are used to identifying words as subjects (nouns, noun phrases, and words acting like nouns) according to their form may experience considerable difficulty with sentences such as these.

There is one more problem that students often encounter when attempting to identify the subject of a sentence that combines the features of position and appearance. Because the subjects of sentences can often be followed by a prepositional phrase, inexperienced writers may easily mistake the object of the preposition for the subject. Consider these sentences:

1. The price *of bananas* is outrageous.

2. The children *in the next room* are mysteriously quiet.

In the case of sentence 1, the student might think that since *bananas* is the last noun in the noun phrase and comes directly before the verb, it is functioning as the subject. The student might make the same assumption of *room* in sentence 2. The inability to identify the subject in either case can cause the student to make an error in subject-verb agreement. An example of such an error would be *The children in the next room is mysteriously quiet.*

Because many of the problems students encounter when attempting to identify subjects and verbs arise from confusions between form and function, we suggest that students engage in activities that encourage them to note that form doesn't necessarily denote the role a word or word group plays in a sentence. There are a number of activities that can help students understand this distinction between form and function. Teachers and students can, for instance, bring in examples of sentences that contain a variety of forms that function as nouns, verbs, and other parts of speech from their own writing or from books, magazines, and newspapers. Many of the student examples can come from journal entries or from out-of-class reading. Students may also write examples of their own, contrasting how similar forms may function differently within the context of a sentence.

Another way to help students improve their skill in recognizing subjects and verbs in sentences is to assist them in becoming more conscious of some of the common or "basic" sentence patterns in English, such as *subject–(intransitive) verb, subject–(transitive) verb–object,* and *subject–(linking) verb–subject complement.* Besides learning to recognize the patterns of short simple sentences, working with nonsense-word sentences can help inexperienced writers "tap into" their innate, unconscious knowledge about sentences, as the following example illustrates (and as you may have experienced in Exercise A in Part One of this chapter):

Those slepful abments have zeeged my dooders very loolifly.

Surprisingly, although the majority of the words in the sentence are nonsense words, speakers of English—even youngsters in middle school—know who or what the sentence is about (the subject: *abments*), what the verb is (*zeeged*), and who or what is receiving the action of or is being acted on by the verb (*dooders*). In fact, it is even possible to recognize that the *abments* are described as being *slepful* and that the action occurred in a *loolif* manner. If students are given the opportunity to discover what they "know" about nonsense sentences, they can be led to discover as well that word order (subjects before verbs; direct object after verbs; adjectives before nouns; etc.), word endings (*slep-ful, abment-s, zeeg-ed, dooder-s, loolif-ly*), and function words (*those, have, my, very*) can provide clues that will help them identify basic sentence constituents in "regular" or normal sentences, particularly subjects and verbs.

As students begin to recognize the major parts of sentences, they can be given excerpts of writing and asked to identify sentence patterns. You can also have students collect and bring to class examples of particular sentence pattern types (e.g., subject-verb-object), which can be posted on class bulletin boards. And of course, it is always good practice to have students produce different kinds of sentences once they can recognize them. To that end, small groups of young writers can be invited to the front of the room, given flash cards with nonsense (or real) words on them, and then instructed to rearrange themselves until the cards they are holding form a sentence that illustrates a particular pattern. Students can also (either as individuals or in groups) compose short pieces of discourse (e.g., song lyrics or greeting card slogans) that evidence particular sentence patterns.

After students begin to develop some skill in identifying subjects and verbs in sentences, they can start to remediate subject-verb agreement problems by working on contextualized passages to edit, including paragraphs you create or excerpts from their own writing. Other strategies can include having students read their own papers, circling errors where they suspect that subject-verb agreement may be incorrect. Reading aloud may also be beneficial in that many native speakers can "hear" agreement problems; however, a student's home dialect or native language may limit the effectiveness of this strategy. Finally, we believe that in helping students edit their own work, it is more effective to bring errors to the students' attention than automatically to correct them.

RECOGNIZING SENTENCE BOUNDARIES: THE COMMA SPLICE AND THE FUSED SENTENCE
Recognizing Comma Splices and Fused Sentences

Because the sentence is such a fundamental grammatical unit, the marking of **sentence boundaries**—whether in speech or in writing—is essential. In writing, sentence boundaries are marked with punctuation: capitalization at the beginnings of sentences and terminal punctuation (period, question mark, etc.) at the ends of sentences. In speaking, sentence boundaries are indicated with particular patterns of intonation, which involve changes in pitch, referred to as _juncture._ Rising juncture occurs in **yes-no questions** (e.g., _Do you understand?_), and falling juncture occurs in **statements** (e.g., _I'm going home at five-thirty tonight._) and **information questions** (e.g., _Where do you live?_). Despite the fact that children ordinarily acquire the ability to understand and produce complete, grammatical sentences before they enter primary school, transferring this knowledge to writing can be difficult. That is to say, in written texts, students are sometimes unable to recognize and mark sentence boundaries, a confusion that leads to two types of problems: comma splices and fused (**run-on**) sentences.

Comma splices are quite common in student writing and occur when two (or more) sentences are inappropriately joined using a comma (,). Here are some examples of comma splices:

1. *She went home, she took a shower.

2. *My room is warm and receptive, it is painted yellow.

3. *I studied all night long, however, I didn't pass the test.

In examples 1 and 2, two sentences are inappropriately joined with a comma. Example 3 illustrates that comma splices can also occur with connecting words; we will discuss this problem more extensively in Chapters 5 and 7.

Like comma splices, *fused sentences* are brought about by the confusion of apprentice writers over punctuation and how it marks sentence boundaries. Fused sentences occur when two or more sentences are punctuated as if they formed a single sentence:

1. *She went home she took a shower.

2. *My room is warm and receptive it is painted yellow.

3. *I studied all night long however I didn't pass the test.

Fused sentences can occur with no intervening connecting words (examples 1 and 2) or with inappropriately punctuated connecting words such as *however* or *therefore* (example 3). Fused sentences are often referred to as "run-on sentences"; however, sentences that are overly long and rambling, though grammatically correct, can also be called "run-on sentences," so *fused* is clearer for identifying the error.

Although we cannot be certain about the origin of difficulties that inexperienced writers encounter as they attempt to recognize and properly punctuate sentence boundaries, we believe that one cause of comma splices and fused sentences is a lack of experience with reading, which results in a lack of familiarity with written conventions. The conventions that govern writing display not only appropriate punctuation usage but also stylistic options in using punctuation that may help students clarify the relationships between the ideas they wish to express and also the role punctuation plays in expressing those relationships. For instance, let's revisit our first example of a comma splice:

*She went home, she took a shower.

We see that the connection between sentences (a comma) does not convey any type of cause-and-effect or temporal relationship that might be expressed by combining these sentences in other ways; for example:

> Before she went home, she took a shower.
> After she went home, she took a shower.
> Since she went home, she took a shower.

Inexperienced writers who don't see *She went home* and *She took a shower* as separate sentences may not recognize the misuse of the comma and may also be unfamiliar with the range of stylistic options available for expressing the relationship between these sentences more precisely. Alert reading (that is, paying attention to written conventions in a text) may help apprentice writers develop a sense of the range of stylistic options and an inventory of punctuation conventions that help convey those options. The assigning of regular reading also allows for an interplay between reading and writing. Students who practice both reading and writing frequently have more of an opportunity to read from the perspective of writers and to write from the perspective of readers. To be effective, however, teachers must ensure that assigned readings are appropriate to the level of skill and ability of the students. Moreover, students must have frequent opportunities to apply the textual conventions they find within their in-class and out-of-class reading to a range of writing genres.

Remediating Comma Splices and Fused Sentences

Although comma splices and fused sentences are both problems with which apprentice writers struggle, comma splices occur far more frequently in student writing. Teachers of writing probably ought to be grateful for this disparity because a comma splice is a less serious error than a fused sentence. A comma splice, although a violation of a punctuation convention, does provide a marker of the sentence boundary for the reader. Writers who inadvertently create comma splices therefore do indicate their knowledge of a sentence boundary by placing a comma at that juncture. Quite often, then, writers who use comma splices need merely to familiarize themselves with and apply appropriate punctuation conventions in order to eradicate the problem.

There are numerous ways to revise comma splices, some of which are illustrated in this example:

Comma splice:	*The dog whined, we took him outside.
Revised:	The dog whined. We took him outside.
Revised:	Because the dog whined, we took him outside.
Revised:	The dog whined; we took him outside.
Revised:	The dog whined, so we took him outside.
Revised:	The dog whined; therefore, we took him outside.

As these examples show, the simplest—if not the best—way to eliminate a comma splice is to replace the comma with a period, as in the first revised sentence above. However, since part of helping students remediate problems in their writing is to acquaint them with options for rewriting and **revision**, we will be more fully discussing problems that students encounter when they improperly combine sentences in subsequent chapters. Chapter 10, in particular, will revisit the problem of comma splices within the context of a discussion of compound (conjoined) sentences and stylistic options for joining two or more clauses.

At this point, beyond suggesting a simple means of correcting comma splices, we also want to suggest that students who use comma splices need to recognize the comma as a signal to which they should alert themselves. Because a comma splice contains two (or more) sentences joined with a comma alone, students need to carefully examine the structures on either side of a comma whenever they have the slightest doubt about the presence of a comma splice. A simple procedure they might follow is as follows: (1) Examine the structure to the *left* of the comma: Does it have a complete subject? A complete predicate? If the answer is no, the procedure stops; the possibility of a comma splice has been eliminated. (2) If the answer is yes, examine the structure to the *right* of the comma. Does it have a complete subject? A complete predicate? If the answer is no, the possibility of a comma splice has been eliminated. If the answer is yes, the student has identified a comma splice and should eliminate it.

As we noted earlier, fused sentences are more serious errors than comma splices because fused sentences fail to indicate sentence boundaries altogether. Because they lack clear boundaries, fused sentences may interfere with the reading process; they also suggest that a writer who uses them frequently has little experience with written texts. It is important to stress, however, that even writers who produce a great many fused sentences in a relatively short piece of writing *do* nonetheless have an innate knowledge of sentence structure. Relatively young children provide evidence of this knowledge in their use of oral language. Furthermore, studies by Kenneth Goodman and other researchers of miscues in the reading of young learners—including those who are not proficient at reading—have provided additional evidence that even children in the early grades of primary school possess an innate knowledge of the structure of their language (Weaver 45–48).

The problem for students who are producing fused sentences, then, is not in their ability to produce or comprehend what constitutes a grammatical sentence in English. Rather, it has to do with recognizing sentence units when they are produced *in writing*. Writers who produce an occasional fused sentence can benefit from an explanation of what constitutes a fused sentence and perhaps some additional practice in **editing** paragraphs or short essays that contain these kinds of sentences. Writers who habitually produce final drafts with multiple fused sentences require more sustained attention, however. It is also likely that such writers will produce inappropriate **sentence fragments**, since the problem of misapprehending sentence boundaries in writing may cause a writer to place terminal punctuation markers (periods, semicolons) in places where they do not belong in addition to omitting them altogether. (Problems with sentence fragments will be discussed in subsequent chapters.)

To reiterate, for writers who have severe problems with fused sentences, simply illustrating the problem and reviewing conventions for punctuating sentences appropriately is inadequate. Instead, we recommend a comprehensive strategy that involves helping students form realistic expectations about both the difficulty of remediating the problem and the length of time it will take to eradicate it from their writing. We also recommend regular practice in writing from dictation and editing. Regarding expectations, it has been our experience that writers who repeatedly create fused sentences in each draft they write will not be able to eradicate the problem in a few weeks. Instead, eliminating fused sentences may require regular, ongoing attention both in and outside of class for the duration of the course (for a quarter, semester, or year). In addition, students who write fused sentences need to understand that the process of correcting these errors may cause them to insert terminal punctuation in the wrong places, in which case more fragments may appear in their writing. To help students form expectations that will encourage rather than discourage them, some sort of ongoing record keeping may be helpful. In this way, students will be able to chart their efforts and perhaps recognize other errors with sentence fragments as a sign of progress.

Besides helping students form realistic expectations, teachers must also provide regular exercises and activities that include dictation, reading, and editing. Dictation activities should probably begin with the teacher (who is a skillful reader) dictating a passage (a short paragraph) to students, who should attempt to punctuate the passage appropriately. Although teachers shouldn't exaggerate terminal punctuation while reading, they should make sentence boundaries as clear as possible. As a course progresses, students (rather than the teacher) should read passages aloud to one another. Those who read should attempt to make terminal boundaries clear (without exaggerating them); those who are listening should attempt to punctuate passages appropriately on their own copy. Teachers can and should regularly provide such students with passages, increasing in length, in which various terminal punctuation marks have been removed. Students need to identify and replace the missing punctuation.

Depending on the number of students in a class who have a problem with fused sentences, group activities can be useful and instructive. A common—and fun—activity is to divide a class into groups of four to five each and give every student a copy of a page-long passage that has some terminal punctuation removed. Each group must together decide what punctuation should be replaced; the "winning" group is the first one to make the appropriate changes on a transparency (in an overhead projector). Group or peer editing activities, in which students read and correct each other's papers for this type of error, are also beneficial, provided that the students have been instructed in identifying and revising fused sentences. Some teachers also recommend that students whose writing evidences a particular error become charged with being the "class experts" regarding that problem. Under these circumstances, students who have begun to successfully identify and eradicate fused sentences in their own writing can become experts in providing editing help to other students who experience occasional problems in this area.

COMMON COMMA FOIBLES

One of the most common yet most difficult punctuation marks to use appropriately is the comma. There are numerous rules for comma usage, and many of them depend on a sophisticated knowledge of sentence structure, which often disadvantages the apprentice writer. It may be challenging, for example, for an inexperienced writer to follow the rule regarding the punctuation of introductory adverb clauses (e.g., as in the sentence *When I got home, I called the doctor right away*) if he has difficulty recognizing these structures in his own writing. Comma rules are also difficult to deploy because they are optional in many sentence contexts.

In response to the difficulties presented by commas, sure-fire "rules" and maxims abound. One the most common of these—which we believe is also the cause of many comma punctuation problems—is the often cited advice to place a comma "wherever a pause occurs in a sentence." The unfortunate consequence of the widespread use of this rule by inexperienced writers is that the rule presupposes a skilled oral reader. That is to say, this rule cannot help a reader who is not familiar with the conventions of reading aloud. Not surprisingly, apprentice writers are often inexperienced readers who pause in inappropriate places when reading aloud. This can lead to a common comma placement error: the placement of a comma between major sentence constituents, such as subject and predicate or between verb and complement or verb and direct object.

Students sometimes place commas between subjects and predicates because they recognize that sentences are composed of these two important constituents. Also, as part of their grammar instruction, students often engage in exercises in their language arts classes that invite them to identify and mark the separation between subjects and predicates. Here are two examples of sentences in which a comma inappropriately separates major sentence constituents:

*1. The angry kitty, scratched her owner.

*2. The winner of the contest is, my cousin from Peoria.

A student might put a comma between *kitty* and *scratched,* recognizing them as the subject and predicate (noun phrase and **verb phrase**). However, this punctuation does not assist the reader. In fact, it cues the reader to look for a modifier or parenthetical phrase (e.g., *The angry kitty, who had not been fed, scratched her owner*) when in fact there is none. In sentence 2, the writer has perhaps recognized, unconsciously or consciously, a division between the linking verb and the complement, or the writer may have been influenced by conversational patterns—but in any case, she has mistakenly signaled a pause that can potentially confuse a reader. For students who regularly commit this kind of punctuation error, practice in recognizing basic sentence constituents (as we described earlier) is crucial. Once students can identify subjects, verbs, objects, and complements, they can be advised to look for—and remove punctuation from—junctures between these constituents when they edit their writing.

RECALLING FAMILIAR TERMS AND CONCEPTS

As you've been reading, you may have recognized many of the terms and concepts we have covered in this chapter. Throughout the process of acquiring knowledge about English grammar, it is important to be conscious of how much you already know regarding the construction of English sentences because your awareness of and appreciation for language is important to acknowledge and build on. As a future language arts teacher, you will want to feel comfortable with and confident about language whenever you enter the classroom because one of your aims as a teacher will be to help your students become confident language users. Unfortunately, too often the teaching of grammar stresses the memorization of terms and concepts divorced from any purposeful context, an approach that does not ordinarily build a student's appreciation for or facility with language.

Recall, for example, your experience with the term *predicate nominative*. When surveyed, the vast majority of our students, who are preservice language arts teachers, have heard this term but don't recall what it means. And sadly, most associate the term with their past inability to understand complicated grammatical concepts. In fact, there's nothing complicated about the concept "predicate nominative": it merely signifies a linking verb complement that is a noun, as in the following example:

Sheila is *president.*

Despite the relative simplicity of the concept "predicate nominative," however, we wonder what is accomplished by focusing on such terms during the K–12 experience. It may be that teaching students terms such as *predicate nominative* as the focus of grammar study has negative effects, the worst of which is to undermine students' confidence in their knowledge of their own language. Moreover, such an emphasis shifts the focus of language arts classes from helping students increase their facility in language use to memorization of terms without providing direct meaning and application to the learner. *like the SOL's*

To conclude, our goal in this chapter has been to help you recognize what you already know about basic sentence constituents in English and to help you expand on this knowledge. The distinction between form and function is particularly important because this distinction is the basis for leading student learners to detect misunderstandings they might have about language and how it is used. (Understanding this distinction may help you clarify some previously confusing grammatical terms or concepts as well.) As students experience a variety of writing activities and assignments, their familiarity with this concept may help them avoid common errors.

EXERCISES FOR PRACTICE

A. The following sentences exhibit challenges regarding form and function. Some sentences, for example, have words that look like nouns functioning as subjects but aren't, and others have words that do not look like nouns but are functioning as subjects. First, identify the subject and the predicate of each sentence. Separate them with a line. Then indicate what type of potential problem is illustrated by the sentence. (Note that some sentences may contain more than one potential problem.)

Example:	Until last year, swimming / was fun.
Potential problem:	*Swimming* appears to be a verb but is in fact functioning as a subject.

1. Bill shouldn't mess with that electrical outlet.

2. Sometimes sorrow dogs my steps.

3. Running is a common way to stay fit.

4. The jump was too dangerous for the children.

5. Attending concerts is costly.

6. In the hallway is where Fluffy sleeps.

7. *Wonderful* is the word for it.

8. Maybe they'll bus the children to another school.

9. You can leap over that puddle.

10. Yesterday was a snowy day.

11. Loving your neighbor is an ideal.

12. The door of the barn was wide open.

13. Tomorrow I sign my annual contract.

14. You mustn't smoke in the lavatory on airplanes.

15. Wednesday falls in the middle of the week.

B. In the following sentences, every noun functioning as a subject is followed by a prepositional phrase. In each sentence, separate the subject and predicate with a line, and put the prepositional phrase that follows the subject in brackets.

> **Example:**   The last chapter [of the book] / revealed the identity of the killer.

1. The door to the hallway was ajar.

2. The speaker for the stereo wouldn't work.

3. The people in the living room are strangers to me.

4. The price of oranges is high all year round.

5. The dirt around the potted plant is very dry.

6. The workers at the factory voted for a strike.

7. The back of the computer contains a lot of jacks.

8. The front of your shirt is covered with spilled food.

9. A map of the world is hanging on that wall over there.

10. The center of the campus is a large, grassy oval.

C. Find a passage from something you are reading—a magazine or a book—with sentences containing hard-to-identify subjects. Explain why the subjects are hard to identify.

D. The following passage may have one or more comma splices and fused sentences. Identify and correct each of them.

> One of the controversial issues regarding public education these days is the public funding of charter schools. Proponents of charter schools argue that they are more adaptable to the needs of students in particular communities they claim as well that charter schools are more responsive to students with special needs or talents. Those who argue against public funding of charter schools express concern that such funding may undermine public education, they also cite data that suggest that students in charter schools do not demonstrate improved academic performance. It

is unfortunate that persons who have opposing opinions regarding this issue and who have students' best interests at heart have not as yet been able to work out opportunities for compromise, politicians, in particular, need to show leadership in creating compromise for the benefit of all their constituents.

E. Review the following brief paragraph for errors involving incorrectly used commas between sentence constituents. Circle each misused comma.

Last night I watched a popular game show on TV. These types of programs, have become more popular in recent years. It's interesting to speculate as to what the appeal of these shows tells us about our culture. Do they suggest that we are a nation of gamblers? I suspect the answer to that question, is "probably not." Everyone likes a contest. Everyone likes to win. The day I win a contest I will buy, a new car and a larger house.

F. The following is a set of song lyrics and a short written passage without punctuation. Provide the punctuation for each of them. Then compare your newly punctuated version with those of a classmate. Did you punctuate the texts in the same manner? If not, how do they differ? How does the different punctuation affect each text? What kinds of questions does this activity raise about punctuation? (Remember that punctuation can include capitalization.)

1. From "The *Titanic*"

> oh they built the ship *Titanic* to sail the ocean blue
> and they thought they had a ship that the sea would not
> > leak through
> but the Lord's almighty hand knew this ship would never stand
> it was sad when that great ship went down
> oh it was sad Lord sad oh it was sad Lord sad
> husbands and wives little children lost their lives
> it was sad when that great ship went down

2. Adapted from *Roughing It* by Mark Twain

> on some of those mountains to the southwest it had been raining every day for two weeks but not a drop had fallen in the city on hot days in late spring and early autumn the citizens could quit fanning themselves and growling they could go out and cool off by looking at the luxury of a glorious snowstorm going on in the mountains they could enjoy it at a distance in those seasons every day but no snow would fall in their streets or anywhere near them

G. Select a term or concept from this chapter (such as *predicate nominative* or *transitive verb*) and recall your first experience with the term, how it was taught to you, and any frustrations you encountered. Then try to recall any other terms or concepts that are a source of confusion and anxiety for you.

● EXERCISES FOR CLASSROOM APPLICATION

A. Design an activity or exercise that requires students to identify subjects that are hard to recognize because of their form or position.

B. Find examples either from your own writing or the writing of others that exemplify comma splices and fused sentences. How would you explain to your students the problems that you find in these examples?

C. Design an activity or exercise that will help students remediate either comma splices or fused sentences.

NOUNS AND NOUN PHRASES

Chapter Preview

Chapter 3 explains how to identify the many forms that nouns can take and their functions in sentences.

In **Part I** you will learn about

- How nouns function
- Noun types
- Possessives
- Plurals, both regular and irregular
- Function words that accompany nouns
- Adjectives
- Pronouns
- Gerunds and infinitives

In **Part II** you will learn about challenges writers may face with

- Noun inflections
- Noun form
- Pronoun agreement and reference
- Form, function, and fragments
- Modification, misguided stylistic choices, and problems with form

PART I   IMPORTANT CONCEPTS ABOUT NOUNS

In Chapter 2 we gave a very simple definition of a *noun phrase* as a *group of words that consists of a noun together with its related words*. This is an oversimplified definition, for several reasons. First, grammarians often define a noun phrase as any structure that contains a noun as its main or "**head**" word. By this definition, a noun phrase can consist of just one noun, as in this sentence: *John ran*. Because the common concept of a phrase suggests a group of words, we have defined a noun phrase as consisting of more than just a noun. Besides simplifying the definition of a noun phrase in this way in Chapter 2, we also simplified it by providing very little information about the "related words" that make up a noun phrase. It is our aim in this chapter, then, to provide more detail about the types of words that make up this important and common English structure.

To begin, before we can more fully discuss what makes up a noun phrase, we need to modify our original definition somewhat by adding another alternative: *a noun phrase is a group of words that consists of a noun together with its related words or a group of words that functions together as a noun*. As you can see, this definition accounts for two different types of noun phrases. One type of noun phrase contains a noun (the main or "head" word) plus related words. The other type of noun phrase consists of a group of words that together function as a noun. Here are some examples of both types; each noun phrase is underlined:

1. The smiling, charismatic *politician* charmed many young *voters*.

2. Those noisy *children* acted quite irresponsibly.

3. John's singing off key last night was really awful.   *gerund*

4. For Kal to have lied so convincingly was astounding.   *past participle*

In these examples, the noun phrases in sentences 1 and 2 clearly have a main or "head" noun (in italics). In sentences 3 and 4, however, it's harder to separate the noun from the rest of the words in the noun phrase because *singing* and *to have lied* seem to require the words in the rest of the phrase to make sense. That is, the words in the noun phrases in sentences 3 and 4 function together as one unit. Now that we have provided a definition of the noun phrase, we will devote the remainder of this part of the chapter to explaining how nouns function, the forms they take, and the types of words that can accompany them.

HOW NOUNS FUNCTION

Because we have stressed the importance of recognizing the difference between form and function in English sentences, it seems appropriate to begin our discussion of nouns by examining how they function in English sentences. Nouns (as well as noun phrases and noun clauses, which we discuss more fully in Chapter 9) can function in a variety of ways in English. As you may recall from Chapter 2, *subjects, direct objects,* and *indirect objects* in sentences must be nouns; *subject complements* and *object complements* may be nouns. Beyond these five functions of nouns, there are two more: *objects of prepositions* and **appositives**. We will discuss these structures and other types of words and word groups that function as nouns—often referred to as **nominals**—more fully in Chapter 9. But for now, here are simple definitions and examples of each. *Objects of prepositions* are the main or head words in prepositional phrases; objects of prepositions must be nouns or nominals. In the following sentences, the prepositional phrases are underlined, and the nouns or noun phrases that are the objects of the prepositions are in italics.

1. The dog ran up *the hill*.
2. The man from *Toledo* won the raffle at *the barbecue*.
3. A dog with *piercing blue eyes* chased the children under *the stairs*.

Appositives are words or groups of words that rename nouns; appositives must also be nouns or nominals. In the following examples, the appositives are underlined; notice how each appositive renames a noun.

1. John, my husband, is a science teacher. [*My husband* renames *John*.]
2. She gave her friend Ellie a big hug. [*Ellie* renames *her friend*.]
3. We are holding a reception for John Ellis, our new governor. [*Our new governor* renames *John Ellis*.]
4. My favorite hobby, collecting stamps, can become expensive. [*Collecting stamps* renames *hobby*.]

In sum, then, there are a total of seven ways in which nouns or nominals can function in sentences. The first five of these functions *always* require nouns or nominals; as for the other two, *subject complements* and *object complements*, nouns or nominals may function as these structures, but they don't necessarily have to do so.

1. *Subject:* The angry *aliens* roared incessantly.
   For Bill to argue is futile.
2. *Direct object:* I love for Khani to play.
   We ended the sad *charade*.
3. *Indirect object:* The study group bought *Cinda* a beautiful scarf.
   Mariana gave violin playing her total devotion.
4. *Object of preposition:* The students with high *marks* won't take the final.
   The thick foliage hid the hospital from *tourists*.

5. *Appositive:*   My dog <u>*Tuffy*</u> eats everything in sight.

                                Lonny brought an incredible costume, <u>a rubber alien *suit*</u>.

6. *Subject complement:*   The lilac remains <u>my favorite *flower*</u>.

                                Desk-size water gardens are <u>great holiday *gifts*</u>.

                                My favorite hobby is <u>reading mystery novels</u>.

7. *Object complement:*   John considers Tuffy <u>his best *friend*</u>.

                                The club members called Eben <u>a *prince*</u>.

Now that you have learned how nouns and noun phrases function and have become familiar with the types of nouns that may head a noun phrase, let's expand that knowledge to include more information about nouns so that you may recognize and manipulate them in sentences more fully. When you are distinguishing nouns from other words in a sentence, it may help you to notice the *forms* they can take as well as the roles or functions that they can fill. Two common distinguishing types of endings—or *inflections*—that nouns can take are the **possessive** *'s* and the **plural** *-s*. Besides identifying nouns, these endings alter the meanings of the nouns to which they are added or indicate a possessive relationship. We will discuss possessives and plurals more fully in the next two sections.

NOUN TYPES

Common Versus Proper Nouns

Although it may be handy to define a noun as "a person, place, or thing," there are further useful distinctions. For instance, **common nouns** *are words that name generic classes or types of persons, places, or things.* Because of their generic nature, these nouns are not capitalized. **Proper nouns**, *by contrast, name specific, unique persons, places, or things and require capitalization.* Distinguishing between common and proper nouns is usually not difficult, as the following list indicates. Note that in the preceding section we have been focusing on words or word groups that *function* as nouns; these are called *nominals.* Here, however, the emphasis is on the form of individual words, so we will be using the term *nouns* to refer to single-word units that meet the criteria of being nouns in terms of both form and function.

<u>Common</u>	<u>Proper</u>
dog	Fido
professor	Dr. Martin
corporation	Ford Motor Corporation
building	University Hall
laptop	Apple iBook
country	Zimbabwe

Sometimes proper nouns become so common in a culture that they come to substitute for common nouns. These are usually brand names. One way to determine whether a noun is common or proper is to conduct the "*a* test": put the **article** *a* before the noun in question. If it makes sense, as in "a dog," that means *dog* is a generic and is therefore a common noun. By contrast, "a Fido" would not make sense, indicating that *Fido* is a proper noun.

An interesting aspect of English is the use of compound nouns, combining two separate nouns to designate a single entity, as in *football, motorcycle,* and *shoebox*. Terms and expressions that develop in response to social, technological, and cultural changes exhibit the tendency to combine into a single new word, as in the case of *gridlock, homepage,* and *laptop*.

Count Versus Noncount Nouns

Within the category of common nouns, there are some nouns that can be both singular or plural and others that can only be singular because they are considered indivisible. An easy way to distinguish between them is to ask whether what the nouns stand for can be *counted* or not. Consequently, we refer to these two subgroups of common nouns as **count** and **noncount nouns**. Count nouns include words such as *class, cookie,* and *dish*. You can have one of these things, or you can have more than one or even any number of *classes, cookies,* or *dishes*. Noncount nouns most often represent substances or abstract concepts that can't be enumerated. Here are some examples of noncount nouns:

Materials:	cotton, gold, silver, plastic, wood
Foods and liquids:	cheese, meat, rice, milk, water, sugar
Abstractions:	truth, justice, freedom, beauty, goodness, evil, time

Within the context of sentences, distinguishing between count and noncount nouns is relatively easy for native speakers of English:

1. The papers were scattered all over the desk.

2. Evil lurks among us.

Recognizing count and noncount nouns includes determining whether a given noun should be preceded by an **indefinite article** (*a* or *an*) or the **definite article** (*the*). If the noun makes sense with *a* or *an* in the context of the sentence, it is countable (*a party, an objection*); if not, it is probably not countable (**a gravity; *a glamour*). When trying to distinguish between count and noncount nouns, it may be useful to classify them as either *concrete* nouns, representing physical properties (*stars, planets, leaves, trees*), or *abstract* nouns, representing ideas, beliefs, and values that are not physical but more emotional and psychological (*anticipation, democracy, idealism*).

1. His *idealism* was infectious.

2. *Anticipation* is making me crazy.

In these sentences, *idealism* and *anticipation* are not countable nouns; indeed, most abstract nouns are noncount nouns and are therefore always used in the singular.

Be aware, however, that certain nouns can fall into both categories, with different shades of meaning. The word *meat*, for example, can be used as either a count noun or a noncount noun. You can say, "I love meat" (noncount), referring to all animal flesh. You can also say, "There were three different meats on the buffet table" (count), referring to specific types of meat. As this example illustrates, the context in which words are used can also determine whether a noun is countable or not countable.

POSSESSIVES

So far in this chapter we have been talking about nouns and how to identify them in a sentence. You have learned how to identify nouns and noun phrases from their function in a sentence; for example, subjects of sentences are always noun or noun phrases, and so are appositives. You have also learned about two types of nouns—count and noncount—and how to recognize them. Another common way to identify nouns—particularly count nouns—is by the endings they can take. Nouns can take two types of endings: the possessive *'s* and the plural *-s.*

As we have suggested, then, one way to recognize nouns in English is by the fact that they can take the possessive *'s* ("apostrophe *s*") ending. Let us examine how possessives are formed and how they function in a sentence. When forming possessives, there are several points to remember. First, as you may have learned in school, possessives are most commonly formed by adding *'s* to a noun, as the following examples illustrate:

1. Mary Helene's new house is around the corner.

2. The dog's supper dish needs washing.

3. The moon's glow cast a bright shadow on the snow below.

In all of these examples, the *'s* is attached to the noun to indicate possession. When a singular noun ends in *s*, you may add *'s* or elect to use only the apostrophe (') and omit the *s* as the following examples illustrate:

1. Mr. Rogers' book was a bestseller.

2. Thomas's new business is flourishing.

3. The grass's color left much to be desired.

As you can see, when forming the possessive of *Mr. Rogers* in sentence 1, only the apostrophe was used; in forming the possessive of *Thomas* and *grass* in sentences 2 and 3, *'s* was used. For singular possessive nouns that end in *s*, this choice is left up to the writer, as long as the use or omission of *s* is consistent throughout a piece of writing.

If, however, a noun ends in *s* because it is plural, only the apostrophe is added to make the plural noun possessive:

4. The apples' remains lay strewn around the floor.

5. We cleaned the boys' room.

Note how important the position of the apostrophe is in showing whether the remains of one apple or more than one apple are strewn on the floor or whether the room that was cleaned belonged to one boy or more than one boy.

Now that you've seen how to form possessives, let's look at how they function. When a noun has been made into a possessive, it precedes a noun and indicates to whom or what that noun belongs (or some other type of close, possessive relationship). In example 1, *the book* belongs to *Mr. Rogers* either by ownership or authorship. In example 2, *the new business* belongs to *Thomas*. In example 3, *the grass* has a specific color. In example 4, *the remains* originated from and thus belong to *the apples*. In example 5, *the room* belongs to or is occupied by *the boys*. As you may have deduced, possessives can be used with both count and noncount nouns.

Another important aspect of using possessives is that in most contexts, they may be replaced with a prepositional phrase using *of:* for example, instead of *the grass's color*, one may express the same thought as *the color of the grass*. This is often a stylistic choice that is dictated by matters such as the formality or nature of the context. Possessives that are formed with a prepositional phrase may seem more formal or more "literary" than those formed with inflections. Compare the following alternatives and see what you think:

her dog's ear	the ear of her dog
her eye's color	the color of her eyes
the plants' holder	the holder of the plants.
our forefathers' plan	the plan of our forefathers.

PLURALS

In addition to the fact that they can show possession or ownership, another way to identify nouns is by the fact that they often can take an *-s* ending when they are plural. When identifying plurals of count nouns, however, it is important to remember that plurals of nouns in English take two forms, regular and irregular.

Regular Plurals

Although the regular plural inflection is *-s*, the way in which it is attached to a word may vary and so needs some discussion. You may have heard the rule "to form a plural, just add *-s*," but it is a little more complicated than that. *Regular plurals* are indeed usually formed by adding *-s,* but sometimes other letters need to be added as well, or the original spelling of the word being pluralized needs to be changed in order to accommodate the inflection. The following are the most common rules for creating regular plurals and some examples:

1. Most nouns form the plural by adding –s only:

    Examples: hat   hat*s*

    dog   dog*s*

    name   name*s*

2. Nouns that end in *sh, ch, s, z,* and *x* usually form the plural by adding –*es:*

    Examples: wish   wish*es*

    church   church*es*

    boss   boss*es*

    buzz   buzz*es*

    fox   fox*es*

3. Nouns that end in *y* usually form the plural by dropping *y* and adding –*ies:*

    Examples: lady   lad*ies*

    puppy   pupp*ies*

    city   cit*ies*

    candy   cand*ies*

There are also some rules for creating plurals that apply to some words but not to others. For example, some nouns that end in *o* make their plural by adding –*es,* but many others make their plural by adding only –*s.* There are also some that can be spelled either way, as shown here:

Forms Plural with -*es*		Forms Plural with -*s*		Forms Plural Either Way	
echo	echo*es*	auto	auto*s*	zero	zero*es* or zero*s*
hero	hero*es*	radio	radio*s*	tornado	tornado*es* or tornado*s*

Similar variation occurs with nouns that end in *f.* Many nouns that end in *f* form their plural by changing the *f* to *v* and adding –*es.* A smaller group of nouns that end in *f* form their plural by simply adding –*s,* as shown here:

Forms Plural with -*ves*		Forms Plural with -*s*	
calf	cal*ves*	belief	belie*fs*
self	sel*ves*	roof	roo*fs*

Irregular Plurals

Among irregular plurals, there are three primary groupings. One grouping is of nouns that do not change their form when pluralized. Most of these words relate to the animal kingdom:

Singular	Plural
deer	deer
sheep	sheep
fish	fish
species	species

A second group consists of words borrowed from other languages, particularly Latin, that retain plural endings from those languages. There are six patterns that these borrowed words follow. In pattern 1, the singular form ends in *on* and the plural form ends in *a*. In pattern 2, the singular form ends in *us* and the plural form ends in *i*. In pattern 3, the singular form ends in *a,* and the plural form ends in *ae*. In pattern 4, the singular form ends in *is* and the plural form ends in *es*. In pattern 5, the singular form ends in *ex* and the plural form ends in *ices*. In pattern 6, the singular form ends in *um* and the plural form ends in *a*. (Some words that follow these patterns, especially patterns 5 and 6, may also have alternative plurals formed regularly, as shown in parentheses.)

Pattern	Singular	Plural
Pattern 1:	criteri*on*	criteri*a*
Pattern 2:	fung*us*	fung*i*
Pattern 3:	vertebr*a*	vertebr*ae*
Pattern 4:	cris*is*	cris*es*
Pattern 5:	ind*ex*	ind*ices* (*or* indexes)
Pattern 6:	medi*um*	medi*a* (*or* mediums)

The third group of words that form irregular plurals is a miscellaneous category. The rules that apply to the words in this group are not easily explained and seem more arbitrary, although they follow patterns that were more common in earlier forms of English but have fallen out of use. As with the other classes of nouns, the plural is formed by either adding an ending to the word or changing the spelling of the word in some way. The following are some of the more common irregular plurals in this miscellaneous group.

Singular	Plural
man	men
woman	women (*continued*)

Singular	Plural
child	children
ox	oxen
foot	feet
goose	geese
tooth	teeth
mouse	mice

FUNCTION WORDS THAT ACCOMPANY NOUNS

Now that we've completed our discussion of the endings nouns often take—plurals and possessives—we want to focus on the related words that can accompany nouns in phrases. Two types of words can accompany nouns in noun phrases: *adjectives* and *function words*. Function words, which include prepositions and articles, act primarily to relate grammatical information. Function words can also help identify content words, such as nouns, verbs, and their modifiers. In this section we will look at several types of function words. These words usually precede the noun and answer questions such as *Which one?* or *How many?* Often these function words are referred to collectively as **determiners**. Common determiners are *articles, demonstratives,* **numbers, quantifiers,** and **possessive pronouns**.

Articles

There are three articles in English: *a, an,* and *the. A* and *an* are known as *indefinite articles* because they identify nouns that refer to one representative of a general class of objects, persons, or entities.

1. *A* watched *pot* never boils.

2. *An application* must be on file.

3. *A cat* can be a good companion.

4. *An albatross* is a rare sight.

In these sentences, each of the noun phrases (the article plus the noun) refers not to a specific object or entity—a specific *pot, application, cat,* or *albatross*—but rather to a single member of a class or group (*any* pot that is watched, *any* application, *any* cat, etc.). Note that *a* or *an* is used only with singular count nouns because it always indicates *one* member of the class or group. Note also that the meanings of *a* and *an* are identical: which word is used is determined by the sound (not the spelling) of the following noun. *A* is used with nouns that begin with a consonant sound, and *an* is used with nouns that begin with a vowel sound, as in the following examples:

a dog	an albatross
a fish	an egg

a window	an inch
a home	an otter
a truck	an undertow
a union	an hour
a YMCA	an MGB

The *definite article, the,* is used with singular or plural nouns that refer to specific or particular entities or objects; its use is influenced by a variety of factors—including whether the nouns are count or noncount, abstract or concrete—and the overall context of the sentence or paragraph. Consider the following examples:

1. The justice left the room.

2. Justice is sweet.

3. The fish is stale.

4. Fish is good for you.

5. The cats are noisy

6. Cats need attention.

In sentences 1 and 2, the use of *justice* makes a distinction between a specific justice, the person who left the room, and the abstract, noncount concept of justice, which would not require the use of an article. Examples 3 and 4 are similar in that sentence 3 refers to a specific fish, and sentence 4 refers to fish in general as a noncount noun and so does not require the use of an article. Sentence 5 refers to a specific group of cats, and sentence 6 refers to cats in general. An easy test is to remember that for count nouns, *a* or *an* refers to a single member of a larger group, and *the* refers to a specific or known member of that group. Any word that makes sense after *a* or *an* can be used with *the.* If a noun fails this test, it is a noncount noun and should not be preceded by an article.

Demonstratives

Another type of determiner is the *demonstrative.* Demonstratives are similar to definite articles but provide more information by pointing to specific objects, ideas, or entities and detailing proximity or contrast. The four demonstratives are *this, that, these,* and *those.* The demonstratives *this* and *that,* for instance, accompany singular count nouns or noncount nouns; *these* and *those* accompany plural nouns:

1. *This* window is broken. *That* window is not.

2. *That* pail is empty. *This* pail is full.

3. *These* cookies are fresh. *Those* cookies are stale.

4. *Those* letters have been postmarked. *These* letters have not.

As these examples illustrate, the demonstratives are useful for making contrasts between objects. Although in some cases the decision to use *this or that* (or *these* or *those*) may be arbitrary, most often the context of the passage in which such sentences occur dictates which demonstrative to use. Generally, especially when both words are used in a given context, *this* or *these* refers to whatever is closer to the speaker and *that* or *those* to what is farther away.

Numbers and Quantifiers

So far you have seen how determiners such as articles and demonstratives help you to recognize nouns in a sentence or phrase. Two other types of determiners, numbers and quantifiers, which are even more specific than demonstratives and articles, can also help you identify nouns and provide detailed information about quantity. *Numbers* provide precise detail (e.g., *five* pails, *one hundred* light bulbs, the *first* word) whereas *quantifiers* suggest a range in quantity or selection (e.g., *some* candy, *a lot of* snow). Quantifiers can be single words or phrases. Some quantifiers are used specifically with count nouns and others with noncount nouns.

NUMBERS.   Numbers can tell how many objects there are or in which order the objects appear. Look at the following examples:

1. Kris ate *one* apple. [*One* tells how many *apple*s Kris ate.]

2. The *first* person in the room can eat an apple. [*First* tells the order in which people come into the room.]

In both sentences, the presence of a number indicates that a noun is to follow. Note that numbers can be used only with count nouns; by definition, noncount nouns consist of things that cannot be counted, so numbers cannot apply to them, as the following sentences demonstrate:

1. We ate two bananas. [*Bananas* is a count noun, so this makes sense.]

2. *We bought two furniture. [*Furniture* is a noncount noun, so this does not make sense.]

QUANTIFIERS.   Look again at sentence 2; clearly, it is an unacceptable sentence in English. Even making *furniture* plural would not work, because *furniture* is a noncount noun, so it cannot have a plural. To turn this into a meaningful sentence—in effect, to "count" noncount nouns—you need to use *quantifiers*. Thus you can make the unacceptable sentence *They bought two furniture* acceptable by specifying the quantity of the individual items or pieces of furniture, as in *They bought two pieces of furniture.* In this sentence, *pieces of* tells how much furniture was bought. Other examples of quantifiers specifying the amount of noncount nouns can be seen in the following sentences:

1. I want *a lot of* bologna.

2. They drank *a liter of* soda with their pizza.

3. Joanne used *a spool of* thread in making the dress.

4. Zelma bought *a package* of gum.

Another point to make about quantifiers is that they can also be used with count nouns to indicate general amounts (e.g., *many* apples, *a lot of* cookies) or specific amounts (e.g., *a pound of* apples). Also, as you can see from the examples, quantifiers can be in two forms: one word (*David bought some novels*) or phrasal (*Deb used five pounds of sugar in the cake*). Here are some examples of single-word and phrasal quantifiers used with both count and noncount nouns:

1. Alice ate *some* cake for dessert.

2. Kris ate *a few* cookies.

3. Virginia ate *a lot of* pie.

4. John prepared *many* sandwiches.

5. Kevin cooked *much* chicken.

6. David ate *all of* the food

A final point about quantifiers is that they often influence subject-verb agreement, as you can see from the following examples:

1. One piece of furniture *is* in the living room. [*One piece* is singular, so the verb is in the singular form to *agree with* the singular subject.]

2. Two pieces of pie *were* left in the pan. [*Two pieces* is plural, so the verb is in the plural form to *agree with* the plural subject.]

However, at times subject-verb agreement with subjects that include quantifiers may not be clear, as the following examples illustrate:

1. Some of the evidence *is* believable. [The singular form of the verb agrees with the noncount noun *evidence*. This makes sense because *evidence* is not countable, so it is always treated as a singular noun.]

2. Some of the people *are* trustworthy. [The plural form of the verb is used to agree with the plural noun *people*. This makes sense because if *people* is plural, a

portion them must also be plural; otherwise, the writer would have written *One of the people is trustworthy.*]

3. <u>Two packages</u> of gum *is* too many. [Two packages is being regarded as a single quantity, so the singular form of the verb is used.]

Possessive Pronouns

<u>A final type of function</u> word that can accompany nouns in noun phrases is the *possessive pronoun*. Like definite articles and demonstratives, possessive pronouns precede nouns and make them specific to particular members of a class rather than to the whole class. That is, in the sentence *A dog makes a good companion,* the noun *dog* refers to any member of the class of nouns referred to by the word *dog;* similarly, in the sentence *Dogs make good companions,* the noun *dogs* refers to all members of the class of nouns referred to by that word. In contrast, in the sentences <u>*His*</u> *dog makes a good companion* or <u>*Their*</u> *dogs make good companions,* the possessive pronouns *his* and *their* limit the class of dogs to particular ones: *his* (the man's) dog or *their* (the men's) dogs.

Besides delimiting the nouns that they precede, possessive pronouns can provide different kinds of information. Sometimes they show ownership, as in the sentence *Her purse is missing;* sometimes they indicate other possessive relationships that aren't, strictly speaking, based on ownership, as in these sentences:

1. *Her* head is really bothering her. [Her head is a part of her body.]

2. *Her* courage astonished us. [She *has* courage but doesn't *own* it.]

3. We admired *her* sculpture. [Either she owns the sculpture or she made the sculpture.]

There are a total of eight possessive pronouns that can precede nouns in noun phrases:

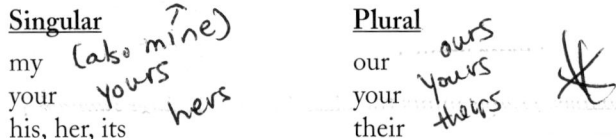

Singular	Plural
my	our
your	your
his, her, its	their

As you examined this list, you probably remembered that possessive pronouns agree in number and sometimes in gender with the nouns to which they refer. Notice this agreement in the following sentences:

1. Every day Chelsea administers a home remedy to *her* children. [*Chelsea* is singular and female; therefore, *her* is singular and marked for feminine gender.]

2. *Her* children hate *their* medicine. [Because the children are Chelsea's, and Chelsea is female and singular, they are *her* children. But the children have to take the medicine, so the medicine is *their* (plural) medicine.]

3. One day the children poured *their* medicine into a plant, and the plant dropped *its* leaves. [It's still the children's (*their*) medicine, but the leaves belong to the plant (which is singular and has no gender), so the plant dropped *its* leaves.]

In addition to possessive pronouns that resemble articles and demonstratives, there are also possessive pronouns that resemble pronouns because they replace or stand for noun phrases:

Which book does she want?   She wants *my book.*
She wants *mine.* [*Mine* stands for *my book.*]

Which car will Bill borrow?   He will borrow *her car.*
He will borrow *hers.* [*Hers* stands for *her car.*]

Because possessive pronouns such as *mine* and *hers* resemble pronouns (words that replace nouns) rather than determiners (words that accompany nouns), we will explain them more fully later in this chapter when we cover pronouns.

ADJECTIVES

The types of words that accompany nouns discussed to this point have been *function words*, words that point out grammatical relationships, amplify meaning, and otherwise clarify sentences. Now we will introduce a common and useful class of words that frequently accompany nouns: *adjectives.* Although we will cover adjectives more thoroughly in Chapter 8, it's important to introduce them at this time because they frequently accompany nouns in noun phrases.

Quite often, adjectives are defined as "words that modify nouns"—although this is quite a broad definition. What exactly does "modify" mean in this context? Like function words that can accompany nouns (articles, demonstratives, etc.), adjectives can and often do limit nouns to a particular subgroup:

1. I want *fresh* bananas. [*Fresh* limits the class *bananas* to *fresh bananas.*]

2. I want *large* bananas. [*Large* limits the class *bananas* to *large bananas.*]

Adjectives also often provide detail and information about a noun that is already limited or identified:

1. The children are playing in our *beautiful, shady* yard.

2. My *lovely, brown, fuzzy* dog is named King.

In these two sentences, the nouns *yard* and *dog* are already limited by the words *our* and *my*, respectively. Which yard? *My* yard. Which dog? *My* dog. The adjectives *beautiful, shady, lovely, brown,* and *fuzzy* function to provide more descriptive detail rather than to limit or point to a particular group of nouns.

Because adjectives provide more detail about nouns, one adjective is often considered insufficient to describe nouns. That is, speakers and writers often elect to use two or more adjectives to modify a noun, as illustrated in the last two examples. In speech, using two or more adjectives to describe a noun doesn't ordinarily cause problems for native speakers of English, but in written English, punctuating a series of adjectives can be problematic. Because the order of two or more adjectives can sometimes be altered and sometimes not, adjectives sometimes require commas to separate them and sometimes don't. Consider these two sentences:

1. I bought a *healthy, vigorous* plant.

2. I love my *new brick* house.

The adjectives *healthy* and *vigorous* can be reversed (*I bought a vigorous, healthy plant*) without changing the meaning of the sentence; *healthy* and *vigorous* could also be separated by the word *and* (*I bought a healthy and vigorous plant*) without altering the sense. These "interchangeable" adjectives—known as *coordinate adjectives*—are therefore separated with a comma. However, in the second sentence, if you switch the order of the adjectives or insert the word *and*, the sentence no longer makes sense (**I love my brick new house* sounds odd, and so does **I love my new and brick house*). Consequently, a comma does not belong between these adjectives in this sentence.

Let's look at a few more examples:

1. The *beautiful, happy* children smiled.

2. The *tall concrete* bunker collapsed.

In sentence 1, *beautiful* and *happy* are coordinate adjectives because the order can be reversed (*The happy, beautiful children smiled*) and *and* can be inserted (*The beautiful and happy children smiled*). In sentence 2, *tall* and *concrete* are not coordinate adjectives because the order cannot be reversed (**The concrete tall bunker collapsed*) and *and* cannot be inserted (**The concrete and tall bunker collapsed*).

As many of these examples illustrate, adjectives ordinarily precede the nouns they modify. However, in Chapter 2 several exceptions to this general rule were explained. Linking verbs can take adjective subject complements, and some transitive verbs can take direct objects with objective complements that are adjectives. Here are examples of sentences with adjective modifiers in the positions we've just described:

1. The *beautiful* kitten gobbled up its food. [*Beautiful* is in the usual adjective position and modifies *kitten*.]

2. The kitten is *beautiful*. [*Beautiful* is a subject complement that modifies *kitten*.]

3. Our neighbor considers our kitten *beautiful*. [*Beautiful* is an object complement that modifies *kitten*.]

Although single-word adjectives (and words functioning as adjectives) ordinarily precede the noun they modify, groups of words that function together as adjectives ordinarily come directly after the nouns they modify:

1. I bought a *tall, green* plant. [*Tall* and *green* are adjectives that modify *plant.*]

2. I bought a plant *that is tall and green.* [*That is tall and green* is an **adjective clause** that modifies *plant.*]

3. I bought a plant *with green leaves.* [*With green leaves* is an **adjective phrase** that modifies *plant.*]

In describing the placement of adjectives, you may have noted that we have been using words like *ordinarily* and *usually.* This is because under certain circumstances, adjective modifiers can be moved to create varying stylistic alternatives. Notice how the placement of the adjectives and the adjective phrases varies in each of the following sentences:

1. The *tired, cranky* <u>children</u> annoyed everyone.
   The <u>children</u>, *tired and cranky,* annoyed everyone.

2. The children, *whining about lunch,* annoyed everyone.
   Whining about lunch, the children annoyed everyone.

The placement of adjective modifiers, an interesting and important aspect of a writer's style, will be covered more fully in Chapter 8.

PRONOUNS

Another type of word that can function in many of the same ways as a noun or nominal (subject, object, object of preposition, etc.) is the *pronoun,* which is commonly defined as "a word that takes the place of a noun." This common definition is a bit misleading, however, because pronouns can substitute for nouns or nominals; that is, they can replace one word or more than one word:

1. I hate <u>liver</u>, and I never eat *it.* [*It* replaces *liver.*]

2. <u>The terrified ponies</u> ran for the hills when *they* saw the mountain lion. [*They* replaces *the terrified ponies.*]

3. <u>Reading in bed</u> is pleasant, but many people don't like to do *it.* [*It* replaces *reading in bed.*]

Notice in these examples that the pronouns (*it* and *they*) can replace one word (*liver*) or more than one word (*the terrified ponies*; *reading in bed*).

Although pronouns are used for a number of reasons, probably the most common use is to avoid repetition. When pronouns are used to avoid repetition, they replace nouns or nominals that might otherwise be restated:

1. I want a new dress so that I can wear the new dress on vacation.
   I want a new dress so that I can wear *it* on vacation.

2. John is a science teacher, and John teaches in Toledo.
   John is a science teacher, and *he* teaches in Toledo.

As these sentence pairs illustrate, the first sentence in each pair is not only repetitious but also more difficult to understand than the alternatives, in which pronouns replace the repeated nouns. Correct use of pronouns, then, can enhance the intelligibility of speaking or writing.

Another common use for pronouns is to stand for entities whose identity is not known. If, for example, you have an aquarium in which the fish are dying but you are unsure of the cause, you might say "*Something is killing the fish in my aquarium.*" *Something* is a pronoun. Similarly, if you get a mysterious message on your answering machine, you might tell your roommate "*Someone left a weird message on our machine.*" *Someone* is a pronoun. In these two examples, pronouns (*something; someone*) were used because the noun or nominal they replaced was unknown.

The Importance of Reference

Because pronouns are used to replace nouns or nominals, what pronouns stand for must always be clear, both in speech and in writing. Imagine, for example, the following conversation:

MARY LOU: *I can't go to dinner tonight.*
BETTY: *Why not?*
MARY LOU: *I'm too upset about it.*
BETTY: *Huh?*

Because Mary Lou hasn't made it clear earlier in the conversation what has been upsetting her, Betty is at a loss. Just exactly what is Mary Lou upset about? What does *it* stand for? The circumstances relating to dinner? Something else entirely? Betty's problem is a problem with *reference,* which is the relationship between a pronoun and the noun or nominal it stands for. Because of a problem with reference, Betty doesn't understand what *it* stands for or refers to. Problems with reference are particularly vexing in writing, because ordinarily, a reader can't ask the writer what he or she means. Passages of writing that exhibit unclear reference (e.g., "If you haven't experienced *this* ..." and the reader isn't sure what *this* refers to) are difficult, if not impossible, to interpret.

Pronoun–Antecedent Agreement

The technical term that designates the noun or nominal that a pronoun stands for or refers to is *antecedent*. Look at the following sentences:

1. I hate <u>liver</u>, and I never eat *it*. [*It* replaces *liver;* the noun *liver* is the antecedent of the pronoun *it*.]

2. <u>The terrified ponies</u> ran for the hills when *they* saw the mountain lion. [*They* replaces *the terrified ponies*; the noun phrase *the terrified ponies* is the antecedent of the pronoun *they*.]

3. <u>Reading in bed</u> is pleasant, but many people don't like to do *it*. [*It* replaces *reading in bed*; the nominal *reading in bed* is the antecedent of the pronoun *it*.]

4. <u>The angry princess</u> dismissed *Bill* after *he* insulted *her*. [*Her* replaces the noun phrase *the angry princess*; the noun phrase *the angry princess* is the antecedent of the pronoun *her*. *He* replaces the noun *Bill; Bill* is the antecedent of the pronoun *he*.]

5. <u>The terrified pony</u> ran for the hills when *he* saw the mountain lion. [(*He* replaces *the terrified pony*; the noun phrase *the terrified pony* is the antecedent of the pronoun *he*.]

In English, the form of pronouns can reflect agreement with their antecedents to show number and gender. In sentence 1, the noun *liver* (the antecedent) is singular and neither masculine nor feminine; the pronoun *it*—which replaces *liver*—reflects these qualities. The antecedent in sentence 2 is plural (more than one pony), but plural pronouns do not reflect gender, so the pronoun *they* reflects number only. Likewise, in sentence 3, the nominal (antecedent) *reading in bed* is singular and neither masculine nor feminine, so *it* is the appropriate pronoun. Although agreement isn't always necessary to clearly tie a pronoun to its antecedent, it can often be helpful in this regard, as sentence 4 illustrates, pronoun agreement indicates that *Bill* insulted the *princess* rather than the opposite. (Consider this alternative: *The angry princess dismissed Bill after she insulted him.*)

Sentence 5 highlights an interesting phenomenon with regard to pronoun agreement: a pronoun that refers to an animal can show agreement with its antecedent in several ways. A pronoun that refers to an animal can indicate the gender of the animal, as in the example (*The terrified pony . . . he*). Or an animal can be referred to as *it*, regardless of gender (e.g., *The terrified pony ran for the hills when it saw the mountain lion*). Furthermore, because gender stereotypes are sometimes conferred on animals, people select pronouns that reflect these stereotypes. For this reason, a kitten whose gender is unknown may be referred to as *she*, or a lion whose gender is unknown may be referred to as *he*. Inanimate objects such as nations and ships are also sometimes imbued with characteristics that reflect gender for particular cultures, which accounts for sentences such as the following:

1. <u>Italy</u> was deluged by tourists last year. *She* is preparing for a larger onslaught this summer. [*Italy,* the antecedent, is referred to by a pronoun (*she*) that shows feminine agreement.]

2. *The Enterprise* was a good ship. When *she* was destroyed, the crew wept. [*The Enterprise,* the antecedent, is referred to by a pronoun (*she*) that shows feminine agreement.]

Pronoun Case

Nouns—except for possessives—don't change their form to reflect their function in a sentence; pronouns, however, do modify their form to reflect the various roles they play. The form that pronouns take to reflect their function in a sentence is often referred to as their *case*. Notice that in the following sentences, the nouns do not change regardless of whether they function as subjects or direct objects, but their pronouns do.

<u>The man</u> ran a red light.   A police officer arrested <u>the man</u>.
  subject   direct object

<u>He</u> ran a red light.   A police officer arrested <u>him</u>.
subject   direct object

Pronoun case forms in English are commonly referred to as *subjective* (or *nominative*), *objective,* and *possessive.* Here is a list of common pronoun forms that reflect these categories.

<u>Subjective</u>	<u>Objective</u>	<u>Possessive</u>
I	me	mine
you	you	yours
he, she, it	him, her, it	his, hers, its

When pronouns function as subjects or subject complements in sentences, they take the subjective form. When pronouns function in other ways (as direct objects, objects of prepositions, indirect objects, and objective complements), they take the objective form. You can see this contrast in the following examples:

1. Mary hit *him.* [*Him* takes the objective form; *him* is the direct object.]

2. *She* is my friend. [*She* takes the subjective form; *she* is the subject.]

3. I am tired of *him.* [*Him* takes the objective form; *him* is the object of the preposition *of.*]

Pronouns that function as appositives reflect the function of the noun they rename. That is, if the pronoun appositive renames a direct object, the pronoun takes the objective form; if the pronoun appositive renames a subject, the pronoun takes the subjective form; and so on. You can see the application of this rule in the following sentences:

1. The winners are *she* and *I*. [*She* and *I* take the subjective form; *she* are *I* are subject complements following the linking verb *are*.]

2. Both winners, *she* and *I,* were delighted. [*She* and *I* take the subjective form because they are appositives that rename the subject, *winners.*]

3. The new senator annoyed many citizens, including Bill and *me*. [*Me* takes the objective form because it is an appositive that renames the direct object, *many citizens*, which includes *Bill* and *me*.]

The possessive pronoun form acts a little differently, however. Unlike the other pronoun case forms, which reflect the function of pronouns in sentences, the form of a possessive pronoun merely indicates that it has replaced a noun in a possessive relationship. That is, whether a possessive pronoun is a subject, direct object, indirect object, or other part of speech does not influence the form it takes, as these examples illustrate:

1. *Direct object:*   Bill likes *my office*.   Bill likes *mine*. [*Mine* replaces *my office*.]

   Subject: *My office* is wonderful.   *Mine* is wonderful. [*Mine* replaces *my office*.]

2. *Direct object:*   Bill wants *her cell phone*. Bill wants *hers*. [*Hers* replaces *her cell phone*.]

   Subject: *Her cell phone* is small.   *Hers* is small. [*Hers* replaces *Her cell phone*.]

Types of Pronouns

In the foregoing discussion, we have introduced two common types of pronouns: ***personal pronouns*** (*I, me, you, he, she, it*, etc.) and *possessive pronouns* (*mine, hers, theirs*, etc.). Earlier in this chapter we also discussed the *demonstratives* (*this, that, these, those*). When demonstratives accompany nouns (e.g., *this book, these dancers*), they function as articles. However, demonstratives can also function as pronouns. ***Demonstrative pronouns***, then, are demonstratives that replace a noun or nominal, as in the following examples:

1. I love lasagna.   I love *that*. [The demonstrative pronoun *that* replaces the noun *lasagna*.]

2. This book is fabulous.   *This* is fabulous. [The demonstrative pronoun *this* replaces the noun phrase *this book*.]

3. Bill wants the little yellow bananas.   Bill wants *those*. [The demonstrative pronoun *those* replaces the noun phrase *the little yellow bananas*.]

4. <u>These kittens</u> are the cutest I've ever seen.

These are the cutest I've ever seen. [The demonstrative pronoun *these* replaces the noun phrase *these kittens*.]

Besides personal, possessive, and demonstrative pronouns, there are several other common types. ***Interrogative pronouns*** are used in questions that require information: *What* do you want? *Whose* did you lose? *Who* was it? *Which* is less fattening? ***Relative pronouns***, which often resemble interrogative pronouns but function differently, occur in relative clauses. We will examine relative clauses in more depth in Chapter 8, but for now, here are several examples of sentences that contain **relative clauses** (underlined) with relative pronouns (in italics):

1. The man <u>*who* won the lottery</u> quit his job.
2. We love plants <u>*that* don't need much care</u>.
3. Her latest best-seller, <u>*which* was reviewed in the tabloids</u>, shocked everyone.

Reflexive pronouns also occur quite frequently because they allow speakers and writers to refer to themselves. Contrast the sentences *Betty hurt her* and *Betty hurt herself*. The first one indicates that someone other than Betty got hurt; in the second, the reflexive pronoun *herself* conveys the fact that Betty was the one who was hurt. Here are some more examples of sentences with reflexive pronouns:

1. John likes *himself* a great deal.
2. People who are obsessed with *themselves* annoy me.
3. I could just kick *myself* for forgetting your birthday.

Finally, another common type of pronoun is the ***indefinite pronoun***, which you saw in the example *Something is killing my fish*. Indefinite pronouns refer to nonspecific or unknown noun antecedents using words such as *someone, something, somewhere, anyone, anything, anybody, anywhere, nothing, nobody, no one, none*, and *nowhere*. Indefinite pronouns can be particularly vexing to writers (and to language arts teachers) because they can refer to more than one **referent** and yet are grammatically singular. For example in the sentence *Nobody wants his or her possessions stolen*, the indefinite pronoun *nobody* clearly refers to a class of people (all who don't want their possessions stolen). Nevertheless, *nobody* is grammatically singular, which is reflected in the agreement of the verb *wants* (rather than *want*) and of the pronouns *his* and *her*. The fact that indefinite pronouns like *nobody* refer to more than one entity accounts for the common occurrence of sentences like *Nobody wants their possessions stolen* or *Anyone who wants their car washed should pay now*. Besides causing problems with agreement, indefinite pronouns also turn up used improperly in negative constructions such as **I don't want nobody to see me like this*. Such constructions, though regularly produced and systematic (rule-governed) in some dialects of American English, are considered inappropriate in most writing.

GERUNDS AND INFINITIVES

Throughout this part of the chapter, we have been discussing how nouns and nominals function, the words that can accompany them, and the various forms they may take. Before we conclude our coverage of nouns and nominals, however, let's take a look at two additional types of nominals (words and phrases that have the capacity to function as nouns): gerunds and infinitives.

Gerunds

What is a *gerund*? The most basic definition of a gerund is "a verb form ending in *-ing* that functions as a noun." In other words, a gerund looks like a verb but functions or acts like a noun. Examine the following sentences:

1. *Walking* makes Kris tired.

2. Kris is *walking* six miles a day.

In sentence 1, *walking* may initially appear to be a verb and so part of the predicate, but the verb is actually the word *makes*. So in this sentence, *walking* is a noun and functions as the subject of the sentence. In sentence 2, by contrast, *walking* is part of the verb phrase *is walking*. In this sentence, *walking* not only looks like a verb but is also functioning as a verb. We will talk more about verbs and the forms they take in Chapter 4, but for now it is important to note that *-ing* forms can function as parts of verbs (as in sentence 2) or as nouns (as in sentence 1).

Here are some additional examples of the types of noun functions gerunds can serve in sentences.

1. *Subject:*   *Fishing* can be a relaxing activity.

2. *Object:*   Kevin and Kris love *fishing*.

3. *Subject complement:*   Their favorite sport is *fishing*.

4. *Object of a preposition:*   This pond is reserved for *fishing*.

5. *Appositive:*   Kevin's favorite activity, *fishing*, is very relaxing.

As you can see from these examples, one aspect of gerunds is that they are very mobile within sentences in terms of placement and function. This is because gerunds can function in most of the same ways that nouns can function (as subjects, objects, and so forth).

Similar to other nominals, gerunds can also be enhanced by modifiers to create *gerund phrases*, which can function in the same way as single-word gerunds. In the following examples, the gerund phrases are underlined and the gerunds are italicized.

1. *Subject:*   His *eating* lasagna was irritating to Alice.

2. *Object of a preposition:* In fact, Alice was livid at <u>his *eating* lasagna</u>.

Overall, gerund phrases can occupy a range of noun positions and functions, as these examples illustrate:

1. *Subject:*   <u>*Kissing* the blarney stone</u> is the goal of many tourists to Ireland.

2. *Object:*   He finds <u>*watching* television</u> a bore.

3. *Subject complement:*   Her major form of exercise is <u>*working* out at the gym</u>.

4. *Object of a preposition:*   Kris learned tai bo by <u>*watching* a video</u>.

5. *Appositive:*   Her new hobby, <u>ballroom *dancing*</u>, was a healthy choice.

One rather simple way to determine whether an *-ing* word is a gerund and thus functioning as a noun is to conduct the "*it* test." If the word *it* can be substituted for the *-ing* word or phrase in question, the word is a gerund, as in the following examples:

1. *Dancing* is fun. [*It* is fun; sentence passes the test.]

2. He finds *watching television* a bore. [He finds *it* a bore; sentence passes the test.]

3. He is *dancing in the kitchen.* [He is *it;* sentence does not pass the test.]

In the case of some noun functions, it may be necessary to rearrange the sentence to use the "*it* test," especially when the gerund is the object of a preposition:

Kris learned tai bo by *watching a video.*

Watching a video was how Kris learned tai bo.

It was how Kris learned tai bo.

As we shall explain in more detail in Chapter 8, *-ing* words can also function as adjectives. For now, the important thing about *-ing* words is to recognize that they can function as parts of verbs, as nominals, or as adjectives. Therefore, it is important not to confuse them.

Infinitives

Infinitives and infinitive phrases look like verb forms. They are, however, nominals. Like gerunds, they function in ways that nouns do, as well as in other capacities that we will address in another chapter. Infinitives are easily formed from the base or uninflected form of the verb (*eat, breathe, go*) simply by adding the word *to* before it:

To breathe is natural.

I want *to go.*

Infinitives and infinitive phrases can also take expanded verb forms:

1. *To have breathed* that foul air seemed impossible.

2. *To be breathing* again felt good.

3. *To have danced* all night was an incredible thing.

4. *To be forgiving* is noble.

There is a specific set of verbs that can be followed by gerunds (e.g., *deny, enjoy, quit*) and a specific set that can be followed by infinitives (e.g., *plan, hope, require*). There is also a small set of verbs (e.g., *begin, start, continue, like, love, prefer, hate*) after which infinitives are interchangeable with gerunds with no difference in meaning. And there is an even smaller set of verbs that allow either an infinitive or a gerund to follow but with a difference in meaning. For example, compare the following two pairs of sentences:

1. I like *fishing*.
   I like *to fish*.

2. I regret *telling* you.
   I regret *to tell* you.

In sentence pair 1, what the person likes—the activity of catching fish—is conveyed regardless of the choice of infinitive or gerund to follow the verb *like*. In sentence pair 2, however, the meaning is substantially changed by the choice of infinitive or gerund. In the first sentence, the speaker regrets having divulged something in the past; in the second, the speaker is preparing the listener to receive bad news.

Many native speakers of English instinctively recognize the way in which they can use gerunds and infinitives interchangeably without a change in meaning; however, gerunds and infinitives, and the verbs that they can follow, often pose a great deal of confusion for nonnative speakers of English. Regardless of whether infinitives can be interchangeable with gerunds following specific verbs, they can act like gerunds in that they are nominals that can function in many ways that nouns do (e.g., as subject, direct object, subject complement, or appositive), as the following examples illustrate:

1. *Subject:*   *To fish* is Kevin's favorite activity.

2. *Object:*   Kevin wants *to fish* this weekend

3. *Subject complement:*   Kevin's favorite activity is *to fish*.

4. *Appositive:*   Kevin's favorite activity, *to fish*, is relaxing for him.

Unlike gerunds, however, infinitives cannot occupy the role of *object of a preposition*. Moreover, the fact that infinitives are formed with the word *to* can lead students to confuse them with prepositional phrases. In the following two sentences, notice how the word *to* functions as part of an infinitive and as a preposition:

1. *Infinitive:*   I want <u>*to* sing</u>.

2. *Preposition:*   I went <u>*to* the farm</u>.

Another similarity infinitives share with gerunds is that they can be expanded with modifiers and other words to create phrases. *Infinitive phrases* are formed by including not just the infinitive but all of its modifications, as the following examples illustrate:

1. *Subject:*   ☆   <u>*To exercise* daily</u> requires discipline.

2. *Direct object:*   Kris vows <u>*to exercise* more often</u>.

3. *Subject complement:*   Jim's goal is <u>*to exercise* his mind</u>.

4. *Appositive:*   Jane's routine, <u>*to exercise* each morning</u>, is a good one.

Notice in each of these sentences that the infinitive phrase is made up of the infinitive plus adverbials or direct objects. A final similarity between infinitives and gerunds is that they can be replaced by the word *it* and are thus subject to the *"it* test" in the same manner as gerunds. Compare the following sets of sentences, all of which pass the test:

1. <u>*Exercising* daily</u> requires discipline. [*It* requires discipline.]

2. <u>To exercise *daily*</u> requires discipline. [*It* requires discipline.]

3. I like <u>*to exercise*</u>. [I like *it*.]

4. I like <u>*exercising*</u>. [I like *it*.]

Because of the similar roles gerunds and infinitives play in forming nominals, the choice whether to use a gerund or infinitive is largely a matter of the word and stylistic choices the writer makes.

● EXERCISES FOR PRACTICE

A. In the following simple sentences, identify the nouns or nominals and the function of each underlined noun, noun phrase, or nominal: subject, direct object, indirect object, appositive, object of a preposition, subject complement.

Example: <u>Swimming in the ocean</u> is <u>my hobby</u>.
                    subject   subject complement

Example: <u>She</u> gave <u>Bob</u> <u>her full attention</u>.
                subject   indirect   direct object
                            object

1. <u>Alice</u> visited <u>Italy</u> last summer.

2. <u>John</u> traveled by <u>bus</u> from <u>Chicago</u> to <u>New York</u>.

3. <u>He</u> gave <u>Kris</u> the <u>book</u>.

4. The <u>idea</u> is fine with <u>me</u>.

5. <u>Bill Clinton</u>, the former <u>president</u>, is a <u>Democrat</u>.

6. <u>Vinnie's</u> favorite sport is <u>tennis</u>.

7. Shakespeare's play *<u>Hamlet</u>* is world famous.

8. The <u>scientists</u> were researching the <u>planets</u>.

9. <u>California</u> is the <u>home</u> of the <u>Raiders</u>.

10. Susan held Tom responsible for the <u>accident</u>.

B. Write one sentence containing a noun, a noun phrase, or a nominal for each of the functions indicated (a total of six sentences):

1. *Subject:*
2. *Object:*
3. *Indirect object:*
4. *Object of a preposition:*
5. *Subject complement:*
6. *Appositive:*

C. In the following sentences, one or more nouns are underlined. If the underlined noun is a common noun, revise it to be a proper noun. If the underlined noun is a proper noun, revise it to be a common noun.

Example: <u>Martha</u> hates grits. *That woman* hates grits.

Example: Those children are annoying <u>the dog</u>. Those children are annoying *Fido*.

1. <u>Our cat</u> is eating less than it normally does.

2. <u>Dr. Smith</u> is a big fan of exercises.

3. <u>Morrison Hall</u> is just one block away.

4. My sister works for <u>that corporation</u>.

5. I want to buy <u>a computer</u>.

6. He plans to revisit <u>the country</u> very soon.

7. <u>Rover</u> seems to be happy with his new food dish.

8. <u>My friends</u> like to golf.

9. <u>The new administrator</u> is very competent at her job.

10. How will you help <u>Jim</u> pass his geography test?

D. Each of the following sentences contains nouns that are preceded by definite articles, indefinite articles, or demonstratives. Underline and identify each of these according to type.

> **Example:**   My brother hates <u>the</u> Cleveland Browns. Definite article

> **Example:**   Kris hates <u>that</u> idea. Demonstrative

1. She drove a Ferrari to the party.

2. An aardvark can also be called an anteater.

3. This book is very good.

4. I brought these cookies for Sarah.

5. His name was one in a series.

6. A funny thing happened on the way over here.

7. Kris was looking for that house with the green shutters.

8. He remembered that the address had an odd number in it.

9. A house in the country has always been my dream.

10. He went to the dentist for an X-ray of his wisdom teeth.

E. In the following paragraph, you will find mistakes in the usage of count and noncount nouns, articles, numbers, and quantifiers. Find these mistakes, correct them, and explain why they are mistakes.

> Nonnative speaker of the English can experience much difficulties when learning some English grammar. One, they may have troubles learning to use the -*s* plural inflection accurately. Especially at a stage of learning, they may add -*s* to noun that isn't plural. Second, they may have many difficulty with learning irregular plural form.

F. The following sentences contain both regular and irregular plurals and possessives. Underline and identify each one according to type.

> **Example:**   I hate <u>Terry's</u> attitude. Singular possessive

> **Example:**   Those <u>fraternities'</u> houses are being renovated.
> Plural possessive

1. The women's clinic is on Main Street.

2. Her teeth were causing great pain.

3. Our students' grades improved significantly.

4. Kris's family is from New York.

5. After the cart tipped over, loaves of bread were scattered in the aisle.

6. My mother-in-law's business is really doing well.

7. Children often play in the park until dark.

8. Yesterday's agenda was well organized.

9. Her beliefs were not shared by all.

10. The server placed the knives next to the forks.

G. In the following sentences, underline all of the adjective modifiers. Some of the adjective modifiers will be single-word modifiers, and some will be groups of words acting together as adjectives.

> **Example:** The <u>loud, feisty</u> children <u>from Toledo</u> annoyed everyone <u>who was at the hockey game</u>.
>
> **Example:** You should toss those <u>smelly, overripe</u> bananas away.

1. As I left that awful party, Bartilda gave me a nasty look.

2. Those little brown bats in our basement gave me a terrible scare.

3. Won't anyone in our class tell me why I failed that preposterous test?

4. Before you come to my new house, our wonderful friend, Bob, is going to fix our leaky roof.

5. The plants in the kitchen wilted after John gave them that cheap fertilizer.

6. Long-haired dogs should be groomed regularly because otherwise they will have matted coats with lots of dead fur.

7. Before those new machines are installed, a qualified electrician who has experience in the area of computing should examine the outlets.

8. The small, shivering kitty with the weepy eye was taken to the vet after work yesterday.

9. At Sue's southern dinner, where every wonderful food imaginable was served, everyone ate too much rich food.

10. Alice, especially, overextended herself by gorging on fresh turnip greens, black-eyed peas, and yellow squash casserole that was out of this world.

H. Each of the following sentences contains one or more groups of adjectives in a series. Punctuate the adjectives properly with commas, and underline each coordinate adjective you find. If the sentence is OK as it stands, write OK.

> **Example:**   We replaced our broken flagstone walk with a new wooden deck. OK

> **Example:**   John likes chewy peanut butter cookies accompanied by <u>fresh</u>, <u>cold</u> milk.

1. Please help! There's a mangy stray cat in my yard.

2. Last summer our friends bought a red brick house.

3. Plants with dark green foliage are my favorite.

4. All of the students cried when their warm energetic teacher retired.

5. Don't you think that is a sad depressing story?

6. Every day on my way to work, I pass a small picket fence.

7. Those tired cranky children are going to annoy that small yappy dog.

8. Who opened the window and let in that giant scary wasp?

9. When Ruth described her latest backpacking trip, we were all impressed.

10. Our faded torn draperies will have to be replaced with pale aluminum shades.

I. Write ten sentences of your own that contain adjective modifiers—either single-word or multiword. Edit each of your sentences carefully to ensure that you've used commas where appropriate. Then put brackets around each of the adjective modifiers in your sentences.

> **Example:**   Yesterday after [math] class, I had a [pepperoni] pizza with [old] friends [from Toledo].

> **Example:**   Don't you hate [yappy], [little] dogs [that are always barking]?

J. In the following sentences are some underlined pronouns and nouns or noun phrases. Substitute a noun when the sentence contains a pronoun, and substitute a pronoun when the sentence contains a noun or noun phrase.

> **Example:**   <u>My sister Laura</u> hates her job. *She* hates her job.

> **Example:**   Alice loves <u>John</u>. Alice loves *him*.

1. John is <u>her</u> friend.

2. <u>She</u> is walking six miles a day.

3. Kevin gave <u>Kris</u> a ring.

4. <u>Someone</u> ate <u>all the cookies.</u>

5. Tony wouldn't stand for <u>it.</u>

6. <u>This</u> is another fine story.

7. No one knows <u>his</u> name.

8. <u>That</u> is <u>hers.</u>

9. How do <u>they</u> work under such conditions?

10. The group gossiped about <u>them.</u>

K. In the following paragraph, you will find mistakes in the use of pronouns. Find each mistake, correct it, and explain why it is a mistake.

> Yesterday, I went for a long walk in the woods because I wanted to enjoy the beauty of the spring weather. It was very nice. While walking, I saw many children riding their bikes and playing games with each other. This was fun. Everyone was enjoying theirself in the pretty weather. It was enjoyable to watch. After a while, I got tired. While I was sitting on a bench resting, a bird came and sat next to myself. Overall, we had a pleasant afternoon.

L. In the following sentences, underline each gerund phrase or infinitive phrase. Then indicate how it functions in the context of its sentence.

Example: Committee members enjoy <u>reading files</u>. Gerund phrase as direct object

Example: <u>To read a thousand files</u> is a demanding task. Infinitive phrase as subject

1. To walk three miles a day is impressive.

2. Swimming in the shark-infested waters is dangerous.

3. Her mother's hobby, collecting Beanie Babies, was becoming an obsession.

4. Terry loves washing his new car.

5. Kris likes to eat Japanese food.

6. The big plan, investing in Starbucks, turned out to be a good one.

7. Her next plan is to visit Ireland.

8. He needed an excuse for leaving the party early.

9. Her favorite springtime activity is planting flowers.

10. He wanted to cook her a special meal.

M. Construct ten sentences of your own, five using infinitives and five using gerunds in each of the following functions: subject, direct object, object of a preposition, object complement, and appositive. Be sure to identify the form and function of each nominal you use.

> **Example:**   Her goal, to end world hunger, was a noble one. (infinitive phrase as appositive)

> **Example:**   Ending world hunger is a noble goal. (gerund phrase as subject)

PART II   CHALLENGES FOR WRITERS

TROUBLE WITH NOUN INFLECTIONS

Several of the most common editing problems for inexperienced writers involve the **inflections** that nouns can take. Because both regular noun inflections (plural and possessive) involve the letter *s*, apprentice writers often confuse these inflections to produce sentences such as these:

1. *I couldn't study because of the noise those *boys'* were making all night long.

2. *Please don't give me *Marthas* phone number now because I'll just lose it.

In the first sentence, the noun *boy* is marked with an inflection (*-s'*) that indicates both the plural and the possessive, when only the plural inflection (*-s*) is appropriate. In sentence 2, the noun *Martha* is marked with an inflection (*-s*) that marks it as plural when in fact the noun *Martha* is singular, but in a possessive relationship with *phone number* (*Whose* phone number? *Martha's* phone number). These kinds of confusions involving the two noun inflections (plural *-s* and possessive *'s*) occur quite frequently in the writing of many students and persist well into college.

Besides the letter *s*, the other marker associated with noun inflections is the apostrophe ('). And like the letter *s*, the apostrophe also serves two different purposes. One purpose of the apostrophe is to help mark the *possessive* relationship in conjunction with nouns, as in *John's guitar* or *the children's birthdays* or *the boys' toys*. The other function of the apostrophe is to indicate the omission of one or more letters in contractions: *We're tired* (for *We are tired*); *I'm sick of this* (for *I am sick of this*); *I can't go* (for *I cannot go*). To confuse matters further, possessive pronouns do *not* take apostrophes: *his guitar, their birthday, their toys*. To make matters even more potentially confusing, common contractions often involve pronouns: *I'm tired; They're hungry; It's a miracle; You're too emotional.* This association of the apostrophe with both possessives and contractions undoubtedly contributes to the widespread confusion of *their* with *they're*, *your* with *you're*, and *its* with *it's*.

On 7-11 website

Besides editing problems caused by confusion associated with the -*s* inflection and the apostrophe—which are widespread and affect many inexperienced writers—there are editing issues with respect to the -*s* inflection that are particular to certain populations of writers. Writers whose first language is not English often overgeneralize the -*s* ending and add it in contexts where it doesn't belong:

*Only one *girls* wants to study later. (-*s* added to singular noun)

*The *childrens* are leaving. (regular -*s* inflection added to irregular plural)

There are also dialects of American English that regularly omit the plural -*s* inflection in some contexts. Some dialects, for example, provide the option of omitting a plural -*s* if the noun is preceded by a plural quantifier, as in *Mary read five book*. Other dialects allow the plural -*s* to be omitted with nouns of measurement, as in *five mile up the road* or *about forty pound of manure*. Similarly, dialects can also produce different possessive forms. Some varieties of American English indicate possessive relationships principally by word order, thus rendering the possessive -*s* inflection as unnecessary in many contexts: *I saw the man car on the street*. As another example of how dialects can affect possessive forms, speakers of some American English dialects make the possessive pronoun *mine* consistent with all others (which already end in *s: yours, his, ours,* etc.) by adding -*s* to *mine,* as in *Those are mines*. Although it is not possible to describe the extent to which every dialect speech variant manifests itself in writing, such variants do have an effect on writing and may contribute to particular editing problems that involve the use of noun inflections. The acquisition of comprehensive, effective editing skills is a long-term process and is therefore no small feat for any writer. However, two important keys to this process, which we cannot overemphasize, are that students must learn to recognize patterns in their own writing to which they must become sensitive and that students need to acquire techniques that force them to attend to detail. In regard to addressing problems involving noun inflections, both of these are important.

Students whose speech habits affect their production of -*s* inflections in particular ways need to become aware of these patterns so that they can attend to them when proofreading their writing. As for attention to detail, any inflectional ending—and the -*s* is no exception—is quite small and therefore a "detail" that students need to train themselves to see. Perhaps the best and most comprehensive approach to such training is illustrated in Mina Shaughnessy's *Errors and Expectations*. In Chapter 4, "Common Errors," Shaughnessy provides a fifteen-page series of activities (which she refers to as a "lesson") with one objective: to help students understand the difference between the noun -*s* inflection and the verb -*s* inflection and develop a strategy for knowing how to use each inflection appropriately. Some of the activities include a test for "hearing" the -*s* by having students read aloud various phrases and noting the difference between those with inflections and those without. Other options include a section on "seeing" the *-s* by asking students to read words with various inflections and "writing" the *-s* by asking students to respond to questions containing inflections in the answer (e.g., *Does Jerline usually <u>get</u> to class on time? Yes, Jerline usually <u>gets</u> to class on time*). Because the lesson doesn't assume any conscious knowledge of grammatical concepts on the part of the student writer, it includes exercises that help students determine if they're apprehending inflections in the first place as well as explanations and activities that explain to students what an inflection is and how to detect one. Our point here, then, is that students who are having editing difficulties that involve noun inflections cannot simply be provided with rules for proper use. They may need help in understanding the function of inflections and in recognizing them, both in speech and in writing. They may need help in understanding the difference between the plural *-s* inflection and the possessive *-s* inflection, as well as how to recognize and produce each properly within written contexts. Shaughnessy's lesson provides an example of how to provide students with a detailed, comprehensive, well-sequenced set of activities that begins with an important foundational concept—the inflection—and then moves on to apply this concept to address particular editing problems that are related to that concept.

TROUBLE WITH NOUN FORM

Irregular Forms

So far you have seen two problems with noun inflections—identifying and using the plural *-s* inflection (e.g., *boys* versus *boys'*) and identifying and using the apostrophe (e.g. *Martha's* versus **Marthas*; *their* versus *they're*) appropriately. You've also seen how speakers of dialects and nonnative speakers of English may have specific problems in identifying and using the plural *-s* inflection and the apostrophe. In addition to these problem areas, student writers may have other problems with noun inflections, especially as they relate to irregular forms of the plural.

In Part One we discussed that plural forms in English can pose two challenges for writers. One possible challenge is that the spelling of a word may change to add the plural *-s* inflection (e.g., *study, studies; echo, echoes*). Another possible challenge for writers is confusion between regular plural forms (which add *-s*, such as *cake, cakes*) and irregular plural forms (which do not add *-s*, such as *ox, oxen* and *curriculum, curricula*). As you have seen, nonnative speakers of English may overgeneralize the *-s* ending and add it where it does not belong, as in **one girls* or **the childrens*. (Note that the word *childrens* has two plural endings, an irregular *-ren* inflection and a regular *-s* inflection.) When writing, nonnative speakers of English often confuse the regular and irregular forms and thus may form the irregular plural and add *-s* as well. This may be especially true of words that do not change their form when made plural, such as *sheep* (**sheeps*) or *deer* (**deers*).

A related confusion with irregular plurals may occur as a result of lack of knowledge of the irregular forms. In such cases, the student writer may create such plurals as *oxes* rather than *oxen* or *gooses* rather than *geese*. To remediate these problems, it is important that the students be made aware of the regular and irregular plural forms and the varieties of spellings plurals can take. One way to help students become aware of such variation is by providing them with lists of common words and the rules related to the spelling of their plural forms. It is also important to give students opportunities to practice applying this information, for example, by completing exercises and participating in other guided editing activities, including ones like the sample passages in the exercises at the end of Part Two of this chapter.

Another way to help students is to encourage the purchase and use of a good dictionary. We discuss the possibilities and the constraints of student use of the dictionary more fully in Chapter 11, "Grammar and the Writing Process." The dictionary can be an especially valuable resource for information on word forms and the endings and inflections words take. Although it is impossible for you as a teacher to provide students with all the information they will ever need to know about noun inflections or usage, you can provide them with knowledge of how to use the dictionary to help them find the answers to questions regarding word forms that may arise as they write. We recommend that you require the purchase of a reliable, hardbound dictionary as part of your course requirements. We also recommend that you find a handbook of English usage and require your students to purchase it along with their other textbooks. In choosing a handbook of English usage, you should look for one that is detailed and comprehensive (not restricted to certain aspects of grammar and usage, such as verbs) and one that is easy to use (tabs indicating the subject matter of individual sections are especially helpful). There are a variety of handbooks on the market that you should take the time to look at and evaluate before recommending one to your students.

While a dictionary is a valuable reference for students to look up irregularities in spelling, they will need to be familiar with the singular form of commonly used nouns that take irregular plurals in order to be able to look these words up. For example, for students to look up the plural form *children*, they will first have to be aware that it is a plural and that the singular is *child*. And although students' understanding of appropriate English usage involves more than memorization of lists, initially it can be useful to have students keep reminders or charts of irregular plurals and any rules that might apply in such cases. Students encounter difficulty with the spelling of regular nouns as well when the spelling requires an addition to or a change in the word, such as *study, studies* or *echo, echoes*. In these cases, it can be helpful for students to learn the various rules that govern such irregular spellings and how to apply them, as well as how to find these rules in the dictionary (all good dictionaries show the forms for both regular and irregular plurals). However, as with most aspects of English grammar, there are exceptions to these rules. As you learned in Part One, there are a number of exceptions regarding the plural forms of words ending in *o* and words ending in *f*. That is, the plural of *echo* is *echoes*—following the rule that words that end in *o* add *-es* to make the plural. However, there are exceptions to this rule, such as *auto, autos,* and plurals that can be written two ways, such as *zero, zeroes, zeros.* We suggest that you help students develop their own strategies for learning how to spell plurals that are exceptions to whatever rules they have learned. You can begin by helping them become aware of such irregularities. One approach to creating such awareness is by having students look at these plurals in context—in a story or paragraph, for example. Another approach is to have students look up words in a dictionary or handbook and note their plural forms. If there is a choice of plural forms, as with the word *zero*, it is important to emphasize that the student writer needs to select a spelling of the plural form (ordinarily, the one given first in the dictionary) and be consistent in its use. Once your students become aware of such exceptions, you may suggest they create their own alphabetized list of words that they may find problematic and use that list for reference when they are editing their writing.

Problems with Pronoun Case

Pronoun case refers to the required form a pronoun must take according to whether it functions as a subject or an object in a sentence. Although pronouns most often take the place of subjects and objects in sentences, there are also possessive case pronouns. As a result, as we have explained earlier, there are three forms of case, the **subjective**, the **objective**, and the possessive:

Subjective Case	Objective Case	Possessive Case
I	me	my, mine
you	you	your, yours
he, she, it, who	him, her, it, whom	his, her, its, whose
we	us	our, ours
you	you	your, yours
they, who	them, whom	their, theirs, whose

(handwritten annotations in left margin: Sing / 1st / 2nd / 3rd / pl. 1st / 2nd / 3rd)

Because the choice between using either the subjective or the objective case can cause student writers the most confusion, we will focus our attention here on these two case forms.

In most instances, determining which pronoun to use does not cause a native speaker of English much difficulty. Consider the following examples:

1. <u>Lara</u> drove <u>Dave</u> to work.
      subject   object

   <u>She</u> drove <u>him</u> to work.
    subjective   objective case
    case pronoun   pronoun

2. I gave the books to <u>the students</u>.
   subject   object of preposition

  I gave the books to <u>them</u>.
subjective case   objective case
   pronoun   pronoun

In the first pair of examples, students should be able to distinguish the correct use of the subjective case in *He drove him to work*. It would be rare to hear the sentence *Him drove he to work*. Similarly, most native speakers of English would recognize an error in substituting the subjective for objective case, such as *I gave the books to they*, or vice versa, in *Me gave the books to them*. Nevertheless, the choice to use the subjective or objective case is not always so clear. The following examples reflect contexts in which case is more likely to be confusing to writers.

PRONOUNS THAT PRECEDE APPOSITIVES.

1. *<u>We</u> cyclists* are concerned about careless motorists.

2. Careless motorists concern *<u>us</u> cyclists*.

In both instances, the pronouns must take the case they would take if the noun that follows were not there: subjective case in sentence 1 and objective case in sentence 2.

PRONOUNS IN COMPOUND SUBJECTS AND OBJECTS.

1. **Julie and <u>me</u>* are leaving tomorrow.
   Julie and <u>I</u> are leaving tomorrow.

2. *The teacher doesn't like <u>*her*</u> and <u>*I*</u>.
   The teacher doesn't like <u>*her*</u> and <u>*me*</u>.

In the first pair of sentences, one way to determine the appropriate pronoun case is to delete the first of the compound subjects, *Julie*. That leaves the following choice: *Me am leaving tomorrow* versus *I am leaving tomorrow*. Again, for native speakers of English, the choice of which pronoun to use is somewhat natural, as *me* as a subject both sounds and reads incorrectly. Similarly, in the second pair of sentences, eliminating the first of the compound subjects, *her*, leaves the following options: *The teacher doesn't like I* or *The teacher doesn't like me*. To most native speakers of English, the grammatically appropriate choice, *The teacher doesn't like me*, simply sounds more grammatically acceptable.

Although we might hear a sentence like *Julie and me are leaving tomorrow* in casual conversation, it reflects faulty pronoun case in that the use of the objective case pronoun *me* is inconsistent with the position of the compound subject *Julie and I*. Another easy way to help students determine the correct pronoun usage in such instances of compound subjects and objects is to remove the compound subjects or objects from the sentence, replacing them with a plural pronoun substitute:

Problem sentence:	*Julie and (I, me)* are leaving tomorrow.
Substitution of plural pronoun:	*We* are leaving tomorrow. (Subjective case)
Resolution of problem:	*Julie and I* are leaving tomorrow. (Subjective case)
Problem sentence:	The teacher doesn't like *her and (I, me).*
Substitution of plural pronoun:	The teacher doesn't like *us.* (Objective case)
Resolution of problem:	The teacher doesn't like *her and me.* (Objective case)

PRONOUNS IN PREPOSITIONAL PHRASES.   Pronouns that are used in prepositional phrases function as objects, just as nouns do. So for that reason, pronouns in prepositional phrases should take the objective case:

It was difficult *for me* to apologize.

Although this is a rather simple rule, numerous problems can occur when two pronouns serve as the objects of the same preposition:

*I want to keep this secret just *between you and I.*   [handwritten: object of prep objective]

Often the prepositional phrase *between you and me* is subject to **hypercorrection**, commonly misstated as *between you and I.* The misconception in this instance involves the presumption that *I* is more formal and therefore "more correct" than *me.* But *between* is a preposition, and the object of a preposition must be in the objective case; consequently, only *me* can be correct.

PRONOUNS AFTER *BE*.   As we explained in Chapter 2, *linking verbs* are verbs that take subject complements to complete their meaning; that is, they complement or complete the subject:

It is *I.*

This is *she.*

As these sentences indicate, when subject complements are pronouns, the pronouns must be in the subjective case. Despite this grammatical convention, it is very common to hear the following, particularly in spoken English:

It is *me.*

This is *her.*

Part of the distinction between these two pairs of sentences may have something to do with formality of language. For instance, although it would be grammatically preferable when responding to a phone call to say *This is she,* it is in fact more natural to say *This is her.* This usage may be acceptable on the phone or even in certain writing contexts because it is a long-established idiom in English. But it still technically reflects an error in that the objective case pronouns *me* and *her* should not be made to function as subject complements. Many of the problems students have with pronoun case can be detected by rewriting sentences in the ways we have described throughout this section or to read sentences aloud. In addition, a general familiarity with the distinction between the subjective and objective case forms will help students tremendously. Finally, because apprentice writers need help in understanding the varying levels of formality in both spoken and written contexts, they should have opportunities to analyze the audience, purpose, and context when making these choices about pronoun case.

PROBLEMS WITH PRONOUN AGREEMENT AND REFERENCE

Agreement

Pronoun agreement ordinarily doesn't cause apprentice writers difficulty. One exception, however, is when a pronoun agrees with a singular noun that refers to a class of individuals or entities. Consider the noun phrase *every student from Toledo.* The noun *student* is in the singular form, yet the entire expression clearly refers to more than one student. Most speakers of English when using a noun in this way understand that the noun—though in singular form—is in fact referring to more than one object, person, or entity. And this understanding can often affect the agreement of pronouns:

1. *Every <u>student</u> from Toledo wants *their* own car.

2. *Each <u>child</u> hugged *their* blanket.

Sentences 1 and 2 illustrate common English usage. Technically, the pronoun in each sentence should be singular (*his* or *her*) to agree with its antecedent (*student, child*):

3. Every <u>student</u> from Toledo wants *his or her* own car.

4. Each <u>child</u> hugged *his or her* blanket.

Yet *student* and *child,* though singular in form, clearly refer to more than one student and more than one child. This accounts for the common, if technically "incorrect," usage shown in sentences 1 and 2.

Also contributing to the use of *their* in sentences such as 1 and 2 is an increasing reluctance on the part of many writers and speakers to use the masculine singular pronoun (*his*) to refer to a group of persons that includes both men and women. That is, despite admonitions that historically, the masculine forms of words are "generic" and can refer to both males and females equally, an increasing number of speakers and writers don't feel comfortable using words in this way (as in the first two of the following sentences) or in making generalizations about groups of individuals (as in sentences 3 and 4):

1. Every <u>student</u> from Toledo wants *his* own car.

2. Each <u>child</u> hugged *his* blanket.

3. A <u>surgeon</u> needs to be calm when talking to *his* patients.

4. A <u>pilot</u> loves *his* plane.

Because the pronoun *their* is being increasingly used to agree with singular antecedents that refer to more than one entity and to avoid the use of the generic masculine, many language arts teachers do not comment negatively regarding sentences such as *Every child wants their own room* or *Every scientist wants their lab to be state-of-the-art*. Still, despite the increasing prevalence of this practice, there are some readers who consider this usage wrong and who can be alienated by writing that contains such constructions. A wise practice, therefore, is to help apprentice writers understand the risks of using *their* in this way and to acquaint them with stylistic alternatives involving the use of plural noun antecedents that avoid this agreement problem altogether:

1. Every <u>student</u> from Toledo wants *his* (or *their*) own car.
   Alternative: <u>Students</u> from Toledo want *their* own cars.

2. Each <u>child</u> hugged *his* (or *their*) blanket.
   Alternative: The <u>children</u> hugged *their* blankets.

3. A <u>surgeon</u> needs to be calm when talking to *his* patients.
   Alternative: <u>Surgeons</u> need to be calm when talking to *their* patients

4. A <u>pilot</u> loves *his* plane.
   Alternative: All <u>pilots</u> love *their* planes.

Another matter regarding pronoun agreement that may cause students difficulty involves the use of collective nouns such as *crowd, faculty,* or *family*. This is because collective nouns may be seen as a single unit or as a group of separate individuals. When a collective noun is considered a single unit, it is usually treated as singular and referred to with a singular pronoun, for example:

1. The <u>crowd</u> went crazy. *It* mobbed the stage.

2. The <u>faculty</u> disagreed with the policies of the dean, so *it* called a meeting of all *its* members.

3. Kris values her <u>family</u>. *It* is important in her life.

However, when a collective noun is regarded as a collection of individuals, it is treated as plural and referred to with a plural pronoun; for example:

1. The <u>crowd</u> turned into an angry mob, and *they* began to loot stores and attack passing motorists and pedestrians.

2. The <u>faculty</u> disagreed so much among *themselves* that *they* failed to present a unified front.

3. Alice adores her <u>family</u>. She treats *them* with love and care.

As a teacher, you can encourage apprentice writers to think about how they visualize and use such collective nouns as *crowd, faculty, family, government, audience, group, team,* and *committee.* It is also useful to encourage inexperienced writers to consider the images they are creating in their reader's mind when choosing either singular or plural pronouns to replace collective nouns.

Reference *My attention to it to clarify writing* —

A far more serious problem in writing than pronoun-antecedent agreement is the problem of unclear pronoun reference. Pronoun reference problems have the potential to render sentences and even entire passages of writing ambiguous, unclear, or confusing. Unclear reference can occur with a personal or demonstrative pronoun by itself, as in these sentences:

1. I'm excited about *it*. [The antecedent of *it* isn't clear.]

2. The principal found *that* disturbing. [The antecedent of *that* isn't clear.]

Unclear reference can also involve a demonstrative used together with a noun. These types of constructions are sometimes referred to as *pronominal phrases:*

1. You need to have *that experience.* [What experience?]

2. *That idea* is dangerous. [What idea?]

Despite the widespread occurrence of writing problems that involve pronoun reference and teachers' best efforts to teach students the importance of clear pronoun reference, problems in this area persist well into college. This is because reference difficulties are manifestations of at least two entirely different aspects of the writing process.

Sometimes problems with unclear reference occur because of inadequate or insufficient editing. That is to say, sometimes student writers know what each unclear pronoun or pronominal phrase stands for, but they have neglected to catch these pronouns and replace them with their referents. Often this happens when an inexperienced writer fails to consider his or her readers; the writer knows what he or she means by *it* or *that* or *this idea*, but audience members don't! Or students may notice problem pronouns but simply don't have the patience or skill (or both) to fix them properly. Reference problems that are largely the result of weak or inadequate editing skills should be addressed through regular practice—both in discovering pronouns or pronominal phrases with unclear reference and in revising such constructions. This sort of practice is necessary because whether or not a pronoun needs to be clarified and the manner in which it should be clarified depends on the written context in which the pronoun or pronominal phrase is used. Since there are no general rules that stipulate when pronouns or pronominal phrases are appropriate and when they are not, practice and regular feedback are essential.

Although inadequate or insufficient editing may be to blame, reference problems can also originate in exploratory drafts that inexperienced writers often mistake for more finished, reader-directed writing. During the exploratory stage of writing, pronouns and pronominal phrases often serve as **placeholders** for ideas that are in the process of being developed. In such instances, then, it is not a simple matter for the writer to replace an *it* or a *this idea* with the words the pronoun or pronominal phrase stands for, because the writer does not yet fully know what she wants to say; she's in the process of articulating this. A good strategy for apprentice writers to employ with a draft that they know to be exploratory is to circle all suspicious pronouns and pronominal phrases and draw arrows that connect them to the words or phrases to which they refer. If too many arrows cannot be connected to referents, it may be that additional activities to help the student clarify her ideas are warranted. These might include listing ideas, drawing groups or clusters of words or phrases and connecting these to clarify relationships, or narrating in an informal way the ideas that one or more pronouns or pronominal phrases might stand for and how these ideas connect to the paper as a whole.

FORM, FUNCTION, AND FRAGMENTS

Throughout the book so far, we have mentioned the importance of distinguishing between form and function. We explained, for example, how the form of the word *bank* can predispose students to consider it a noun despite how it might actually function in a sentence such as *You can bank on that*. A student who automatically assumes that the word *bank* must be a noun, no matter how it is used, may also mistake that word for the subject of a sentence, since subjects are always nouns or nominals. As this errant chain of reasoning suggests, confusion between form and function can sometimes prevent inexperienced writers from recognizing fundamental sentence constituents such as subjects and verbs. This, in turn, can contribute to such writers' inability to recognize whether or not the sentences they've written are complete and grammatical.

Two common types of nominals covered earlier in this chapter are *gerunds* and *infinitives*. These nominals are notable because even though they function as nouns, they resemble verbs:

> *Singing* is fun.
>
> I love *to sing.*
>
> After *exercising,* I feel robust.
>
> Wilbur found *running* to be exhilarating.
>
> My life's desire is *to act.*

However, not only do gerunds and infinitives look like verbs to begin with, but they can often be expanded in ways that make them resemble verbs even more. They can, for example, be preceded by words that appear to be "subjects" because they're performing (or potentially performing) the action suggested by the gerund or infinitive:

1. *John's* singing was awful. [Who is singing? *John.*]

2. *For Betty* to dance is foolish. [Who is dancing? *Betty.*]

Gerunds and infinitives can also take "direct objects":

1. John's *stealing the onion dip* was appalling. [What was stolen? *The onion dip.*]

2. For Bill *to have hit* Woody was unthinkable. [Who was hit? *Woody.*]

Also, because gerunds and infinitives often describe actions, they can even be modified by adverbs and adverb phrases that describe these actions:

1. John's *singing off-key at 2:00 A.M.* annoyed us all.
   adverb   adverb phrase

   [How was John singing? *Off-key.* When was John singing? *At 2:00 A.M.*]

2. I tried *to run quickly up the stairs without falling.*
   adverb   adverb phrase   adverb phrase

   [How did I try to run? *Quickly.* Where did I try to run? *Up the stairs.* How did I try to run? *Without falling.*]

Because they are frequently used and important structures, we will be examining gerunds as well as infinitives that function as nominals more fully in Chapter 9. Our purpose here is to suggest that form-function confusion involving gerunds and infinitives is quite frequent and may have serious consequences for apprentice writers, who are sometimes prone to punctuating gerund and infinitive phrases as if they were sentences. Or to put it another way, since gerunds and infinitives resemble verbs, when they are expanded into lengthy phrases, inexperienced writers can mistake these phrases for sentences. Consider the following examples; in each case, an infinitive or gerund phrase (in italics) is incorrectly punctuated as a sentence:

1. *Spending a lot of money when you don't have it.* It is a bad idea.

2. *For Congress to pass a bill that causes married people to pay more taxes.* That is just wrong.

3. I hate the idea that Brittany had. *To give everyone credit regardless of whether they did the work.*

As these examples illustrate, expanded gerund and infinitive phrases can resembles sentences a good deal, particularly when such phrases seem to contain subjects, verbs, modifiers, direct objects, and the like. The infinitive (*to pass*) in example 2, for instance, seems to take a subject (*Congress*) and a direct object (*bill*), and the additional words create a lengthy phrase that feels a lot like a sentence.

When students fragment gerund and infinitive phrases, then, they are usually responding to cues that signal something sentencelike about these structures. This suggests that there is a "logic" to fragmented gerund and infinitive phrases and that inexperienced writers, even when committing these errors, are attempting to follow the rules that are a part of their innate knowledge of language. It is important to recognize the logic that governs errors committed by apprentice writers because the discovery of such logic can often reveal systematic patterns in error production as well as suggest ways of formulating plans to remediate common problems with sentence structure.

PROBLEMS WITH MODIFICATION

As you know, in English there are two parts of speech that are generally referred to as *modifiers:* adjectives and adverbs. *Adjectives* ordinarily modify (affect the meaning of) nouns or nominals, and adverbs modify verbs, adjectives, and other adverbs. Earlier in this chapter, we explained that in addition to single-word adjectives, groups of words acting together (phrases or clauses) can also modify nouns and nominals. Such modification is an important, pervasive phenomenon among language users; however, just as clear pronoun reference often relies on the novice writer's audience awareness, so does modification. Indeed, modification may pose a challenge for many apprentice writers for similar reasons as pronoun reference does: the writers may have a clear mental image of what they are describing but may not yet have enough control or awareness to convey it clearly. Because many inexperienced writers have difficulty with modification, most handbooks contain explanations of the most predominant problem areas in modification. These have to do with the relationship between the modifier and what it describes, misguided stylistic choices, and inappropriate word form.

Unclear Modification

A common problem for novice writers is that they can fail to make clear the connection between the modifier and what it is describing. Sometimes confusions in modification can arise because modifiers are misplaced. In this case, a modifier is not placed close enough to a noun to make the relationship between them clear. Or a novice writer may fail to provide a noun or nominal to be modified. We will be discussing this is more detail in Chapter 8.

Misguided Stylistic Choices

Another modification problem common among novice writers—and one that may not be easy or obvious to identify because it is not necessarily a grammatical error—is their often misguided choices of modifiers. Attempts to make their writing interesting can result in flowery or unclear sentences like this one:

> The bright blue big beautiful glass ball which you see which I had been given as a young precocious talented child is spinning on the polished top of the wooden dining room table.

As you can see, this sentence is difficult to read because it contains too many modifiers. It might best be rewritten as two or even three sentences.

At the opposite end of the spectrum is a lack of sufficient modification, which may leave the writing dry, choppy, or uninformative, as in the following example:

> The ball belongs to me.

This sentence might be rewritten in a way that both provides more information and catches the reader's interest. For example, *bright blue* might be added to specify what the ball looks like. *That you see spinning on the table* might be added to further specify which ball. These additions would create a more interesting and informative sentence:

> The bright blue ball that you see spinning on the table belongs to me.

For novice writers to gain confidence in modifying their sentences in an interesting, informative, and appropriate manner, then, it is important that they have experience in reading well-written sentences, in comparing well-written sentences with poorly written ones, and in editing their own writing and the writing of their classmates to avoid overuse or underuse of modification. We cover this topic more fully in Chapter 8.

Problems with Form

In addition to problems with modifier placement and use, another problem inexperienced writers may face is in confusing adjective and adverb forms, as can be seen in the following example:

> *I told my brother to run *quick* and fetch the doctor because I was feeling very *badly*.

In this sentence, the adjective form of *quick* is used to modify the verb *run* when the adverb form *quickly* would be more appropriate, and the adverb form *badly* is being used following the linking verb *feel* when the adjective form *bad* is the more appropriate form. These modifications would create the sentence *I told my brother to run quickly and fetch the doctor because I was feeling very bad.* Although confusion regarding the use of appropriate adverb and adjective form may seem to be a trivial matter, unsuspecting novice writers may inadvertently conjure up humorous images when using adverb forms following verbs that can be used as both linking verbs and intransitive or transitive verbs, such as *feel, taste, look,* and *appear.* In the case of the sentence *I was feeling very badly,* for example, the use of the adverb form *badly* literally states that the subject *I* was touching something but not doing a very good job of it!

Errors involving adjective and adverb form are often the result of common usage in oral discourse being transferred to the written. They can also result from a writer's confusion regarding when to use adverbials with transitive and intransitive verbs and when to use adjectives with linking verbs. Or they may also be examples of overcorrection (e.g., using *badly* because it follows the verb), which is brought about when students are unsure of which form is appropriate. To help remediate this type of problem with form, it is important that student writers be able to identify linking, intransitive, and transitive verbs and the type of modification used with each.

Another problem with form that may arise in student writing is the overuse of **comparative** and **superlative** forms, as in

1. Marty is my *most favoritest* cousin.

2. Mary Helene is my *bestest* friend.

In such cases, it is important that the writers become familiar with the rules governing comparative and superlative forms of adjectives—particularly irregular ones—and that they have opportunities to apply these rules either in creating sentences of their own or by editing sentences to correct misused forms.

EXERCISES FOR PRACTICE

A. Find, fix, and explain any problems with plurals, possessives, and irregular forms in the paragraphs that follow.

Example: Its a good day to take a walk.
Problem: Its is possessive; it should be *it's,* a contraction.
Revision: It's a good day to take a walk.

1. Terry's house is on a small lot. On this lot there are many trees—maples, birchs, and oaks—with just as many leafs. When its windy, the leafs blow into the neighbor's yards. Because there are so many trees,

branchs also sometimes fly onto their roofs. The neighbors get upset with Terry for not trimming her trees. They have strong believes in being good citizens. They think Terry is a bad neighbor. Echos of this turn up every week in the local police chiefs' reports.

2. The thiefs stole more than a million dollars's worth of livestock, including cows and sheeps and ox. The sheep's, cows, and ox's owners were very upset because they had come to regard their livestocks as childs. The owners trust in their neighbors was violated. But when they consulted the police, they indicated the likely suspects were a band of womens rustlers. Attornies for the owners said that it was possible to sue for punitive damages because of the owner's suffering so much.

B. Revise each sentence to read more acceptably, explaining the rationale for your choice. In some instances, the sentence may be correct. If so, explain why.

> **Example:**   Lisa and me are good friends.
> *Revision:*   Lisa and I are good friends.
> *Explanation:* Lisa and (me, I) is the subject of the sentence; therefore, replace objective case *me* with subjective case *I*.

1. Ms. Smith asked Julie and I to stay after school.

2. Us guys are going to the movies on Saturday.

3. They gave the award to him and me.

4. Just between you and I, I don't like opera.

5. Hardworking students always impress we teachers.

6. We are tired because John and me worked late.

7. When him and Terry called, I was in the garden.

8. He gave his best baseball cards to he and Kevin.

9. "Is this Kris?" "Yes, this is she."

10. The watch was given to her for Christmas.

C. The following sentences may contain improperly used adjectives and adverbs. Find, fix, and explain each error in a sentence, or indicate why the sentence is correct as is. Also indicate whether the sentence contains a linking, transitive, or intransitive verb.

> **Example:**   She smiled sweet at the baby.
> *Explanation:*   *Smiled* is an intransitive verb. Therefore, the adjective *sweet* should be an adverb, *sweetly*, indicating how she smiled.
> *Correction:*   She smiled sweetly at the baby.

1. The guests looked gratefully for the break in the boring conversation.

2. The students complained consistently.

3. Sally feels badly about the misunderstanding.

4. Joe sings so awful that it drives us crazy.

5. She gave the book to her sister quick before anyone else noticed.

6. The dog smells so terribly.

7. I don't feel so good.

8. Rover snores real loud.

9. Karen returned the gift prompt.

10. He held the pipe tight in his mouth.

D. In the following paragraph, identify and revise the pronoun agreement problems for consistency, acceptability, and gender fairness.

A student always has to work hard to improves their grades. One priority is to have them turn in his assignment on time. A student may ignore their deadlines, but they can eliminate their weaknesses by careful planning and attention to her schedules. It will help tremendously. Each student should be responsible to himself. Putting this first is always the sign of a successful undergraduate. They might even graduate first in her class.

E. Identify whether any fragments exist in the following sentence pairs. For each fragment you find, explain why you think the fragment occurred and how it might be corrected to serve its gerund or infinitive function.

Example:	Walking five miles a day. That is Julia's favorite form of exercise.
Explanation:	The gerund phrase *Walking five miles a day* is a fragment because it isn't connected to a predicate.
Revision:	Walking five miles a day is Julia's favorite form of exercise.
Example:	His dieting routine was rigid. To consume no more than 1,000 calories each day.
Explanation:	The infinitive phrase *To consume no more than 1,000 calories each day* functions as an appositive and so is a fragment.
Revision:	His dieting routine, to consume no more than 1,000 calories each day, was rigid.

1. To walk up a hill backward. This is the way to get a really good workout.

2. Giving her all every day. This makes her a great worker.

3. Taking a vacation at Christmas. Scrooge wouldn't have liked that.

4. Karen's fundraising idea was a good one. To have a raffle.

5. Eating pizza every day for lunch. This is not a recipe for good health.

6. To take one day at a time. That is his philosophy.

7. I have a dream. Traveling to China.

8. Getting up early, studying hard, and making good grades. These were her goals.

9. For Congress to vote themselves a raise. This is appalling.

10. To swim across the English Channel. Very few have dared try it.

EXERCISES FOR CLASSROOM APPLICATION

A. Create an activity for your own students in which they must find and fix pronoun case errors other than by correcting individual sentences.

B. Devise a series of writing or speaking contexts in which students must work together to determine the level of formality and appropriateness of pronoun agreement.

C. Select a piece of your own writing to share with your future students to demonstrate your own use of pronoun reference, with particular discussion of unclear reference.

D. Have students make up writing and speaking scenarios to determine when it is or is not appropriate to use phrases such as *I don't feel good* and *I don't feel well.*

E. Create an activity that allows students to work with popular advertisements to find fragments in order to compare and contrast them with complete sentences. Have students discuss in what ways the fragments are effective as well as the features of this context that make fragments more permissible.

MORE ABOUT VERBS

Chapter Preview

Chapter 4 explains the role of verbs in sentences.

In **Part I** you will learn about

- Verb forms and verb function
- The structure of the predicate, including the role of helping verbs
- The concepts of tense and aspect
- Expressing negation
- Subject-verb agreement
- Words that modify verbs
- Form versus function

In **Part II** you will learn about challenges writers may face with

- Verb inflections
- Verb form
- Subject-verb agreement
- Contractions
- Negation
- Adverbs

PART I   VERBS AND PREDICATES

In Chapter 2 we introduced you to the concept of the predicate and discussed various types of verbs and the words necessary to accompany them in order to create a complete predicate. In Chapter 3 we explained that nouns can be described with respect to both their form and their function. This is also true of verbs. Thus in the first part of this chapter, as we describe verbs more fully, we will explain the forms verbs take as well as how they function in sentences. In addition, we will further explore the predicate, the part of the sentence that contains the verb and its related words.

VERB FORMS

As we discussed briefly in Chapter 2, most of us have learned in school to define a verb as a word that "describes an action" (e.g., *run*). But if we try to recognize the verb in a sentence based on this narrow definition, we may find it difficult. That is because this definition is quite limiting and even confusing, since verbs can consist of more than one word (e.g., *ask out, get out of*) and can express much more than action. In addition, verbs can describe, among other things, a sense (e.g., *smell, feel*), a perception (e.g., *seem*), a process (e.g., *become*), or a mental state (e.g., *anticipate*). Verbs can also serve merely to connect two parts of the same sentence (e.g., *be*). Therefore, similar to the challenges of recognizing nouns, we cannot recognize verbs based solely on a summary description of them. It is more effective to identify verbs by what they look like (their form) and what they do (their function). That is, verbs have specific similarities in form and function that can help us identify them in a sentence.

Recognizing Verbs by Their Form

There are several ways to identify verbs by their form. All verbs have what is generally called a *base form* or an *uninflected form*, which is the verb without endings (e.g., *bank, chase,* or *charge*). But unless we know the meaning of these words in a specific context, it would be difficult to recognize them as verbs from their form alone. Nevertheless, some verb forms are easier to recognize than others. For example, knowing that some **suffixes**, such as *-ify* (*intensify*), *-ize* (*memorialize*), or *-ate* (*deliberate*), may signify verbs can help in recognizing them. Knowing the infinitive form, created by placing *to* before the base form (e.g., *to sing, to decide, to interrupt*), may also help in recognizing verbs. However, verbs may most easily be recognized by the endings they can take (*-s, -ing,* and *-ed*) and by how they function in a sentence.

One similarity in form common to verbs is that they can have one of three different types of *inflectional endings* (i.e., letters attached to the ends of words that carry grammatical meaning). In discussing these endings, we will make references to tense, which is discussed more thoroughly later in this chapter. For now, we merely want to introduce you to the types of endings English verbs have and the information these endings can carry.

The first type of inflectional ending that the vast majority of verbs can have is -*s* added to the third person singular: *Josh runs every day, Kris writes on weekends,* and so on. The second type of ending is -*ing* to designate the **present participle:**

> Edie is scream*ing* at the top of her lungs. [verb + -*ing* = present participle, *screaming*]

The third common type of ending is -*ed* to mark the **past tense** or past participle:

1. Marie skat*ed* across the lake alone. [verb + -*ed* = past tense, *skated*]

2. Peter has review*ed* the test results. [verb + -*ed* = past participle, *reviewed*]

Recognizing verbs by the -*ed* endings alone can be limiting, however, because not all verbs add -*ed* to form the past tense or past participle; only **regular verbs** do. Indeed, English has a large set of irregular verbs in which the word itself is changed to form the past tense and the past participle (e.g., *swim, swam, swum*). We will discuss irregular verbs in more detail later in the chapter.

In addition to carrying meaning, adding endings to regular verbs can cause minor rule-governed changes in their spelling. In Chapter 3 we discussed how adding -*s* to create a plural form follows specific rules that can require the change or addition of some letters to a word. This is true also of adding -*s*, -*ing*, or -*ed* to a verb. That is, certain irregularities in spelling occur when these endings are attached to the ends of verbs.

Adding -*s*

When adding -*s* to a verb to form the third person singular, sometimes it is necessary to add letters to the word (e.g., *go, goes*) or to change a letter (*cry, cries*). In general, the spelling rules for creating plural nouns that we discussed in Chapter 3 apply to adding the -*s* of the third person singular to verbs as well, as these examples illustrate:

1. Jamal *runs* every day. [If the verb ends in a consonant, add only -*s*.]

2. Carol *bakes* on weekends. [If the verb ends in *e*, add only -*s*.]

3. Amiyalli *dresses* her dolls in her sister's baby clothes. [If the verb ends in *ss*, add -*es*.]

4. Sue *quizzes* her daughter regularly about her boyfriends. [If a one-syllable verb ends in *s* or *z*, double the consonant and add -*es*.]

5. Brian *cries* at sad movies. [If a verb ends in *y*, change the *y* to *i* and add -*es*.]

Only two verbs in English change their spelling when forming the third person singular, *be* and *have*. *Be* changes its form to *is* (*She is sleepy*), and *have* becomes *has* (*He has a headache*). We will discuss the variety of forms of *be* in depth later.

Adding *-ing*

The rules of spelling when forming the present participle by adding *-ing* to the verb (e.g., *hunt, hunting*) generally follow the rules for adding *-s* in that sometimes extra letters are added (e.g., *hit, hitting*) or a letter must be changed (e.g., *lie, lying*). However, there are three areas in which the spelling of verbs when adding *-ing* differ from when adding *-s*: (1) rules can vary according to the number of syllables in a word, (2) there are fewer instances of these changes in the spelling of verbs, and (3) there are no verbs that change their spelling completely as *be* and *have* do in the third person singular. Here are some examples of *-ing* added to the verb to create the present participle:

1. Jamal is *running* nowadays. [If a one-syllable word ends in a single consonant, double the consonant and add *-ing*.]

2. Amiyalli is *dressing* her dolls in her sister's baby clothes. [If a one-syllable word ends in two or more consonants, add only *-ing*.]

3. I like Carol's *baking*. [If the word ends in *e*, drop the *e* and add *-ing*.]

4. They found the dog *lying* on the couch. [If a verb ends in *ie*, change the *ie* to *y* and add *-ing*.]

5. The firemen were *offering* to help. [If a word of more than one syllable is stressed on the first syllable, add only *-ing*.]

6. Maria was *referring* to the car in the garage. [If a word of more than one syllable is stressed on the final syllable, double the final consonant after a vowel and add *-ing*.]

Adding *-ed*

Although adding *-ed* to the verb to form the past tense or the past participle also follows many of the rules for adding *-s* or *-ing* to words, there are many more exceptions to these rules. That is, although it is sometimes necessary when adding *-ed* to add extra letters to the original word (e.g., *spot, spotted*) or to change a letter (e.g., *fry, fried*), there are many more occasions when *-ed* is not added and when at least part of the word itself changes. Because there are so many verbs that do not add *-ed* to form the past tense or the past participle, they constitute their own special group known as the *irregular verbs*. Only *regular* verbs add *-ed*, as these examples show:

1. The police *spotted* the car a mile away. [If a one-syllable verb ends in a single consonant, double the consonant and add *-ed*.]

2. Amiyalli *dressed* her dolls. [If a verb ends in two or more consonants, add only -*ed*.]

3. Laura *baked* her uncle a cake. [If the word ends in *e*, add only -*d*.]

4. The teething baby *cried* all day. [If a verb ends in *y*, change the *y* to *i* and add -*ed*.]

Despite the slight variation in spelling when adding -*ed* to a verb, it is still easy to recognize regular verbs by this -*ed* ending. However, recognizing irregular verbs can be more complicated and difficult because they do not add -*ed* and the spelling of the base form itself may change, at least in part, as this chart of examples illustrates:

Base Form	Past Tense	Past Participle *(uses have as helping verb)*
bite	bit	bitten
buy	bought	bought
cost	cost	cost
do	did	done
fly	flew	flown
forget	forgot	forgotten
have	had	had
go	went	gone
sing	sang	sung

You may have noticed, while reading this abbreviated list, that other irregular verbs in your vocabulary follow these various patterns when forming the past tense and the past participle. Can you think of some verbs that follow the pattern of *cost* or *sing*, for example?

Of all the irregular verbs, *be* is the most irregular in that it takes different forms, depending on whether the verb is in the first person (*I, we*), second person (*you*), or third person (*he, she, it, they*). The form also changes dramatically, depending on whether *be* is in the present or the past tense. Notice the many different forms of *be* in the following chart and how none of these forms resemble its base form.

Person	Present Singular	Present Plural	Past Singular	Past Plural
first	I *am*	We *are*	I *was*	We *were*
second	You *are*	You *are*	You *were*	You *were*
third	She *is*	They *are*	She *was*	They *were*

Knowing the endings that verbs can take is one way to recognize them. However, verbs plus their endings may not always function as the main verb in a predicate. For example, as we discussed in Chapter 3, a verb + -ing can function as a noun (e.g., *Running is my favorite pastime*) or as an adjective (e.g., *Who is the candidate's running mate?*). In addition, a verb + -ed can also function as an adjective (e.g., *The agent wanted to meet the interested parties*). Finally, verbs in their infinitive form (e.g., *to swing*) can function as nouns but can never be the main verb (or any other kind of verb) in a predicate. Consequently, because an ending on a verb does not always indicate that it is functioning as a verb, it is not only important to know the endings and other forms of the verb but also essential to know how verbs function in a sentence.

HOW VERBS FUNCTION

Although the forms verbs take can help us identify them, how they function in a sentence is of primary importance. For example, as we have explained, it is quite common for a word to resemble a verb although it may function as a noun (e.g., *Swimming is fun*) or as an adjective (e.g., *She took swimming lessons*). When we look at what verbs do in sentences, we can see that they have two important functions: to convey the essential meaning of a predicate and to carry tense. In addition, some verbs can also serve as **helping verbs.**

In Chapters 2 and 3 we explained that a sentence is made up of a subject and a predicate. For a word to function as a verb, it must be the principal, indispensable element of a predicate in a sentence or a clause. To put this another way, *the most important function of a verb is to convey the essential meaning of a predicate.* (Because the verb is the most important word in the predicate, it is often referred to as the *head of the predicate.*) No predicate—and therefore no sentence or clause—can be complete without a verb, as the following sentences illustrate:

1. Jose *went to the zoo last Friday.* [*Went* is the essential word in the predicate *went to the zoo.*]

   *Jose *to the zoo last Friday.* [The predicate is incomplete without a verb.]

2. Ahmed *loves swimming in the ocean.* [*Loves* is the essential word in the predicate *loves swimming in the ocean.*]

   *Ahmed *swimming in the ocean.* [The predicate is incomplete without a verb.]

3. Marco *is a high school science teacher.* [*Is* is the essential word in the predicate *is a high school science teacher.*]

   *Marco *a high school science teacher.* [The predicate is incomplete without a verb.]

4. Seja *seems tired lately.* [*Seems* is the essential word in the predicate *seems tired lately.*]

   *Seja *tired lately.* [The predicate is incomplete without a verb.]

The second important function of a verb (or verb phrase, which includes a helping verb + main verb) is to carry tense. English sentences can convey a variety of meanings with respect to time, and verbs play an important role in this regard because they carry tense. Notice how time is conveyed in the verb tense of the following sentences:

Jose *goes* to the zoo every Friday. (shows present tense)

Jose *went* to the zoo last Friday. (shows past tense)

Ahmed *loves* swimming in the ocean. (shows present tense)

Ahmed *loved* swimming in the ocean. (shows past tense)

Marco *is* a high school science teacher. (shows present tense)

Marco *was* once a language teacher. (shows past tense)

Seja *seems* tired lately. (shows present tense)

You *seemed* tired yesterday. (shows past tense)

In these examples, some verbs show whether they are in the present or past tense by the endings they take. As you may have noticed—and as we explained earlier in the chapter—a change in the form of a verb usually involves the addition of an ending to the verb, but not always, as in the sentence *Jose went to the zoo last Friday* or *Marco was once a language teacher.*

THE STRUCTURE OF THE PREDICATE

You may recall our discussion of the predicate in Chapter 2. We would like to reiterate some of the main points of that discussion here, particularly the characteristic structure of the predicate and forms necessary to complete it. You may be saying to yourself, "Well, a predicate has to contain a verb" and you would be right. That is its primary characteristic. The smallest possible predicate, then, consists of one word, a verb. Here are some examples of sentences with one-word predicates:

John *swims.*

The woman who won the lottery *laughed.*

My neighbors, Myrtle and Frieda, who moved here from Canada, *garden.*

Of course, one-word predicates are not as common as longer predicates, for several reasons. In Chapter 2 we explained the various types of verbs and how they might need additional words to form a complete predicate. The following is a review of the various verb types—with the exception of *be*—and the pattern of their predicates:

1. Shannon *gardens*. (predicate with intransitive verb)

2. Shannon *grows* asparagus. (predicate with transitive verb + direct object)

3. Shannon *gave* Penny a gift. (predicate with transitive verb + direct object + indirect object)

4. Shannon *considered* Frank a genius. (predicate with transitive verb + direct object + objective complement)

5. Shannon *put* the cap on the bottle. (predicate with transitive verb + direct object + adverbial

6. Shannon *seems* excited. (predicate with linking verb + subject complement)

These examples are short and succinct to illustrate the respective sentence patterns. However, as you know as a language user and writer, all of the predicates in these sentences and all other sentences can be expanded by using various modifiers, including adjectives and adverbial modifiers (which we will discuss later in this chapter). Here are examples of the same six sentences with a variety of modifiers in the predicates. The modifiers are underlined.

1. Shannon *gardens in her backyard every day*.

2. Shannon *grows the best asparagus in the valley*.

3. Shannon *gave her friend Penny a very special gift for her birthday*.

4. Shannon *considered Frank a bona fide genius at cutting hair*.

5. Shannon *put the small plastic cap on the large bottle of catsup*.

6. Shannon *seems very excited about her new boyfriend*.

In all of our examples so far, the sentences are presented in "regular" subject-verb-object word order. However, writers may choose to vary that regularity by shifting the order of words in the predicate to achieve a certain style or effect. The words and forms that are necessary to complete the predicate do not change (e.g., a transitive verb will always need a direct object), but their position in a sentence may. We will explore these variations on sentence structure in depth in other chapters of this text, particularly in Chapters 5 and 10.

In this section, we have provided a review of the predicate by focusing on the constituents of a complete predicate. In addition to optional modifiers and other words necessary to complete the predicate (e.g., a direct object), an important element in many a predicate is the ***auxiliary verb***, also known as the *helping verb*.

Helping Verbs

Verbs in predicates can appear in their simplest, one-word form (e.g., *Max exercises every day; Juanita left yesterday*) and still convey meaning with respect to the time or nature of an action by expressing the present tense or the past tense.

However, we may want to express more subtle differences in time. We may want to know when, exactly, did a particular action occur? If it began in the past, is it still ongoing? Did the action occur on a regular basis or just once? If an action is yet to happen, how certain is it that the action will take place? How much does the speaker care as to whether the action will or won't take place? Helping verbs (auxiliary verbs), used in combination with the main verb in a predicate, provide answers to these questions—and others as well. For example, notice the combination of helping verb and main verb in the following sentences and what type of time information these combinations provide (the combinations are italicized, and the helping verbs are underlined):

1. For several years, I *have been jogging*. [The action began in the past and is still occurring.]

2. By the time Brenda arrived, John *had washed* the dishes. [Both Brenda's arriving and John's washing the dishes happened in the past; but John washed the dishes first.]

3. Nick *will have been studying* photography for two years by this time next summer. [Nick has been studying photography for one year and plans to continue studying it next year.]

As these sentences illustrate, helping or auxiliary verbs are a vital part of the predicate of a sentence. In fact, the main verb plus its helping or auxiliary elements is often called the *verb phrase* to distinguish it from the rest of the predicate. That is the terminology we will use throughout this text.

Despite the broad range of meanings auxiliary verbs can convey, only three main verbs can also function as helping verbs: *be, have,* and *do.* In the following sets of examples, compare how *be, have,* and *do* function as helping verbs in the first set but as main verbs in the second set:

Be, Have, and *Do* as Helping Verbs
I *was singing.* [*Be (was)* is the helping verb; *sing* is the main verb.]
I *had been* sad. [*Have* is the helping verb; *be (been)* is the main verb.]
I *don't like* Bob. [*Do* is the helping verb; *like* is the main verb.]

Be, Have, and *Do* as Main Verbs
I *am* tired. [*Be (am)* is the main verb.]
I *have* a dog. [*Have* is the main verb.]
I *did* my homework. [*Do* is the main verb.]

As these examples show, *be, have,* and *do* can be either main verbs or helping verbs. However, there is a much larger class of words or expressions, known as modal auxiliaries or simply *modals*, that function *only* as helping verbs. You are probably quite familiar with these verbs. Most are single words: *can, could, may, might, must, will, would, shall, should.* But modals can also consist of more than one word: expressions such as *used to, have to, ought to,* and *be going to* are also modals (the term used to refer to them is *phrasal modals*). The primary difference between *be, have,* and *do* as helping verbs and modals is in the type of information they carry in the verb phrase. Here are some examples of sentences with predicates that contain modals as helping verbs. Notice the type of information each one provides:

go over

> You *ought to* study. [The speaker or writer urges that the studying take place. *Ought to* is the helping verb; *study* is the main verb.]
>
> We *might* go to Italy the summer after next. [Going to Italy is not certain. *Might* is the helping verb; *go* is the main verb.]
>
> We *will* go to Malaysia the summer after next. [Going to Malaysia is certain. *Will* is the helping verb; *go* is the main verb.]
>
> All Americans *must* pay taxes. [Paying taxes is obligatory. *Must* is the helping verb; *pay* is the main verb.]
>
> You *could have been* drinking bad water. [There is a possibility that you were consuming bad water. *Could, have,* and *been* are all helping verbs, but *could* is the modal that expresses possibility; *drinking* is the main verb.]

As these examples illustrate, an important function of most modals as helping verbs is to work with the main verb to convey a variety of meanings with respect to the nature of an action (e.g., its probability), the speaker's or writer's attitude toward the action, and so forth. By contrast, *be, have,* and *do*—along with some of the modals—have the important function as helping verbs of conveying the *time* when the action of the main verb takes place. For this reason, auxiliaries are necessary for the formation of all of the other tenses in English besides present and past: the future (*I will study*), present perfect (*I have studied*), past perfect (*By the time Marguerite got home, her husband had cooked dinner*), and future perfect (*By this time next year, I will have retired*). (We will review the tenses later in this chapter.)

Besides their function to help convey time and other information related to the action of the main verb, auxiliaries are also necessary in modern English to convey questions and negatives in sentences with main verbs other than *be.* Notice in the following example that *be* does not require a helping verb to form yes-no questions or a negative:

Be as the Main Verb

You *are* tired. (statement)

Are you tired? (yes-no question)

You *are* not tired. (negative)

That *is* a dog. (statement)

What *is* that? (information question)

Compare these examples with the next set of sentences, which contain a verb other than *be* as the main verb. In comparing them, notice how *do* is required as a helping verb in questions and negatives:

Verbs Other than *Be* as the Main Verb

I *love* eating in new restaurants. (statement)

Do you *love* eating in new restaurants? (yes-no question)

Love you eating in new restaurants? [The sentence is ungrammatical (and the predicate incomplete) without the required auxiliary *do.*]

I *want* a new car. (statement)

I *do* not *want* a new car. (negative)

*I not *want* a new car. [The sentence is ungrammatical (and the predicate incomplete) without the required auxiliary *do.*]

Jisu *lived* in Maryland in 1989. (statement)

Where *did* you *live* in 1989? (information question)

*Where you *lived*? [The sentence is ungrammatical (and the predicate incomplete) without the required auxiliary *do.*]

We will discuss the formation of questions and other types of sentences in Chapter 5 and the formation of negatives later in this chapter. Right now our purpose is to introduce you to the ways helping verbs should be used in these types of sentences. As the examples show, sentences with *be* as the main verb form questions by inversion (placing the verb first in the sentence: *Are you happy?*) and form negatives by the insertion of the word *not.* In contrast, main verbs other than *be* must take a form of the helping verb *do* to form questions and negatives in present and past tense. (An exception to this general rule is that *be* needs the helping verb *do* to form a negative command: *Don't be silly!*)

A final important matter to note about the structure of the predicate is the order of the verb phrase within it. As we have mentioned, although English sentences do allow rule-governed variations, normal or regular word order in the predicate requires that verbs come before the words that complete the predicate (e.g., direct objects) and that helping verbs come before main verbs. Helping verbs within the verb phrases also come in a particular order:

Predicate = Verb + Direct Object
Eric Clapton sang "I Shot the Sheriff."

Verb Phrase = Modal + Have + Be + Main Verb
I could have been skiing.

What these formulas indicate is that a verb phrase must have a main verb. But if a verb phrase has one or more helping verbs, they must come in the order of *modal* first, *have* next, and *be* last:

I *cook* dinner. [*Cook* is the main verb of the verb phrase.]

I *might cook* dinner. (modal + main verb only)

I *have cooked* dinner. (*have* + main verb only)

I *am cooking* dinner. (*be* + main verb only)

I *have been cooking* dinner. (*have* + *be* + main verb)

I *might have cooked* dinner. (modal + *have* + main verb)

I *might be cooking* dinner. (modal + *be* + main verb)

I might have been cooking dinner. (modal + *have* + *be* + main verb)

Another important matter to note about helping verbs is how they affect the form of the verb that follows them. That is, when a modal or *do* is used, the verb that follows it in the verb phrase is not inflected. (We will discuss the use of *do* as a helping verb in more detail in Chapter 5 and later in this chapter.) Instead, it remains in its bare form (e.g., *can see, might look*). But when *have* and *be* function as auxiliary verbs, the verb that follows is not in its bare form. As you may have noticed from the examples, when *have* functions as a helping verb, it must be followed by a verb in the past participle form (*I have danced; I have sung*). When *be* functions as a helping verb (except in passive sentences, which we discuss in Chapter 5), it must be followed by a verb in the present participle form (*I was dancing; I am singing*). Following are some sentences that illustrate how the helping verbs *have* and *be* affect the form of the verbs that come immediately after them. Notice that the past or present participle form of the verb is required in order for the sentence to be grammatical.

1. I *have finished* dinner. [*Have* is a helping verb; the verb that follows is in the past participle form.]

2. He *might have arrived* earlier. [*Have* is a helping verb; the verb that follows is in the past participle form.]

3. Kitty *has swum* seven laps. [*Have* is a helping verb; the verb that follows is in the past participle form.]

4. The students *are arriving* soon. [*Are* (a form of *be*) is a helping verb; the verb that follows is in present participle form.]

5. Edna *might be studying*. [*Be* is a helping verb; the verb that follows is in present participle form. (Since *be* follows a modal—*might*—it remains in its base form *be*.)]

6. My dog *has been playing*. [*Have* and *been* (a form of *be*) are helping verbs; since *been* follows the helping verb *have*, it is in the past participle form; the main verb—*playing*—follows the helping verb *been* (a form of *be*) and is in the present participle form.]

We have covered a great deal of important information about the structure of predicate in this section, which we would like to summarize before introducing you to more new information regarding verbs. First, all predicates must contain a verb, which is called the *main verb*. Second, predicates can consist of a single word (in the form of an intransitive verb), but they ordinarily contain both the verb and any other words necessary to complete the verb (such as a direct object). Third, predicates can contain modifiers, giving optional information the writer wishes to add. Fourth, the verb phrases in the predicate can contain one or more helping verbs, which enable verbs to convey information about the time or nature of an action. Helping verbs are also used in the formation of questions and negatives. Finally, helping verbs in the verb phrase affect the form of the verb that directly follows them.

TENSE VERSUS ASPECT

Earlier in this chapter, we explained that one of the important functions of the verb phrase in the predicate is to carry tense. In the examples we provided, we showed how verbs can show present tense (*John loves swimming*) or past tense (*John* loved *swimming*) by attaching an ending to their base form. Tense, then, is a way of referring to or describing the particular *form* a verb may take. This is why grammarians often say a distinctive feature of verbs is that they can be *inflected* for tense (*inflected* means to attach an ending that adds meaning to a word). Tenses provide information about the time of an action. Although many people think of tense and time as synonymous, tense *can* be closely related to the time a verb expresses, but it doesn't have to be. This is because tense has to do with the form a verb takes; time has to do with the verb's *meaning*. You may have been taught that there are twelve tenses in English. In recent years, grammarians have postulated that there are actually only two—present and past—and that the other tenses are all aspects of those two tenses. We will discuss both of these concepts here. Let us begin by refreshing your memory of the twelve "tenses" in English and how they are formed. The following chart shows the form for each of the twelve "tenses" and the name by which each is designated:

Present:	People dance.
Past:	People danced.
Future:	People will dance.
Present progressive:	People are dancing.
Past progressive:	People were dancing.
Future progressive:	People will be dancing.
Present perfect:	People have danced.

Past perfect:	People had danced.
Future perfect:	People will have danced.
Present perfect progressive:	People have been dancing.
Past perfect progressive:	People had been dancing.
Future perfect progressive:	People will have been dancing.

In some languages, tense (form) and time (meaning) correspond rather closely. But in English, tense and time are often quite different. Examine the following sentence, for example:

Tomorrow we *go* to Chicago.

Clearly, the time expressed in the sentence is the future; however, the verb is in the present tense. In this sentence, time is expressed by the word *tomorrow* rather than by the tense of the verb. Now take a look at these sentences:

Every morning Marsha *brushes* her teeth.

Infants *are* helpless.

The verbs in both sentences are in present tense form (*brushes, are*), yet the action being expressed by each verb is not necessarily taking place at this very moment. In fact, when an English sentence has one verb (no helping verbs) in the present tense, it expresses actions in a variety of time frames:

1. Action that takes place regularly or habitually: *Every morning Marsha brushes her teeth.*
2. A general truth or widely held belief: *Infants are helpless.*
3. Future action: *Tomorrow we go to Chicago.*

As you can see from these examples, the distinction between tense and time is an important one that may help apprentice writers who experience difficulty with *tense shifts*. In general, the tense forms of the verbs in a piece of writing should be consistent.

It is easy to see how a verb without an auxiliary shows either present or past tense form. But what about sentences that have helping verbs? In general, if a verb phrase (the auxiliary plus the main verb) has one or more helping verbs in it, the first helping verb is in either present or past tense form. If the first verb is the helping verb *have*, then *have* must be in the present or past tense form, as these examples in the present and past perfect indicate:

She *has studied* hard. [*Have* shows present tense form.]

I *have bought* a dog. [*Have* shows present tense form.]

She *had studied* hard. [*Have* shows past tense form.]

If the first verb in the verb phrase is the helping verb *be*, then *be* must take either a present or past tense form, as these examples in the present and past progressive indicate:

> She *is* studying hard. [*Be* shows present tense.]
>
> They *are* studying hard. [*Be* shows present tense.]
>
> She *was* studying hard. [*Be* shows past tense.]

If the first auxiliary verb is a modal, it may on the surface appear to show either present or past form, although—as the following examples illustrate—there is virtually no correspondence between the tense (form) and meaning (time) of the modals *can/could, may/might, shall/should,* and *will/would*:

> She *may* have studied. [*May* shows present tense.]
>
> She *might* have studied. [*Might* shows past tense but does not represent past time.]
>
> She *can* be studying. [*Can* shows present tense.]
>
> She *could* be studying. [*Could* shows past tense but does not represent past time.]
>
> She *will* have been studying. [*Will* shows present tense.]
>
> She *would* have been studying. [*Would* shows past tense but does not represent past time.]

The exception is the phrasal verb *have to,* which does represent past time when it is inflected for past tense (*had to*). Although most modals can show present or past tense by changing their form, some modals do not. Some examples of modals that don't show tense by changing form are *ought to* and *must.*

Despite the fact that English verbs can show only two tense forms—present and past—English sentences can nevertheless express a variety of meanings with respect to time. As we explained earlier, English verb phrases can describe actions that take place in the past, present, or future. Verb phrases can also express when an action occurs relative to another one, whether the action is continuous or repeated, what the speaker or writer's attitude toward the action is, how probable the action is, and so forth. These additional qualities that clarify an action are generally referred to as **aspect**. Most grammar books refer to two aspects, **progressive aspect** and **perfect aspect**.

Progressive aspect is used to express a number of meanings but is commonly described as conveying a continuous or repeated action or state or an action that is in progress. To form the progressive aspect requires the helping verb *be* followed by a verb in the present participle form. Here are some examples of sentences with verb phrases that show the progressive aspect. Notice that the helping verb carries the tense but does not indicate the complete time frame in which an action has taken place:

I *am* hammering nails into wood. [The action is in progress in the present.]

I *was* petting my dog, Woody. [The action was in progress in the past.]

I *will* be thinking about your offer. [The action is to occur in the future.]

I *am* starving. [The verb expresses a current condition.]

She *is* studying for her calculus exam. [The action is in progress in the present or is occurring repeatedly over a period of time extending into the future.]

Perfect aspect is often said to designate an action that is "completed." Perfect aspect is also used to describe the time of an action or a state in relation to another action or state. Suppose, for example, Denzel wants to express the fact that he lives in a town now and that he started living in that town seven years ago. He could use perfect aspect to convey this relationship: *I have lived in this town for seven years.* Or suppose he wants to describe two events that occurred in the past, indicating that one occurred before the other. He could use perfect aspect to tell that one action occurred before the other one, both having occurred in the past: *By the time I got your address, you had already moved again.* Finally, suppose he wants to describe two events that will occur in the future, one further into the future than the other. He could use perfect aspect to show the earlier action in relation to the later one: *By the time I get home, Anita will have cooked dinner.* Both Denzel's getting home and Anita's cooking dinner will occur in the future. But perfect aspect (*will have cooked*) shows that the action described will occur earlier in the future than Denzel's getting home.

As you may have noticed from these examples, perfect aspect is formed with the helping verb *have* followed by a verb in the past participle form. Here are some examples of sentences with verb phrases that show perfect aspect. Consider the time frame that is represented in each clause containing perfect aspect and the tense represented in the form of the helping verb. Which clauses or sentences relate to the present? Which ones relate to the past? Which ones relate to the future?

1. I *have tried* to study.

2. She *may have been* the most beautiful.

3. By the time I got home, the delivery boy *had dropped off* the box.

4. Norma *has been listening* to Beethoven.

5. By the time I get home, John *will have walked* Woody.

As these examples show, perfect aspect can be combined with progressive aspect or with modals to convey many different meanings. Because perfect aspect is often used to express two different actions with respect to one another, sentences that employ perfect aspect may require two verb phrases in sequence, as in sentences 3 and 5.

As we have explained, although there are, strictly speaking, only two tenses in English, most grammar handbooks, in trying to simplify rules and concepts for language users, refer to the twelve most common combinations of tense and aspect as the twelve tenses of English. How you wish to refer to these combinations is up to you. What is most important is that you understand the complicated and sometimes subtle time frames they represent.

Ended 10/3

EXPRESSING NEGATION IN SENTENCES

Creating Negatives with *Not*

We include **negation** in this chapter because it quite often affects the verb phrase. Still, there are a number of ways to express negation in English sentences. Usually, the word *not* performs this function in the verb phrase of a sentence and in conjunction with an auxiliary. *Do* is added as an auxiliary in present and past tense verb phrases that contain only a main verb (e.g., *Agnes doesn't like pastrami*). With the exception of verb phrases that contain only *be* (e.g., *I am not tired*), *not* is positioned between the auxiliary and the verb that follows it (e.g., *I haven't seen you for ages; Bill hasn't been playing ball much lately*). For this reason, *not* will appear with the auxiliary when it is placed at the front of the sentence in yes-no questions (e.g., *Didn't you want potatoes? Hasn't Bill been playing ball lately?*). However, English also permits other ways to convey negation using pronouns, **prefixes**, adjectives, adverbs, or **conjunctions**.

As we have said, the most common way negation can be expressed in English sentences is by adding the word *not* to the verb phrase. Notice that the main verb appears in its bare form when used in conjunction with *do* and that *not* appears between the helping verb and the main verb:

David *does not like* freeways.

English teachers *do not* always *speak* grammatically.

My sister *did not feed* the dog.

In questions and other types of sentences that are not in the normal subject-predicate order, the word *not* may be moved along with an element of the auxiliary to the front of the sentence. Notice the different positions of the auxiliary in the different types of sentences in the following examples:

Doesn't Clare *like* peaches?

Don't English teachers always *speak* grammatically?

Don't feed the dog.

Haven't you ever *been* to San Francisco?

Aren't you *coming* with us?

Why *didn't* the dogs *bark* at the car?

To whom *haven't* you *spoken* recently?

As you can see from the two sets of examples just given, when using *not* as a part of the verb phrase in present and past tense, *do* is a required auxiliary. However, the auxiliary *do* is not used when using *be*, in the progressive or perfect aspect, or with most modal auxiliaries, as the following sentences show:

Bradley *is not* younger than Zelma.

Terry and Sergio *are not going* to the movies tonight.

Toni's neighbors *are not being invited* to the party

The mountains *have not changed.*

The faculty *have not been attending* meetings very regularly.

Young children *must not be left* alone.

I *cannot read* your handwriting.

A second point to make about negatives with *not*, which you have certainly noticed by now, is that *not* can be (and usually is) contracted by attaching it to the auxiliary (*be, have, do, can, must,* etc.). When it is attached, the letter *o* is dropped and replaced by an apostrophe: verb + *n't* = verb*n't*. Here are some examples:

Those kids *aren't* happy. (*be* + *n't*)

Julia *isn't getting* any younger. (auxiliary *be* + *n't*)

We *haven't talked* for ages. (auxiliary *have* + *n't*)

Tom *didn't get* much sleep last night. (auxiliary *did* + *n't*)

The U.S. president *can't declare* war without approval from Congress. (modal *can* + *n't*)

As we explained earlier, in most cases, *not* is attached to *be* because unlike other verbs, when *be* functions as a main verb, it doesn't require the helping verb *do* to form negatives. But there is one exception: when giving a negative command using *be*, the helping verb *do* is required. Notice in the following contrasted examples how outdated or excessively formal it sounds when *do* is not used to create a negative **command** with *be:*

Be *not* unhappy. [The preferred form is *Don't be unhappy.*]

Be *not* silly. [The preferred form is *Don't be silly.*]

Be *not* a stranger. [The preferred form is *Don't be a stranger.*]

Creating Negatives Without *Not*

Although the most common way to show negation is by using *not* (or its contracted form) and attaching it to a part of the verb phrase (e.g., *They aren't showing a movie tonight*), there are several other ways to express negation in English using a pronoun, a prefix, an adjective, an adverb, or even a conjunction. As you may know, the pronouns *nobody, nothing,* and *none* are commonly used to express negation. Notice in the following groups of sentences how the second sentence carries a negative meaning when *nobody, nothing,* or *none* is used. Notice, too, how different the sentence may sound—or even how the meaning may change—when *not* is used in the verb phrase to express the same meaning as the pronouns, as it is in the third sentence in each of the following sets:

Positive:	*Somebody ate* my sandwich!
Negative without *not:*	*Nobody ate* your sandwich!
Negative using *not:*	*Somebody didn't eat* your sandwich!
Positive:	I *bought something* for you today.
Negative without *not:*	I *bought nothing* for you today.
Negative using *not:*	I *didn't buy anything* for you today.
Positive:	The raccoons *ate some* of the grapes.
Negative without *not:*	The raccoons *ate none* of the grapes.
Negative using *not:*	The raccoons *didn't eat any* of the grapes.

Another way for English speakers to express negation is by attaching a prefix to the noun or verb. Frequently used negative prefixes are *un-, in-, il-, im-, dis-,* and *mis-.* Notice in the following groups of sentences how the addition of the prefix to the noun or verb changes the meaning of the sentence from positive to negative. Then compare the meaning and sound of the second sentence with *not* used in the verb phrase.

Positive:	They are *a happy* couple.
Negative using an **affix**:	They are *an unhappy* couple.
Negative using *not:*	They are *not a happy* couple.
Positive:	That rich man *is tolerant* of beggars.
Negative using an affix:	That rich man *is intolerant* of beggars.
Negative using *not:*	That rich man *is not tolerant* of beggars.
Positive:	That is *a logical* solution.
Negative using an affix:	That is *an illogical* solution
Negative using *not:*	That is *not a logical* solution.
Positive:	That *is* quite *probable.*
Negative using an affix:	That *is* quite *improbable.*
Negative using *not:*	That *is not* quite *probable.*

Positive:	She is *an agreeable* person.
Negative using an affix:	She is *a disagreeable* person.
Negative using *not:*	She is *not an agreeable* person.

Positive:	I *understood* what you said.
Negative using an affix:	I *misunderstood* what you said.
Negative using *not:*	I *did not understand* what you said.

As you can see from these examples, choosing between using *not* in the verb phrase or showing negation by another means, such as in a pronoun or by attaching an affix to a word, can be a stylistic choice as well as a grammatical one. It can also require a change in the words used. Stylistic choices using forms of negation and the possible need to change wording is especially evident when using adjectives and adverbs. The following sets of sentences show these changes when using adjectives such as *less, fewer,* or *no* to change the meaning of a sentence from positive to negative:

Negative:	I *have less* money than I thought.
Negative using *not:*	I *don't have as much* money as I thought.

Negative:	There *are fewer* people than we expected.
Negative using *not:*	There *aren't as many* people as we expected.

Negative:	There *is no other* way to solve this problem.
Negative using *not:*	There *isn't any other* way to solve this problem.

These sentences and the next set illustrate how using *not* in the verb phrase can result in a longer, wordier sentence than using a pronoun, an affix, or some other construction does. Furthermore, it's important to note that most of the adverbs that can be used for negating a sentence, such as *never, seldom, rarely,* and *barely,* may sometimes not easily be replaced by using *not* in the verb phrase without causing at least a subtle change in meaning. Do you sense any difference in meaning in the following pairs of sentences?

We *never go* to the movies.

We *don't ever go* to the movies.

We *seldom go* to the movies.

We *don't go* to the movies *often.*

We *rarely go* to the movies.

We *don't go* to the movies *often.*

We *barely got out* alive!

We *almost didn't get out* alive!

A final way of showing negation in a sentence that we will discuss here is by using the **correlative conjunction** *neither…nor,* as in *Neither Dick nor Andrew has had dinner. Neither* can also be used as a pronoun, as in *Neither one of us wants to argue.* Compare these two sentences using *neither…nor* or *neither* with the following sentences using *not* in the verb phrase:

Dick and Andrew *haven't had* dinner.

We don't want to argue.

These two sentences—although grammatically correct—do not have the same effect or convey quite the same information as their *neither…nor* and *neither* counterparts, do they? It is obvious from these examples, as well as the ones given in our discussion of negation, that using *not* in the verb phrase may not always be the choice of writers who wish to provide detail and exactness in their writing.

While there are many alternatives to using *not* + verb for expressing negation, some of these alternatives may be more appropriate in certain contexts than in others. This is particularly true of the word *no,* which can be used in a variety of ways. For example, as we've illustrated, *no* can be an adjective as in *There is no way out of here, We have no bananas for sale,* and *There is no alternative.* Using *no* in this way, however, is restricted to certain specific combinations, such as beginning the sentence with *there* or before words such as *way, reason,* or *alternative.* When *no* is used in sentences such as *We have no bananas for sale,* it may cause the sentence to sound overly formal, extremely emphatic, or slightly awkward. Another use of *no* is as the opposite of *yes* when replying to a question, and this is perhaps the most common and most easily recognizable use of *no* in English. Often when *no* is used as a response, the speaker follows up with a more complete restatement. Notice in the following examples that each sentence amplifies the negative expressed by the word *no.*

Are you going to study tonight?

No, I'm *not.*

Did she work last year?

No, she was *unemployed.*

Do you have a lot of students in your class?

No, I have *fewer* than last year.

You're not going to the football game?

No, I'm *not.* I have to study.

A final way that *no* is used to show negation is to combine it with words such as *where* (*There is nowhere to hide*), *one* (*No one wants to know*), and *body* (*Nobody has an answer*).

As you may have determined from the information we've given you in this section, because there are so many ways to express negation in English, using negation appropriately and effectively can be a source of trouble for students, especially if their first language isn't English. Therefore, in Part Two of this chapter, we will address some of the more common difficulties apprentice writers experience with negative constructions.

SUBJECT-VERB AGREEMENT

Although the forms verbs take can help us recognize them, some of the rule-governed changes in form can be troublesome. This is especially true of the conventions of subject-verb agreement, especially when writing. As we explained earlier, the subject's *number* (singular versus plural) and *person* (first, second, or third) determine the form that a verb must take if the verb is in the present tense. Third person singular subjects (*he, she, it, one,* and most singular nouns) require a form of the verb that is inflected with the ending -*s* (with the exception of *be* and *have*). This form is often referred to as *third person singular.* All other subjects (*I, you, we, they,* and most plural nouns) require the plain or uninflected form of the verb (with the exception of *be*). Notice this distinction in the following examples:

Third-Person Singular Form of the Verb	Plain, Uninflected Form of the Verb
He <u>walks</u> to school every day.	*I <u>walk</u> to school everyday.*
She <u>studies</u> biology.	*You <u>study</u> biology.*
It <u>needs</u> light.	*We <u>need</u> light.*
One <u>studies</u> to succeed in school.	*They <u>study</u> to succeed in school.*
That baby <u>cries</u> all the time.	*Those babies <u>cry</u> all the time.*
Woody <u>loves</u> dog food.	*Woody and Max <u>love</u> dog food.*
Honesty sometimes <u>requires</u> courage.	*Truth and honesty <u>require</u> courage.*

Sometimes grammar books illustrate subject-verb agreement with a chart such as the following that shows each person and number with respect to a series of subjects, along with the attendant verb form that agrees with each subject:

	Singular	Plural
First person	*I walk*	*we walk*
Second person	*you walk*	*you walk*
Third person	*he, she, it, walks*	*they walk*

Of course, such simple charts show the various verb forms only in the present tense. In doing so they imply that subject-verb agreement is much less complicated than many language users find it to be. Subject-verb agreement can in fact sometimes require a great deal of awareness and thought on the part of the writer, for several reasons. For one thing, the irregular verbs *be* and *have* require more than just the addition of a third person singular -*s*. The verb *have* takes the third person singular form of *has*. And the verb *be* not only takes three different present tense agreement forms (*I am; you, we, they are; he, she, it is*), it also changes form to agree with the subject even when it is in the past tense (*I, he, she, it was; you, we, they were*).

Besides the exceptions regarding subject-verb agreement posed by the irregular verbs *be* and *have* and compound subjects (which we discuss in depth in Chapter 5), collective nouns also require special rules for particular circumstances. Compound subjects are ordinarily treated as plural subjects with respect to subject-verb agreement (e.g., *The dog and the cat want the same food.*). However, compound subjects that are connected with correlative conjunctions such as *either...or* or *neither...nor* are an exception because the verb agrees with whichever compound subject or noun is closer to the verb:

> *Either the dog or the cats get* the special treat.
>
> *Either the cats or the dog gets* the special treat.

Collective nouns (e.g., *team, committee, group*), which we discussed in an earlier chapter, also require an exception to the general rule for agreement because they can sometimes be interpreted as either singular or plural. Whether the speaker or writer wishes to portray a collective noun as one entity or to emphasize the individual things or persons that compose it can determine the form of the verb: *The flock are eating all of the seeds. The flock is taking flight this very minute.*

A final complication of subject-verb agreement crops up when words that modify the subject appear between the noun and the verb phrase or predicate. In particular, prepositional phrases that modify subjects (e.g., *of the children* in the sentence *None of the children wants to go to bed*) can cause confusion. Because such modifying phrases come immediately after the subject, the object of the preposition can be mistaken for the subject of the sentence. For example, the sentence **One of my dogs need a new collar* has faulty subject-verb agreement because the final noun (*dogs*) before the verb phrase (*need*) has mistakenly been identified as the subject. To have appropriate subject-verb agreement, the sentence should be *One of my dogs needs a new collar* because the subject of the sentence is *one*, which is singular. We will return to issues of subject-verb agreement in a later chapter.

WORDS THAT MODIFY VERBS

In English, the most common way to modify a verb—that is, to provide extra information about it—is by using adverbs. For this reason, we will discuss single-word adverbs only briefly in this section and leave fuller discussion for Chapters 6 and 7. In Chapter 3, we explained how nominals can be modified by single-word adjectives. Similar to single-word adjectives, single-word adverbs can perform several functions and come in a variety of forms.

What Adverbs Do

One of the easiest ways to recognize adverbs is by how they function. The most common functions of adverbs are to modify verbs, adjectives, and other adverbs:

1. Katie talks *incessantly*. [*Incessantly* is an adverb that modifies the verb *talk*.]

2. Katie is *very* bright. [*Very* is an adverb that modifies the adjective *bright*.]

3. Courtney, Katie's sister, speaks *somewhat* softly. [*Somewhat* is an adverb that modifies another adverb, *softly*.]

In sentence 1, *incessantly* modifies the verb *talk* (How does she talk? *Incessantly*). Notice, however, that in the other two examples, *very* modifies the adjective *bright* (How bright is she? *Very* bright) and *somewhat* modifies the adverb *softly* (How softly does she speak? *Somewhat* softly). That is because when an adverb is used to modify an adjective or another adverb, it is usually used to intensify or qualify. The most common intensifiers are *very, quite, too, somewhat,* and *extremely*. In fact, intensifiers comprise a relatively small group of adverbs. By contrast, we use many different adverbs to modify verbs. These adverbs can provide a variety of information, including when (e.g., *now*), where (e.g., *nowhere*), how often or frequently (e.g., *daily*), in what manner (e.g., *happily*), or for how long (e.g., *forever*). Here are some examples of single-word adverbs and the information they can provide:

1. Nathaniel went to the zoo *yesterday*. [*Yesterday* tells when.]

2. Stacy is going *home*. [*Home* tells where.]

3. Brianna *seldom* drinks whiskey. [*Seldom* tells how often or frequently.]

4. Anthony speaks *quietly*. [*Quietly* tells in what manner.]

5. He promised to love her *forever*. [*Forever* tells for how long.]

Information such as reason, purpose, or conditions is usually expressed in word groups, such as phrases or clauses, known as *adverbials,* that function as adverbs; these will be discussed in great detail in Chapters 6 and 7.

What Adverbs Look Like

Sometimes it is possible to recognize adverbs by what they look like. The most common and most easily recognizable form of adverb is a word with an *-ly* ending, such as *quickly* or *suddenly*. In fact, most people have been taught to distinguish adverbs from adjectives by looking for that ending. However, this tactic does not always work because many adverbs do not end in *-ly* (e.g., *never, now, there*) and because some adjectives do end in *-ly* (e.g., *lovely, homely*). In addition to sharing some endings with adjectives, adverbs share other similarities in form with adjectives as well. For instance, many adverbs—but not all—can be compared by using *more* (e.g., *He worked more diligently when meeting a deadline*) and *most* (e.g., *The winner ran the most quickly*) or by attaching *-er* (e.g., *Fred jumped higher*) or *-est* (*The small baby cried the loudest*). Similarly, the irregular comparative adverb forms for *well* and *bad* are the same as for when these words function as adjectives: *well, better, best; bad, worse, worst.*

Because the forms of adverbs and adjectives are not always distinguishable from each other, it is more reliable to recognize adverbs by their function, as we have described. Another possible way to recognize adverbs is by where they appear in a sentence. Generally, adverbs appear at the end of the predicate, but sometimes they can be moved to other parts of a sentence. This movability distinguishes them from adjectives, which are much less flexible in terms of where they are placed in a sentence. Notice the movability of the adverb *slowly* in the following sentences:

Scott ate his hamburger *slowly.*

Scott *slowly* ate his hamburger.

Slowly, Scott ate his hamburger.

Although it is usually possible to move the adverb from the end of the predicate to other parts of the sentence without changing the meaning of a sentence, there are certain adverbs, such as *only,* which cause the meaning of the sentence to change depending on where it is placed (e.g., *Only I can cook chicken* versus *I can cook only chicken*). We will further investigate the movability of adverbs in Chapters 6 and 7.

FORM VERSUS FUNCTION

Throughout this text, we emphasize the importance of differentiating form from function. This distinction is no less crucial for verbs and adverbs than it is for nouns and adjectives because words that *look like* verbs or adverbs may not be functioning as verbs or adverbs. Conversely, words that *don't look like* (take the form of) verbs or adverbs may indeed be functioning as verbs or adverbs. Thus distinguishing between form and function can help identify main verbs in a predicate. In the following sets of sentences, we provide you with some examples of words whose form may be confusing.

Words That Take the Form of Verbs but Don't Function as Verbs

Swimming is lots of fun. [*Swimming* looks like a verb but functions as a noun.]

You are a *roaring* success. [*Roaring* looks like a verb but functions as an adjective.]

I bought a *used* book. [*Used* looks like a verb but functions as an adjective.]

Words That Take the Form of Adverbs but Don't Function as Adverbs

Slowly is the way they walked. [*Slowly* looks like an adverb but functions as a noun.]

The leaves blew in a *downward* spiral. [*Downward* looks like an adverb but functions as an adjective.]

Words That Function as Verbs but Don't Look like Verbs

Hearsay can *fuel* rumors. [*Fuel* looks like a noun but functions as a verb.]

Can you *up* my credit limit? [*Up* looks like a preposition but functions as a verb.]

Coffee *yellows* my teeth. [*Yellow* looks like an adjective but functions as a verb.]

Words That Function as Adverbs but Don't Look like Adverbs:

I'm going *home*. [*Home* looks like a noun but functions as an adverb.]

The students will take the test *tomorrow*. [*Tomorrow* looks like a noun but functions as an adverb.]

We drove *slow*. [*Slow* looks like an adjective but functions as an adverb.]

He sings *loud*. [*Loud* looks like an adjective but functions as an adverb.]

As you read the final two examples, you might have wondered whether it was fair to include them, since many speakers of English would consider the forms *slow* and *loud* to be incorrect in those contexts. Yet it can be argued that because adjectives and adverbs often resemble one another closely with respect to both form and function, English speakers do use them interchangeably:

I feel *bad*. / I feel *badly*. [should be the adjective *bad*, not the adverb *badly*]

I feel *good*. / I feel *well*. [should be the adjective *good*, not the adverb *well*]

Please drive *slowly*. / Please drive *slow*. [should be the adverb *slowly*, not the adjective *slow*]

Enid talks *loudly*. / Enid talks *loud*. [should be the adverb *loudly*, not the adjective *loud*]

In fact, for some adjective-adverb pairs, the forms and functions have become so interchangeable that many native speakers of English prefer the "incorrect" construction rather than the technically correct one because the incorrect construction sounds better (e.g., *I feel well* sounds better to many people than *I feel good*) or because the correct construction sounds stilted or hyperformal (*Enid talks loudly* sounds stilted or overly formal). Though we don't mean to suggest that the form-function distinction isn't important with respect to adjectives and adverbs, we want you to be aware that the distinction can be blurred in certain pairs of similar adjectives and adverbs. This blurred distinction can pose a challenge to language arts teachers when they are instructing students on correct forms to use in their writing.

EXERCISES FOR PRACTICE

A. In each of the following sentences or sets of sentences, underline the verb or verb phrase in the predicate.

Example: I <u>would walk</u> a million miles for one of your smiles.

1. I have seen the truth, and it makes no sense. (Anonymous)

2. A combustion engine can use gasoline as fuel.

3. Margaret elbowed her way onto the crowded bus.

4. I was looking at the stars.

5. I am giving up procrastination. I'll start tomorrow.

6. Rick and Caitlin have visited Italy many times.

7. Each man must look to himself to teach him the meaning of life. (Antoine de Saint-Exupéry)

8. I have been waiting an hour for the bus.

9. The microwave buzzer went off an hour ago.

10. David got off the bus at the corner of Wooster and Manville.

B. In each of the following sentences, put brackets around the predicate, underline the auxiliaries, and circle the main verb.

Example: We [<u>have</u> (had) a very cold winter.]

1. The president will arrive at the airport at noon.

2. A physicist can extrapolate the origins of the universe.

3. Pavlov had trained his dogs to associate the ringing of a bell with the presence of food.

4. Walking the dog is Barb's favorite form of exercise.

5. Many people don't understand the president's explanations.

6. A lot of learning can be a little thing. (Spike Mulligan)

7. Babies cry for no reason at all sometimes.

8. Everybody needs some hugging every once in a while.

9. That comedian is running for president.

10. The radio has been playing for several hours now.

C. In each of the following sentences, underline the auxiliaries, and describe what meaning they help the main verb convey.

> **Example:**   You <u>must</u> call the doctor at once! [*Must* carries the meaning of requirement. There is no choice but to call the doctor.]

> **Example:**   Sally <u>had</u> felt dejected before she met Kim. [*Had* combined with *felt* creates a past perfect. It tells us that this action in the past occurred before another action in the past.]

1. Miguel has lived in Spain all of his life.

2. You ought to wear a coat in this cold weather.

3. Would you help me with this zipper?

4. The majority of people are willing to help others.

5. Kevin will paint the house next year.

6. Eric Clapton has been performing since the 1960s.

7. Jody had already heard the news before it appeared in the newspaper.

8. Jason might move to another state.

9. Meredith has been studying for her final exams.

10. John will have left by the time I get home.

D. Compose nine sentences. In three sentences, use *be, have,* and *do* each as a main verb. In another set of three sentences, use *be, have,* and *do* as helping verbs. In the final set of three sentences, use *be, have,* and *do* each as both the main verb and as the auxiliary.

> **Examples:**   Set 1 (for *be*):   I *am* sorry.
> Set 2 (for *have*):   Jakimba *has* lost her homework.
> Set 3 (for *do*):   *Did* you *do* what I asked you to?

E. In the following sentences, some of the verb forms are incorrect. Find the mistakes, correct them, and then briefly explain why you made the correction.

> **Example:**   The sun rise in the east. [Change *rise* to *rises* because it is in the third person singular.]

1. That car stoped right in front of me.

2. The elevator had pass my floor before I realized it.

3. I runned down the road yesterday.

4. She have called home several times today.

5. Everybody could understood the problem.

6. The sheep are grazeing in the meadow.

7. I wonderied what you were doing.

8. Rosie plays in the creek with Lefty every chance she gets.

9. Grass will be greener on the other side.

10. Eva partyed all the time in college.

F. In each of the following sentences, identify the "tense" using one of the twelve listed in this chapter. Then explain the time being conveyed by the use of the "tense." (In sentences 1 and 5, identify the tense of the first verb phrase only.)

> **Example:**   Everybody needs love. [Present tense: conveys a general truth.]
>
> **Example:**   Jane is teaching in Slovenia. [Present progressive: conveys what Jane is doing right now.]

1. I was talking to myself when you called.

2. Have you gotten a flu shot yet?

3. Justice lies in the truth.

4. Did you get a lot of sleep last night?

5. Holly had already seen the movie before I read the book.

6. Roxanne is going to California in December.

7. Ram has been living in Bowling Green for thirty years.

8. Are you talking to me?

9. Bananas are expensive nowadays.

10. Jason had been watching TV when the electricity went off.

G. The following is a passage from Abraham Lincoln's Gettysburg Address. Try to identify the various "tenses" used in this portion of the speech, and underline the verbs that carry them. Then discuss the various time frames addressed or evoked within the context of the speech.

It is for us the living, rather, to be dedicated here to the unfinished work which they who fought here have thus far so nobly advanced. It is rather for us to be here dedicated to the great task remaining before us—that from these honored dead we take increased devotion to that cause for which they gave the last full measure of devotion; that we here highly resolve that these dead shall not have died in vain; that this nation, under God, shall have a new birth of freedom; and that government of the people, by the people, for the people, shall not perish from the earth.

H. Transform each of the following sentences into a negative as instructed in brackets.

> **Example:**   Will likes cornbread. [Use *not.*]
> Will doesn't like cornbread.

> **Example:**   Aaron likes cornbread. [Use *dis-.*]
> Aaron *dislikes* cornbread.

1. Charlie lives in Florida. [Use *not.*]

2. Mary Helene had opened the door. [Use *hardly.*]

3. Somebody likes applesauce on his mashed potatoes. [Use *nobody.*]

4. Miyuki was happy after her retirement. [Use *un-.*]

5. I have heard something from the college about admissions. [Use *nothing.*]

6. Terry and Sergio are going somewhere. [Use *nowhere.*]

7. I ate food to lose weight. [Use *less.*]

8. Audrey often goes to the movies. [Use *never.*]

9. Which one do you want? [Respond using *neither.*]

10. Do you have an idea about this? [Respond using *no.*]

I. In each of the following sentences, underline the verb form in parentheses that best agrees with the subject.

> **Example:**   Neither Marlin nor his students (<u>write</u>, writes) term papers.

1. Some class members (is, are) leaving early today.

2. The members of Congress (votes, vote) on the agriculture bill today.

3. One of my friends (is, are) traveling to a reunion this summer.

4. Either the president or his wife and daughter (has, have) to meet with the press.

5. Some of these apples (is, are) going into a pie.

6. Apples and oranges (mix, mixes) very well in a fruit salad.

7. The scale of measurement (is, are) difficult.

8. The jury (has, have) investigated the crime themselves.

9. The three desires of a dog's heart (is, are) to eat, to sleep, and to be petted.

10. Each of the delegates (has, have) a vote.

J. Underline every adverb in the following sentences. Draw an arrow to the word or words each adverb modifies and tell what type of information the adverb is providing (when, where, etc.).

> **Example:**   Sharon exercises <u>daily</u>. [*Daily* tells how frequently Sharon exercises.]

1. Marty's cat is very quiet.

2. Put the sofa down.

3. The giraffe wants its supper now.

4. Never enter a dark alley alone.

5. The baby seems surprisingly contented.

6. The jury gave a response quite quickly.

7. Ron ran too fast, and now he can't catch his breath.

8. Do you sometimes wonder if Friday will ever come?

9. Susan leaves Friday.

10. Please go home right now.

K. Write two sentences using each word. In the first sentence, use the word as an adverb. In the second sentence, use the word as another part of speech. Then identify how you've used each word.

> **Example:**   I go home Monday. [*Monday* is used as an adverb.]
> Monday is my day to rest. [*Monday* is used as a noun, the subject.]

1. home

2. well

3. pretty

4. yesterday

5. never

6. interestingly

7. better

8. bad

9. loud

10. funny

PART II CHALLENGES FOR WRITERS

Because verbs are such an integral part of every sentence and because they convey tense and aspect (time), using verbs appropriately can be a challenge for inexperienced writers, especially those who don't read regularly. In fact, it is not unusual for a detailed grammar handbook to devote thirty or more pages to discussing concepts and rules related to verbs. Although it is not our purpose to offer such detailed coverage regarding verbs here, we do wish to provide a brief overview of the range of problems that may confront apprentice writers as they learn to use verbs appropriately. We will also discuss some of the causes that underlie problems with verb use and offer strategies for remediating them.

PROBLEMS WITH VERB INFLECTIONS

As we explained earlier in this chapter, there are three regular inflections that verbs in English can have: (1) *-ed* to mark the past tense or past participle (e.g., *I walked home; I have walked home regularly for years*), (2) *-s* to mark the third person singular (e.g., *Mary walks home every day*), and (3) *-ing* to mark the present participle (e.g., *I was singing in the shower*). For the most part, native speakers of English do not omit the *-ing* inflection or use it incorrectly. However, many apprentice writers experience spelling difficulties with all three inflections. When using the *-ing* inflection, for example, they may not know when a final consonant should be doubled (e.g., *plan, planning*) or that a final *e* should be dropped (e.g., *plane, planing*). Also, adding the regular *-ed* or *-s* inflection to a verb requires knowledge of quite a few spelling rules, such as doubling a final consonant (e.g., *plan, planned*) or changing *y* to *i* and adding *-es* (e.g., *study, studies*). Indeed, for beginning writers who have difficulty with spelling, the addition of any kind of prefix or suffix (including regular verb inflections) is likely to pose a challenge.

To develop good spelling habits, apprentice writers need to become careful observers of their own writing to determine what sorts of words give them

problems. For example, a writer may know how to add an -*ed* inflection to verbs that end in *y* (e.g., *copy, copied*) but may be unsure of when to double a final consonant when adding -*ed* (e.g., past tense of *plan: planed* or *planned?*). The best way to help writers become critical observers of their spelling difficulties is to encourage (or require) them to keep a spelling log. In such a log, students can keep a running list of the words they misspell and periodically examine their list to discover error patterns. Once an error pattern in spelling is discovered, students should be helped to locate relevant rules, which they can copy into their log and illustrate with their own examples. Before students are able to understand and apply particular spelling rules, however, they may need instruction in related concepts (and attendant terminology), such as *syllable, consonant,* and *vowel.* Be aware that finding properly spelled forms in a reference work isn't always simple or easy for the inexperienced; for example, because the word *plan* can be used as both a noun and a verb, novice dictionary users may not read sufficiently far into the entry to find the spelling of the past tense (*planned*) listed. Therefore, it is advisable to provide regular in-class exercises and activities (finding the proper spelling of particular inflected forms, editing passages, etc.) that afford students practice in locating information in and properly using a dictionary or handbook. Finally, to assist students with a variety of spelling difficulties—including those that arise from the addition of regular verb inflections—Chapter 5 in Mina Shaughnessy's *Errors and Expectations* contains an outstanding explanation of pertinent spelling rules as well as a comprehensive collection of tried-and-true strategies.

Besides posing challenges with respect to spelling, the -*ed* and -*s* inflections also vex writers in other ways. One problem regarding the -*ed* inflection is that it is often omitted by apprentice writers. Moreover, since the -*ed* inflection is used to form the past tense and past participle of regular verbs and is required on past participles of regular verbs that function as adjectives, there are quite a few contexts in which this ending can potentially be omitted:

-*ed* Inflection Omitted from Past Tense Verbs

> Last week we visit Las Vegas for the first time and had a wonderful time! As soon as we got there, we walk up and down the "Strip" and gawk at all of the fancy hotels.

-*ed* Inflection Omitted from Past Participles in Verb Phrases

> For some time now I have live in a small college town. Although many of my friends have move, I still stay right here. Many of my buddies have ask me why I don't leave, but I just shrug and tell them that I like it here.

-ed Inflection Omitted from Past Participles Used as Adjectives

> As soon as I got to town I began to look for a furnish apartment, but no apartments were available. Unfortunately, I had to rent an unfurnish apartment and to buy my own bed, tables, chairs, sofa, etc. So to save money I got lots of use things at a nearby antique mall.

Although apprentice writers may not eliminate the *-ed* every time it is required, as in the examples, it is not unusual for students to omit this ending quite regularly in a piece of writing. Moreover, students who omit the *-ed* in one context, such as the past tense, are likely to omit it in other contexts (past participles in verb phrases, past participles used as adjectives) as well.

Writers who omit the *-ed* ending may also be inclined to omit the *-s* ending (*Mary walk to school every day*). Sometimes this omission is caused because writers experience difficulty with subject-verb agreement, which we will discuss shortly. Other times, however, inexperienced writers may regularly leave out the *-s* inflection for the same reasons that they omit the *-ed* inflection. Both *-ed* and *-s* are ordinarily unstressed in speech and therefore not enunciated clearly. In addition, many Americans speak dialects that omit the *-ed* or *-s* ending in speech, as we discussed in Chapter 1. Writers inexperienced in the conventions of standard American English as it appears in print tend to produce language the way it sounds to them in conversation. Or to put it another way, apprentice writers—unless they do a good deal of reading—are inclined to write what they hear. If such writers don't hear *-ed* or *-s* inflections in speech, they tend to omit them from their writing.

To help apprentice writers who leave out the *-ed* or *-s* inflection with some regularity, it may first be necessary to acquaint them with the concept of "inflection." That is, you may need to help such writers become conscious of the function of inflectional affixes so that they will note their absence and add the appropriate forms where necessary. To acquaint students with the concept of inflection, they can be given a group of words and asked to underline any endings that add "extra meaning to the word of which they are a part" and to explain how each ending affects the meaning of the word to which it has been added. Such a list should contain words that do and do not contain inflections (e.g., *girls, walked, glass, ladies, dog, class*). Once students understand what inflections are and how they affect meaning, the students need to determine (with your help) which inflections they tend to omit. This can be accomplished through a careful examination of their own writing; students may also find it helpful to keep a record of the kinds of inflections they omit and (if it is possible to recognize this) the particular environments where these omissions occur most frequently. As students discover which inflections they tend to leave out and in what contexts, they may also require some assistance in understanding how to apply the various rules of standard usage regarding the *-ed* and *-s* endings.

Finally, once students discover what inflections they omit most frequently, they need a good deal of practice in recognizing and revising words from which inflections have been omitted. Apprentice writers can first be given opportunities to revise improper forms in individual sentences. However, once student writers can add the proper inflections to verbs in individual sentences, they are ready for practice in editing longer passages. This practice is crucial if students are to become proficient at editing their own writing. To this end, you can give students passages to read out loud and note (mark) inflections; you can also encourage them to identify verb inflections in excerpts from books, newspapers, and magazines that they bring to class; in song lyrics and cartoons; or in dialogues and texts that they create. And of course, apprentice writers need frequent opportunities to edit passages of text from a variety of sources as well as excerpts from their own and their peers' writing. For additional information about how to assist students who are having difficulty with verb (and other) inflections, Mina Shaughnessy offers an outstanding series of sample lessons in *Errors and Expectations* (137–52).

PROBLEMS WITH VERB FORM

Besides having difficulty with verb inflections, inexperienced writers may encounter problems with irregular verb forms. These tend to manifest themselves in several ways. Sometimes apprentice writers use an inappropriate past tense or past participle form, often substituting one form for the other, as in the following examples:

Past Participle Form Instead of Past Tense Form

*I *seen* that lecture several times. [I *saw* that lecture several times.]

*They *done* that work already. [They *did* that work already.]

*They *swum* the mile in record time. [They *swam* the mile in record time.]

Past Tense Form Instead of Past Participle Form

*The children *have did* their lesson. [The children *have done* their lesson.]

*I *have went* to Disneyland. [I *have gone* to Disneyland.]

*She *has chose* another stylist. [She *has chosen* another stylist.]

Because constructions such as *I seen* or *They have did* are common to the speech patterns for some dialect speakers of American English, these forms can find their way into written contexts. However, since most written contexts tend to be more formal in style, irregular verb forms used in nonstandard ways are usually perceived as incorrect. It is also worth noting that some incorrect verb forms are more noticeable than others. For example, incorrect constructions such as *They swum the mile* or confusions regarding the past tense and past participle form of the irregular verbs *lie* and *lay* (e.g., *I laid around the house all day*) often escape people's notice, whereas constructions such as *They seen* and *I have went* rarely do and are considered examples of "bad grammar."

Along with other irregular verbs, the verb *be* can also pose special problems for writers because it is so highly irregular. Sometimes the past participle form (*been*) is used without the helping verb *have* in perfect aspect, as in *I been tired* or *I been working*. In addition, some dialects of American English permit *be* to be omitted in some contexts (e.g., *She at work now*) or to not change form in others (*Sometimes she be busy*). As with other irregular verb forms, nonstandard constructions with *be* are usually considered inappropriate for most written contexts.

Finally, apprentice writers may experience difficulty in constructing conventionally correct verb phrases because the variety of English they speak may permit other alternatives regarding the forms or structure of the auxiliary. For example, some varieties of American English permit the helping verb *done* instead of a form of the helping verb *have* in perfect constructions, as in *I done cleaned the furnace* (instead of *I have cleaned the furnace*). Some dialects permit the use of two modals (rather than one only) to indicate probability, as in *I might could go to the festival*. The point here is the form of irregular verbs and the structure of the auxiliary can stray from standard English according to the variety of American English that is spoken and find their way into print.

Because of the variety of forms irregular verbs may take and the ways in which the auxiliary can be structured in American English dialects, however, most students need to acquire skill in using standard forms and structures in their writing. To that end, students should be given opportunities to examine and discuss verb phrases in written passages and to practice writing a variety of verb phrases that convey a range of tenses and aspects. Working with fiction dialogue is especially useful in accomplishing this end because fiction writers often attempt to approximate natural language patterns in the speech of their characters. This speech, which may employ nonstandard verb forms, can be contrasted with other narrative passages, which generally reflect standard English usage. Besides examining verb phrases that contrast standard and nonstandard usage, students can examine such phrases in various passages and discuss how different formations of tense and aspect convey different meanings. To supplement such class activities, you can also ask students to find and bring to class an excerpt (around a page or two) of dialogue in which one or more characters use nonstandard verb forms in their speech. Students can take turns performing these dialogues (or excerpts from them), and following each reading, the class can describe the attributes (economic status, education level, region of the country, occupation, etc.) of the characters that their speech suggests. Subsequent to this exercise, students can rewrite the verb phrases in the speech of various characters so that these verb phrases reflect standard usage. (Time permitting, students can discuss how these modifications might affect readers' perceptions of and attitudes toward various characters.) Another similar "translation" activity might be having students rewrite and perform popular or original song lyrics with nonstandard verb forms into language that reflects standard American English usage (e.g., *She done me wrong* might become *She has treated me badly*). Or you might assign students (as individuals or groups) to write two letters that express similar content to two different audiences—one letter in which nonstandard forms are acceptable and one in which standard forms are required. Assignments and activities that invite students to discover and appropriately use language variants in different contexts should be supplemented with exercises that give them opportunities to practice writing sentences with different auxiliaries and verb forms. Finally, as students attempt exercises, activities, and assignments that require them to use a variety of verb forms in appropriate ways, they may need assistance in using handbooks to find and apply rules regarding the use of such forms. In-class problem-solving sessions, in which students practice finding and applying handbook rules, are always appreciated.

PROBLEMS WITH SUBJECT–VERB AGREEMENT

As we've just discussed, some problems with subject-verb agreement can be related to common variants in speech, such as saying *They was busy*. Subject-verb agreement problems are also common in embedded sentences, which we will discuss in Chapter 10. Other reasons for problems in subject-verb agreement include confusion over whether collective nouns are singular or plural (e.g., *the committee is* versus *the committee are*), confusion when a prepositional phrase separates the subject from the verb (e.g., *The members of the wedding are getting impatient*), and confusion with certain compound subjects.

Collective Nouns

Judging whether a collective noun is singular or plural can be confusing to writers, for two reasons. First, the word appears singular in form (e.g., *team, orchestra, family, committee, jury*) but refers to a group of people. Second, because a collective noun refers to a group of people, whether it is singular or plural depends on how the writer is visualizing the word; that is, it depends on whether the writer is referring to the group as a single unit or to the many individuals that make up the group. Here are some examples:

1. The family *is* getting together this weekend. [*Family* refers to single group.]

2. My family *are* traveling in from all over the country for our reunion. [*Family* refers to the many members of the group.]

the faculties —

In sentence 1, *family* refers to a single unit and so is considered singular (*family is*). In sentence 2, *family* refers to the various individuals that make up the family, and so it is considered plural (*family are*). Only one collective noun lacks this flexibility—*number*. When *number* is preceded by the article *a*, it is always considered plural; when it is preceded by *the*, it is always singular:

1. *A* number of pigeons *were* sitting on the park bench. [plural]

2. *The* number of pigeons *was* astounding. [singular]

Because the writer can choose between singular or plural verbs depending on his intention—with the exception of the word *number*—subject-verb agreement with collective nouns can be somewhat complicated. There is rarely a "right" way to ensure subject-verb agreement. Sometimes, however, the writer's intention is obvious depending on the remaining information provided in a sentence. For example, in the sentence *My class was arguing among themselves*, it is evident that the writer intends to refer to the individuals in the group. Therefore, the subject-verb agreement should be with a plural verb, and the sentence should be changed to *My class were arguing among themselves;* this change also takes care of the inconsistency between the singular verb form (*was*) and the plural pronoun form (*themselves*) in the original sentence. Since it may sound awkward to say *my class were*, the writer has another option and that is to change the sentence to show that the group is made up of individuals, as in *The members of my class were arguing among themselves.* Specifying the individuals in a collective noun by using words such as *members* can create a second problem in subject-verb agreement, however, because it causes the subject (*the members*) to be separated from the verb phrase (*are arguing*) by an intervening prepositional phrase (*of my class*).

Prepositional Phrase Between Subject and Verb

Problems with subject-verb agreement commonly occur when novice writers write sentences in which either a noun subject, singular or plural, is separated from the verb phrase by a prepositional phrase containing a noun object of the opposite number. Here are some examples:

Singular Noun, Plural Object

*The *life* of our parties <u>are</u> always the children. [This should be *The life of our parties <u>is</u> always the children* because *life* is the subject. Subject-verb agreement is confusing because *parties,* the object of the preposition *of,* is plural and stands next to the verb.]

Plural Noun, Singular Object

*The *items* in our question <u>is</u> answerable. [This should be *The items in our question <u>are</u> answerable* because *items* is the subject. Subject-verb agreement is confusing because *question,* the object of the preposition *in,* is singular and stands next to the verb.]

*The *members* of the jury *is* sequestered at a downtown motel. [This should be *The members of the jury are sequestered* because *members* is the subject of the sentence. Subject-verb agreement is confusing because *jury,* the object of the preposition *of,* appears singular in form and stands next to the verb.]

Teachers can help students achieve appropriate subject-verb agreement in these circumstances by giving them practice in omitting the prepositional phrase that separates the subject from the verb. Students, for example, can bracket or underline prepositional phrases in sentences and then circle the grammatical subject in each sentence. Or they can expand sentences by adding prepositional phrases that modify the subject (e.g., *The cost was too high* to *The cost of Marcia's new dresses was too high*). Because students always find it interesting to work with excerpts from actual language, you might also ask them to bring in examples of a particular genre (such as a recipe) and mark intervening prepositional phrases wherever they find them (e.g. *Next, the mixture with the olives is folded gently into the batter*). Following such an activity, students might find it fun to compose a cookbook of their own recipes, which must include some sentences with prepositional phrases that separate the subject from the verb.

Compound Subjects

Most novice writers do not have difficulty with subject-verb agreement in **compound structures** when the subjects are combined using *and* (e.g., *Bob and his family are on vacation*). This is because it is obvious that a plural results when *and* is used to combine two or more things. However, writers do have problems with subject-verb agreement when subjects are combined using expressions such as *as well as* (e.g., *Ruth as well as Bette*), *or,* or *either...or.* The reason for the confusion is that the conjunctions seem to be creating compounds of more than one but really aren't, as these examples show:

Either the teacher or her students *are* attending the conference. [The subject of the sentence consists of nouns joined by the conjunctions *either...or.* The verb should agree with the noun that is closer to it, *students.*]

My parents or Joe *is* picking you up at the airport. [The subject of the sentence consists of nouns joined by the conjunction *or.* The verb should agree with the noun that is closer to it, *Joe.*]

To help students with their problems with subject-verb agreement, teachers need to help apprentice writers to recognize their own pattern of errors and to learn the underlying rule that pertains to that problem. It is important that students become familiar with handbooks at this stage and comfortable in using them to search out rules as well as exceptions to those rules. Students also need to have practice in applying rules pertaining to subject-verb agreement in sentences and in larger passages, including their own writing.

PROBLEMS WITH CONTRACTIONS

Although contractions used to be discouraged in writing, today they are considered appropriate in all but the most formal written contexts. Contemporary writing teachers, then, tend not to address the issue of contraction use except to note that contractions lower the formality of language. As the following examples illustrate, the first sentence in each of the pairs is more formal than the second:

1. I *cannot* attend the play.
   I *can't* attend the play.
2. *I am* sad that you are leaving.
   I'm sad that you're leaving.
3. *We will* examine the errors in due time.
   We'll examine the errors in due time.

Because the majority of written contexts are not so formal as to prohibit the use of contractions—even in school-sponsored or academic writing—inexperienced writers employ them frequently and therefore experience a few common problems. One problem involving contractions is caused by the fact that several of the most common contracted forms sound very much like other words (e.g., *you're* and *your*). This similarity can cause writers confusion. Perhaps the most widespread error with contractions is the use of *of* instead of *have* in constructions involving modals, especially *would* and *could*:

> *I *would of gone* but had to work. [This should be *would've gone* or *would have gone*.]
>
> *I *could of studied* but didn't. [This should be *could've studied* or *could have studied*.]

In speech, of course, the *ve* in *could've* sounds very much like the word *of*, which explains why inexperienced writers commonly make the substitutions shown in the examples. A related problem that derives from the same cause—similar-sounding structures—explains the common confusion of *it's* and *its*, *they're* and *their*, *you're* and *your*:

> *I like *you're* car a lot. [should be *your*]
>
> *My dog licks *it's* tail all the time. [should be *its*]
>
> **Their* going to Orlando this weekend. [should be *They're*]
>
> **Your* not really sick. [should be *You're*]

Writers who confuse contracted forms with like-sounding or homophonous words need to become aware of the patterns of use of these words so that they can practice and become proficient at identifying "suspicious" constructions in their writing. Then whenever they encounter sentences with either a "suspicious" contraction (*it's, you're*, etc.) or its homophone (*its, your*, etc.), they can substitute the full, uncontracted form and use their knowledge of what "makes sense" to determine which option is correct:

Suspicious construction:	I wonder if *their* going on vacation. Check: I wonder if *they are* going on vacation. [The substitution makes sense; therefore, *they're* is correct.]
Correct sentence:	I wonder if *they're* going on vacation.
Suspicious construction:	I *would of* bought that coat if I had the money.
Check:	I *would have* bought the coat.... [The substitution makes sense; therefore, *would've* is correct.]
Correct sentence:	I *would've* bought the coat if I had the money.
Suspicious construction:	*They're* yard is really beautiful.
Check:	*They are* yard is really beautiful. [Substitution does not make sense; therefore; *their* (not *they're*) is correct.]
Correct sentence:	*Their* yard is really beautiful.

Another problem with contractions that writers experience, especially if English isn't their native language, is in placing the apostrophe correctly. In contractions, the apostrophe must be positioned to show where one or more letters have been omitted. For example, in the contraction *I'm*, the apostrophe is placed to show that the letter *a* has been omitted from *I am*. In the contraction *weren't*, the apostrophe indicates the omission of the letter *o* from the word *not*. Writers who don't understand the principle behind contractions or who don't attend to detail when they write can produce constructions such as *She is'nt very respectful*. Although attending to minutiae like apostrophe placement can seem tedious to apprentice writers, most readers do notice such details. Therefore, writers who wish to use contractions need to understand how to place the apostrophe and may require practice recognizing and rewriting misplaced apostrophes in sentence exercises as well as in larger pieces of discourse.

PROBLEMS WITH NEGATION

Whereas problems with contractions are related to correct form, problems with negation are a matter of correct grammatical usage. The most common problems student writers have in using negation is with putting two or more negatives together in the same sentence, which produces what is called a *double negative*. Here are some examples of possible double negatives:

The store doesn't have *no* milk.

*We are*n't* going *nowhere.*

*You ca*n't* meet *none* of my friends.

*They are*n't hardly* talking to each other.

*I do*n't never* eat *no* bananas. [This is a *triple* negative.]

Even though such variants may be common in informal speech, multiple negatives are usually considered ungrammatical, especially in writing. Sometimes multiple negation occurs because the speaker or writer is trying to be consistent in using negatives; that is, if the verb is negative, the person reasons, then everything else in the sentence should agree. However, in English, negative agreement does not exist. Rather, one negative in a sentence suffices to negate the entire sentence.

In addition to multiple negatives in a sentence, another type of negative that is common in some informal speech is the word *ain't*. Although grammarians have argued for years whether *ain't* is a legitimate word, they do generally agree that it is unacceptable grammar. Moreover, in English, using multiple negatives in the same sentence or using the word *ain't* (especially in sentences such as **I ain't got no energy*) is often associated with certain regional or social groups and with a lack of education.

To help students avoid using multiple negatives in a sentence, it is useful for them to become familiar with the rules of usage concerning negatives and then to have practice negating sentences in a variety of ways (with *not* in the verb phrase, with *nobody,* etc.). Students can, for example, do exercises that require them to paraphrase negative sentences using alternate forms of negation (e.g., *I want no ketchup on my fries* rewritten as *I don't want any ketchup on my fries; Volunteers didn't step forward* rewritten as *No volunteers stepped forward*). Or they can compose a brief story (or dialogue or song or political speech) in which they use at least three different forms of negation. Along with engaging in these kinds of activities, students need to practice identifying and fixing double negatives in their own writing and in the writing of others. An activity related to this kind of practice is to have students rewrite the speech of various fictional characters that use multiple negation so that the negatives reflect standard English usage and then discuss, if time permits, the effect that such rewrites have on the reader's perception of and attitude toward the characters.

PROBLEMS WITH ADVERBS

Although students may experience a number of difficulties with adverb phrases and clauses (which we will cover in Chapters 6 and 7), single-word adverbs can also pose problems for inexperienced writers. Sometimes students may have problems with sentence ambiguity caused by the awkward placement of words such as *only* or *even,* with the formation of comparative and superlative forms of adverbs, or with confusing some irregular forms of adverbs with similar adjective forms.

Using *Only* and *Even*

As we have explained, one important feature of single-word adverbs is that many of them can be moved to different places in a sentence without changing the meaning of that sentence. Notice, for example, how the adverb *often* can be positioned in different places in the sentence *Alan likes to go to the movies on Saturdays* without changing the meaning of the sentence:

> *Often* Alan likes to go to the movies on Saturdays.
>
> Alan *often* likes to go to the movies on Saturdays.
>
> Alan likes to go to the movies on Saturdays *often*.

As the examples show, the placement of a single-word adverb ordinarily reflects the writer's desire to create **sentence variety**, emphasize one aspect of the sentence, or follow a particular style. However, with the adverbs *only* and *even*, placement can change the meaning of the sentence, depending on where *only* or *even* is located in the sentence. Notice, in the following examples, how the meaning of the sentence *Alan likes to go to the movies on Saturdays* shifts and changes depending on the location of *only* or *even*:

Using *Only*

> *Only* Alan likes to go to the movies on Saturdays. [No other person but Alan likes to go to the movies on Saturdays.]
>
> Alan likes *only* to go to the movies on Saturdays. [Alan doesn't like anything else on Saturdays.]
>
> Alan likes to go *only* to the movies on Saturdays. [Alan doesn't like to go anywhere else on Saturdays.]
>
> Alan likes to go to the movies *only* on Saturdays. [Alan doesn't like to go to the movies on any other day.]

Using *Even*

> *Even* Alan likes to go to the movies on Saturdays. [It's something of a surprise that Alan likes this.]
>
> Alan *even* likes to go to the movies on Saturdays. [Going to the movies on Saturdays may be unusual, but Alan likes doing so.]
>
> Alan likes to go to the movies *even* on Saturdays. [Alan goes to the movies so much that we don't expect him to go on Saturdays, but he does.]

Knowing whether student writers are having a problem using *only* or *even* effectively can be a challenge for teachers because using *only* or *even* effectively depends on the meaning the writer is trying to convey. However, sometimes a student's misuse of *only* or *even* can be evident from the context of the writing. For example, if a student has written *Only my mom knows how to cook* but then proceeds to write about the cooking of other family members, it would be probable that the writer has created an ambiguous passage by misplacing *only*. Conversely, if the student has written *Even my mom knows how to cook* but then writes that no one in the family can cook, it might be safe to presume that the student is having trouble using *even*. To help student writers learn the power of these small words, we suggest they be given ample practice in deciphering the intended meaning of sentences that contain *only* or *even* in different positions in sets of sentences as we have just done. After students have become familiar with how *only* or *even* can affect the meaning of a sentence, they should then be given opportunities to apply this awareness by creating sentences that use *only* or *even* in a variety of ways.

One activity that students might enjoy would be to have them individually or in groups create cartoons whose humor hinges on the misuse of *only* or *even*. For example, a cartoon might have two cells. In the first cell, a boy is shown talking to his friend; the caption reads, "My mom knows only how to cook." In the second cell, the two boys are in the garage with Mom, who is fixing the lawn mower by taking the engine apart. The caption for this cell reads "I thought your mom knew only how to cook!" A related exercise might be to have students narrate events or create dialogue that includes humorous—or not so humorous—misunderstandings that arise from the misplacement of *only* or *even*.

Comparative and Superlative Forms

Perhaps the most common problem student writers may have in using single-word adverbs is in the formation of comparatives (e.g., *faster, more easily*) and superlatives (e.g., *fastest, most easily*). In addition to misspelling words when adding -*er* or -*est* to an adverb (e.g., *easyer* in place of *easier*), quite often student writers may be confused regarding whether a word takes the -*er* or -*est* suffix or should be preceded by *more* or *most* instead. Due to this confusion, writers may mix forms (e.g., *more prettier*) or add suffixes inappropriately (e.g., *beautifulest*).

To learn how to create the comparative and superlative forms of single-word adverbs more accurately, student writers need to become familiar with the rules that govern the creation of such forms and have practice applying them. So that students can see how the forms correlate with particular meanings, they can be encouraged to dramatize differences between sentences that contain the comparative and superlative forms. One way you can accomplish this is to hand out slips of paper to groups of two or three students and require each group to dramatize what is on its piece of paper. (For example, three students might be given a slip of paper with the sentences *Ed reads fast; Armando reads faster than Ed; Michael reads the fastest.*) Conversely, to give students practice writing comparative and superlative forms properly, groups of two or three students can dramatize actions, which the rest of the class must describe in sentences that use these forms. After students have familiarized themselves with comparatives and superlatives, they need opportunities to practice using them in a variety of contexts. You can ask students to create greeting card lines (e.g., *Get well sooner than later!*), slogans for advertisements (e.g., *Let Swift tennis shoes help you run faster*), song lyrics (e.g., *My heart beats faster every time you are near*), and fairy tales (e.g., about three little turtles named Slow, Slower, and Slowest).

Besides forming comparatives and superlatives properly with *-er* and *-est*, student writers may be unfamiliar with the forms of a small group of single-word adverbs (e.g., *badly, well*) that have irregular comparative and superlative forms (e.g., *badly, worse, worst; well, better, best*). In addition, students may become confused when using these words because they are similar to their counterpart adjective forms (e.g., *bad, good*). As a result of this confusion, student writers may produce sentences such as these:

> The car ran *badder* after the accident. [should be *worse*]
>
> My foot hurts *the worstest*. [should be *worst*]

In addition to using the irregular forms of some single-word adverbs inappropriately, student writers often confuse the adverbs *badly* and *well* with the adjectives *bad* and *good,* thus producing such sentences as *She sang good* or *I feel badly.* Although this usage has become so common—especially in spoken English—that it is barely noticeable, the confusion of the irregular forms (e.g., *worser, badlier*) is quite noticeable. To eliminate problems with irregular adverbs, students may need assistance in understanding and applying the rules governing the irregular forms of single-word adverbs (including words such as *far* and *less* in addition to *badly* and *well*). In addition, students need the opportunity to use this knowledge in editing their own writing and that of others.

● EXERCISES FOR PRACTICE

A. In the following passage, some *-ed* and *-s* inflections are missing. Find and correct each error by adding the appropriate inflection. Then explain in each instance why an *-ed* or an *-s* inflection was required.

> Dear Colleagues,
>   I am writing to you today to ask for your assistance with our annual neighborhood park cleanup. Last year the city receive over a hundred volunteers for this important activity. We were touch by the overwhelming response, and our mayor hope to receive a similar one this year. You may wonder, What did the folks who volunteer last year do? They did a variety of things. Some picked up use containers and pack them into large receptacles that the park provide for this purpose. Others rake up dead leaves. Still others

repaired and painted some of the shelters in the park. This year we have prepare lots of snacks and exciting activities to keep you motivate while you work! So come one, come all, and make this year's the best park cleanup day ever. As always, the city count on you for your support.

Sincerely,

Bob Parks

B. In the following passage, some of the sentences contain problems in the verb phrase. Find these problems and fix them. For each error, explain the problem.

My friend, Mary, has did many interesting things in her life. You might could say she's a world traveler. She has lived with her family in Indonesia, Malaysia, South Africa, Burundi, and Korea. When I visited her home, I seen pictures of her that she had took while living in those countries. They seem so foreign to me! I haven't travel much in the world. I haven't went anywhere as adventurous as Mary has.

C. Some of the following sentences contain subject-verb agreement problems. Find each one and fix it. Then explain the cause of each problem.

Example: Either Randy or the children wants a haircut.

Either Randy or the children *want* a haircut. [The verb (*want*) must agree with the noun that is closest, *children*.]

1. The cost of those glittery socks make me angry.

2. John and his friend from college wants lower taxes.

3. Bettina, Marketta, and Zoolita play tennis together every Saturday.

4. Nandy or her sisters shops for the family's groceries every Wednesday.

5. The high price of fossil fuels are disturbing many consumers.

6. The tiny beagle with the big eyes plays with everyone in the store.

7. The fish on the menu are all fresh.

8. The students and their teacher wants the proficiency testing to be over.

9. All residents of East Hall, including Ralph, is delighted by the news.

10. Much of the time, unripe fruit make me sick.

D. Write a sentence using each phrase as its subject. Cast the verb in each predicate in the present tense, and pay close attention to subject-verb agreement.

Example: John and his teammates

John and his teammates hope to win the game tonight.

Example: Woody or his friends
             Woody or his friends eat pizza whenever possible.

1. The price of silver

2. Either Dopey or one of the other dwarfs

3. The cost of freedom

4. Fresh meat

5. The man with the distinguished sideburns

6. The slippery mud

7. Ned or his friends

8. Sidney and his fellow administrators

9. Neither of us

10. Our dogs or our cat

E. In the following paragraph, contractions are used incorrectly in some instances. Find these errors and fix them.

> If anyone asks me what's exciting about my life right now, Id say that its my sons engagement. My husband and I are both ecstatic about it even though theres not much time until the wedding. As the wedding approaches, wer'e landscaping our front yard in anticipation of the reception. Some people ask us, "Are'nt you worried about whether you'll get along with your daughter-in-law?" But we just shake our heads and smile because we know that our son has chosen wisely. As our friend Clarissa says, "Youve planted the seed; now enjoy the shade of the tree!"

F. Find and underline the various negations that Mark Twain has used in the following passages from *Huckleberry Finn*. Then experiment by rewriting the passages in another way. What is the challenge in rewriting the negatives? How do the rewrites change the effect of the content of the passage?

> You don't know about me without you have read a book by the name of *The Adventures of Tom Sawyer;* but that ain't no matter. That book was made by Mr. Mark Twain, and he told the truth, mainly. There was things which he stretched, but mainly he told the truth. That is nothing. I never seen anybody but lied one time or another, without it was Aunt Polly, or the widow, or maybe Mary. Aunt Polly—Tom's Aunt Polly, she is—and

Mary, and the Widow Douglas is all told about in that book, which is mostly a true book, with some stretches as I said before.

...The Widow Douglas, she took me for her son, and allowed she would sivilize me; but it was rough living in the house all the time, considering how dismal regular and decent the widow was in all her ways; and so when I couldn't stand it no longer I lit out.

G. Some of the following sentences contain errors with single-word adverbs. Find each one, fix it, and explain why it's a problem.

1. I felt well when the teacher complimented my handwriting.

2. I've been sick, but I feel good today.

3. She thinks really quick on her feet.

4. Katie talks more louder than Courtney.

5. What is the baddest thing you've ever done?

6. Soaking your feet in hot water will make them feel more better.

7. This drink with crème de menthe tastes the worstest of all.

8. You'll look a lot more prettier if you comb your hair.

9. The students all ran fastly to the bus when the bell rang.

10. Number 6 is the most hard question.

H. For each of the following sentences, explain what *only* modifies and what its placement causes the sentence to mean.

1. Only I have five dollars.

2. I only have five dollars.

3. I have only five dollars.

4. I have five dollars only.

I. For each of the following sentences, explain what *even* modifies and what its placement causes the sentence to mean.

1. Even I can dance the cha-cha.

2. I can even dance the cha-cha.

3. I can dance even the cha-cha.

4. I can dance the cha-cha even.

EXERCISES FOR CLASSROOM APPLICATION

A. Assume that your students have problems with subject-verb agreement. Explain how you would diagnose the causes of the problems (modifying prepositional phrases, deletion of the -*s* inflection, etc.). Then describe a lesson you would devise to help your students understand and remediate this problem completely. Write out one activity or exercise.

B. Devise an activity that requires your students to look in commonly available print media (newspapers, magazines) to find examples of nonstandard uses of verbs or adverbs that are now becoming standard. In what contexts are these forms prevalent? Why is this so?

C. Choose a problem regarding verb use that you anticipate your students might experience, and devise a class editing activity that would help them find and fix this problem. Don't just describe the activity; rather, make all the materials that you would hand out in class, and plan how and when you would use them as part of your lesson.

SIMPLE SENTENCE VARIATION

Chapter Preview

Chapter 5 describes ways to create variation in simple sentences.

In **Part I** you will learn about

- Sentence types
- Compound structures in simple sentences
- Stylistic variation
- Passive voice

In **Part II** you will learn about the challenges writers may face with sentence variation

- When they are nonnative speakers
- When subject-verb agreement is not obvious
- When using passive voice

In **Part III** you will learn about the options developing writers have

- When choosing stylistic variations
- When choosing point of view

PART I   VARIETY IN THE SIMPLE SENTENCE

In Chapter Two you were introduced to the simple sentence and its components. In this chapter, while still focusing on simple sentences, we introduce you to sentence types (or the functions of sentences) and to the various structures that may occur in simple sentences.

SENTENCE TYPES

Statements, Questions, Commands, and Exclamations

In earlier chapters we have discussed and provided examples of the basic underlying structures for the majority of English sentences. As we explained, English sentences are made up of clauses, and each clause consists of at least one subject and a predicate. These basic constituents, in turn, can be composed of a limited set of necessary elements (nouns, verbs, etc.) that may be expanded in predictable, rule-governed ways. However, as you may have noticed, the structures we have described thus far reflect what linguists and grammarians refer to as *statements* (or ***declarative*** sentences). The function of such sentences is to state a fact or an opinion. But users of English often produce sentences that are altered or transformed from this statement pattern in particular ways:

1. I am going home for dinner.

2. Are you going home for dinner?

3. Go home for dinner.

4. What a wonderful dinner that was!

In these examples, only sentence 1 functions as a statement or a "regular" declarative sentence; the others function to ask a question (sentence 2), to give an order (sentence 3), or to express a strong feeling (sentence 4). Look at these same sentences again in terms of how you might understand them when you hear or see them:

1. I am going home for dinner. (she *said*)

2. Are you going home for dinner? (she *asked*)

3. Go home for dinner. (she *commanded*)

4. What a wonderful dinner that was! (she *exclaimed*)

Because the majority of expressions that users of English produce seem to fall into these broad categories, many grammar books classify English sentences into four main types: (1) statements, (2) questions, (3) commands, and (4) exclamations. You may also be familiar with the more technical terms that are associated with each of these types of sentences: statements are often referred to as *declarative* sentences; questions, as *interrogative* sentences; commands, as **imperative** sentences; and exclamations, as **exclamatory sentences**.

As to the relative prevalence of these sentence types, by far the most dominant type of sentence in writing is the declarative. However, in some written contexts (e.g., in dialogue), the other types may appear more frequently. Questions, commands, and exclamations are also often used to produce stylistic effects. In speech, especially in informal conversation, questions abound, and commands and exclamations also occur more frequently than in writing.

The Form of Statements, Questions, Commands, and Exclamations

One of the ways that speakers of English recognize and interpret expressions is by their form or structure. We have already devoted a good deal of attention to the structure of statements in previous chapters, but what about the form of questions, commands, or exclamations? The structure of each of these variants can differ from that of a declarative sentence in significant ways.

QUESTIONS.   In English there are two broad types of questions (interrogatives): *yes–no questions* and *information questions* (sometimes called **wh- questions**). Yes-no questions can be answered with yes or no:

"Do you understand?" "Yes."

"Do you find this interesting?" "No."

Information questions, by contrast, require information to be provided:

"What don't you understand?" "I don't understand the difference between these two types of questions."

"How will you figure this out?" "I will talk to my teacher."

As you can see, the declarative form changes when forming both types of questions. The primary change is that the subject and verb are inverted (the subject is italicized in each of the following sentences):

You don't understand. [Declarative sentence—the subject begins the sentence and precedes the verb.]

Don't *you* understand? [Yes-no question—the auxiliary (helping) verb precedes the subject.]

What don't *you* understand? [*Wh-* question—the direct object takes the form of a question word, and the auxiliary verb precedes the subject.]

These examples illustrate how the subject of the sentence in questions changes position. It is generally preceded by either an auxiliary or the verb itself (depending on the type of question it is), instead of coming before the verb and all of its auxiliaries, as it does in declarative sentences. In addition to the examples, this variation in form can be noted in each of the following sentences. (In each sentence, the subject is underlined and the complete verb phrase—the main verb plus its auxiliaries—is italicized).

> Statement: <u>You</u> *are writing.*
> Yes-no question: *Are* <u>you</u> *writing?*
> Information question: What *are* <u>you</u> *writing?*

Also notable with respect to the form of information questions is that they begin with words (called *interrogative pronouns*) like *who, what, where, when, how,* and *why:*

> *What* do you want?
> *Where* are you going?
> *Why* are you angry?
> *How* are you going to get to Las Vegas?

Besides their change in word order or sentence structure, both types of questions are also marked in writing by a particular type of punctuation and in speech by an intonation pattern that is characteristic for each.

COMMANDS.   Like questions, commands (imperatives) have a characteristic form or structure. In most commands, the implied subject, *you,* is omitted, and the verb is in the base or uninflected form:

> *Go* home.
> *Pick* that *up.*
> *Clean* your room.

Written commands are usually punctuated with a period but may be punctuated with an exclamation point for added emphasis:

> Go home!
> Pick that up!
> Clean your room!

Like questions and statements, commands are marked by characteristic intonation patterns in speech.

EXCLAMATIONS.   In some ways the exclamation is the most difficult to describe in terms of form. This is because we often think of exclamations as being expressions of strong emotion, and such expressions can and do take a variety of forms in English:

> 1. I love this house!

2. What a dump!

3. How dare you!

4. Get that smile off your face!

5. Are you kidding!

Of course, all of these statements convey strong emotion, but sentence 1 has the form of a regular declarative statement; sentence 4 has the form of a command; sentence 5 looks like a yes-no question; and sentences 2 and 3 aren't complete sentences at all! Some grammar books solve this problem by strictly classifying as "true" exclamations only sentences that begin with *What* or *How* and that transpose the word order:

> What a lousy president he was! [*What* + subject complement + subject + verb phrase]
>
> How scared you must have been! [*How* + subject complement + subject + verb phrase]

Some people might argue that in writing, the exclamation point is more important in signifying whether an expression should be considered an exclamation than the form the expression takes. And in speech, intonation plays a particularly important role in helping listeners make this determination.

Form Versus Function

In focusing our discussion about statements, questions, commands, and exclamations on the *form* they take, we do not wish to imply that *function* is not an important factor or that form and function are always congruent with one another with respect to these expressions. In fact, as our examples of exclamations indicate, statements that look like (take the form of) statements, questions, or commands often *function* as exclamations: *I hate this sweater! Are they serious! Get out of my way!*

In speech, sentences that are structured as statements can function as yes-no questions when uttered with the appropriate intonation pattern. And written sentences that take the form of statements can function as yes-no questions with the addition of a question mark, as the following examples illustrate:

> You understand the situation?
>
> The children ate all the lasagna?

In some speech contexts, the structure of information questions may also vary from the standard form and resemble statements in terms of subject-verb order:

> You ate how many bagels?
>
> Heather went where?

Similarly, commands don't necessarily have to take the standard form with the implied subject *you* omitted and can therefore more closely resemble declarative statements in terms of structure: *You boys stop that noise.*

Moreover, to make matters more complicated, particularly in speech contexts, speakers may avoid a form that marks a particular type of expression for reasons such as tact or politeness. Consider the following scenario, in which two roommates are together in their residence hall room, and one is sitting near the only window, which is closed. Letty is very warm:

LETTY: *Betty, it's hot in here. (She looks pointedly at the window.)*

BETTY: *Want me to open the window?*

LETTY: *Oh, yes, please.*

As this brief dialogue suggests, although Letty may have wanted to command Betty to open the window, she chose instead to make a statement about the temperature and hoped that Betty would guess (and act on) the intention—and open the window. Here are some other examples of how individuals might fashion a sentence in one form (e.g., a declarative statement or a question)—even though their intention might be to accomplish something else altogether:

Situation: Betty sees a box of chocolates on an acquaintance's coffee table.

What she says: Godiva chocolates are my favorite. (declarative statement)

What she means: May I have a chocolate? (yes-no question)

Situation: Betty is at the counter at a fast-food restaurant.

What she says: May I have a Bazooka Burger and Fritter Fries? (yes-no question)

What she means: Give me a Bazooka Burger and Fries. (command) [This intent is clearly a command because the employee does not have the option to say no.]

As we have suggested on numerous occasions, it is always wise to encourage students to consider both *form* and *function* when they are working with words, phrases, or sentences.

COMPOUND STRUCTURES IN SIMPLE SENTENCES

As you just saw, there are four basic types of simple sentences. As you also saw, regardless of the type, simple sentences all are made up of a subject and a verb. They can also contain direct objects, subject complements, and many other types of words, depending on the information being given. The examples in the chapter so far have all involved single subjects and direct objects, but there is no limit to the number of forms (nouns, noun phrases, adjectives, verbs, adverbs, etc.) that may appear within a function (subject, direct object, verb phrase, etc.). For example, in the following sentences, there is one noun in the subject of sentence 1, two in sentence 2, and two nouns and three noun phrases in sentence 3:

1. *Peter* likes to take Spot for long walks. (one noun as the subject)

2. *Mike* and *Peter* like to take Spot for long walks. (two nouns as the subject)

3. *Mike, Peter, their friend Sherry, her boyfriend Gus,* and *a neighbor* all like to take Spot for long walks. (two nouns and three noun phrases as the subject)

As you can see, although there are five nouns or noun phrases in the subject of sentence 3, the fact that they constitute the subject does not change. That is, in sentence 3 a group of five different nouns and noun phrases make up one subject. To illustrate this, let's look at sentence 3 broken down into individual sentences:

Mike likes to take Spot for long walks.

Peter likes to take Spot for long walks.

Their friend Sherry likes to take Spot for long walks.

Her boyfriend Gus likes to take Spot for long walks.

A neighbor likes to take Spot for long walks.

In both writing and speaking in English, to repeat the predicate when several people or things are involved doing the same action (or to repeat the subject when several people are doing different things) can be quite repetitious. And so we combine the information to make it shorter and more concise (e.g., compare *Mike, Peter, their friend Sherry, her boyfriend Gus, and a neighbor all like to take Spot for long walks* with the five individual sentences, which all repeat the same information). This combining of similar structures performing the same type of function to reduce repetition in a sentence is called *compounding*. (It may also be known as *conjoining, conjunction,* or *coordination*.) By combining more than one subject, we can produce a *compound subject* (as in *Mike and Peter like to take Spot for long walks* or *Mike, Peter, their friend Sherry, her boyfriend Gus, and a neighbor all like to take Spot for long walks*). We discuss compound sentences in Chapter 10.

As you can see from the following sentences, we can also create compound verb phrases, compound direct objects, compound subject complements, and so on. The structures are usually joined using *and, or,* or *but,* which are generally known as ***coordinating conjunctions***.

1. Annie <u>walks five miles</u> every day. Annie <u>works out at the gym</u> every day.
     verb phrase   verb phrase

   Compound verb phrase: Annie <u>walks five miles and works out at the gym</u> every day. [Annie does two things every day: she walks five miles and she works out at the gym. Since the same person is doing two different things in the same **time** frame (every day), we combine them into one sentence using *and*. In so doing, we create a compound verb phrase.]

2. Travis made <u>pasta</u> for dinner. Travis made <u>salad</u> for dinner.
     direct object   direct object

   Compound direct object: Travis made <u>pasta and salad</u> for dinner. [Travis made two things, pasta and salad. Since the same person made two things at the same time, we combine them into one sentence using *and*. In so doing, we create a compound direct object.]

3. Wayne is <u>very intelligent</u>. Wayne is <u>quite humorous</u>.
     subject complement   subject complement

   Compound subject complement: Wayne is <u>very intelligent and quite humorous</u>. [Wayne is two things, very intelligent and quite humorous. Since the same person has the two qualities, we combine them into one sentence using *and*. In so doing, we create a compound subject complement.]

As you may deduce, we can create compound forms of every function in English (subject, verb phrase, direct object, indirect object, subject complement, appositive, object complement, object of a preposition, etc.) using every form (nouns, noun phrases, nominals, verbs, prepositions, etc.). The following sentences illustrate this versatility:

1. *Joanne and Jessica* work very hard. (compound subject)

2. Jessica *works and plays* very hard. (compound verb phrase)

3. Joanne wrote *a letter and a memo*. (compound direct object)

4. Jessica sent *students and faculty* the memo. (compound indirect object)

5. Joanne is both *organized and detail-oriented*. (compound subject complement)

6. Jessica, *the department secretary and a great person*, is indispensable. (compound appositive)

7. Tom painted his house *blue and purple*. (compound object complement)

8. There are cockroaches in *the bedroom and the bathroom*. (compound object of a preposition)

9. The couple liked the neighbors *immediately and without reservation*. (compound adverbial)

10. The *old and worn-out* table was discarded with the rest of the junk. (compound **adjectival**)

So far we have looked only at examples of compounding using *and*, which functions to add information. However, as we have said, *or* (which functions to indicate choice) and *but* (which functions to indicate contrast) can also be used in compound structures. The following are some examples of *or* and *but* being used in a variety of compound structures:

Compound Structures with *Or*

1. *Steve or Lori* will meet you at the door when you arrive. [Steve will meet you or Lori will meet you, but not both.]

2. They will *take your coat or let you hang it up yourself.* [Two actions are possible, taking your coat or letting you hang it up yourself, but not both.]

3. They will give you *tea or coffee* to drink. [You will be given one or the other but not both.]

Compound Structures with *But*

4. I like *Steve but not Lori.* [I am contrasting my liking for Steve with my not liking Lori.]

5. They ran *slowly but energetically.* [Because they ran slowly, we do not expect them to be energetic. The sentence thus expresses a contrast between those aspects of the way they ran.]

6. Joely is *naughty but nice.* [If Joely is naughty, it is surprising that she is also nice.]

Sometimes additional words are used to add emphasis and focus to the structure that is being compounded. The most common expressions for combining structures are *both ... and* (*Jacy is both bright and talented*), *either ... or* (*Either put on a sweater or turn up the heat*), *neither ... nor* (*The children are neither hungry nor sick*), and *not only ... but also* (*Today it is not only foggy but also chilly*). What is important to remember in these expressions is that they are all compound structures being used to conjoin information in simple sentences.

Some of the challenges student writers encounter when using compound structures are in using them effectively to avoid repetition, in creating **parallel** structures within a compound structure, in ensuring subject-verb agreement, and in making changes that reflect the order of the elements in the compound structure. We discuss these challenges in Part Two of this chapter.

STYLISTIC VARIATION IN SIMPLE SENTENCES

In addition to compounding structures, there are other rule-governed ways we as writers and users of English can alter the content and form of simple sentences to create variety and avoid repetition. In fact, you are likely not aware of the changes you make when you move (rearrange), substitute, delete, or add structures in sentences, since your focus is more often on the meaning being conveyed by those structures than on the forms themselves.

Movement

As you have learned, the "normal" word order in English is subject-verb-object (SVO), as in *Agnes likes ice cream* (*Agnes* is the subject, *likes* is the verb, and *ice cream* is the object). Furthermore, we can augment this basic structure by adding a number of modifiers that add information within the confines of the rules for word order in English, as in *The young, beautiful, but indulgent Agnes really likes to eat chocolate ice cream with hot fudge sauce on a cold winter's day.* Although a lot of extra information has been added, the SVO word order has not changed.

Because English has this basic SVO word order, any change from it sends the message "I am stressing this part of the sentence" or "I am being creative." There are rules in English that permit us to manipulate and rearrange the structures in a sentence to emphasize certain words or add variety. One of the most movable parts of speech in English is the adverbial, which can appear pretty much anywhere in a sentence. Look how the adverb *slowly* can be moved within the same sentence:

> *Slowly,* she went down the hill.
>
> She *slowly* went down the hill.
>
> She went *slowly* down the hill.
>
> She went down the hill *slowly.*

You may have noticed as you read these sentences a slight change of nuance according to the position of *slowly* in each sentence. For example, placing *slowly* at the beginning of the sentence stresses the slow movement, and this stress varies according to each location. It is important to note, though, that moving *slowly* changes neither its function nor the basic meaning of the sentence of which it is a part; by moving it, the writer has merely chosen to add variety or to stress certain parts of the sentence over others according to the context in which the sentence is used. However, sometimes moving a word within a sentence can change the function and to that extent the meaning of the sentence, as you may recall from our discussion of the adverbs *only* and *even* in Chapter 4. To refresh your memory, let's look at the following sentences using *only*. Notice how the meaning of the sentence changes as *only* is placed in different parts of the sentence *I love you:*

> *Only* I love you. [Placed before the noun, *only* modifies *I* and restricts it to say that no other person but *I* love you.]
>
> I *only* love you. [Placed between the subject and verb, *only* modifies the verb and restricts it to say that *I* have no other feelings but love for you.]

I love *only* you. [Placed between the verb and the direct object, *only* modifies the direct object and restricts it to say that there is no other person I love.]

I love you *only*. [*Only* again modifies the direct object, emphasizing that there is no other person I love.]

In addition to moving adverbials for sentence variation or emphasis, other parts of a sentence may be moved. For example, a direct object or indirect object may be moved to the beginning of a sentence. Compare the following pairs of sentences:

1. She ate *pie.*
   Pie she ate.

2. We called *this new idea* fantastic.
   This new idea we called fantastic.

3. You don't like *him?*
   Him you don't like?

4. You are giving this *to me?*
   To me you are giving this?

In reading these sentences aloud, most people will find a difference of rhythm as well as stress, and indeed often the intonation is important when moving direct or indirect objects to the front of a sentence. That is because this movement may be more common in speech, and some variants may be more commonly used by speakers of various dialects of English.

Another type of movement more common in speech than in writing is the shifting of a *wh-* word from the beginning of a *wh-* question to the end, as in

1. *Where* are you going? (functions as a question)
   You are going *where?* (functions as both question and exclamation)

2. *What* did you give him? (functions as a question)
   You gave him *what?* (functions as both question and exclamation)

In such cases the movement not only adds emphasis but also causes the function of the sentence to change from questioning to both questioning and exclaiming.

A final point about movement that is important for writers is that this variation may change a simple sentence to a more complex one. Notice that the writer must replace the phrase with a clause when rearranging (moving) the structures in these pairs of sentences:

1. She likes *ice cream.*
   Ice cream is what she likes. [Moving the direct object *ice cream* requires a noun clause, *what she likes.*]

2. They named the baby *Evan.*
   Evan is what they named the baby. [Moving the object complement *Evan* requires a noun clause, *what they named the baby.*]

3. She is *terrific.*
   Terrific is what she is. [Moving the subject complement *terrific* requires a noun clause, *what she is.*]

4. The criminals are going *straight to jail.*
   Straight to jail is where the criminals are going. [Moving the adverbial *straight to jail* requires a noun clause, *where the criminals are going.*]

We will discuss complex sentences such as these in more depth in Chapter 9.

Substitution

Whereas moving sentence structures can provide variety and emphasis, another common variation of the simple sentence, substitution, helps reduce repetition within and between sentences. A common form of substitution is the use of pronouns:

1. Ryan went home, and *Ryan* called the police right away.
   Ryan went home, and *he* called the police right away. [Substituting *he* for *Ryan* reduces the repetition within the sentence.]

2. Ryan called the police. *Ryan* then went to the window to watch for them.
   Ryan called the police. *He* then went to the window to watch for them. [Substituting *he* for *Ryan* reduces repetition between sentences.]

As you can see from these examples, not only does substitution help stylistically by reducing repetition, but it also helps relate ideas within and between sentences. That is, it provides a form of **cohesion**. This is especially true when substituting forms other than noun phrases, such as verb phrases, whole predicate phrases, or prepositional phrases. Notice how each of these structures is substituted in the following sentences:

1. Mary *went to the zoo.* Beth *went to the zoo.*
   Mary *went to the zoo.* Beth *did too.* [*Did* substitutes for the entire predicate *went to the zoo. Too* is added to express the repetition of action.]

2. Mary went to the zoo. Beth *met Mary at the zoo.*
   Beth met *her there.* [*Her* substitutes for Mary; *there* substitutes for the prepositional phrase *at the zoo.*]

In example 2, the sentence *Beth met her there* illustrates the fact that there is no limit to the amount of substitution within and between sentences as long as the meaning is clear and comprehensible. However, too much substitution—especially when using such pronouns as *this* and *that*, which can refer to previously given information in the form of one word or several sentences—can cause difficulty for writers, a challenge that we will discuss in Part Two of this chapter.

Deletion

In our discussion of compounding, we illustrated how sentences can be combined by deleting parts of a sentence and then merging the structures. For example, the combined sentence *Mary and Beth went to the zoo* is a compound of *Mary went to the zoo* and *Beth went to the zoo*. In compounding it, we have deleted the second predicate to create *Mary and Beth went to the zoo*. This is a common use of deletion as a way to create variety in simple sentences.

Another form of deletion also involves deleting all or parts of sentences. This deletion is more common in speech than in writing—especially when responding to questions—as these examples illustrate:

1. Can Johnny go to the park?
   Yes, he can. [Part of the verb phrase (*go*) and the rest of the predicate phrase (*to the park*) are deleted.]

2. Who is going to wash the dishes?
   Norma. [The entire predicate (*is going to wash the dishes*) is deleted.]

As when using substitution, the challenge for writers when using deletion is to make sure that cohesion, and hence comprehensibility, is not lost. It is especially important when using deletion (also known as *ellipsis*) that the context (the deleted information) is known to the reader.

Addition

Adding information to a sentence usually means that the basic information in that sentence has changed. However, certain stylistic variations in the simple sentence do not change the basic information, although words may be added. For example, in the variations we have described so far—compounding, movement, substitution, and deletion—it is sometimes necessary to add words or even structures (as when movement requires conversion of a simple sentence to a complex one, as in *Pizza is what I want tonight*) in order to keep the sentence comprehensible or grammatical. The following sentences illustrate this point.

Original sentence: The storm destroyed the crops.

Movement: It was the storm *that* destroyed the crops.

To move the subject, a placeholder (*it*) plus a verb (*was*) must be added. A relative pronoun (*that*) must also be added to follow the subject. This same information could also be expressed by using *there,* as in *There was a storm that destroyed the crops.* Despite these additions of words and structures and the movement of the subject to a position after the verb phrase, no new information has been added to the sentence, and the meaning has not changed. That is, the fact that the storm destroyed the crops has not changed regardless of how we expressed it in words. (This type of variation is called ***extraposition***.)

Original sentence:	Nick goes to high school.
Substitution:	Angela does *too.*

Too has been added to express repetition of an activity (*goes to high school*), yet it does not alter that fact in any way.

Original sentences:	Molly can't cook tonight. Jim can't cook tonight.
Deletion:	*Neither* Molly *nor* Jim can cook tonight.

To combine these two sentences, *neither* and *nor* must be used to replace *not*, yet no new information has been added to the sentence, and the meaning has not changed.

In addition to the above examples, a final common usage of both movement and addition is the creation of the passive voice, which we discuss next.

MORE ABOUT VARIATION: THE PASSIVE VOICE

Another common stylistic variant is the *passive voice,* which involves two of the operations we discussed earlier, movement and addition. Passive constructions occur frequently in both speech and writing. In conversation, for example, it is not unusual to encounter the passive:

MARTHA:	*Oh, my! What happened to you?*
MEENA:	*I was attacked by a dog on my way to work.*

Likewise, some written genres, such as reports, make frequent use of the passive voice:

One thousand grams of analgesic *was administered to the child* upon admission to the hospital.

Calcium chloride *was gradually added* to the solution until a pH of 7 was obtained.

The Form of the Passive

For a sentence in the **active voice** to be transformed into the passive, it must contain a transitive verb and a direct object:

Active:	My neighbor's children <u>*rake my lawn*</u> on Mondays.
	transitive verb direct object
Passive:	*My lawn is raked* by my neighbor's children on Mondays.

The passive form is usually easy to recognize because it differs from the active or "regular" form of the simple sentence in three basic ways.

1. The order of subject and direct object is reversed.

   Active: My neighbor's children rake my lawn on Mondays.

                subject   direct object

   Passive: My lawn is raked by my neighbor's children on Mondays.

            new subject   former subject, now agent

   In the active sentence, the subject (*my neighbor's children*) precedes the verb (*rake*), and the verb precedes the direct object (*my lawn*). In passive sentences, the former direct object (*my lawn*) becomes the grammatical subject of the sentence. The former subject (*my neighbor's children*)—now the actor or **agent** performing the action—is moved to follow the verb.

2. The word *by* is added immediately before the former subject.

   Active: My neighbor's children rake my lawn on Mondays.
   Passive: My lawn is raked *by* my neighbor's children on Mondays.

3. A form of *be* is added as an auxiliary in the verb phrase, and the main verb is changed to the past participle form.

   Active: My neighbor's children *rake* my lawn on Mondays.

                                          present

   Passive: My lawn *is raked* by my neighbor's children on Mondays.

            be + past participle

Note in point 3 that the active sentence doesn't contain a form of *be;* the passive transformation adds a *be* form. If the active sentence already contains a form of *be,* the passive transformation adds an *additional be* form: *My neighbor's children were raking my lawn on Mondays* would be transformed into *My lawn was being raked by my neighbor's children on Mondays.* And as you can see, in passive sentences the main verb (*rake* in the example) is changed to the past participle form (*raked*).

Indirect Objects in the Passive

One notable variation in the process of forming a sentence in the passive voice occurs when the sentence contains an indirect object. As we have explained, the passive voice is created by switching the subject and the direct object of the active sentence. However, active sentences that contain *both* a direct and an indirect object can often be changed or transformed into the passive through one of two options: either the direct object can become the subject of the passive sentence, or the indirect object can become the subject of the passive sentence:

Active: The nurse gave the patient a powerful painkiller.
             subject   indirect object   direct object

Passive option 1: A powerful painkiller was given to the patient by the nurse.
         new subject (former direct object)

Passive option 2: The patient was given a powerful painkiller by the nurse.
         new subject (former indirect object)

In either case, the former subject (in these sentences, *nurse*) becomes the agent of the newly constructed passive sentence. In determining whether to use the direct object or the indirect object as the new subject, language users make the subject of the passive sentence the word or phrase they wish to emphasize, for whatever reason. In the examples, passive option 1 calls attention to the *painkiller;* in passive option 2, the focus is on the *patient.*

Other Variations with the Passive

Besides the option of forming the passive voice in two different ways when an active sentence has both a direct and an indirect object, English language users have at their disposal several other options when forming a passive. Passive sentences, for example, can often be formed with the word *get:*

Active: A car *hit me* on the way home.
Passive: I *was hit* by a car on the way home.
Passive with *get:* I *got hit* by a car on the way home.

Active: The fire alarm *startled me.*
Passive: I *was startled* by the fire alarm.
Passive with *get:* I *got startled* by the fire alarm.

Active: My teacher *caught me* cheating.
Passive: I *was caught* cheating by my teacher.
Passive with *get:* I *got caught* cheating by my teacher.

As these examples suggest, with **get passives**, the word *get* is used instead of a form of *be.* Passives formed with *get* are usually considered more informal than passives formed with *be.* *Get* passives can also convey additional nuances of meaning in some circumstances. In the third example, for instance, the *get* passive alternative might suggest to some readers more of a possibility that the teacher caught the unfortunate writer *in the act* of cheating.

Another less common passive variant is the passive formed with the word *have* as an auxiliary. Such passives are possible with only a select group of verbs and are permitted only in certain contexts:

Active:	Edith *cut* my hair.
Passive:	My hair *was cut* by Edith.
Passive with *have:*	I *had* my hair *cut* by Edith.

Nearly all passives formed using *have* as an auxiliary involve the performance of a task by a person other than the speaker or writer, as in these examples:

Bill had his shoes shined.

I had my house painted.

I had my nails done.

I had my car washed.

As you may have noticed, in these examples, passive sentences often reflect an additional stylistic option: to delete the word *by* and the former subject. That is, *Bill had his shoes shined* is a shortened version of *Bill had his shoes shined by the man at the mall.* And *Bill had his shoes shined by the man at the mall* is a passive variation of the active sentence *The man at the mall shined Bill's shoes.* It is common in both speech and writing for passive sentences to exhibit the additional stylistic option of deleting the word *by* and the former subject, particularly when the identity of the agent is obvious, unimportant, or unknown:

Active:	The police arrested Tabitha.
Passive:	Tabitha was arrested by the police.
Passive + deletion:	Tabitha was arrested. [The agent is obvious.]
Active:	The officials tallied the results after the election.
Passive:	The results were tallied by the officials after the election.
Passive + deletion:	The results were tallied after the election. [It may not be important to know the agent.]
Active:	Some unknown workers built the bridge in 1782.
Passive:	The bridge was built by some unknown workers in 1782.
Passive + deletion:	The bridge was built in 1782. [The agent is not known.]

We will return shortly to the option of *by* deletion. Earlier we said that passive sentences are usually easy to recognize, but the key word is *usually.* In fact, inexperienced writers—who can overuse or misuse the passive—often don't recognize passive sentences when the former subject plus the word *by* are deleted.

Why Use the Passive Voice?

Because apprentice writers often have difficulty constructing sentences in the passive voice or using them appropriately, teachers sometimes tell their students, "Don't use the passive." Indeed, passive sentences may be longer—and more "wordy"—than their active counterparts. Furthermore, an accumulation of ineffective, inappropriate passive sentences in a piece of writing can create all kinds of unintended effects, including reduced readability and a stilted, distant tone. Still, the passive, when used properly, is a powerful alternative that should be a part of every writer's stylistic repertoire.

Style manuals and grammar books offer a number of legitimate uses of the passive. In many instances when the passive variant is preferred, it is accompanied by the additional option of deleting the word *by* plus the former subject. Here are some of the more common instances when the passive is recommended:

1. Use the passive when the actor or agent performing the action of the verb is unknown or unimportant. Note that *by* and the identity of the agent are omitted because that identity is either unknown or unimportant.

   Active: Someone left the lights on all night long.

   Passive: The lights were left on all night long.

   Active: Something clogged our fountain during the summer.

   Passive: Our fountain was clogged during the summer.

2. Use the passive when it is more important to emphasize the object or the indirect object than the subject. To put it another way, sometimes a writer or speaker might wish to emphasize the object or receiver of an action rather than the performer of that action.

   Active: All of her visitors cheered Jan during her illness.

   Passive: Jan was cheered by all of her visitors during her illness. [The emphasis is on *Jan* rather than on *her visitors*.]

   Active: The school administrators awarded the top students silver candlesticks.

   Passive option 1: Silver candlesticks were awarded to the top students. [The emphasis is on *what* was awarded.]

   Passive option 2: The top students were awarded silver candlesticks. [The emphasis is on *who* received the awards.]

3. Use the passive when it is necessary to be polite or tactful. Sometimes it's polite not to call attention to who did a particular deed. In this use of the passive, the former subject and the word *by* are omitted.

Active: Here is another copy of the report that *you misplaced.*

Passive: Here is another copy of the report that *was misplaced.* [Only the italicized portion is passive.]

4. Use the passive when it is necessary to appear objective or impartial. Academic writing often employs the passive, with *by* and the former subject deleted.

Active: I observed the subjects daily for two consecutive weeks.

Passive: The subjects were observed daily for two consecutive weeks.

5. Use the passive when repeating the same subject would be monotonous. Especially in describing a process or procedure, the passive can help writers avoid frequent repetition of the subject, which is omitted (along with the word *by*).

Active: First, I sorted the essays into topic areas. Then, I reexamined each piece to confirm my original placement. Next, I developed a set of evaluation criteria. Following these steps, I ...

Passive: First, the essays were sorted into topic areas. Then each piece was reexamined to confirm the original placement. Next, a set of evaluation criteria was developed. Following these steps,...

This list of uses for the passive is not meant to be exhaustive. In fact, there are many other contexts in which the passive variant may be more appropriate and effective than its active counterpart. As the many uses for the passive suggest, then, this stylistic alternative is a potent tool for both writers and speakers.

EXERCISES FOR PRACTICE

A. Indicate whether each sentence is in the form of a statement, a yes-no question, an information question, a command, or an exclamation.

Example: Take that animal out of here now. (command)

Example: Won't Martha be upset by your attitude? (yes-no question)

1. New Yorkers stood in line for hours to get into the new restaurant.

2. What do you think you're doing?

3. What a marvelous person she is!

4. Do you have any idea about Bill's latest project to renovate the old theater?

5. All five of the pups in the litter found a "feeding station" on their mother's belly except for the little black-and-white fellow.

6. Oh, how lucky my students are to be in my class!

7. Won't you take a moment to answer this questionnaire?

8. Wipe that smirk off your face.

9. Each of the plants was treated with pesticide.

10. Who will staff the front desk next week?

B. Transform each of the following sentences into the form indicated in parentheses. (For some sentences, more than one right answer may be possible.)

Example: Clean the filing cabinet in the back office. (yes-no question)
Will you clean the filing cabinet in the back office?

Example: What caused the seedlings in the greenhouse to die? (statement)
The intense heat caused the seedlings in the greenhouse to die.

1. Tie that sail down. (yes-no question)

2. What caused Maria to run out of hall screaming? (yes-no question)

3. Did Matt spill the vanilla shake all over Debby's black dress? (statement)

4. Many of the voters decided not to participate after the election. (information question)

5. Carlos is a marvelous fiction writer. (exclamation)

6. Will you create a new file for this investor? (command)

7. How long do you think Betty's hair is? (exclamation)

8. Try standing in my shoes for a while. (yes-no question)

9. After examining the data carefully, the auditors made several recommendations. (information question)

10. What strategies did the consultant recommend? (statement)

C. In each of the following newspaper headlines, identify the type of sentence that is being used. Explain why you identify the sentence as such.

Example: "A Partnership Brings College Curriculum to High School Classes"

Statement.: The sentence is in "normal" word order, and its content does not imply an exclamation or a question.

1. "Akron Rallies for Win"

2. "Is Town Center Taking Shape?"

3. "What Would You Do?"

4. "Landowners Oppose Nuclear Waste Dump"

5. "How the Locals Are Taking Charge"

D. In the following dialogues, identify the types of sentences and how they are being used.

Example: TOM: *My, it's hot in here. Someone should open a window.* (statement used as a request for opening a window)

PENNY: *Here, I'll open a window for you.* (statement)

1. JAIME: *Have you seen my new baby?*
   BRIAN: *He's such a big boy.*

2. MOM: *This room is a mess.*
   SON: *I don't have time to clean it.*

3. JULIE: *Are you really going to eat that whole pie?*
   TIM: *Why shouldn't I?*

4. CLERK: *May I help you?*
   CUSTOMER: *What kind of purple paint do you have?*

5. CLERK: *The counter is open.*
   CUSTOMER: *Oh, yes. I'd like a cup of coffee, please.*

E. The following sentences contain compound structures. Underline the structures and identify them.

Example: The birds and the bees play together in the spring. (compound subject)

1. George is doing very well in history and math at this new school.

2. Barb is washing dishes and talking on the phone right now.

3. Jacky dyed her hair blue and orange.

4. You are the most stubborn and most difficult person I've ever met!

5. Either Deb or Sue is going to the movies this weekend.

6. Carol, my boyfriend's sister and my friend, works for the state government as a translator.

7. J.J. and Jakimba ate <u>pizza and ice cream</u> while they watched the movie.

8. They gave Shirley and Jim an award for their new book.

9. The tired but delighted new mother took the baby in her arms.

10. The football players jumped on the bus quickly and with determination.

F. The following is a short passage from *The Battle of Life* by Charles Dickens. In literature, writers often use unusual means of compounding. Why is it difficult to identify some of these compound structures? Try to identify as many as you can by underlining them. The first compound structure is identified for you as an example.

> The door <u>was barred and locked</u> again, and once again she stood beneath her father's roof. Not bowed down by the secret that she brought there, though so young; but with that same expression on her face for which I had no name before, and shining through her tears.
>
> Again she thanked and thanked her humble friend, and trusted to her, as she said, implicitly, with confidence. Her chamber safely reached, she fell upon her knees; and with her secret weighing on her heart, could pray!
>
> Could rise up from her prayers, so tranquil and serene, and bending over her fond sister in her slumber, look upon her face and smile—though sadly: murmuring as she kissed her forehead, how that Grace had been a mother to her, ever, and she loved her as a child.

G. Select five of the ten compound structures from the following list, and write your own sentences. Be sure to combine the sentences using a variety of conjunctions, including *and, but,* and *or.*

> **Example:**   compound adjectival
>
> The naughty but nice children had their stockings filled by Santa.
>
> The cold and bitter wind made us all long for summer.
>
> Call him silly or serious, he is still a good writer.

1. compound subject

2. compound direct object

3. compound indirect object

✗ 4. compound subject complement

✗ 5. compound appositive

6. compound adverbial

7. compound adjectival

8. compound verb phrase

9. compound object of a preposition

10. compound object complement

H. Combine each pair of sentences to produce one sentence with a compound structure. Be sure to use a variety of conjunctions (*and, but, or,* etc.) to join the sentences.

> **Example:**   The potatoes are delicious. The chicken is delicious.
> The potatoes and chicken are delicious.

1. Nancy ran all the way on her first day at school. Nancy skipped all the way on her first day at school.

2. The soup is hot. The soup is creamy.

3. Josh loves his mom. Josh loves his dad.

4. They went to the zoo. They went to the park.

5. Stanley, Angie's older brother, lives in Florida. Stanley, Angie's good-looking brother, lives in Florida.

6. Books for classes are expensive. Notebooks for classes are expensive.

7. Randle left Julia his money. Randle left Clarence his money.

8. They named one twin Ronald. They named one twin Donald.

9. The young woman became a doctor. The talented woman became a doctor.

10. The cheerleaders shouted loudly. The cheerleaders shouted boldly.

I. Using the prompt provided, create stylistic variation in each of the following sentences. Be sure to make new sentences that convey the same basic information. (There may be several ways to create variety. You do not have to provide every option.)

> **Example:**   John marched to the back of the room slowly. (movement)
> Slowly, John marched to the back of the room.

1. The tornado uprooted all the trees in the park. (addition)

2. Suddenly, the wind had begun to blow hard. (movement)

3. The book was written by somebody in the twelfth century. (deletion)

4. John went to the movies last week. Alice went to the movies last week. (substitution)

5. Simon and Kim read a newspaper only on Sundays. (movement)

6. Can you translate this sentence for me? (deletion)

7. Suat had a baby last year. Suat named him Daniel. (substitution)

8. You don't like scuba diving? (movement)

9. Everybody wants ice cream for dessert. (addition and movement)

10. Who went to the Democratic National Convention? (deletion)

J. Some of the following sentences are in the active voice; others are in the passive voice. Transform the active sentences to passive and the passive sentences to active.

    Example: My suggestions were taken literally.
                    My children took my suggestions literally. (passive to active)

    Example: The magazine subcommittee selected a two-color cover.
                    A two-color cover was selected by the magazine subcommittee. (active to passive)

1. The notebook format was voted on by the class.

2. Our neighbors renovated the porch on their house last summer.

3. Tabby cornered a tiny little chipmunk near the garage.

4. Since last summer, the essays have been assessed by external evaluators.

5. Several concerned citizens proposed a comprehensive solution.

6. The discontinued computer model was purchased by quite a few smart consumers.

7. Our daughter-in-law, Emma, designed a Web page full of beautiful graphics.

8. After remodeling, the attic was taken over by our children.

9. The manager of the local coffeehouse renovated and remodeled a historic theater in our town.

10. All of the residents of our town owe Kelly a debt of gratitude.

K. All of the following sentences are in the active voice; transform each into the passive. Where you think it appropriate, delete the word *by* plus the former subject and explain why you think this additional operation was necessary or beneficial.

> **Example:**   The transfer students will use the new computer lab.
>
> The new computer lab will be used by the transfer students.

> **Example:**   Something dented my car door.
>
> My car door was dented. [*By* + *something* has been deleted because what dented the door is not known and so need not be mentioned.]

1. My supervisor lost all of the invitations.

2. The tidal wave devastated the small coastal village.

3. First, you add the dry ingredients to the mixture. Then, you add the marinated vegetables. Finally, you toss everything in a large pasta bowl.

4. I observed each of the subjects of the experiment on two different occasions.

5. The tourists from Belgium bought the handcrafted dolls.

6. Something is eating my tulip bulbs.

7. Someone is vacuuming my office on a regular basis.

8. All of the politicians felt the hostility of the crowd.

9. The nurse administered the entire dose of painkiller to the patient.

10. Anybody can open the screen door easily.

L. Obtain several examples of two different types (genres) of writing. For example, newspapers contain different types of writing (letters to the editors, feature articles, news reports, film reviews, etc.), and so do magazines. You might also take a look at the textbooks you own, since textbooks themselves represent a genre of writing. Even your medicine cabinet or linen closet will contain bottles or packages that include written directions (also a genre of writing). Once you've selected several examples of writing from each of the two genres you've chosen, examine these for passive sentences. Do the examples of writing from the two genres you've chosen seem to contain the same or a different percentage of passive sentences? If one genre seems to contain more passive sentences than the other, what might account for this? If neither of the genres you've selected seems to contain very many passives, do you think this is typical? Explain why or why not.

PART II   CHALLENGES FOR WRITERS

Developing control of simple sentence variation and using it effectively in writing can be the source of several challenges for novice writers. In Part Two we discuss in particular the challenge simple sentence variation poses for nonnative speakers of English and the challenges subject-verb agreement in inverted sentences and using the passive voice pose for all novice writers.

SENTENCE TYPES: PROBLEMS FOR NONNATIVE SPEAKERS

One of the first challenges for any speaker of another language when learning English is the possible interference of the learner's native language. Certain aspects of the learner's mother tongue, both grammatically and rhetorically, may differ from their English counterparts. For example, some languages do not have pronouns, and some languages have more verb tenses than English has. One of the most basic differences that challenge nonnative speakers learning English is word order. As we mentioned earlier, English has a subject-verb-object (SVO) word order. However, some languages have an SOV word order or some other order, and the grammar constraints and concepts may be quite different as well. What all these differences may mean for learners of English is that they find basic simple sentence structure hard enough to control when using English and thus find variations on this form especially challenging.

Nonnative Speakers and Sentence Types

As nonnative speakers who are learning English develop a command over the rules of English, they are likely to first develop control over the word order of statements (e.g., *Mohammed likes potatoes*). Likewise, most nonnative speakers usually develop proficiency with the form of exclamatory sentences (e.g., *These potatoes are delicious!)* because it can resemble the statement in form (exclamations using other sentence types, such as *What a beautiful sunset!* may be more challenging). However, nonnative speakers may have some difficulty with the form and function of imperatives. Although imperatives are more commonly used in speech than in writing, they can appear in writing, particularly in reported speech or written directions. In terms of form, one difficulty ESL learners may have is in understanding the limits of using a subject in imperatives (e.g., *Be good* versus *You be good*, *Turn off the light* versus *Somebody turn off the light*, *Be quiet* versus *Let's be quiet*). It can even be more confusing when the basic rules of constructing imperatives (verb + modifier or object) seem to be contradicted (e.g., *Somebody put out that fire!*). For this reason, students may produce sentences such as these:

*He sit down. [The learner mistakenly thinks imperatives can be used in the third person and so replaces *you* with *he.*]

*Turn somebody off the lights. [The learner mistakenly has the subject, *somebody*, follow the verb, *turn.*]

*Let quiet. [The learner mistakenly omits both the subject and *be*, which is required when *let* is used (e.g., *Let's be quiet*).]

To help students with these types of problems, it is important to make certain that they are familiar with the rules for using subjects with imperatives and to give them enough practice in applying those rules. Some possible activities that give students practice are to have them play "Simon Says" or give instructions or directions to another person (either oral or written) that the other person must follow. Another activity may be having each student write a short recipe.

An important challenge for nonnative speakers when learning to use imperatives in English can be negative constructions (e.g., *Don't you laugh* versus *Don't laugh* versus *Do not laugh*). This is especially true when the verb *be* is involved (e.g., *Be happy* versus *Don't be gloomy*) since *be* in other contexts does not require *do* as an auxiliary. As we discussed in Chapter 4 and will discuss in the next section on forming questions, using *do* as an auxiliary can be a great challenge for nonnative speakers, who may produce such constructions as the following:

*Don't sad. [The learner has mistakenly understood *do* to be the main verb and thus omitted *be.*]

*Be not sad. [The learner has mistakenly omitted the necessary auxiliary, *do*, and changed the order of the verb phrase.]

*Not sad. [The learner has mistakenly omitted the verb phrase.]

*Do not you go away. [The learner has not understood the necessity of contracting *do* + *not* (or of deleting *you*).]

A possible way to remediate this difficulty for nonnative speakers is to provide ample practice, both in oral and written form, in using negation with imperatives. With respect to oral practice, the simplest kind of drill is to have students practice transforming imperatives into negative imperatives (e.g., *Go home* becomes *Don't go home*); such drill is helpful in that it provides speakers with an opportunity to practice forming a difficult structure. However, because such drill can become tedious, students require other opportunities to produce negatives with imperatives. In this regard, brief skits that students dramatize can be of help. For example, students can act out short dialogues that you construct and give to them (e.g., *"Don't go away. I need to talk with you." "OK. What's the problem?" "I'm not sure my roommate likes me." "Don't worry; I'm sure she likes you."*) Or they can write and then perform brief skits of their own, especially if you provide them with prompts (*Write and perform a four- to six-line dialogue that includes at least one sentence with a negative imperative. Some examples of negative imperatives are "Don't be afraid," "Don't leave without me," and "Don't be sad.").* For students who have sufficient skills to comprehend television commercials, a related oral activity can be to compose and read (or perform) a brief commercial with a slogan that contains a negative imperative (e.g., *"Don't get mad. Get Glad!"*).

With respect to written practice in using negation with imperatives, simple exercises might require students to transform a series of imperative sentences into negative imperatives, to write individual sentences of their own with verbs that you provide, or to rewrite sentences that contain incorrectly formed negative imperatives. Students can also find examples of negation with imperatives in short passages that they come across, record instances of these sentences and bring them to class, edit excerpts from their own or other's writing that contain errors with respect to these structures, and so forth. Finally, so that students can understand the range of contexts in which negative imperatives are used, they can be asked to bring in, discuss, and then write their own versions of genres that use negation with imperatives; these genres might include advertisements (*"Don't wait another minute. Buy a new Free Spirit now and SAVE!"*), greeting cards (*"Don't think for a minute that I forgot your birthday"*), political speeches (*"Don't settle for four more years of tax and spend …"*), and recipes (*"Don't be concerned if the mixture turns brown; if it does, simply stir in 1 to 2 tbs. of milk"*).

A final challenge for nonnative speakers in forming imperatives can be in overgeneralizing the third person singular inflection, which might produce a sentence like this:

> *Walks on this side. [The learner has mistakenly used the third person singular inflection for the imperative.]

In such an instance, the teacher needs to provide both oral and written practice of the sort we have described that would help the student understand that the verb should not be inflected because the sentence is in fact in the second person singular (*you*).

As the foregoing discussion suggests, in addition to *forming* the imperative properly, nonnative speakers may find *using* imperatives appropriately equally challenging. We therefore suggest that students be provided with many different examples of imperatives being used appropriately in a variety of contexts (in an emergency, when making a request of a friend, when making a request of a teacher, etc.) and with opportunities to use these structures in different circumstances to produce different effects.

Although forming and using the imperative can be challenging for nonnative speakers, the greatest challenge with sentence types is in forming questions in English. This is because many languages, particularly Asian languages, do not use inversion for asking questions. That is, these languages do not change the word order; instead, they use a change in intonation or some other language-specific way to signal a question. The fact that English not only changes the word order but also adds the *do* auxiliary (e.g., *Do you like pizza? You like pizza, don't you?*), splits the verb phrase (e.g., *Would you like some pizza?*), or begins the question with a *wh-* word (e.g., *What would you like for supper?*) can be especially confusing. Nonnative speakers may produce questions such as these:

*You like some pizza?

*You no like pizza?

*You don't like spaghetti, don't you?

*Would like you some pizza?

*What like you for supper?

To help nonnative speakers learn to form questions appropriately in English, it is important to give them ample practice in converting statements to questions (in both oral and written contexts) with drill, simple dialogues, and other, more ambitious exercises and assignments that we have described earlier. Besides these types of activities, students can also practice forming questions if you give them one or more "real" tasks to perform. If, for instance, you compile a list of occupations (librarian, server at a restaurant, assistant at a financial aid office, etc.) and a group of questions that might be appropriately asked of a person performing each occupation (e.g., librarian: *Where is the reference section? How do I use this computer to do a search? Is this the periodicals section?*), you can ask your students to go to two or more venues where they must ask and then write out the answers to at least three different questions. Other variations of this type of assignment might include assigning students to ask directions from someone they pass (*Where is the student union?*), raise questions in class (*Would you repeat that, please?*), or solicit opinions from friends or roommates (*What do you think of the new restaurant on the corner?*).

Besides practice in asking questions, practice in answering questions is equally important, since it is necessary to use the *do* auxiliary in the answers to yes-no questions and tag questions (e.g., *You write poetry, don't you?*) as well. "Naturalistic" assignments such as we have described are helpful in this context also, since these kinds of assignments can give students practice in forming answers to questions in English; they also provide students with opportunities to experience the various ways in which questions can appropriately be used (questions as exclamations, questions that genuinely request information, questions as polite requests, questions that don't expect answers, etc.). Besides practice in posing and answering questions orally, we also suggest giving students opportunities to find, discuss, and craft questions in a variety of written forms (titles of articles, captions to cartoons, direct quotations, etc.).

Nonnative Speakers and Simple Sentence Variations

In terms of movement, most nonnative speakers may with continual practice be able to control the concept of moving adverbs (e.g., *Michael shops only for shoes; Suddenly, Cheryl let out a cry*). However, they may find it a challenge to understand the particular change in word stress associated with other types of movement. For example, a student who consistently writes sentences such as *To there you are going?* or *Home I went* may not have control over English word order and may therefore be unaware of the effect such variation of the basic word order might have on the reader. That is, the writer may not yet have command of English word order and thus not be making a conscious choice to vary the sentence. (Misplaced modifiers, which we discuss in Chapters 7 and 8, may also be a challenge for nonnative speaker writers for this same reason.) If students seem to use such variants regularly, we recommend giving them a lot of practice in rearranging such sentences into "regular" word order. Often only the very advanced nonnative speakers will be able to use movement for stylistic effect, and so teaching or allowing such students to do so should be saved for advanced writing classes.

Like native speakers, nonnative speakers sometimes find extraposition—the movement of subjects and the addition of the placeholder *it* or *there*, as in *There is poverty in many countries*—to be a challenge, especially as such structures relate to subject-verb agreement. Omitting the placeholder *it* or *there*, as in **Is busy* or **Is cloudy*, can be a common error because it translates into an appropriate construction in many languages. Likewise, few languages have a part of speech that corresponds to the placeholder *there*. Consequently, using *there* appropriately as a placeholder can be confusing to many nonnative speakers. Here are the types of sentences nonnative speakers might produce as a result of their confusion:

- *There is happy at the party. [The writer mistakenly uses *there* to mean *at the party*.]
- *There is pleasant in Kenya. [The writer mistakenly uses *there* to mean *in Kenya*.]
- *It's a dog in the road. [The writer mistakenly substitutes *it* for *there*, meaning *There is a dog in the road*.]
- *There is windy today. [The writer mistakenly substitutes *there* for *it*, meaning *It is windy today*.]

One way to help students use *it* and *there* appropriately is to give them practice using the placeholders in an appropriate context, such as using *it* when discussing the weather (e.g., *It is cold in Minnesota in the winter*) or *there* as a placeholder for extraposed subjects (e.g., *There is pleasant weather in Nairobi*). After students begin to understand how *it* and *there* can be used as placeholders in these common contexts, it would be appropriate to give them extra practice on subject-verb agreement in these contexts. After learning these basics of using *it* and *there*, students would then be ready for the challenge of using *it* and *there* as placeholders for moved subjects that contain nominal phrases and clauses (which we discuss in Chapter 9).

Nonnative Speakers and the Passive Voice

In addition to the concept of active versus passive sentences and appropriate usage, inverted word order and sequence of subject-verb-object can be a challenge for nonnative speakers. For example, nonnative speakers may produce questionable passive constructions such as these:

> *Kathy and Greg was enjoyed their honeymoon. [The subject and object have not been inverted.]
>
> *Depoe Bay is sped up its tourism. [The subject and object have not been inverted.]

It could be argued that the students' problem in these sentences is not only subject-object inversion but also in knowing which transitive verbs lend themselves to being used in the passive. This lack of knowledge of the limitations of transitive and intransitive verbs could also lead nonnative speakers to produce a sentence such as *My mother was suffered by the disease.*

In addition, nonnative speakers may have more varied difficulties with knowing and using regular and irregular past participle forms than most native speakers might:

> *This paper was wrote by my friend.
>
> *My boyfriend's letter was sended by airmail.

A final problem nonnative speakers may have with passive form is the omission of *be* as a helping word (e.g., *The Congress surprised by the president's sudden resignation*). Since nonnative speakers don't have a native speaker's advantage of having been aware of passive constructions since childhood, special care needs to be taken in helping nonnative speakers learn the form of sentences in the passive voice. To that end, such students should have opportunities to examine and discuss the meanings of both active and passive sentences, to dramatize the meanings of both active and passive sentences with their own examples, to practice converting active sentences to passive (and vice versa), and to compose passive sentences of their own. Besides engaging in these "sentence-level" exercises, nonnative speakers also need to find and discuss passive constructions in a variety of contexts (lab reports, recipes, instructions, etc.) and to produce larger pieces of discourse that employ the passive.

The many challenges nonnative speakers may have in learning the rules of English with respect to simple sentence variation is in itself worthy of a text. Useful works written specifically for nonnative speakers and their teachers are listed in the Recommended Resources at the back of this book. *The Grammar Book* by Marianne Celce-Murcia and Diane Larsen-Freeman is a comprehensive grammar text that includes specific suggestions for dealing with the types of challenges nonnative speakers face in learning English. Many current English handbooks for native speakers also have a section devoted specifically to the challenges that nonnative speakers may face in learning to master the rules of grammar.

The field of study known as English as a second language (ESL) trains teachers for working specifically with nonnative speakers. If you are likely to have a preponderance of nonnative speakers in your classroom, you may need to investigate the possibility of taking some ESL classes or pursuing a degree in ESL. You might also want to investigate whether your state offers ESL certification.

SUBJECT-VERB AGREEMENT IN SENTENCES WITH VARIETY

In Chapter 4 we discussed how subject-verb agreement can be a challenge for writers when using quantifiers, as in *One of the children is missing* or *All of the weeds were pulled.* In such sentences, it can be difficult to determine which part of the noun phrase is the subject and hence which word must agree with the verb. For example, in *One of the children is missing,* the writer must determine whether *one* or *children* is the subject (*one* is) and then use the third person singular form of the verb (in this case, *is*) to agree with the subject. Subject-verb agreement can also be a challenge when there is a compound subject, as in *Spaghetti and meatballs is Jesse's favorite dish* or *Dee and Craig are a team.* In such cases, the challenge is to determine whether the compound subject is regarded as one item (as in *spaghetti and meatballs*) or two distinct items (as in *Dee and Craig*).

Another occasion when the subject may be difficult to identify—and therefore pose a challenge for subject-verb agreement—is when the subject or other parts of the sentence are inverted, as in these sentences:

> There was a lot of money on the dresser. [The subject, *a lot of money,* has been moved to a position following the verb phrase.]

> There were potatoes, onions, and mushrooms in the shopping cart. [The compound subject, *potatoes, onions, and mushrooms,* has been moved to a position following the verb phrase.]

In general, sentences using *there* as a placeholder for the moved (extraposed) subject may be a challenge for students because *there* is in the subject position and resembles a subject. Indeed, students may not produce sentences such as **There were a lot of money on the dresser,* in which the extraposed subject rather obviously takes the third person singular. But they would be likely to produce **There was a potato, onions, and mushrooms in the shopping cart,* in which the extraposed subject is plural.

In addition to sentences with extraposed subjects that begin with the placeholder *there,* subject-verb agreement can be a challenge in other forms of subject inversion as well:

> **Next to a clear stream stands the shelters for the horses. [*The shelters* is the moved (extraposed) subject, so the verb should be *stand,* not *stands.*]

*Home goes the children. [*The children* is the extraposed subject, so the verb should be *go*, not *goes*.]

In such sentences, the subject follows the verb, so the writer might erroneously identify a noun that precedes the verb as the subject, thus producing a grammatically incorrect sentence similar to our examples. As the examples indicate, writers are likely to make mistakes with subject-verb agreement when the extraposed subject is plural but the noun preceding the verb is singular:

*Out by the <u>barn</u> *burns* the newly lit <u>torches</u>. [The verb form should be *burn*,
    singular object of preposition   plural subject
to agree with the plural subject <u>torches</u>.]

Another situation where some writers may make mistakes with subject-verb agreement arises when the direct object precedes the subject, as in these examples:

*<u>This food</u> <u>the children</u> *doesn't* like? [*This food* is the moved direct object.
  direct object   plural subject
The children is the plural subject. The verb should agree with *the children*; it should therefore be *don't* rather than *doesn't*.]

*<u>Those shoes</u> <u>the baby</u> don't like? [*Those shoes* is the moved plural direct object.
  plural direct   singular subject
  object
The baby is the singular subject. The verb should agree with *the baby*; it should therefore be *doesn't* rather than *don't*.]

Other types of inverted subjects, as in passive constructions or in questions, can also be sources of confusion for writers. In passive constructions, the challenge can be in retaining the number (singular or plural) of the former subject, as in these sentences:

Active: That dog *bites* children. [The subject is *dog* and so takes the third person singular inflection of the verb, *bites*.]

Passive: *Children *is bitten* by that dog. [The new subject is *children*, which must take the plural form of the verb, *are bitten*.]

In questions, a plural noun at or near the beginning of a sentence may also cause difficulty by being mistaken for a subject:

*Which books *do* the new neighbor want? [The verb form should be *does*, to agree with the subject, *new neighbor*.]

Overall, for helping novice writers who persistently make errors with subject-verb agreement in sentences whose structures have been varied, we recommend providing exercises that require the writers to identify the subjects of the sentences and then to rearrange the sentences to "regular" word order. Occasionally, students may have trouble identifying the subjects of such sentences and might find it easier to determine the verb first. Once they've found the verb, they can identify the subject by asking, "*Who* or *what* is doing the action expressed by the verb?" or "*Who* or *what* is being described by the verb?" For instance, with respect to the sentence *Which books do the new neighbor want?* if a novice writer can't immediately identify the subject, he or she may find it easier to find the verb *want* and then ask, "*Who* wants?" The answer to that question, *the new neighbor,* is the subject. As students become adept at identifying subjects in sentences with varied structure and converting these to "normal" word order, they should be given sets of sentences that contain occasional errors in subject-verb agreement to identify and fix. Finally, because subject-verb agreement problems in inverted sentences may be difficult to find and fix in larger passages of text, students need ample opportunity to edit passages that they and others have written.

PASSIVE PITFALLS

With respect to what constitutes good writing and writing instruction, all of us frequently encounter rules that seek to apply to all situations (e.g., "Don't end a sentence with a preposition"; "Don't write in the first person"), and it is our sense that the passive voice is another commonly proscribed option. That is, apprentice writers are often counseled to use the passive sparingly or even to avoid it altogether. Yet as we explained earlier, the passive can be an enormously useful stylistic option. It can help a writer avoid repetition, emphasize important points or concepts, be courteous and tactful, or eliminate vague or overly general subjects. Because the passive voice can potentially afford a writer so many benefits, it is an important stylistic tool. Therefore, each writer should be given the opportunity to practice writing appropriate passive sentences and to develop a sense of when and when not to use the passive. However, in the process of becoming proficient in forming and using the passive voice, apprentice writers often experience difficulty in several areas that may require attention.

Forming the Passive Correctly

Although persons whose native language isn't English may have difficulty rearranging sentences to form the passive, native speakers rarely evidence this kind of problem. Instead, the major challenge for native speakers in forming the passive is determining the form of the past participle. As you know, passive sentences require the addition of a form of *be* (*is, am, was, were,* etc.), and the main verb must be changed to the past participle form:

John *kissed* the baby.	The baby *was kissed* by John.
Ed *furnishes* all the rooms.	All the rooms *are furnished* by Ed.
Mira *sang* the solo.	The solo *was sung* by Mira.
Edith *bought* the soap.	The soap *was bought* by Edith.

Regular verbs (e.g., *kiss, furnish*) form the past participle in the same way as they form the past tense, by adding *-ed*, while irregular verbs (e.g., *sing, buy*) form their past participle in different ways.

As we have noted, the regular past participle verb form often creates problems for writers—whether it functions as part of a verb phrase or as an adjectival. In speech, for example, people often don't pronounce or hear the *-ed* ending, and this can be reflected in writing:

> *I have *furnish* my apartment in a modern style.
>
> *Nola wants a *furnish* apartment.
>
> *We have lots of *use* books in our garage.

When forming the passive, then, writers who leave off the *-ed* endings of past participles in other contexts will do so here as well:

> *He *was trick* by the politician's promises.
>
> *Lilly *was ambush* by her enemy.
>
> *The toothpaste *was use* by everyone on the floor.
>
> *The job *will be finish* by noon.

In assisting students who form passives improperly because of the form of the past participle, the same kinds of strategies that can help them recognize and appropriately use the *-ed* inflection in other contexts are helpful here as well. In fact, writers who delete the *-ed* ending of past participles in passive constructions are likely to omit the ending in regular past tense forms (*She _furnish_ her apartment last week*), in past participles functioning as verbs in perfect tense formations (*She _had furnish_ them with the answers*), and in past participles functioning as adjectivals (*She lives in a _furnish_ apartment*). Such students need instruction in recognizing the variety of contexts in which regular past tense and past participles can appear. Want ads (e.g., "Wanted: Furnished Apartment" or "Wanted: Used Vacuum Cleaner. Will pay cash") or classified ads (e.g., "For Sale: Used 1990 Buick. Low Mileage. Runs like New. $1,500 firm"), for example, are a particularly rich source of past participles used as adjectivals.

Once students have practice identifying past tense and past participle forms in a variety of written contexts, they can be asked to produce these forms in writing of their own. For example, they can be asked to create their own classified page using as many past tense and past participle forms as possible (e.g., "Have changed jobs. Must sell refinished Fender guitar"). As an accompaniment to these types of activities and exercises, students can be assigned exercises that require them to convert active sentences into passive ones or to edit passages that contain errors in passive past participle forms.

Overused and Awkward Passive

Because many inexperienced writers have the faulty impression that the passive variant makes them sound "intelligent" or "well educated," overuse of the passive is a common problem in their writing. This is probably because many novice writers think that anything said in a concise, straightforward manner might be considered too simple; so they are often motivated to create sentences that are less accessible to the reader in an effort to sound more sophisticated. As we explained earlier, however, an accumulation of passive sentences in a text can render it excessively formal, distant, and more difficult to comprehend. Too much passive can also lessen syntactic variety in a text and diminish its crispness, making it seem vague and monotonous.

Besides a tendency to overuse passive constructions, inexperienced writers—who are often inexperienced readers—may not have developed an ear to help them detect when the passive sentences they produce sound awkward or even silly:

1. Marcia's personal hygiene should be watched by her if she wishes to continue being befriended by me.

2. A letter to one's congressional representative should be written by a person if he or she wants action to be taken by him or her.

3. A fraternity or sorority should be joined by a person if he or she wishes a good social life to be enjoyed.

When writing teachers who have encountered passive constructions similar to these ask students why they wrote them, the answer they receive is often a variant of "I wanted to sound intelligent." And even when students who write such sentences are asked to read them aloud and listen to them, they may not necessarily recognize that the sentences are long or awkward because they expect that sentences in certain written genres should be long and complex.

In a sense, the underlying problem with respect to both of these problems regarding the passive—excessive use and awkward construction—is that student writers don't yet have the skill to ascertain when a text sounds overly formal or when it feels too distant from the audience it wishes to address. Nor do they have the skill to assess when complicated sentences will strike the majority of their readers as sounding refined or just plain awkward. Unfortunately, the skills that enable writers to assess how their writing will sound or feel to their readers are sophisticated and not easily mastered by learning a set of rules. Despite this fact, however, there are three strategies that teachers can use to help their students make progress with these skills and with the ability to use passive more effectively. Let's look at each one.

1. *Assign students reading in different genres.* We cannot state emphatically enough how important it is for students to read if they are to become competent writers. At every opportunity, then, students should be afforded opportu-

nities to read in different genres (fiction, political speeches, reports, instructions, business correspondence, etc.) and to make note of the relationship between the passive structures of the sentences and the genre in which they are found. If students examine a laboratory report or an article from a science journal and rewrite some of the sentences in the active voice (e.g., *The experimenter decanted the liquid…. The experimenter heated the solution….* etc.), they may see how the passive voice can eliminate repetition, focus the reader's attention on what was done rather than who was doing it, contribute to the "objectivity" of the text, and so forth. Similarly, if students discuss pieces of correspondence that contain examples of "tactful" passive (e.g., *Enclosed is another copy of the materials that were misplaced*), they will see how passive constructions can be used to document accurately what has been done (an original set of materials was sent) and yet minimize the accusatory tone that might result from an active construction: *Enclosed is another copy of the materials that you misplaced.* Political speeches and reports are also an interesting source of passive constructions because passives with deleted agents are often employed to disconnect actions from the people who commit them: *Several errors in judgment were made* versus *My staff made several errors in judgment.*

2. *Encourage students to read their sentences aloud.* Sentences have sound as well as meaning, and apprentice writers should be encouraged to exploit this quality of language, rather than to have it work against them. Particularly for apprentice writers who tend to overuse the passive voice or to produce awkward-sounding passives, reading their writing out loud and attempting to assess its overall feel can be beneficial. Students who are particularly prone to creating odd passive constructions can be encouraged to do a separate edit just for these structures by reading each suspicious-looking sentence out loud and listening to how it sounds. If students have difficulty assessing when passive constructions do and do not sound all right, class activities in which you or your students read passive sentences aloud can be helpful. For example, you can gather excerpts with acceptable and awkward-sounding passives, read (or have your students read) these out loud, have students vote as to whether or not each passive does or does not sound awkward, and discuss the results of each vote. (As a variation on this activity, you might have the class rank all the passive constructions from best-sounding to worst-sounding; the disagreements that are likely to occur about rankings will stimulate lively debate.)

3. *Have students learn the circumstances when the passive is appropriate.* Students who wish to use the passive appropriately should be encouraged to become aware of the specific circumstances when it is most effective. It is particularly helpful if students are assigned to examine the various types of writing they encounter to find actual instances of effective, appropriate passive use, as we have already suggested in the section on genres. Students also need practice writing passive constructions to achieve a particular sought-after

effect. Ideally, apprentice writers should be conscious of when they are using the passive voice and of the effects they are trying to achieve by using it. To this end, they can be assigned activities in which they must find and revise excessive or ineffective passive constructions in excerpts of writing or exercises in which they must use passive constructions judiciously and effectively and explain why they elected to use them and the effects they intended to create. Or they can be asked to find a genre of discourse (or an excerpt) in which the passive is used effectively and craft their own version of that genre (or their own excerpt), using the passive appropriately.

EXERCISES FOR PRACTICE

A. The following paragraph is from an essay written by a nonnative speaker of English. Try to identify any sentence problems the student may be having with regard to rearranging word order appropriately. Note that some sentences may require movement of the subject.

On the other hand, a lot of plants have installed in some industrialized areas for the purpose of exporting goods. As a result, the manufactured goods are a variety of models, shades, colors, and so on. Those materials have influenced the spirit of Korea. They have influenced the daily life of Korea. The youth now have no respect for old people. Old people now try to enjoy themselves outside of their homes. As a result, there a significant gap appears between the old and the young. So visitors to Korea are easy to get a bad impression about Korea. They are easy to find bad clichés about Korean people.

B. In the following sentences, identify and underline the subjects that appear in an order other than their "usual" word order. (*Hint:* To identify the actual subject, you may find it helpful to first find the verb.)

Example: Which shoes did <u>LaRuth</u> decide to buy?

Example: It was sad <u>to leave</u>.

1. Where was Erma Jean going yesterday?

2. After dinner, will the children attend the special memorial service?

3. It was the owner who prepared our pasta.

4. What new trick is Livia playing on us now?

5. Over the hills and through the woods ran the fox.

6. It bothered me that you didn't attend my wedding.

7. With her you're studying?

8. Why didn't you study harder for that exam?

9. It was wonderful for Bill to help us.

10. To whom have the voters complained now?

C. The following sentences have rearranged word order and may therefore pose a challenge for subject-verb agreement. Select the appropriate verb form in parentheses to ensure subject-verb agreement.

> **Example:** Which books (*do, does*) Emily want for her collection?

> **Example:** It (*was, were*) the cats who messed up the laundry room.

1. What new hobbies (*has, have*) Tabitha been pursuing these days?

2. To whom (*does, do*) I have the pleasure of speaking?

3. All last week where (*has, have*) Mindy and her sisters been studying?

4. It (*was, were*) the storms that devastated my hometown.

5. Those red kitties (*is, are*) what she wants now?

6. The open-toed sandals (*was, were*) admired most by my sister.

7. It (*doesn't, don't*) bother me that Sandra got the prize.

8. Which wedding dress (*does, do*) the bridesmaids love the best?

9. It (*has been, have been*) extraordinarily hard to clean under the sink.

10. (*Doesn't, Don't*) the new mayors have any obligations to find a solution?

D. The following letter relies excessively on the passive voice. Decide which sentences should be changed, and rewrite them in the active voice. Be prepared to explain your decisions.

Dear Friends and Colleagues:

This week marks the kickoff of Master State University's annual fundraising campaign. A few minutes of your time are needed for the goals of this campaign to be explained to you. As you are all aware, MSU already does many great things for its students and staff, but more can and should be done! Currently, all of our resources are used by the many programs and opportunities offered by MSU. Yet we need to do more. More scholarships need to be offered by our various departments and programs. More support needs to be received by our students as they conduct research, travel to conferences, and pursue their studies.

Not only are MSU resources depleted by personnel costs, but huge sums of money are also consumed by maintenance costs for buildings and facilities. But a new century has been entered, and we are challenged by this new era. We are challenged to provide new technology for our students, faculty, and staff—new technology that will be used to spur new ideas and build new hopes.

A moment should be taken out of your busy schedule to think about what program or initiative might benefit from your generous gift. Your contribution will, of course, be tax-deductible. But most important, the education of generations of future students will be enhanced by your kindness.

Sincerely,

Your Campaign Committee

E. Select one of the appropriate uses of the passive discussed in Part One of this chapter. Compose a half-page to one-page draft or excerpt of an essay, letter, or set of directions that demonstrates this particular use of the passive voice. Then explain how your writing illustrates the effective use of the passive.

F. Each of the following sentences contains either an incorrectly formed or an excessively awkward passive. Rewrite each sentence in the active voice.

Example: That problem was solve months ago.
            We *solved* that problem months ago.

Example: That juice should be drunk by someone before it goes sour.
            Someone *should drink* that juice before it goes sour.

1. That dog should be shampooed and groomed by its owner if she expects it to be petted by anyone.

2. Fluffy the cat was watched by Sid as the mouse was attacked by it.

3. That last taco should be eaten by someone or it will get thrown away by me.

4. The dentist told Joe that some of his teeth needed to capped.

5. Joe was astonish by the cost of the procedure.

6. Prior to his visit for a routine teeth cleaning, it was assumed by him that a new car could be purchased with his savings.

7. Now this was not to be; instead, his meager savings would be consume by dental work.

8. Joe knew that his teeth needed to be cared for by him because only one permanent set was given.

9. Still, he was irk by the idea of spending money on his teeth.

10. If we are honest, most of us will admit that spending money on new things that can be enjoy by us is prefer by us.

G. The following sentences are in either the active or the passive voice. Where appropriate, convert the active sentences to passive ones, and convert passive sentences to active ones, deleting the word *by* plus the former subject and otherwise revising so that the sentences are grammatically correct. If a sentence is appropriate as written, do not change it.

> **Example:**   The bus was stop by the police officer directing traffic.
> The police officer directing traffic *stopped* the bus.

> **Example:**   Marcia's attitude should be watched by her if she wants to be liked by people.
> Marcia *should watch* her attitude if she wants people to like her.

> **Example**:   Someone tallied the results of the vote.
> The results of the vote *were tallied*.

1. Last week I volunteered to help out with a new fundraising initiative.

2. All alumni were encourage by Dean Whorf to express their opinions regarding the new program.

3. Something swept the leaves off every lawn on the street.

4. Amazingly, that cold coffee was finished by someone.

5. We were amazed by the fact that Ginny Lou didn't finish the exam.

6. That congressman was written to by me last month.

7. I thought that he would be sympathetic to my view.

8. Because my congressman was contacted by so many irate voters in the district, action on this particular issue will be taken by him.

9. Someone ate all of the grapes in the English Department refrigerator by the time we left work.

10. The photocopier was use by virtually everyone in the office.

EXERCISES FOR CLASSROOM APPLICATION

A. Devise an activity that requires your students to identify instances of the passive voice in two of the following: novel, textbook, reference book, magazine, newspaper, scholarly journal, instruction, recipe. Then have them explain why or how the passive is being used. Is it being used appropriately or inappropriately? What are the effects of its use?

B. Assume that your students are having a problem with either forming the passive properly, using the passive excessively, or writing awkward passive sentences. Describe a lesson or series of exercises or activities that would address this problem. Then create a sample activity or exercise that would be a part of this lesson.

PART III   STYLE, CHOICE, AND CONVENTION

As we have indicated, English allows its users remarkable flexibility in varying sentence order to create particular effects with the language. In Part One we discussed simple sentence types and how variety is achieved in them and with them. In Part Two we discussed some of the challenges for writers that these variants pose. In this section we discuss why writers might choose one variant over another. We also discuss the effects of shifting point of view and of choosing one verb tense over another.

CHOOSING STYLISTIC VARIATIONS

Choosing a particular style to write in, which dictates to a degree the type and amount of simple sentence variation a writer chooses, depends on the audience to which the author is writing and the overall effect the writer wishes to create. For example, compare the following sentences:

1. Once upon a time, long, long ago, there lived deep in the woods a poor cobbler and his three adoring daughters.

2. A poor cobbler and his three adoring daughters lived deep in the woods a long, long time ago, once upon a time.

In the first sentence, the writer creates the effect of an age-old story and a sense of time by moving the adverbials *once upon a time* and *long, long ago* to the front of the sentence. The writer then creates a sense of mystery and distance by using the placeholder *there* and moving the subject (*a poor cobbler and his three adoring daughters*). The sense of distance is then extenuated by rearranging the description of the location (*deep in the woods*) to come before the subject. By placing time and distance first and making the reader wait to find out *whom* this story is about, the writer has not only created an atmosphere but also piqued the reader's interest in finding out just whom this story is about. By using the possibilities of English sentence variation, the writer has established an interesting storytelling style that will continue throughout the text. The second sentence reads more as a statement of facts and resembles a newspaper report.

When should a writer choose to use movement and other forms of rearrangement, the passive voice, questions, or exclamations? As our examples illustrate, choosing a style of variation often depends on what the writer wishes to achieve.

Throughout this chapter, we have discussed some of the "rules" often given to writers, such as "Don't use the passive voice." Another such rule is to avoid using *there* and *it* as placeholders, as in *There are many children on the playground* or *It is necessary for all students to hang up their coats.* The rule makers might argue that such constructions are wordy and that such sentences should be written more concisely as *Many children are on the playground* or *All students need to hang up their coats.* And indeed there are occasions when it is best not to move sentence elements around. However, there are also times when such movement can be used quite effectively. For example, compare the style and effect of the following sentences.

1. The stormy waters sank the unsuspecting ship. [This sentence is a strong, matter-of-fact presentation of details in standard word order; putting *the stormy waters* first in the sentence also places emphasis on it. A writer might choose this word order when telling the details of a story or perhaps when telling a sequence of events.]

2. It was the stormy waters that sank the unsuspecting ship. [By moving (extraposing) *the stormy waters,* even more stress is placed on it than in sentence 1. A writer might choose to use this variation when wanting to grab the reader's attention at the beginning of a story or when discussing several possibilities for the sinking of the ship (e.g., *John didn't sink the ship. Rather, it was the stormy waters that sank the unsuspecting ship.*).]

3. Three passengers were left on the boat. [This is a matter-of-fact statement in standard word order. By placing the subject first, the focus of the sentence is on the subject. A writer might choose to use this word order when detailing facts or explaining a sequence of events (e.g., *During ten days of intense storms, the high waves continually knocked the passengers overboard into the roiling seas below. When the Coast Guard finally found the distressed vessel, three passengers were left on the boat.*).]

4. There were three passengers left on the boat. [By moving (extraposing) *three passengers,* the writer sets a scene in which *three passengers* play a part. A writer might also choose to use this variation for emphasis, especially in answer to doubt about the number of passengers left (e.g., *There weren't twelve passengers left. There were three passengers left on the boat.*).]

In addition to the reasons given in these examples, a writer might prefer to use movement or extraposition when explaining rules (e.g., *There are seven players, and they each …*) or for academic distance (e.g., *It can be preferable to use extraposition when …*). What is important is that the novice writer be made aware of the various options to choose from and given the opportunity to make those choices.

Using the passive voice, too, is a choice writers can make depending on the situation. Unlike movement—which is normally a matter of choice—there are some occasions when it is better to use the passive voice, as we discussed in Part Two of this chapter. And students need to be given an opportunity to "play" with passive by using it in a variety of ways in their writing.

Finally, there are also occasions when it is appropriate to use questions, exclamations, and commands for emphasis or to create a certain style. For example, a writer might choose to use questions for headings of sections (we have used questions in this way throughout this text—for example, "Why Use the Passive Voice?"), for chapter headings, in direct quotes, to reflect an internal dialogue, or to create closeness to the audience. A writer may use exclamations for most of these same reasons, as well as to emphasize a point (e.g., *I thought Kim would never give me a second glance, but then one day she asked me for a date!*). Commands, too, can be an effective stylistic device. In addition to using them in direct quotes, a writer may use commands because of the genre (e.g., writing directions or instructions, as in technical manuals or recipes). Using commands can also create a closeness between the reader and the information (e.g., *Look at the following examples* or *Let me tell you about what happened last Saturday*). Sometimes a writer may choose to use questions, exclamations, and commands together, as in

> Would you ever want to be involved in a long-distance relationship? Yes, of course! Take my friend's situation for example....

What is important in teaching novice writers to use sentence variety is to emphasize that it is not necessarily right or wrong to use some variant over another but rather a matter of the circumstances of the writing and what the writer is trying to accomplish. The form that sentences might take can depend on the emphasis the writer wants to place in a sentence or paragraph, the genre the writer is using, or even the necessity of being concise.

Given the infinite number of ways a writer can choose to express ideas and create effect, teaching novice writers to make choices in sentence variety can seem like a daunting task. After all, isn't it difficult enough to teach them to use the basic conventions? However, we believe that introducing students to using sentence variety helps them appreciate the ways that they can step beyond basic conventions and have fun with language. And when students play with language in this way, they can become aware of their own possibilities as more creative and effective writers.

CHOOSING POINT OF VIEW

In preceding chapters we discussed nouns, pronouns, and verbs, as well as common challenges writers experience with these types of words—agreement, proper form, clear reference, and so forth. In covering these challenges for writers in the earlier chapters, we tended to devote most of our attention to what might be considered word- or sentence-level problems. Problems in subject-verb agreement, for example, are word- or sentence-level problems because they rarely interfere with a reader's ability to process a piece of writing at the text level; such word- and sentence-level problems rarely cause incoherence, illogicality, and so forth. However, despite the fact that many of the challenges that nouns, verbs, and pronouns present for apprentice writers are at the level of the word or sentence, the forms that these words—especially pronouns and verbs—take can affect broader, text-level matters such as *point of view*.

Pronouns and Point of View

The concept of "point of view" is commonly explained as *the relationship a piece of writing manifests among the writer, the audience, and the subject matter.* What this definition suggests is that the point of view of a piece of writing reveals whether an author has elected to create and maintain a formal, distant relationship among himself, his readers, and his topic, as in example 1, or a closer, more informal relationship, as in example 2:

1. Formal: Consumers should take responsibility for their health by
                  exercising regularly.   objective - 3rd person

2. Informal: It is really important for you to take care of your body
                  by exercising regularly. - subjective - 1st + 2nd p.

As these examples suggest, point of view is controlled by a number of factors such as word choice (*take responsibility for* versus *take care of*) and sentence structure (*should take responsibility* versus *it is really important*). However, also of paramount importance in controlling point of view is the selection of pronouns.

In fact, pronoun selection is so significant that three different points of view are commonly identified according to the pronouns the writer chooses. Consistent use of the pronoun *I* (or *we, us, our*) is identified as the first person point of view, consistent use of the pronoun *you* is called the second person point of view, and consistent use of the pronouns *he, she, it, they,* and *one* together with other nouns is called the third person point of view. Here are examples of each:

First Person

I began exercising about a year ago and noticed that my health really began to improve. Now I'm a believer in the benefits of physical activity and have even begun to advocate it to my friends.

Second Person

You should exercise if you want to notice your health begin to improve. Once you begin exercising, you will become a believer in the benefits of physical activity and even advocate it to your friends.

So you began exercising about a year ago and noticed that your health began to improve? Now you're a believer in the benefits of physical activity and have even begun to advocate it to your friends.

Third Person

Eric began exercising about a year ago and noticed that his health had really begun to improve. Now he's a believer in the benefits of physical activity and has begun to advocate it to his friends.

Persons who begin exercising may notice their health improve in a relatively short period of time. It is also often the case that once they engage in physical activity, people become believers in the benefits of such activity and readily advocate it to their friends.

Despite the fact that many other elements besides pronoun form contribute to creating a relationship among the writer, reader, and subject matter, the examples just given do show that pronoun form plays a major role. The use of the first person, for example, tends to create a closer, more informal relationship between the reader and the writer.

It is also difficult to make generalizations when using the first person (e.g., *Jogging is good* is a generalization), because the first person tends to suggest that the writer is relating his or her own experience (*I began jogging and found it to be wonderful*). It's up to the reader to decide whether to identify with the writer and assume that the writer's experience is relevant. Like the first person, the second person creates more closeness between the reader and writer, but the second person can be used to generalize: *You should jog if you want to improve your health.* The third person creates the most formal and most distant relationship between the writer and his or her audience and is also conventionally used to show that the writer is sufficiently distant from the subject matter to be "objective" (as in the example *Jogging is good*).

Because academic genres often require objectivity, writing instructors may tell apprentice writers to avoid using the first and second person. Writing teachers also often ban the use of *you* in their students' writing because the second person *you* figures prominently in two common kinds of inappropriate shifts in point of view:

Inappropriate Shift in the First Person Point of View

I began exercising a few months ago, and I'm glad I did. Soon after I started, you could detect a significant difference in energy level. I even began to get sick less often. But the most exciting changes happened when my clothes got looser. My muscles got tighter, and you could even notice changes in the way I looked.

who is
you here?

Inappropriate Shift in the Third Person Point of View

Americans are becoming too lax about their personal health and well-being. Everyone wants an easy path to youth and vitality, but there is no quick fix. If people are going to maintain—or improve on—their youth and vigor, exercise is a must. An exercise regimen isn't hard to begin; you should start slowly and work up to your own comfort level, and before long, everyone will be taking responsibility for his or her own healthfulness.

Despite the difficulties the pronoun *you* often causes and despite the fact that much academic writing requires the third person point of view, we believe that apprentice writers ought to receive both instruction and practice in selecting and crafting different kinds of relationships among themselves, their readers, and their subject matter. To this end, students should be given the opportunity to read and discuss the effects of writing in the first, second, and third person point of view and also to practice crafting texts that create different relationships among reader, writer, and subject matter.

Practice in identifying and writing from different points of view is vital not only because it helps writers develop their overall skill in adapting their writing to different audiences to meet different aims or purposes in a variety of contexts but also because when students learn to attend to overall patterns of pronoun use in their drafts, they may become more conscious about the range of the decisions they can make as writers. Many apprentice writers don't realize, for example, that an assignment to write about a significant person (say, Ruth) can be approached as a personal narrative that focuses primarily on the writer (how Ruth influenced *me*) or as a more informative piece of discourse in which the author minimizes her presence and focuses principally on Ruth. In examining a first draft of such an essay, if the student writer discovers that she began in the third person (e.g., *Ruth ... she*) but ended up in the first person (e.g., *Because of Ruth, I became more aware of ...*), it may be that she hasn't yet decided on the primary focus for her essay.

Verb Tense and Point of View

Besides pronoun selection, writers need to be conscious about their choice of verb tenses because these, too, contribute to the point of view of a piece of writing. Selection of verb tenses can influence matters such as the feeling of closeness or immediacy of a piece of writing. Verb tenses can also influence a reader's perception about the likelihood of a particular event. In writing about the possibility of a future trip to Scotland, for example, the use of *will* or *would* increases or decreases probability:

Probable: If I travel to Scotland, I will visit castles and go to Loch Ness to see if I can see the monster, Nessie, for myself. I will also be sure to

	experience the beautiful green hills I have heard so much about.
Less Probable:	If I traveled to Scotland, I would visit castles and go to Loch Ness to see if I can see the monster, Nessie, for myself. I would also be sure to experience the beautiful green hills I have heard so much about.

Although some academic and other types of genres do prescribe the use of a particular tense, there is often no clear-cut rule to guide the writer. Furthermore, as the Scotland examples show, differences in meaning created by one verb tense or another can be subtle. Still, the principle for selecting the verb tenses in a piece of writing is the same one that should guide pronoun selection. In each case, it's important for the writer to make a conscious decision to create a particular effect.

With regard to the selection of verb tenses, besides helping writers control the outcomes of their writing, a conscious choice of tense can also help inexperienced writers recognize and eliminate inappropriate tense shifts. In writing about an upcoming trip to Scotland, for instance, using either *will* or *would* is appropriate. But switching back and forth between these two forms for no reason might confuse readers. Or for another example, many contexts may offer the apprentice writer a choice between the present tense and the past tense. However, failure to make a conscious decision about that choice may lead to inappropriate tense shifts:

Inappropriate Tense Shifts

I decided that my couch potato days were over; it was time to exercise! Knowing myself as well as I do, I chose to begin my regimen modestly and started with just ten minutes of activity three times a week. But before I know it, I notice that it is getting much easier to exercise a little longer.

Consistent Past Tense

I decided that my couch potato days were over; it was time to exercise! Knowing myself as well as I do, I chose to begin my regimen modestly and started with just ten minutes of activity three times a week. But before I knew it, I noticed that it was getting much easier to exercise a little longer.

Consistent Present Tense

I decide that my couch potato days are over; it is time to exercise! Knowing myself as well as I do, I choose to begin my regimen modestly and start with just ten minutes of activity three times a week. But before I know it, I notice that it's getting much easier to exercise a little longer.

As with controlling point of view through the selection of the first, second, or third person, apprentice writers should be given opportunity to read and discuss the effects of different tenses on their audience and their purpose for writing, as well as the opportunity to practice writing with different verb tenses to create a variety of outcomes.

● EXERCISES FOR PRACTICE

A. For each of the following quotations, comment on the writer or speaker's use of imperatives and questions. Why do you think the writer or speaker used that form? Try rewriting each quote as a statement. How does this rewrite change the form?

1. And so I urge you: go after experience rather than knowledge. (*The Cloud of Unknowing*)

2. Remember your stories. They can save your life a little at a time. (Kim R. Stafford)

3. What good are laws where Money is king? (Petronius, *The Satyricon*)

B. Music and poetry often use a variety of sentence types to create a desired effect on the listener or reader. Choose from one of the following sets of folk song lyrics, and comment on the song's use of various sentence types. What variety did the writer use? What effect does this variety create? What would the effect be had the writer used only statements or declarative sentences?

1. (From "Hangman, Hangman")

> Hangman, hangman, slack your rope. Slack it for a while.
> I think I see my sister coming, traveling many a mile.
> Sister, did you bring me silver?
> Sister, did you bring me gold?
> Did you bring me anything to keep me from the gallows pole?
>
> I've brought you no silver.
> I've brought you no gold.
> I've come for to see you hanging from the gallows pole.

2. (From "Silver Dagger")

> Don't sing love songs. You'll wake my mother.
> She's sleeping here right by my side.
> And in her right hand is a silver dagger.
> She says that I can't be your bride.

Go court another tender maiden
And hope that she will be your wife.
For I've been warned and I've decided
To sleep alone all of my life.

C. Find a book intended for children four to eight years of age. Read the book out loud. Examine the structure of the sentences. What types of variations do you find? What effects do the variations have on the reader?

D. Select the work of at least two different fiction writers, such as Hemingway and Faulkner. Compare two excerpts of about one-half to one page in length. Compare the sentence variety in each of the excerpts. In terms of this feature, how do the styles of the two writers vary? What effect does each style create? Why?

E. Find examples of writing—at least one paragraph in length—from two very different genres (textbook, advertising, directions, magazine feature articles, letters to the editor, scholarly articles, etc.). Contrast the excerpts in terms of sentence variety. How does the sentence variety relate to the genre? What effect does the structure of the sentences have on the reader?

F. Select two pieces of writing written in two different points of view (e.g., one in the third person and the other in the first person). For each piece of writing, explain why you think the author chose that particular point of view. Some issues you might consider: What was the author trying to accomplish, and how does the selected point of view help accomplish that purpose? What audience was the author addressing, and why might that point of view be appropriate for that audience? If you think the point of view was dictated by the conventions of a particular genre, how does the point of view function in that genre?

G. Find a short piece of writing (one to two pages), and rewrite it in a different point of view. For example, if it is written in the third person, change it to the first or the second person. Compare the two versions. In what way might each version affect audiences differently? Why? Which version is more formal? Why? Which version seems more believable? Why? (Reading the versions aloud might help you discover differences between them.)

H. Select a piece of academic or professional writing in a book or journal. Examine the tenses of the verbs. What effect do the tenses of the verbs create overall?

● EXERCISES FOR CLASSROOM APPLICATION

A. Design an activity that requires your students to use sentence variation to create a particular effect on a potential audience that they've chosen.

B. Assume that many of your (future) students are having difficulty with tense shifts. Describe a series of activities that would help them increase their skill in consciously choosing tense to maintain a particular point of view. Be sure to specify the age and skill level of the students for whom your activities are intended. After you have described the activities, completely prepare at least one activity for distribution to your imagined class of students.

INTRODUCING SENTENCE COMPLEXITY: ADVERBIALS, ADJECTIVALS, AND NOMINALS

Chapter Preview

Chapter 6 introduces concepts you will study in greater depth in subsequent chapters.

In **Part I** you will learn about making sentences more complex by

- Embedding and conjoining sentences
- Using adverbials, adjectivals, and nominals

In **Part II** you will learn about challenges writers may face with

- Embedding, especially as it relates to fragments and other problems
- Conjoining, especially as it relates to sentence boundaries

---

PART I   MAKING SENTENCES COMPLEX

Thus far, we have been discussing *simple* sentences. In the course of this discussion, we've explained how to recognize forms (nouns, noun phrases, verbs, verb phrases, etc.) and their many functions (subject, direct object, subject complement, object of a preposition, etc.). We have also discussed how to combine structures within sentences (e.g., compound nouns: *Bill and Joe*) as well as how simple sentences are combined (e.g., compound sentence: *I went to the store, and my husband mowed the lawn*). In this chapter we preview some of the ways that sentences may be combined to make them increasingly complex. We will expand these options in Chapters 7 through 10.

EMBEDDING VERSUS CONJOINING

Most grammar books make a distinction between at least three types of sentences—*simple, compound,* and *complex:*

Simple sentence:	George likes pizza. [consisting of a subject and a predicate]
Compound sentence:	George likes pizza, but Barbara doesn't. [two simple sentences joined by a conjunction]
Complex sentence:	The pizza that George likes best usually gives him stomachaches. [simple sentence with a dependent clause]

As you can see from these examples, a simple sentence (also referred to by linguists as a ***kernel sentence***) is made up of a subject and a predicate. Even if a sentence has a compound subject or many modifiers in the predicate (e.g., *Stanley and his son, Steve, drove to Florida last November*), it is still a simple sentence. Here are some examples of simple sentences with various compound structures or with many modifiers in the predicate:

The frog *jumped and skipped* across the bright green water. [compound verbs]

In gratitude, Alice sent *Di and Josh* a bouquet of flowers. [compound indirect objects]

In spring, the *trees and bushes bud and become green and beautiful.* [compound subject complement]

These simple sentences all contain compound structures such as compound verbs (*jumped and skipped, bud and become*), compound indirect objects (*Di and Josh*), compound subjects (*the trees and bushes*), and compound subject complements (*green and beautiful*). Besides elements within sentences, sentences themselves can be compounded (conjoined) by using conjunctions such as *and, or, so, but, for,* and *yet*. Other conjunctions can also be used to combine sentences (e.g., *however, therefore, whereas, consequently*). We will cover options for combining sentences more fully in Chapter 10. Here are some examples of compound (conjoined) sentences combined using various conjunctions:

1. The dog yipped, *and* its owner petted it.

2. Life is a mystery; *however,* some people try to find the answer.

3. Everyone likes swimming, *so* the beaches are crowded in the summer.

4. *Either* my maternal grandparents came from Ireland *or* my paternal ones did.

5. Grandma was craving ice cream; *therefore,* we bought some at the store.

All of these are compound sentences. The difference between a conjoined (or compound) sentence and a complex sentence is that a conjoined sentence is made up of two independent sentences combined using a conjunction. A complex sentence, by contrast, is one sentence made up of two parts: a kernel sentence (simple sentence) and one or more dependent clauses that give extra or needed information about the kernel sentence. For example, in the sentence *I saw the new puppy that you bought, I saw the new puppy* is the kernel sentence and *that you bought* is a clause that provides extra information about the kernel sentence. Structures containing both subjects and verbs that appear as part of a complex sentence are ordinarily known as *clauses.* Most grammarians refer to the original sentence being modified or expanded as an *independent clause* because it is a complete sentence and would make sense standing on its own. For example, *David loves his dog* and *My mother ate a lot of coconut cookies* are complete sentences, and they are also independent clauses. As kernel sentences, they become the main clauses of complex sentences when another clause is added to them as a modifier or to provide necessary information. The added clause is usually referred to as a *dependent clause* because it cannot stand alone as a sentence; it needs the independent clause to "support" it. Here are some examples of complex sentences made up of one main (independent) clause and one or more dependent clauses.

1. Because she was nervous, Deb ate handfuls of chocolate. [*Because she was*
         dependent clause   main clause
   nervous modifies *ate;* it provides additional information about why or how Deb ate.]

2. They waited until the cows came home. [*Until the cows came home* modifies
      main clause   dependent clause
   waited; it provides information about how long they waited.]

3. The van that we rented wouldn't start. [*That we rented* modifies *van;* it tells
    subject of   dependent   predicate of
 main clause clause   main clause
   which van.]

4. The police found the contraband, which had been smuggled into the country.
           main clause   dependent clause
   [*Which had been smuggled into the country* modifies *contraband;* it provides more information about *contraband.*]

5. I saw what you did. [*What you did* is the direct object; it tells what I saw.]
   main   dependent
clause clause

6. <u>There is doubt</u> <u>that the president will be reelected</u>. [*That the president will be*
    main clause   dependent clause
reelected is an extraposed subject.]

In examples 1 and 2, the dependent clauses are clearly separate sentences connected to the main clauses by connecting words (e.g., *because, until*). However, in examples 3 through 6, the dependent clauses are integral components of the larger main clause. <u>When this happens—when a dependent clause is found within an independent clause—we call it **embedding**</u>. Notice what structures are embedded in the main clause of each of the following sentences; the embedded clauses are italicized.

1. The van *that we rented* wouldn't start.

2. The police found the contraband, *which had been smuggled into the country*.

3. I saw *what you did*.

4. There is doubt *that the president will be reelected*.

As you can see, embedding as a source of sentence complexity is a common occurrence in English. In the next section we discuss two common ways of embedding in English—with adjective clauses and noun clauses—along with another source of sentence complexity, adverbial clauses.

ADVERBIALS, ADJECTIVALS, AND NOMINALS

In earlier chapters we have discussed adverbs (*quickly, very*, etc.), adjectives (*blue, happy*, etc.), and nouns (*nut, chimpanzee*, etc.). In discussing these forms, we have described the various ways they can function (as subjects, object complements, noun modifiers, verb modifiers, etc.) and how to recognize adverbs, adjectives, and nouns in sentences. In Chapter 5 we described how a noun can be the head of a phrase (*the gigantic <u>spider</u>, the private <u>detective</u>*, etc.). In fact, adverbs, adjectives, and nouns can appear either as single words or in phrases. Here are some examples of adverbs, adjectives, and nouns appearing as single words or in phrases:

Adverbs

    The duck walked *awkwardly*. [*Awkwardly* is a single-word adverb.]

    Joe spoke *very loudly*. [*Loudly* is in an adverb phrase.]

Adjectives

    Woody is a *happy* dog! [*Happy* is a single-word adjective.]

    That news is *quite sad*. [*Sad* is in an adjective phrase.]

Nouns

Mom always liked you best. [*Mom* is a single-word noun.]

The wee babe slept in *its crib.* [*Babe* and *crib* are in noun phrases.]

At this point it is important to revisit the concepts of form and function. In the sample sentences, the adverbs, adjectives, and nouns—both single words and phrases—can fairly easily be recognized by their form. We also recognize them by their functions—verb modifier, noun modifier, subject complement, subject, and so on. Let's look again at these sentences. Notice how the words and phrases function in each sentence.

The duck walked *awkwardly.* [*Awkwardly* functions to modify the verb *walked.*]

Joe spoke *very loudly.* [*Very loudly* functions to modify the verb *spoke.*]

Woody is a *happy* dog! [*Happy* functions to modify the noun *dog.*]

That news was *quite sad.* [*Quite sad* functions as a subject complement.]

Mom always liked you best. [*Mom* functions as the subject.]

The wee babe slept in *its crib.* [*The wee babe* functions as the subject; *its crib* functions as the object of a preposition, *in.*]

As is evident from these examples, it is important to look at both form and function. As we've explained in earlier chapters, one reason this is important is because form can be deceiving. A word may look like a noun but function as an adjective (to modify a noun) or an adverb (to modify a verb), and vice versa. For example, in the sentence *Tomorrow is Tuesday, tomorrow,* which might otherwise be considered an adverb, in this sentence functions as a noun does, as the subject of the sentence. Furthermore, in *Tomorrow is Tuesday,* the word *Tuesday* functions as a noun—it is a subject complement. Notice how this function changes, however, in the sentence *Her Tuesday outfit is at the cleaners.* In this sentence, *Tuesday* functions as an adjective modifying the noun *outfit.*

Because words may function in a variety of ways, it is important to look at how they function in individual sentences, not just at the form they take. In fact, not only single words but also phrases and even clauses can function as adverbs (which we call *adverbials*), as adjectives (which we call *adjectivals*), and as nouns (which we call *nominals*). That is, adverbials, adjectivals, and nominals are all *functions,* and a variety of forms can fill these functions. The following sentences show how different forms can function as adverbials, adjectivals, and nominals.

Adverbials

I want to go *home.* [*Home* looks like a noun but functions as an adverbial.]

They robbed the bank *to pay for her operation.* [*To pay for her operation* is an infinitive phrase that functions as an adverbial.]

They hiked *in the mountains.* [*In the mountains* is a prepositional phrase that functions as an adverbial.]

Call me *when supper is ready.* [*When supper is ready* is an adverb clause functioning as an adverbial.]

Adjectivals

Did you bring your *dinner* jacket? [*Dinner* looks like a noun but functions as an adjectival.]

The cat *in the living room* is Siamese. [*In the living room* is a prepositional phrase that functions as an adjectival.]

The house *that we bought last year* is being auctioned off next week. [*That we bought last year* is an adjective clause that functions as an adjectival.]

The man *who stole your wallet* just walked out the door. [*Who stole your wallet* is an adjective clause functioning as an adjectival.]

Nominals

Yesterday is gone. [*Yesterday* looks like an adverb but functions as the subject and is a nominal.]

Singing makes David happy. [*Singing* is a gerund and functions as the subject of the sentence and is a nominal.]

Tammy hated *Sam's constant bridge playing.* [*Sam's constant bridge playing* is a gerund phrase that functions as the direct object and is a nominal.]

Michael wants *to ski.* [*To ski* is an infinitive that functions as the direct object and is a nominal.]

Damon's ambition was *to design airplanes.* [*To design airplanes* is an infinitive phrase that functions as the subject complement and is a nominal.]

Take back *what you said.* [*What you said* is a noun clause functioning as a direct object and is a nominal.]

Whenever you arrive will be fine by me. [*Whenever you arrive* is a noun clause functioning as the subject and is a nominal.]

Because a variety of single words, phrases, and clauses can function in the ways that adverbs, adjectives, and nouns do, recognizing their functions in sentences can become complex. For this reason, we give each function its own chapter. Chapter 7 will detail the words, phrases, and clauses that function as adverbials, Chapter 8 will detail the forms that function as adjectivals, and Chapter 9, devoted to nominals, will detail the many forms that function in the ways that nouns do.

● EXERCISES FOR PRACTICE

A. Identify which of the following sentences are simple, which are compound, and which are complex.

    Example: David and John like to read. (simple)

    Example: The cow jumped over the moon, and the dish ran away with the spoon. (compound)

    Example: Please tell me when you want me to pick you up. (complex)

1. Statistics lie forty percent of the time.

2. My sister doesn't like coffee, yet she buys it every time she goes to the grocery.

3. We are not born all at once, but by bits. (Mary Antin)

4. Did you understand what the speech was about?

5. Experience, which destroys innocence, also leads one back to it. (James Baldwin)

6. I know that Julia likes candy.

7. Although it is dark and cold, I like getting up early on winter mornings.

8. Nothing is more real than nothing. (Samuel Beckett)

9. Ethel likes warm temperatures; nevertheless, she's lived in Minnesota most of her life.

10. All of the chocolate ice cream was sold out, so I bought strawberry instead.

B. Each of the following sentences contains one or more embedded sentences. Identify the embedded sentences by underlining them.

    Example: Do you know <u>where you'll be living next year</u>?

    Example: Are you the thief <u>who stole her heart</u>?

    Example: What happened <u>when you got home</u>?

1. That the sun sets in the west is indisputable.

2. Do you know where my keys are?

3. We carry with us the wonders we seek without us. (Sir Thomas Browne)

4. My favorite piece of music is the one we hear all of the time if we are quiet. (John Cage)

5. Where they went was what the sheriff wanted to know.

6. All of the animals excepting man know that the principal business of life is to enjoy it. (Samuel Butler)

7. Parents who stay up all night with sick children know the meaning of the word *commitment.*

8. He that wrestles with us strengthens our nerves and sharpens our skill. (Edmund Burke)

C. Each of the following sentences or sets of sentences contains one or more adverbials. Underline the adverbials, and tell whether they are single-word adverbs, phrases, or clauses. Then tell what each one modifies.

> **Example:** The truck backfired <u>noisily</u>. (single-word adverb, modifies *backfired*)
>
> **Example:** The truck sped <u>down the road</u>. (phrase, modifies *sped*)
>
> **Example:** The truck stopped <u>after its engine fell out</u>. (clause, modifies *stopped*)

1. The waitress hastily put out the fire.

2. What is life? It is a flash of a firefly in the night. It is a breath of a buffalo in the winter time. It is as the little shadow that runs across the grass and loses itself in the sunset. (Chief Crowfoot)

3. Did you buy this book to give it as a present?

4. So long as little children are allowed to suffer, there is no true love in this world. (Isadora Duncan)

5. The past would be startled if it could see itself on the pages of the historian. (Will Durant)

6. The president's train will stop in many small towns because he wants to reach as many people as possible during this campaign.

7. One must be poor to know the luxury of giving. (George Eliot)

8. Put the box of books there and the box of dishes in the kitchen.

D. Each of the following sentences contains one or more adjectivals. Underline the adjectivals, and tell whether they are single-word adjectives, phrases, or clauses. Then tell what they modify.

> **Example:** What a <u>pretty</u> baby! (single-word adjective, modifies *baby*)
>
> **Example:** The cake <u>on this plate</u> is stale. (phrase, modifies *cake*)

> **Example:** The man <u>that you are looking for</u> is not here. (clause, modifies *man*)

1. We seldom see anybody who is not uneasy and afraid to live. (Ralph Waldo Emerson)

2. Cary Grant was a popular Hollywood actor in the 1930s, 1940s, and 1950s.

3. The many-colored photographs on her desk and walls were pictures of dearly loved friends and relatives.

4. The street where I live is being repaved.

5. Any man who is any good is different from anybody else. (Felix Frankfurter)

6. We could hear the beautiful, clear sound of the musician's piano all the way out on the street, beyond the walls of the concert hall.

7. Believe those who are seeking the truth; doubt those who find it. (André Gide)

8. The dog in the next room caught our attention by barking.

E. Each of the following sentences contains one or more nominals. Identify the nominal, and tell whether it is a single word, phrase, or clause. Then tell how it functions in the sentence.

> **Example:** <u>Running</u> can be fun. (single-word gerund functioning as the subject)

> **Example:** <u>To be late</u> is inexcusable. (infinitive phrase functioning as the subject)

> **Example:** I know <u>what you did</u>. (pronoun functioning as the subject; and noun clause functioning as the direct object.)

1. The invariable mark of wisdom is to see the miraculous in the common. (Ralph Waldo Emerson)

2. What Jesse doesn't know is that his wife is planning a party for him.

3. If you don't know where you are going, you can't get lost. (Bernard Glassman)

4. Giving fair grades can be challenging for teachers.

5. Van Gogh just wanted to be understood.

6. Do not seek to follow in the footsteps of the men of old; seek what they sought. (Basho)

7. According to the legend, Daniel Boone always knew where he was going and what he wanted to find after he got there.

8. Many people like communicating over the Internet.

F. Fiction and nonfiction writers usually develop a specific style that helps them convey a desired tone or atmosphere. This style sometimes depends on complex or creative sentence structures or creative combinations of words. The following passage from "The Legend of Sleepy Hollow," written by Washington Irving in 1819, is an example of the author's use of long sentences and embedding as part of his descriptive style. What effect does Irving create by using this style? Identify the embedded sentences in the three-sentence paragraph in the excerpt, and then try to rewrite the paragraph using shorter sentences. Does your rewritten version have the same effect as the original version? Why or why not?

> In the bosom of one of those spacious coves which indent the eastern shore of the Hudson, at that broad expansion of the river denominated by the ancient Dutch navigators the Tappaan Zee, and where they always prudently shortened sail, and implored the protection of St. Nicholas when they crossed, there lies a small market town or rural port, which by some is called Greensburgh, but which is more generally and properly known by the name of Tarry Town. This name was given it, we are told, in former days, by the good housewives of the adjacent bands to linger about the village tavern on market days. Be that as it may, I do not vouch for the fact, but merely advert to it, for the sake of being precise and authentic.

PART II   PREVIEW OF CHALLENGES FOR WRITERS

Although apprentice writers often experience difficulty with noun and verb forms, agreement, and punctuation within simple sentences, the most challenging problems arise when they combine kernel sentences to form longer, more complex structures. Because students need to see error patterns in order to eradicate particular problems, successful writing teachers usually become proficient in recognizing and explaining common sentence structure difficulties to their students in accessible language. Each of the next four chapters will therefore explain common problems for writers associated with the particular embedded or **conjoined structures** that are covered. We preview that coverage here.

TROUBLE WITH EMBEDDING

Although difficulties with embedded structures can manifest themselves in many ways, the most common sentence structure problems with respect to embedding involve movable modifiers and appositives. Because these movable structures often resemble sentences, students can and do punctuate them as such, thus creating sentence fragments. Students also frequently lose track of a movable modifier's status as a modifier. When this happens, a modifier can be misplaced or even appear in a sentence that doesn't contain anything for it to modify.

Embedding and Fragments

As we explained in Part One of this chapter, single words, phrases, and clauses can function as adjectivals, adverbials, and nominals:

Function as Adjectivals (all modify *daughter-in-law*)

My *beautiful* daughter-in-law lives in Las Vegas. (single word)

My daughter-in-law *from Las Vegas* is beautiful. (phrase)

My daughter-in-law, *who is from Las Vegas,* is beautiful. (clause)

Function as Adverbials (all modify *studied*)

My son studied *diligently.* (single word)

My son studied *with great care.* (phrase)

My son studied *as if his life depended on it.* (clause)

Function as Nominals (all rename *my idea;* each is therefore an appositive)

My idea, *condominiums,* astounded everyone. (single word)

My idea, *to buy a condominium,* astounded everyone. (phrase)

My idea, *that we should buy a condominium,* astounded everyone. (clause)

As these sentences show, word groups that function as modifiers and appositives—particularly if they are lengthy—can resemble sentences. Clauses, after all, do have subjects and verbs, and phrases can often contain structures such as participles and infinitives that resemble verbs.

It is also the case that modifiers and appositives can often be moved out of their normal or customary position in a sentence:

I went home *because I was sick.*

Because I was sick, I went home.

The boy *standing in line* dropped his pen.

Standing in line, the boy dropped his pen.

The moment *that we were all waiting for* arrived.

The moment arrived *that we were all waiting for.*

The thought *that I might be a grandmother* excited me.

The thought excited me *that I might be a grandmother.*

This combination of qualities, that phrase and clause modifiers can resemble sentences and that they can be moved, often causes apprentice writers to mistake them for—and punctuate them as—sentences. An incomplete structure that is mistakenly punctuated as a sentence is called a *sentence fragment.* Sentence fragments are considered serious errors in academic and professional writing.

Both adverb and adjective embedding can give rise to sentence fragments. Most often when this happens, students inappropriately punctuate adverbials or adjectivals, which are attempting to function as modifiers, as if they were complete sentences. Here are some examples of modifiers punctuated as if they were sentences:

> *Because I became ill.* I left school early. (fragmented adverb clause)
>
> Bill purchased tickets regularly. *To win the lottery with the big payoff.* (fragmented adverbial phrase)
>
> *Waving her arms hysterically at the charging bull.* Reena attempted to divert him from the playground. (fragmented adjectival phrase)

Inexperienced writers can also produce fragments as they attempt to modify nouns and noun phrases with adjective phrases and clauses. Such modified structures (noun plus a phrase or a clause) can sometimes be mistaken for complete sentences. In the following examples, each fragment consists of a noun plus the phrase or clause that modifies it:

> Di wants a special engagement ring. *A quality diamond set in white gold.* (fragmented appositive modified by a past participle phrase)
>
> *The actor who does his own stunts and who is always a hit at the box office.* He is my favorite. (fragmented noun phrase modified by a relative clause)

Other types of challenges with nominal embedding that may cause students to write sentence fragments include structures (often appositives) that begin with the expressions *for instance* or *for example* (e.g., *I do many things when I'm in the garden. For instance, weeding flower beds or clipping hedges.*). Student writers may also punctuate gerund and infinitive phrases as if they were sentences because they contain gerunds and infinitives, which students can mistake for verbs:

> *To obtain the highest grade point average, despite the fact that it was an honors class.* That was Bettina's goal. (fragmented infinitive phrase)
>
> *Wild dancing and gorging on fabulous food.* They were the things that made the party unforgettable. (fragmented gerund phrase)

Other Problems with Embedding

Besides sentence fragments, embedded structures such as movable modifiers can cause apprentice writers other kinds of problems. Modifiers (particularly adjectivals), whether phrases or clauses, can often be placed improperly, rendering sentences ambiguous, awkward, or even humorous. In fact, _misplaced_ _modifiers_ vex so many writers that most grammar handbooks include sections explaining this problem. Here are some examples:

The new principal found lots of trash _walking down the hallways._ (misplaced adjectival modifier, a participial phrase)

We found a new plumber to fix our pipe _that is from Chicago._ (misplaced adjectival modifier, a relative clause)

To pass the driver's test, John told his son to practice regularly. (misplaced adverbial modifier, an infinitive phrase)

In each of these sentences, misplacement causes the modifier to seem as if it's describing the wrong word. In the first sentence, for example, _walking down the hallways_ seems to be describing _trash,_ which is clearly impossible.

In addition to misplacing movable modifiers, students may also include such modifiers—particularly **participial** (adjectival) **phrases**—in sentences that don't contain anything for them to modify. This type of sentence structure problem is also quite common and is referred as a _**dangling modifier:**_

Lying on the steamy beach, the sun felt very hot. [Dangling modifier. _Lying on the steamy beach_ has nothing to modify; _who_ is lying on the steamy beach?]

When walking down the runway in our new dresses, there are lots of appreciative stares. [Dangling modifier. _Who_ is walking down the runway in our new dresses?]

Intimidated by the snarling dogs, it was time to leave. [Dangling modifier. _Who_ was intimidated by the snarling dogs?]

Finally, although adjective and adverb embedding causes writers the most difficulty with sentence structure, the embedding of nominals can also occasionally challenge writers. Because **direct discourse** (e.g., _John said, "I am tired";_ _Marcia wondered, "Should I leave the party early?"_) and **indirect discourse** (e.g., _John said that he was tired; Marcia wondered if she should leave the party early_) involve nominal direct objects, difficulty in writing direct or indirect speech can be considered a problem related to the embedding of nominals and will therefore be discussed in Chapter 9.

TROUBLE WITH CONJOINING

Conjoining and Sentence Boundary Problems

In general, the most serious problems related to conjoined structures that vex apprentice writers have to do with the failure to recognize sentence boundaries or to punctuate them properly. When a sentence boundary isn't recognized and no punctuation (or no appropriate connecting word) is used, a serious sentence structure problem, known as a *fused sentence*, results:

> John went home he took a shower. [Fused sentence. *John went home* and *He took a shower* are both sentences; they cannot be punctuated as one sentence.]

> My favorite place at home is my room it is a soft, golden yellow. [Fused sentence. *My favorite place at home is my room* and *It is a soft, golden yellow* are both sentences; they cannot be punctuated as one sentence.]

Sometimes fused sentences result because the writer has failed to recognize **conjoined sentences**, as in the examples just given. In other instances it is common for inexperienced writers not to understand the conventions regarding the use of coordinating conjunctions (*and, but, or, nor,* etc.) as opposed to conjunctive adverbs (*however, therefore, then, next,* etc.). **Conjunctive adverbs** cannot be used by themselves to conjoin sentences; they must be used with semicolons (e.g., *I was sick; therefore, I left work early*). Coordinating conjunctions, in contrast, can be used without any punctuation and not produce a fused sentence (e.g., *I was sick so I left work early* is not a fused sentence). When inexperienced writers use conjunctive adverbs without punctuation to conjoin sentences, they inadvertently create fused sentences:

> I was sick therefore I left work early. [Fused sentence. The conjunctive adverb *therefore* must be preceded by a semicolon.]

> I went home then I took a shower. [Fused sentence. The conjunctive adverb *then* must be preceded by a semicolon.]

Related to the fused sentence but not as serious is the *comma splice*. Comma splices occur when an inexperienced writer recognizes a sentence boundary but doesn't employ proper punctuation. By themselves, commas generally function to mark structures *within* sentences. They cannot ordinarily be used by themselves to conjoin sentences. When a comma by itself is used (incorrectly) to join two sentences, a comma splice occurs: *I was sick, I went home early*. A comma splice also results when a conjunctive adverb is used with a comma in conjoined sentences instead of a semicolon: *I was sick, therefore, I went home early*. [The conjunctive adverb *therefore* requires a semicolon: *I was sick; therefore, I went home early*.] Comma splices are a very common problem for apprentice writers.

Most often, sentence boundary problems that involve conjoined structures are those in which the writer fails to apprehend, and thus omits (or fails to punctuate properly) a sentence boundary. However, occasionally, conjoined structures can cause writers to see boundaries where they don't exist and therefore to produce sentence fragments. When inexperienced writers construct lengthy sentences with compound predicates, direct objects, and the like, they can potentially lose track of the relationship between a conjoined structure and the rest of the sentence of which it is a part. If this happens, a sentence fragment may result: *Archie Bunker always tries to sound like he's up on current events. But frequently loses track of his train of thought and ends up sounding like a fool.* As this example illustrates, the writer has lost track of the relationship of the compound predicate (*But frequently loses track of his train of thought and ends up sounding like a fool*) to the rest of the sentence and has punctuated it separately as a complete sentence.

Conjoined Structures and Other Problems

In addition to problems in apprehending sentence boundaries appropriately, conjoined structures can cause writers other difficulties. One is *faulty parallelism.* Because parallel structures are common in speech and writing, even inexperienced writers attempt to use them and often do so improperly, creating awkward or even ambiguous sentences:

> I like *swimming, hiking,* and *to ski.* [Faulty parallelism. The structures *swimming, hiking,* and *to ski* are not parallel (in the same grammatical form). *Swimming* and *hiking* are gerunds; *to ski* is an infinitive.]

> Students who major in computer science get *challenging work, flexible hours,* and *the pay is really good.* [Faulty parallelism. The structures *challenging work, flexible jobs,* and *the pay is really good* are not parallel. *Challenging work* and *flexible hours* are both modified nouns; *the pay is really good* is a sentence.]

These examples of faulty parallelism make the sentences sound awkward and unbalanced; however, structures that aren't parallel can also create ambiguity in meaning. For example, in the sentence *Those commencement speakers make students excited and enjoy themselves,* it's not clear whether *enjoy themselves* refers to the commencement speakers or to the students. This is because the sentence is structured in such a way that *enjoy themselves* could be a part of a compound predicate (*speakers make students excited* + *speakers enjoy themselves*) or a part of a compound object complement (*make students excited* + *make students enjoy themselves*).

In addition to problems with faulty parallelism, conjoining can pose challenges in punctuation and in sentence logic. As we explained earlier, sentences can be conjoined with two different kinds of connecting words, coordinating conjunctions (*and, but, for, or,* etc.) and conjunctive adverbs (*however, therefore, moreover, then,* etc.). In order to be used properly in conjoined sentences, these words must be accompanied by the proper punctuation and must create an appropriate relationship between the sentences that are being connected. Inexperienced writers frequently create errors in conjoined sentences that can involve punctuation, inappropriate logic, or a combination of these. The following sentences provide some examples of these kinds of problems:

> Meena studied for a week, nevertheless she didn't do well on the exam. [The conjunctive adverb *nevertheless* should be preceded by a semicolon and followed by a comma.]

The new students became homesick so, they left campus early. [The comma should precede, not follow, the conjunction *so*.]

My desk fountain is nice, the new ones, however are prettier. [The clauses *My desk fountain is nice* and *the new ones...are prettier* should be separated with a semicolon. The conjunctive adverb *however* should be set off (preceded and followed) by commas.]

I don't like Mozart, and I attended a concert of his chamber music. [The sentence logic is confusing. *I don't like Mozart* creates the expectation that the writer wouldn't attend concerts of his music. Therefore, a connecting word that expresses contrast (e.g., *however* or *but*) should be used.]

John worked hard preparing the flower beds for new plantings. For example, he thatched and fertilized the lawn. [The sentence logic is confusing. The conjunctive adverb *for example* has been overgeneralized to extend to activities that aren't related to flower bed preparation. Another, more precise conjunction that creates an appropriate additive relationship (e.g., *in addition* or *not only that*) should be used.]

As student writers become more proficient working with conjoined structures (which will be discussed in detail in Chapter 10), these kinds of difficulties, as well as those that involve sentence boundary problems, gradually diminish.

EXERCISES FOR PRACTICE

A. Some of the numbered items contain inappropriate sentence fragments. Identify each of the fragments, and see if you can explain how the fragmented structure is attempting to function.

> **Example:**   Enid left practice early. Because she felt discouraged.
> *Because she felt discouraged* is a sentence fragment. It is attempting to modify the verb *left*, telling why Enid left early.

1. Nearing the large parking lot. The cars began to pile up in long lines.

2. As far as I can tell. John isn't too upset about not being able to put up a fence.

3. Because of her attitude toward Bill. Edna will not be attending the spring banquet.

4. Because of illness, Jen left the convocation. She got into bed as soon as she got home.

5. The new executive committee revised all of the procedural rules. And passed several new regulations as well.

6. Securing her body carefully with strong, flexible rope. The rock climber scaled the almost vertical face of the mountain.

7. My husband has several hobbies to keep him occupied once he's retired. For example, attending tai chi classes, taking guitar lessons, and studying photography.

8. All of us decided that a special event was in order. A banquet with gourmet food and live entertainment.

B. Some of the following sentences exhibit problems with movable modifiers. Identify each problem, and try to describe what is causing it.

> **Example:**   Standing on the corner, the tuba sounded really loud.
>
> *Dangling modifier:* There is nothing for *standing on the corner* to modify.

> **Example:**   We found a rare shell combing the beaches.
>
> *Misplaced modifier: Combing the beaches* seems to be describing *shell.*

1. We found lots of litter walking down Pennsylvania Avenue.

2. To get admitted to a good college, Mr. Jones advised his students to engage in extracurricular activities.

3. Striding boldly down the catwalk, the audience admired the fashion show.

4. To avoid getting sunburn, people should use a good-quality sun block and apply it regularly and liberally.

5. Examining the data from the investigation, many irregularities were found.

6. Bounding exuberantly, Woody leaped into the strawberry patch and began rolling on his back.

7. Clutching his A exam, excited shouts of glee could be heard all over the house.

8. The department chair greeted the new faculty member extending her hand.

9. Tinkling peacefully, the desk fountain soothed Susan's jangled nerves.

10. Considering every alternative, a selection was finally made.

C. Some of the following items contain comma splices or fused sentences. Identify each error, and try to explain its cause.

> **Example:**   The wind blew open the door it scattered papers everywhere.
>
> *The wind blew open the door* and *it scattered papers everywhere* are both complete sentences. They should not be punctuated as if they were one sentence.

> **Example:** Neela wanted to excel at skiing, therefore, she practiced at every opportunity.
>
> The conjunctive adverb *therefore* requires a semicolon before it.

1. I have only two sisters their names are Laura and Evey.

2. Evey lives in Los Angeles, she is an executive at an insurance company.

3. We were at a comedy club recently, and the comedian made fun of Evey's profession. When he found out what she did for a living, he said, "Follow your dream."

4. Everyone laughed, however, I laughed the loudest.

5. Afterward I hoped I hadn't hurt Evey's feelings, but I didn't say anything.

6. We did talk about the joke later at dinner, though, and Evey seemed to think it was amusing, therefore I assumed that she wasn't annoyed with me.

7. I don't know why people assume that working for an insurance company isn't exciting probably it's just ignorance.

8. My other sister is a securities analyst, she works for a large, international investment company.

9. Laura spends a good deal of her time flying all over the world, especially to Europe.

10. Sometimes I'm jealous of the exotic places she visits regularly, I always realize, however, how very tiring business travel is.

D. Although fragments are considered inappropriate for some kinds of writing, in some genres they are used frequently. Examine easily accessible sources of writing (books, magazines, newspapers, etc.), and make an informal assessment of the sentence fragments that you encounter. In what genres (advertisements, fiction, letters to the editor, informative essays, etc.) are fragments most prevalent? Explain why you think fragments occur more readily in these genres.

E. Whole books have been published containing collections of "blooper" sentences in which the writers have unintentionally created humorous mistakes, often because of a misplaced or dangling modifier (e.g., "Wanted: used table for a large family made of wood"). Survey recent issues of your local newspaper, especially classified ads, for such sentences. (If you can't find many examples in the paper, you might select a few from one of the blooper books.) Bring your selections to class, and together with your classmates, compile a list. Once the list has been compiled, try to explain what makes each sentence unintentionally humorous.

INTRODUCING ADVERBIALS

Chapter Preview

Chapter 7 explains how to recognize adverbials in sentences.

In **Part I** you will learn about

- Phrase adverbials, including prepositional, infinitive, and other types of adverb phrases
- Adverb clauses

In **Part II** you will learn about the challenges
writers can face with

- Conventions and conjunctions, including punctuation issues and conveying logical relationships
- Fragmented adverbials, including clause and phrase fragments and how to fix them
- Punctuation with adverbials

In **Part III** you will learn about stylistic choices
writers make when using

- Adverbials
- Fragmented clauses

PART I   FORMS OF ADVERBIALS

In Chapter 6 you learned how to make sentences more complex through the use of adverbials, adjectivals, and nominals. In this chapter we take a more in-depth look at adverbials. We review adverbials in their various forms—as single-word adverbs (e.g., *well, happily, finally*), as adverbial phrases (e.g., *very fast, in the next room, with delight*), and as adverb clauses (e.g., *because you loved me, after the snow fell*)—and look at the various ways adverbials can be used in sentences to add information and to provide more sentence variety. Indeed, as we demonstrate, adverbials may be the most flexible of all the parts of speech in English. For that very reason, their form and placement in a sentence may be both confusing and a source of error for the writer.

REVIEW OF SINGLE-WORD ADVERBS
What Adverbs Do

As part of their flexible nature, adverbials can modify various parts of speech, primarily verbs, adjectives, and other adverbs, as well as whole sentences. When adverbs function to modify an adjective or another adverbial, they usually tell intensity or degree (e.g., *very pretty, just on time, moderately hopeful*). Here are some additional examples of adverbs that illustrate the various ways that they can function:

1. He dispatched the news *quickly*. [*Quickly* modifies the verb *dispatched*.]

2. He is *very* punctual. [*Very* modifies the adjective *punctual*.]

3. The actors spoke *terribly* loudly. [*Terribly* modifies the adverb *loudly*.]

4. *Suddenly*, a fire broke out in the gymnasium. [*Suddenly* modifies the entire sentence, *a fire broke out in the gymnasium*.]

Because of their flexibility as modifiers, adverbials can also provide a variety of information in a sentence, telling, among other things, when (time), where (place), why (reason or cause), how long (duration), how often (frequency), or how (manner) the action occurred or a condition existed, as these sentences demonstrate:

1. The play starts *at 9:30*. [*At 9:30* tells *when* the play starts.]

2. The play starts at 9:30 *at the local playhouse*. [*At the local playhouse* tells *where* the play starts.]

3. The play starts at 9:30 at the local playhouse *because a fire broke out in the gymnasium*. [*Because a fire broke out in the gymnasium* tells *why* the play is being held at the local playhouse.]

4. The play will run *for two hours*. [*For two hours* tells *how long* the play will run.]

5. The play *seldom* exceeds two hours. [*Seldom* tells *how often* the play exceeds two hours.]

6. The playgoers sit *attentively* throughout the play. [*Attentively* tells *how* the playgoers sit during the play.]

Adverbials of time play an especially important role in narrowing the time frame that is expressed by the verb phrase in a sentence. Notice how the use of specific adverbials focuses the time of the action in the following three sentences:

1. I am playing in the orchestra *now*.

2. I am *currently* playing in the orchestra.

3. I am playing in the orchestra *next week*.

Although all three sentences are in the present progressive tense, the time of the action varies in each sentence, depending on the adverbial used. That is, in sentence 1, the use of *now* tells us that the action is being completed at this very moment. In sentence 2, the use of *currently* conveys the notion that the action is ongoing at present but not necessarily at this very moment. In sentence 3, the use of *next week* focuses the action on a future time.

Finally, another important quality of adverbs is that they are quite movable. When adverbials modify a complete sentence (*Suddenly, the room became very quiet*), for example, they can often be placed in different locations:

The room became very quiet, *suddenly*.

The room *suddenly* became very quiet.

Adverbs of frequency (*always, sometimes, often, never,* etc.) have even greater flexibility in their placement. For example, look at the many ways in which the frequency adverb *often* can be placed in the following sentences:

Often, I go to the movies.

I *often* go to the movies.

I go *often* to the movies.

I go to the movies *often*.

Writers may choose to change the location of adverbs that modify an entire sentence and adverbs of frequency in order to provide sentence variety or to emphasize a specific action. Overall, frequency adverbs and some other single-word adverbs may be more flexible than phrases or clauses in their movability within a sentence, a fact we will discuss further in our discussion of adverbial phrases and adverbial clauses.

A final quality of adverbials is that an unlimited number of adverbials can be strung together to modify a sentence. Note how the adverbials work together in the following example:

> <u>Coincidentally</u>, the bulldozer <u>very suddenly</u> started <u>across the street at 3 A.M.</u> <u>because the driver had left it out of gear</u>.

Ordinarily, when using several adverbials in sequence, there is a specified order with respect to placement. In particular, adverbials of place come before adverbials of time, and both come before adverbials of reason. Compare the following sentences:

1. *The bulldozer started at 3 a.m. across the street.

2. The bulldozer started across the street at 3 a.m.

In sentence 1, the placement of the adverbial of time before the adverbial of place makes the sentence awkward. Likewise, compare this pair of sentences:

3. *The bulldozer started *because the driver had left it out of gear* across the street at 3 A.M.

4. The bulldozer started across the street at 3 A.M. *because the driver had left it out of gear.*

In sentence 3, changing the sequence of the adverbials changes the entire meaning of the sentence. It tells us when the driver had left the bulldozer out of gear rather than when the bulldozer started across the street. In comparison, placing the adverbial of reason at the end of the sentence tells us why the bulldozer started across the street at 3 A.M.

What Single-Word Adverbs Look Like

In describing the many ways in which adverbials can modify a sentence, we have shown that adverbials can take three distinctive forms: single-word adverbs, adverb phrases, and adverb clauses. Of these three forms, single-word adverbs may be the most distinctive but also at times the most difficult to recognize in a sentence. Sometimes, however, single-word adverbs may be recognized by the endings they take. The most commonly recognized form of single-word adverbs may be those created by adding the ending *-ly* to an adjective, which tell the manner in which an action is completed: *lightly, freely, quietly, slowly,* and so on. Another common ending for adverbs is *-ward,* which tells direction, as in *forward* or *backward*. Other common single-word adverbs of manner, such as *well, fast,* and *late,* do not fit into either of these categories (as in *David sings very well* or *Tom types very fast*) because they don't take a recognizable ending.

Besides the endings *-ly* and *-ward,* another common distinguishing feature of single-word adverbs of manner or direction, as well as a few adverbs of time, is that they can be compared by adding *-er* or *-est* to the base word form (e.g., *fast* + *-er* = *faster, fast* + *-est* = *fastest*) or by using *more* or *most* plus the adverb (e.g., *more badly, most frequently*).

Other Ways to Recognize Single-Word Adverbs

As we have suggested, it may not always be easy to recognize single-word adverbials by their form. Rather, single-word adverbs may be easier to recognize by their meaning or function in a sentence because not all single-word adverbs have easily recognizable endings such as *-ly* or *-ward*. In fact, most of the single-word adverbs that tell time, place, or frequency do not have distinguishing endings or suffixes: *soon, tomorrow, forever, here, there, upstairs, outside, never, seldom, sometimes, often, always.* Although many of these adverbs cannot be compared (**He will arrive most here*), they can be qualified or intensified, which is another distinguishing feature of single-word adverbs (*He will arrive very soon*). Some common single-word qualifiers or intensifiers include *quite, almost, really, very, just, somewhat, extremely*, and *undeniably.* These single-word adverbials are most commonly used to modify other adverbs (e.g., <u>*almost*</u> *always,* <u>*quite*</u> *frequently*) and adjectives (<u>*extremely*</u> *difficult,* <u>*undeniably*</u> *outrageous*).

Another way to recognize single-word adverbs that is related to how they function is their ability to modify a whole sentence. As we said earlier, some adverbs can be used to modify complete sentences, as the following examples show:

Happily, the tornado didn't strike.

Obviously, some changes need to be made around here.

Fortunately, she didn't have twins.

Undeniably, presidential candidates should be honest.

As with adverbs of frequency, these adverbs are movable and can be placed after the subject or at the end of the sentence:

The tornado, *happily,* didn't strike.

Some changes need to be made around here, *obviously.*

She *fortunately* didn't have twins.

Included in this set of movable adverbials is a group of words or phrases often referred to as *conjunctive adverbs* (<u>*however, therefore, consequently, in spite of, as a result of,* etc.</u>). As we discussed in Chapter 6, conjunctive adverbs are connecting words that connect two related sentences, as the following sentences illustrate:

I walked to the store in the blizzard. I caught a cold.

I walked to the store in the blizzard. *Consequently,* I caught a cold.

While conjunctive adverbs function as connectors, they also function adverbially in that they give a reason or make a contrast—as many adverb clauses do—or modify the entire sentence. Because using conjunctive adverbs often leads to problems in punctuating sentences, we discuss their use in more depth in Part Two of this chapter.

Form and Function

As we have repeatedly pointed out, there is a distinction between the form of a word and how it functions in a sentence. Indeed, there are words that function as adverbs but look like other parts of speech and, conversely, words that look like adverbs but don't function as adverbs. When reading through the examples of single-word adverbs in our discussion, you may have thought of some other ways in which the words we identified as "adverbs" might be used. For example, compare the following pairs of sentences:

1. Please get that letter to me *soon.*
   The soonest we can get it to you is tomorrow.

2. The family sleeps *upstairs.*
   Can you fix the *upstairs* window?

In the first pair of sentences, *soon* is used both as an adverbial (telling *when* I should get the letter) and as the head of a noun phrase (*The soonest we can get it to you...*). As an adverbial in the first sentence, it tells the time the action should take place; as the head of a noun phrase in the second sentence, it functions (in its superlative form) as the subject of the sentence. In the second pair of sentences, *upstairs* is used as an adverbial (telling *where* the family sleeps) and as an adjectival (to modify *window*). In fact, many words that look like nouns can function as adverbs, such as the days of the week (*I go to the zoo <u>Sundays</u>*), as well as words such as *home* (e.g., *Let's go <u>home</u>*).

Another type of adverbial that may cause confusion is the participle. Participles are particularly vexing because they usually function as adjectivals but may appear to be functioning as adverbs, as in *Screaming, she ran out of the room.* That is, *screaming* may seem to describe how she ran out of the room rather than describing *she,* which is what the participle is actually doing. Yet it is often the placement of a participle that determines whether it is modifying a noun phrase or a verb phrase because *-ly* cannot be added to a participle to distinguish whether it is functioning as an adjectival or an adverbial. Compare the following two sets of sentences:

1. They ran out of the room, *hysterical.*
   They ran out of the room *hysterically.*

2. *Laughing,* the baby jumped up and down.
   The baby jumped up and down, *laughing.*

In pair 1, the adjective form, *hysterical,* is easily distinguishable from the adverb form, *hysterically,* because of the *-ly* ending. However, in pair 2, the participle *laughing* appears to be functioning adverbially only when placed at the end of the sentence. Even then, it might be argued that it has really been moved to the end of the sentence for stylistic purposes and is therefore still modifying the noun phrase (describing a quality of the baby) rather than the constituents of the verb phrase (describing how the baby jumped up and down). The point here is that the exact function of participles is not always easy to identify, even for professional grammarians. The identification of their function is mostly important when their use creates ambiguity in the sentence.

Overall, when trying to determine the function of a word or word group in a sentence, it is helpful to ask what type of information the word or word group provides. If it relates to time, place, manner, or any of the other types of information that adverbials provide, the word or word group is likely functioning as an adverbial.

PHRASE ADVERBIALS

In earlier chapters we explained that sometimes groups of words can work together as a single unit; such word groups are called *phrases* and *clauses*. You will recall that clauses are groups of words that contain subjects and verbs. A phrase, then, is a group of words that acts together but does *not* contain a subject and a verb. Sometimes adverbs form phrases with related words, such as *very* or *quite*, that are themselves adverbs. Here are some examples:

1. Bella ran *very quickly*. [*Quickly* is the adverb; *very* is a related word that tells how quickly.]

2. I ate my sandwich *too fast*. [*Fast* is the adverb; *too* is a related word that tells how fast.]

3. That snail crept up the walk *ever so slowly*. [*Slowly* is the adverb; *ever* and *so* are words that tell how slowly.]

Sometimes, rather than consisting of an adverb and its related words, a phrase can act *as* an adverb. Such phrases can be considered adverbials because they function as adverbs. (Recall that an *adverbial* is a word or word group that functions as an adverb.) Here are some examples of phrases that act as adverbs:

4. I accidentally pushed Woody *down the stairs*. [*Down the stairs* is an adverbial; it tells *where* Woody was pushed.]

5. Tomeka studied *to ace the exam*. [*To ace the exam* is an adverbial; it tells *why* Tomeka studied.]

6. *For years* Ellen has lived in the country. [*For years* is an adverbial; it tells *how long* Ellen has lived in the country.]

As you examined these examples of adverbial phrases, you may have wondered whether the structures *down the stairs* in example 4 and *for years* in example 6 were prepositional phrases. The answer is yes. An adverbial phrase that consists of a group of words acting together as an adverb can be defined by either form or function. If the phrases *down the stairs* and *for years* are identified by their form, they are called prepositional phrases. If the phrases *down the stairs* and *for years* are identified by their function, they can be called adverbials because each functions in the same way as an adverb.

Prepositional Phrases

As you may have anticipated from the discussion so far, one of the common groups of words that act together as an adverb is the *prepositional phrase*. Prepositional phrases are ordinarily defined and described in terms of their form: they begin with a preposition and end with a noun or noun phrase that is called the *object* of the preposition.

What is less commonly emphasized is how prepositional phrases function, despite the fact that the vast majority of prepositional phrases function as modifiers. As we have suggested, besides recognizing their form, it is useful to note that prepositional phrases frequently act or function in the same way as adverbs—which modify verbs, adjectives, and other adverbs. Here are some examples of prepositional phrases that function as adverbials:

1. They live <u>in the fifth-floor apartment</u>. [*In the fifth-floor apartment* modifies the
   preposition object of the preposition
   verb *live;* it tells *where* they live.]

2. <u>After our family reunion</u>, I spent most of the weekend cleaning. [*After our family reunion* modifies the verb *spent;* it tells *when* I spent the weekend cleaning.]
   preposition object of the preposition

3. Maria danced <u>with great abandon</u>. [*With great abandon* modifies the verb
   preposition object of the preposition
   danced; it tells *how* Maria danced.]

4. <u>For many years</u>, I have wondered about you. [*For many years* modifies the
   preposition object of the preposition
   verb have *wondered;* it tells *how long* I have wondered.]

In Chapter 8 we will be explaining and providing examples of prepositional phrases that modify nouns. Prepositional phrases that modify nouns can also be called *adjectivals*. Notice the contrast between the two different functions (as adverbials and as adjectivals) of prepositional phrases in the following sentences:

1. The neighbor *with the broomstick* chased our cat. [*With the broomstick* modifies the noun *neighbor;* it tells *which* neighbor. It's an *adjectival.*]

2. A woman chased our cat *with a broomstick*. [*With a broomstick* modifies the verb *chased;* it tells *how* the woman chased our cat. It's an *adverbial*.]

3. The house *under the overpass* burned down. [*Under the overpass* modifies the noun *house;* it tells *which* house. It's an *adjectival*.]

4. Those wild dogs wandered *under the overpass*. [*Under the overpass* modifies the verb *wandered;* it tells *where* the dogs wandered. It's an *adverbial*.]

Sometimes only context can determine whether a prepositional phrase is an adverbial or an adjectival because the structure of the sentence is ambiguous. For example, the prepositional phrase *from Nebraska* in the sentence *She sent a package to her cousin from Nebraska* might explain from *where* she *sent* her cousin a package: from Nebraska. In this interpretation of the sentence, *from Nebraska* functions as an adverbial. It modifies the verb *sent* (From where was the package sent?). Or she might have two cousins: one from Nebraska and one from Idaho. *Which* cousin did she send the package to? The one from Nebraska. (We don't know where she mailed the package from.) In this interpretation, *from Nebraska* is an adjectival; it modifies the noun *cousin*. Here are a few more examples of sentences with ambiguous prepositional phrases that might function as either adjectivals or adverbials:

1. I chased the puppy *with the stick*. [Does *with the stick* tell how I chased the puppy (adverb phrase) or which puppy I chased—the one with the stick (adjective phrase)?]

2. I e-mailed a student *from Peoria*. [Did I do the e-mailing from Peoria (adverb phrase), or is the student from Peoria (adjective phrase)?]

As we noted earlier in this chapter, one of the characteristics of adverbials is that they can be quite movable. Prepositional phrases functioning as adverbs are no exception; they can often be moved to create sentence variety: *The horses raced through the quiet streets* can be changed to *Through the quiet streets the horses raced.* Sometimes moving an ambiguous prepositional phrase can clarify its function. For example, if the ambiguous prepositional phrase in the sentence *I e-mailed a student from Peoria* is meant to convey from where I e-mailed the student, it can be moved to precede the sentence: *From Peoria, I e-mailed a student.* Later in this chapter we will discuss in more detail the reasons a writer might wish to relocate an adverb phrase from its "normal" spot (following the verb it modifies).

Infinitive Phrases

As you recall from your earlier reading, a common English structure is the *infinitive,* which in its most simple form consists of the word *to* plus the base form of a verb: *to walk, to read, to dance, to swim, to sigh*. Infinitives can also consist of the word *to* plus inflected verb forms, as in *to have walked, to have swum,* and *to be sighing*. Because infinitives and infinitive phrases (*to walk quickly, to swim the English Channel, to dance a tango with abandon*, etc.) can function as nominals, we will be examining these structures again in Chapter 9. Besides acting as nouns, however, infinitives and infinitive phrases can function as adverbials:

1. Evey *left* Pittsburgh <u>to pursue dance</u>. [Why did Evey leave? To pursue dance.]

2. I *came* to the library <u>to study</u>. [Why did I come to the library? To study.]

3. JoBeth *fasted* <u>to lose weight rapidly</u>. [Why did JoBeth fast? To lose weight rapidly.]

4. <u>To call attention to herself</u>, Neela *came* to the party with purple hair. [Why did Neela come to the party with purple hair? To call attention to herself.]

Ordinarily, it is not too difficult to tell the difference between infinitives and infinitive phrases that act as adverbials and those that act as nouns. Nominal infinitives and infinitive phrases must function in the way that nouns function (as subjects, direct objects, appositives, etc.). Adverbial infinitives and infinitive phrases (which function as adverbials) modify verbs, adjectives, and adverbs. By examining what an infinitive phrase *does* (how it functions) in a sentence, you can determine whether it is an adverbial:

1. *To swim* is exciting. [*To swim* is an infinitive acting as a noun; it is the subject of the sentence.]

2. *To swim* all day, Marcia wore a lot of sunblock. [*To swim all day* is an infinitive phrase acting as an adverb. It modifies the verb *wore* by telling *why* Marcia wore sunblock: to swim all day.]

3. John loves *to chase bats*. [*To chase bats* is an infinitive phrase acting as a noun; it is the direct object of the transitive verb *love*. What does John love? To chase bats.]

4. I am afraid *to chase bats*. [*To chase bats* is an infinitive phrase acting as an adverb. It modifies the adjective *afraid* by telling what I am afraid of—chasing bats.]

Finally, it is important to note that infinitives and infinitive phrases, like other adverbials, are movable. The adverbial infinitives and infinitive phrases in all of the examples just given can appear at the end or the beginning of the sentence. Fronted infinitive adverbials (those at the beginning of sentences) are set off by a comma:

1. To pursue dance, Evey left Pittsburgh.

2. To study, I came to the library.

3. To lose weight rapidly, JoBeth fasted.

4. To call attention to herself, Neela came to the party with purple hair.

If the phrase is placed at the end of the sentence, no comma is necessary:

1. Evey left Pittsburgh to pursue dance.

2. I came to the library to study.

3. JoBeth fasted to lose weight rapidly.

4. Neela came to the party with purple hair to call attention to herself.

Other Types of Adverb Phrases

Although infinitive phrases and prepositional phrases are the most common phrasal adverbials, other word groups can function in this way as well. *Absolute phrases* resemble adverb clauses—which will be covered in the next section of this chapter—but strictly speaking aren't clauses because they don't contain subjects and verbs. Contrast these pairs of sentences:

1. [Because *the party* <u>was</u> boring,] we *left* early.

2. [The party being boring,] we *left* early.
   Why did we leave? Because of the boring nature of the party.

3. [Since *my wheels* <u>were embedded</u> in snow], I couldn't *drive*.

4. [My wheels embedded in snow,] I couldn't *drive*.
   Why couldn't I drive? Because of my wheels being embedded in snow.

5. [If *the weather* <u>permits</u> it,] we *will camp* on the hill.

6. [Weather permitting,] we *will camp* on the hill.
   Under what conditions will we camp? If the weather permits camping.

In each of the examples, the bracketed structure is an adverbial that modifies the main verb in the sentence. However, only the bracketed structures in the first sentence in each pair (1, 3, 5) contain both a subject (italicized) and a verb (underlined). The bracketed structures in the second sentence in each pair (2, 4, 6) are reduced versions of the clauses; they are *absolute phrases*.

ADVERB CLAUSES

Another type of adverbial is the adverb clause, also referred to as a dependent clause. Adverb clauses are clauses that consist of a **subordinating conjunction** and a subject and verb. Because they consist of subjects and verbs, adverb clauses can seem like complete sentences:

Before the parade passes by.

Since you went away.

However, despite their sentencelike appearance, adverb clauses are in fact modifiers. That is, they may appear to have the *form* of sentences, but they *function* as modifiers.

In explaining how adverb (and other dependent) clauses differ from sentences, many grammar handbooks describe the concept of dependency in terms of meaning. For this reason a common explanation regarding what makes adverb clauses "dependent" is their need for additional information to complete the relationship expressed by the clause. As we have explained earlier in this chapter, though, it may be advisable not to rely entirely on this approach. That is, while students may find it helpful with respect to the two examples just given—and other similar structures—to note that more information is needed (What needs to be done "before the parade passes by"? What has happened "since you went away"?), we suggest that they also be helped to understand that subordinating conjunctions function to create adverb clauses, which like all other adverbials are modifiers. Modifiers are parts of sentences, not sentences themselves. Adverb clauses must therefore always be connected to a main or independent clause.

Before we delve deeper into dependent adverb clauses, let's look at the words that typically signal the presence of an adverb clause, *subordinating conjunctions.*

COMMON SUBORDINATING CONJUNCTIONS

<u>Time</u>	<u>Cause/Effect</u>	<u>Contrast</u>	<u>Condition</u>
before	because	although	if
after	now that	even though	unless
during	since	while	in case
until			
when			

As the list indicates, subordinating conjunctions modify the independent main clause by signaling specific relationships between the dependent adverb clause and the independent main clause (i.e., a complete sentence consisting of a subject and a verb). Let us look at these various relationships one by one.

Time Relationships

1. *Before she wrote the letter,* <u>Sally sharpened her pencil</u>.
   subordinating   adverb (dependent)   independent clause
   conjunction   clause

2. *After his friends went home,* <u>Jerry did his homework</u>.
   subordinating   adverb (dependent)   independent clause
   conjunction   clasuse

3. *During his annual checkup,* <u>Fido bit the veterinarian</u>.
   subordinating   adverb (dependent)   independent clause
   conjunction   clause

In each of these examples, the italicized part is an adverb clause. In example 1, *Before she wrote the letter* shows an adverbial relationship between the dependent clause and the independent clause *she sharpened her pencil* that is based on time, or *when* Sally sharpened her pencil.

Cause-and-Effect Relationships

1. *Because he was a good speaker,* Jim was elected class president.
   subordinating   adverb (dependent) clause   independent clause
   conjunction

2. *Since she was already at the nursery,* she bought more flowers.
   subordinating   adverb (dependent) clause   independent clause
   conjunction

3. *Now that her mother has moved out,* Sharon feels more independent.
   subordinating   adverb (dependent) clause   independent clause
   conjunction

In example 1, *Because he was a good speaker* indicates a causal relationship that shows *why* Jim was elected class president, thus making the dependent clause adverbial.

Contrastive Relationships

1. *Although she is tough with people,* Karen is tender with animals.
   subordinating   adverb (dependent) clause   independent clause
   conjunction

2. *Whereas Susan loves to go to parties,* she is always the first to leave.
   subordinating   adverb (dependent) clause   independent clause
   conjunction

3. *Even though Tim is very frugal,* he always buys gifts for friends and family.
   subordinating   adverb (dependent) clause   independent clause
   conjunction

In example 1, *Although she is tough with people* is an adverbial that indicates a contrasting relationship between the dependent clause and the independent clause *Karen is tender with animals.*

Conditional Relationships

1. *If you eat your carrots,* your eyesight will improve.
   subordinating   adverb (dependent) clause   independent clause
   conjunction

2. *Unless you develop a tough skin,* unkind comments will always hurt.
   subordinating   adverb (dependent) clause   independent clause
   conjunction

3. *In case her car battery died,* Tina brought jumper cables.
   subordinating   adverb (dependent) clause   independent clause
   conjunction

Finally, a relationship of condition exists between the adverb clause in example 1. *If you eat your carrots,* and the resulting outcome in the main clause, *your eyesight will improve.*

You may have noticed that in all of these examples, the dependent clause precedes the independent clause. However, the advantage of adverb clauses is their mobility: they may either precede or follow the main clause or in some instances be placed in the middle of the sentence. Let's take a look at some of our examples again with the order of the adverb clauses moved to follow the independent clause:

1. <u>Sally sharpened her pencil</u> *before she wrote the letter*.
   independent clause   subordinating   adverb (dependent) clause
                                  conjunction

2. <u>Jim was elected president</u> *because he is a good speaker*.
   independent clause   subordinating   adverb (dependent) clause
                                  conjunction

3. <u>Karen is tender with animals,</u> *although she is tough with people*.
   independent clause   subordinating   adverb (dependent) clause
                                  conjunction

4. <u>Your eyesight will improve</u> *if you eat your carrots*.
   independent clause   subordinating   adverb (dependent) clause
                                  conjunction

As you may also have observed, when adverb clauses precede the main clause, a comma is placed at the end of the clause:

> *Because he was tired,* Tom fell asleep early.

However, when the dependent clause follows the main clause, a comma is ordinarily not required.

> Tom fell asleep early *because he was tired.*

Note also that it is possible to move an adverb clause to the middle of the sentence to follow the subject:

> Tom, *because he was tired,* fell asleep early.

In this case, commas surround the clause because it has been moved away from its expected position in the sentence near the verb phrase *fell asleep early* or at the beginning of the sentence. One advantage of the mobility of adverb clauses in the sentence is the possibility for increased connection and relationships between ideas, as well as for the general **fluency** and variety of student writing.

● EXERCISES FOR PRACTICE

A. In each of the following sentences, underline all the adverbials (single-word adverbs, phrases, and clauses). Tell what word each adverbial modifies and what information it provides.

> **Example:**   <u>Slowly</u>, the children crawled <u>up the ramp</u>.
>   *Slowly* modifies the verb *crawled;* it tells how the children crawled. *Up the ramp* modifies the verb *crawled;* it tells where the children crawled.

Example: The <u>ominously</u> deserted streets frightened us.
Ominously modifies the adjectival *deserted*. It describes in what way the streets seemed deserted.

1. When you are finished eating, you should drive to Toledo.

2. Those cameras are hard to find in the United States.

3. After class, Anita and Juan walked hand-in-hand to the House of Brats.

4. Because she was angry with her sister, Laura cleaned her room agonizingly slowly.

5. Over the mountains and through the woods trotted the three glorious brown stags.

6. If you see my puppy in the neighborhood, please let me know right away.

7. Sue walked seductively across the runway to attract the gaze of the onlookers.

8. Unfortunately, if you don't try harder, you will fail miserably.

9. Despite having a good time, LaRuth and Joyce left the dance early to please their mothers.

10. Between my job and yours, there is not much time for us to travel this year.

B. In each of the following sentences, the underlined words or word groups look like (take the form of) adverbs or adverbials. Sometimes they also function as adverbs, but sometimes they function as nouns or adjectives. In each case, explain how the underlined word or word group functions in the sentence.

Example: He got up from <u>behind the desk</u>. Nominal; object of the preposition *from*.

Example: The mouse ran <u>behind the desk</u>. Adverbial; modifies *ran*.

1. <u>Yesterday</u> was such a happy day.

2. I studied my brains out <u>yesterday</u>.

3. I tripped over Woody <u>at the top of the stairs</u>.

4. <u>At the top of the stairs</u> is where you might slip.

5. I hate <u>Mondays</u>.

6. We are going to be meeting <u>Mondays</u>.

7. Your <u>Monday</u> attitude is depressing and demoralizing.

8. The woman <u>from Bowling Green</u> surprised everyone.

9. I came to Idaho <u>from Bowling Green</u>.

10. Seena requires that we all take our work <u>seriously</u>.

C. Use each of the following words or phrases in two sentences. In the first sentence, use the word or phrase as an adverb or adverbial. In the second sentence, use the word or phrase in some other way (as a noun, noun phrase, or nominal, as an adjective or adjectival).

> **Example:**   last night
>
>   I danced the tango last night. (adverbial)
>   Last night was wonderful. (noun phrase)

1. tomorrow

2. Tuesday

3. downstairs

4. from the next county

5. slowly

6. morning

7. hard

8. fast

9. home

10. in the basement

D. Underline the adverbial phrases and clauses in the following sentences. Identify the form of each, and explain what each one modifies.

> **Example:**   She bought the piano <u>to impress her neighbors</u>. Infinitive
>   phrase; tells why she bought the piano.

1. To free herself from guilt, Grace confessed her sins to a stranger at the bus stop.

2. The wayward bus broke through the guard rail and plunged over a steep cliff.

3. The picture was hanging at an angle against the back wall.

4. The magician always performed in the shadows.

5. Kris sang happily as she prepared a simple dinner.

6. When the clock struck six, a brisk wind suddenly blew the door open.

7. The shot rang out with a loud crack before we could get the gun away from the madman.

8. The computer remains in the bedroom where the delivery man left it.

9. Ethel gave her phone number to the policeman to distract his attention from the speeding ticket he was concentrating on writing.

10. Suddenly, more than fifty birds lifted themselves from the bushes and flew over Agnes's head after she stepped into the garden.

E. Write a brief paragraph using a variety of adverbials (single-word adverbs, phrases, and clauses). Identify their form, explain what they modify, and tell what type of information they provide.

F. In each of the following examples, underline the adverb clause, and identify the type of information it provides or relationship it conveys within the context of the sentence.

>   **Example:**   <u>Even though Carol is over eighty</u>, she still walks a mile every day. Contrastive relationship; shows an unexpected act based on Carol's age

1. Because I was feeling depressed, I didn't go to the party.

2. He made a large charitable donation after he visited the homeless shelter.

3. If the market maintains its stability, the stockbrokers will keep their jobs.

4. She lent him the money, though she doubted she would ever be repaid.

5. George devoted a lifetime to stamp collecting, even though it is an expensive hobby.

6. Since Woody was a puppy, he has always liked to chase squirrels.

7. You'll never improve your grades unless you actually go to class.

8. My mother becomes very nostalgic whenever she listens to Sinatra.

9. After the president approves the tax cut, his rating will go up in the polls.

10. John gave me all the tickets because he didn't want to sell them himself.

G. Use a subordinating conjunction to connect the following pairs of sentences, making sure to punctuate appropriately and create a logical relationship between the ideas.

>   **Example:**   Susan was afraid she would fail the exam. She studied very hard.
>   Because Susan was afraid she would fail the exam, she studied very hard.

1. Jennifer cried with sorrow. Her puppy died.

2. The test was very difficult. Very few people passed it.

3. They need to study more. This would ensure a higher pass rate.

4. The soup was very hot. Tom sipped it slowly.

5. He misses his grandmother very much. She moved away in October.

6. I may not make it to the party. Don't wait for me.

7. She was tired and cranky. She managed to get through the performance.

8. The class was over. Some students stayed behind to talk with the instructor.

9. The trip needs to be within my price range. Otherwise, I can't go.

10. We were sad that Sharon didn't go with us. We managed to have a good time.

H. Each word on the list is a subordinating conjunction. Use each word in two sentences containing adverb clauses, the first with the adverb clause occurring before the main clause and the second with the main clause coming first. Be sure to punctuate properly and to make the relationship between nouns and pronouns clear.

> **Example:** because: Because Tom was tired, he left early.
> Tom left early because he was tired.

1. although

2. unless

3. before

4. since

5. if

6. whenever

PART II   CHALLENGES FOR WRITERS

CONVENTIONS AND CONJUNCTIONS

Part of the process of student writers becoming more confident and fluent stylists is their own experimentation with combining sentences of various sorts and the errors they may make as a result. Because integrating two sentences by converting one sentence into an adverb clause and combining two sentences with a conjunctive adverb (*therefore, however, moreover,* etc.) are strategies that writers use quite often, it is common for apprentice writers to have difficulty with these structures. Although we will be discussing fragmented adverbials and punctuation problems related to adverbials later in the chapter, we wish to begin by providing an overview of the types of difficulties inexperienced writers may encounter when using subordinating conjunctions or conjunctive adverbs to join sentences. Sometimes students use punctuation inappropriately when crafting sentences that contain these conjunctions, and sometimes students have problems using these connecting words appropriately to reflect an appropriate, logical relationship between two clauses or sentences.

Punctuation Issues

As we have suggested, apprentice writers may encounter difficulty with punctuation when they write sentences with adverb clauses or when they create compound sentences with conjunctive adverbs. Sometimes this difficulty can arise from the assumption that punctuation conventions always convey what is "reasonable" or what "makes sense," despite the fact that this may not be the case. Consider the options for combining the following sentences:

Uncombined	Combined
I studied hard. I passed the exam.	I studied hard, *and* I passed the exam,
I studied hard. I passed the exam.	I studied hard; *therefore*, I passed the exam.
I studied hard. I passed the exam.	*Because* I studied hard, I passed the exam.

As you might imagine, it's hard to explain reasons for the differences among the punctuation conventions required by the different types of conjunctions other than "those are the rules." For example, there's really nothing "logical" about the fact that conjunctive adverbs require semicolons, depending on their placement in the sentence, whereas coordinating conjunctions do not. For example, the sentence *I studied hard, and I passed the exam* is grammatical with or without the comma, whereas the sentences *I studied hard therefore I passed the exam* and *I studied hard, therefore I passed the exam* are incorrectly punctuated. The first would be considered a fused or run-on sentence; the second would be considered a comma splice.

Now let's examine the same sentences both when they are combined and when they are left uncombined but with the connecting words (italicized) still in place:

Combined	Uncombined
I studied hard, *and* I passed the exam.	I studied hard. *And* I passed the exam.
I studied hard; *therefore*, I passed the exam.	I studied hard. *Therefore*, I passed the exam.
Because I studied hard, I passed the exam.	*Because* I studied hard. I passed the exam.

As these examples suggest, both coordinating conjunctions (e.g., *and*) and conjunctive adverbs (e.g., *therefore*) can begin an independent clause, but subordinating conjunctions (e.g., *because*) cannot. For this reason, it is acceptable to punctuate *And I passed the exam* and *Therefore, I passed the exam* as sentences, whereas it is not acceptable to punctuate *Because I studied hard* as a sentence. If *Because I studied hard* were punctuated as a sentence, it would be considered a sentence fragment.

What makes this situation confusing and perhaps seem a bit arbitrary is the fact that fragments are often defined as being "incomplete thoughts, " as structures that "can't stand alone" or that are "dependent on another sentence for their meaning." Although these common definitions may be somewhat helpful, it's hard to see much difference among the structures *And I passed the exam* or *Therefore, I passed the exam* or *Because I studied hard* in terms of which ones do or do not express complete thoughts. How can one argue persuasively, for example, that *Because I studied hard* relies on another structure for its meaning while *And I passed the exam* or *Therefore, I passed the exam* do not? Clearly it is impossible to fully interpret what *Therefore, I passed the exam* means on its own. The point here is that what differentiates structures such as *And I passed the exam* or *Therefore, I passed the exam* from structures such as *Because I studied hard* is not something inherent in their meaning (whether or not that meaning expresses a complete idea or thought). Rather, what differentiates these structures is *how the conjunctions in them function*: subordinating conjunctions create dependent clauses; conjunctive adverbs and coordinating conjunctions do not.

As the examples illustrate, then, students who don't understand the function of subordinating conjunctions or conjunctive adverbs may produce serious errors in punctuation such as comma splices and sentence fragments. They may also make errors involving inappropriate comma use. For example, students who are not confident in recognizing and writing adverb clauses may have difficulty punctuating these structures appropriately when they are moved to the front of a sentence. In addition to punctuation problems that may derive from a misunderstanding of how various conjunctions function, difficulties may arise as a consequence of apprentice writers' unfamiliarity with the mobility of conjunctive adverbs. As we will explain later in this section, many inexperienced writers do not understand the various options for placement or the appropriate punctuation of conjunctive adverbs.

Conveying Logical Relationships

Properly punctuating complex sentences with adverb clauses and compound sentences joined with conjunctive adverbs isn't the only challenge inexperienced writers face when crafting these structures. Besides creating grammatical and appropriately punctuated sentences, students also need to use connecting words effectively to convey the logical relationships between their thoughts to their readers. Part of the difficulty with using connective words and expressions effectively, however, is that conjunctions can be classified in one way according to their function and punctuation conventions and classified in another way based on the meaning relationships they convey. Examine the following short lists of conjunctions:

CLASSIFIED ON THE BASIS OF FUNCTION/PUNCTUATION CONVENTIONS

Coordinating Conjunctions	Conjunctive Adverbs	Subordinating Conjunctions
and	however	although
but	therefore	because
yet	also	if
so	in addition	whenever

CLASSIFIED ON THE BASIS OF MEANING RELATIONSHIPS

Adversative	Cause and Effect	Additive
but	so	and
however	because	in addition
although	therefore	also

As the lists suggest, from the perspective of function, the words *and* and *but* can be grouped together. They are both coordinating conjunctions. They function in a similar manner (to create a compound sentence from two or more independent clauses), and they require the same punctuation conventions (to be preceded by a comma). However, when considering the logical relationship *and* and *but* create between the sentences they join, they do not reside in the same group. From this perspective, *but* is more reasonably grouped with *however* and *although* because all three create an adversative relationship (one that is contrary to expectation):

> I hate spinach, *but* I ate quite a lot of it at dinner last night.
>
> I hate spinach; *however,* I ate quite a lot of it at dinner last night.
>
> *Although* I hate spinach, I ate quite a lot of it at dinner last night.

Perhaps because connecting words can be grouped in one way according to their grammatical function and another way according to the logical relationships they convey, or perhaps because apprentice writers don't get sufficient experience in reading and making note of the types of logical relationships connecting words can create, problems in using connecting words and expressions effectively occur quite frequently in student writing. Sometimes students—particularly those whose first language isn't English—overgeneralize the connective *for example* and use it where it is inappropriate, as in the following example:

> Many Americans don't like negative campaigning; *for example,* some citizens have vowed to cast their votes against the first politician who launches negative television ads.

The second sentence doesn't really serve as an example of the first; conjunctive adverbs or adverbials such as *moreover* or *in fact* would be more appropriate:

> Many Americans don't like negative campaigning; *moreover,* some citizens have vowed to cast their votes against the first politician who launches negative television ads.

> Many Americans don't like negative campaigning; *in fact,* some citizens have vowed to cast their votes against the first politician who launches negative television ads.

Besides overgeneralizing with the expression *for example,* inexperienced writers can omit important connective words or expressions, especially those that make adversative or cause-and-effect relationships explicit. It is rare for apprentice writers to omit such connectives in a single sentence that consists of two combined clauses (e.g., *Although I love Grateful Dead recordings, due to my finances I didn't buy any*). Therefore, it is unlikely that either of the following sentences would appear in student writing:

1. I love Grateful Dead recordings; I didn't buy any.

2. The traffic on the freeway was backed up for miles; we were late for our appointment on Wednesday.

However, when inexperienced writers don't combine clauses that express adversative or cause-and-effect relationships into one sentence—when the relationship must span two sentences—it is not unusual for them to omit a helpful or even necessary connecting word or expression:

3. I love Grateful Dead recordings. I didn't buy any.

4. The traffic on the freeway was backed up for miles. We were late for our appointment on Wednesday.

Within the context of an essay, sentences as in examples 3 and 4 can create difficulties, perhaps even incoherence, for a reader because the nature of the relationship between them isn't made clear. In either case, the problem has probably arisen because the writer perceives a *mental* connection between the sentences, whether adversative or cause-and-effect, that she hasn't made explicit for her audience.

As with many matters related to writing, to become more fluent in using connecting words and expressions to create precise relationships, students need to be exposed to a variety of texts that illustrate the use of conjunctive adverbs and subordinating conjunctions in various ways to create different logical relationships. As students examine passages containing such conjunctions, they need to articulate the differences in the logical relationships they perceive, particularly when those differences are subtle.

To gain practice in using conjunctions properly, students can be invited to use related conjunctions that create subtle differences to join sets of sentences and then to explain the differences conveyed by each relationship. Following the creation of compound and complex sentences that evidence different kinds of logical relationships, students can be given passages of writing with inappropriate and omitted conjunctions to edit. If you require help in explaining logical relationships to students or in constructing exercises of the sort we've described, Chapter 5 of Halliday and Hasan's *Cohesion in English* is a readable source that clearly explains and classifies the various logical relationships that connecting words and expressions in English convey.

FRAGMENTED ADVERBIALS

As we have explained, adverbials are widely used, highly movable structures, and so their very flexibility increases the chances that apprentice writers may use them inappropriately from time to time. We have also suggested that one of the problems student writers encounter with adverbials is that they may punctuate them improperly for various reasons. Probably the most serious error inexperienced writers commit with respect to adverbials is to punctuate them as if they were sentences; this practice is especially common with respect to adverb clauses.

Adverb Clause Fragments

Perhaps the most common type of inappropriate sentence fragment that apprentice writers produce is the fragmented adverb clause. Although this structure can appear in the writing of fifth- or sixth-grade students, it is also a "favorite" of first-year college writers who are still having difficulty with the conventions of written English. There are probably several explanations for the rather widespread occurrence of this type of sentence fragment in student writing. One reason that prompts inexperienced writers to punctuate adverb clauses as if they were sentences is that these structures resemble complete sentences because they contain subjects and verbs. Or to put it another way, as we explained in Part One of this chapter, an adverb clause may look like, or take the *form* of, a sentence, but it *functions* as a modifier, which is part of a sentence rather than a sentence itself:

Sentence with adverb clause: I left the party after I ate dinner.

Form: *After* <u>I ate dinner</u>. [resembles a sentence]
            subject verb object

Function: I left the party *after* <u>I ate dinner</u>.
            modifier (tells *when*)

Another reason that students produce adverb clause fragments in their writing is that they are approximating patterns of oral discourse that they commonly hear. In speech, adverb clause fragments often stand alone both in statements and, particularly, as answers to questions, as the following examples illustrate.

1. That's what I'm planning to do. *If I get my chores finished.*

2. You know, I'm only going to do that one time. *When I get there.*

3. Why did you leave work early? *Because I got really sick.*

4. When are you going to the party? *After I finish the dishes.*

5. Are you going to the picnic? *If I get my homework done.*

Just as students may be accustomed to hearing fragments in informal spoken contexts in which they are acceptable, students may also encounter sentence fragments in some genres of written discourse where they are appropriate—for example, magazine or newspaper ads—and this familiarity also increases the probability that students will use these structures in their writing.

Fragmented Phrasal Adverbials

Besides punctuating adverb clauses as sentences, student writers can and do make similar errors with phrasal adverbials, although not as frequently. Like other adverbials, phrasal adverbials are movable, and that can cause inexperienced writers to lose track of their function as modifiers and to punctuate them as if they were sentences:

> <u>To motivate his students to do homework.</u> John assigns extra credit points.
> fragment
>
> <u>With your foot in the stirrup and your body properly positioned.</u> You are
> fragment
>   ready to boost yourself into the saddle.

Also, because a phrasal adverbial can often express a particular meaning—especially causality—that is quite similar to the meaning expressed by an adverb clause, students who punctuate adverb clauses as if they were sentences may do so with some phrasal adverbials. Notice the parallels between the fragmented clausal and phrasal adverbials in the following examples:

1. <u>To motivate his students to do homework.</u> John assigns extra credit points.
   fragmented phrase

2. <u>Because he wants to motivate his students to do homework.</u> John assigns
   fragmented clause
   extra credit points.

3. <u>With your foot in the stirrup and your body properly positioned.</u> You are
   fragmented phrase
   ready to boost yourself into the saddle.

4. <u>After you have placed your foot in the stirrup and positioned your body properly.</u>
fragmented clause

   You are ready to boost yourself into the saddle.

We cannot, of course, predict absolutely that student writers who would tend to produce the clause fragments depicted in examples 2 and 4 would also fragment the phrases that parallel these in examples 1 and 3. However, because the structures are such close paraphrases, students may have difficulty with both.

Finally, as with adverb clauses, in informal speech it is not unusual to encounter phrasal adverbials uttered by themselves:

1. That's what we're going to do next weekend. *With the kids.*

2. Where are you going after work? *To Grounds for Thought for some coffee.*

3. Where did you find those mushrooms? *At that new supermarket in Perrysburg.*

As these examples suggest, the fact that we frequently isolate phrasal adverbials in casual conversation may cause some inexperienced writers to punctuate such structures as if they were sentences.

Fixing Adverbial Fragments

As with any problem that apprentice writers might experience, the best way to help students eradicate that problem is to help them recognize a pattern. Such an approach involves helping students recognize visual cues that might point to a particular problem as well as helping them understand the underlying cause or "logic" that prompts its production. Students who frequently produce inappropriate fragmented adverb clauses should be encouraged to consult a list of words that commonly function as subordinating conjunctions (*although, because, if, before, after,* etc.) as they proofread their writing and to mark structures that they think may be adverb clauses. Students who fragment phrasal adverbials should make a list of the words that head such fragments (e.g., *with, because*) and use this list during their proofreading. Each suspicious-looking structure should be examined carefully to determine whether it is a modifying clause or phrase punctuated as a sentence. Structures that are determined to be fragmented modifiers should be reworded or attached to the sentence that precedes or follows it:

Fragment: Once you have positioned your horse properly and have the reins in your hands, the next step is to climb aboard! <u>With your foot in the stirrup and your body properly positioned.</u> You are ready to boost yourself into the saddle.

Corrected: Once you have positioned your horse properly and have the reins in your hands, the next step is to climb aboard! <u>With your foot in the stirrup and your body properly positioned,</u>

you are ready to boost yourself into the saddle. [corrected by attaching to another sentence]

Corrected: Once you have positioned your horse properly and have the reins in your hands, the next step is to climb aboard! <u>First, place your foot in the stirrup, and position your body properly.</u> Now you are ready to boost yourself into the saddle. [corrected by rewording the fragment to make it an independent clause]

Because identifying and rewriting fragments are separate skills, each of which can be difficult for inexperienced students to master, apprentice writers need assistance with and practice in doing both. To help students build competence in identifying adverbial fragments, they should be assisted in understanding the reasons behind the particular fragments that they write (e.g., the fragment resembles a sentence) and the markers of such fragments (words such as *although, because,* etc.). They should be assigned exercises that require them to identify such fragments, first in individual groups of sentences and then in short passages (e.g., paragraphs, brief essays). Students can also be assigned—both individually and in groups— essays that contain fragments for them to find and identify. Once students begin to acquire the skill of successfully identifying adverbial fragments, they need explanations regarding these structures and practice in revising them. It can often be instructive for a class (or for a group of writers) that is having difficulty with fragmented adverbials to examine a number of these structures, devise several options for rewriting them, and then discuss the relative merits of each revision. In such discussions, students can discover or develop for themselves the criteria for such comparisons, which might include things like how well the resultant sentence fits (or "flows") with the sentences that precede and follow it, how accurately the revised sentence conveys the meaning the writer intends, or the extent to which the revised sentence does or does not add sentence variety to the text.

PUNCTUATION WITH ADVERBIALS

As we have noted several times, students often find punctuating structures that involve adverbials to be a particular challenge. Because, for example, they are not familiar with the structures of clauses and how to use them, they often punctuate them in ways that cause confusion in meaning or that result in fused sentences, comma splices, and fragments. Besides avoiding adverb clause fragments, the most challenging aspects of working with adverbials usually involve the appropriate use of commas after an introductory adverb clause (e.g., *Because I had forgotten my house key, I had to call a locksmith*), the correct use of commas with movable subordinating conjunctions (e.g., *However, he forgot to bring his equipment* versus *He forgot to bring his equipment, however*), and the appropriate use of semicolons with movable subordinating conjunctions.

Commas After Introductory Adverbial Clauses

Introductory adverbial clauses can cause problems for novice writers in two different ways. First, novice writers may confuse the rules for comma use with respect to adverbial clauses that follow the verb phrase as opposed to those that precede the verb phrase or introduce a sentence. Adverb clauses that precede a main clause are ordinarily separated by a comma. Examine these two sentences:

We went to the zoo *because the children wanted to.*

Because the children wanted to, we went to the zoo.

In the first sentence, there is no comma before the adverb clause *because the children wanted to* because it follows the verb phrase of the main clause. In the second sentence, because the adverb clause is used at the beginning of the sentence, a comma separates it from the rest of the sentence. When students are confused about how to punctuate sentences that contain adverb clauses, they may produce sentences such as these in which the comma following an introductory adverb clause is omitted:

*When we left Colorado we cried all day

*Because the children wanted to we went to the zoo.

In these sentences, the writer has not set off the introductory adverb clause with a comma.

To help students punctuate adverb clauses properly, they should become familiar with the basic structural patterns of adverb clauses within sentences. It is also important for them to practice using adverb clauses in a variety of sentences and in various positions. One possibility is to have students rewrite simpler sentences in passages that contain a range of adverbial information (cause, condition, contrast) yet are disconnected from their larger context. Finally, we suggest practice in editing sentences with inappropriately used commas in clauses. Having the students bring their handbooks with them to refer to during such editing activities can be quite useful in helping them associate various structures with the rules that apply to them.

Punctuation and Conjunctive Adverbs

A second problem for novice writers is using commas with movable conjunctive adverbs (*however, consequently, therefore, moreover,* etc.). Conjunctive adverbs not only conjoin sentences but are also movable. That is, they can be placed in various positions within a sentence. It is these two qualities that usually cause confusion for writers when punctuating sentences that contain conjunctive adverbs. Even though writers may recognize that each structure contains two independent clauses, they may nevertheless not understand the conventions of punctuation or may confuse the punctuation of conjunctive adverbs with that of coordinating conjunctions. The common result of this lack of understanding or confusion is fused sentences and comma splices such as these:

*Jessica didn't hear the announcement *however* Mary Jo did.

*Mary Ann likes potatoes *therefore,* she cooks them every night.

Errors such as these may also indicate that the writer is unaware of—or lacks confidence in deploying—the options available in moving conjunctive adverbs. Another possibility is that writers may not recognize when conjunctions mark a sentence boundary. In learning how to use conjunctive adverbs to the fullest, therefore, students need to be aware of the difference among the following sentences:

1. I started to open the door. *However,* I had locked myself out of my apartment.

2. I started to open the door; *however,* I had locked myself out of my apartment.

3. I started to open the door; I had, *however,* locked myself out of my apartment.

4. I started to open the door; I had locked myself out of my apartment, *however.*

Sentence 1 is punctuated as two distinct sentences, with *however* providing the relationship between them. In this instance, it can be clear that they are two distinct sentences and punctuated accordingly. But *however* is a movable part of an independent clause and therefore presents options to the writer. When the writer begins to move *however* (or any conjunctive adverb), she may become confused as to the application of learned rules, or the movability may compound any existing confusion the writer has concerning punctuation. The resulting confusion may result in sentences such as these:

1. *I started to open the door. I had locked myself; *however,* out of my apartment.

2. *I started to open the door *however* I had locked myself out of my apartment.

3. *I started to open the door, *however;* I had locked myself out of my apartment.

4. *I started to open the door; I had locked myself *however* out of my apartment.

Confusion between using a movable conjunctive adverb in the middle of a complete clause or sentence (e.g., *I had, however, locked myself out of my apartment*) and using it to join two clauses or sentences (e.g., *I started to open the door; however, I had locked myself out of my apartment*) may lead students to the misuse or nonuse of semicolons.

To help students overcome such confusion and to punctuate conjunctive adverbs appropriately, we suggest having students punctuate unpunctuated sentences after having marked off the sentence boundaries in each sentence. More specifically, we suggest having them add semicolons only; then, as a next step, adding semicolons with conjunctive adverbs; and finally, having them practice moving conjunctive adverbs to various positions using either commas or semicolons (whichever is appropriate according to the context of the sentence). We also suggest having students break combined sentences down into individual sentences and combine sentences using conjunctive adverbs in various positions.

For students to gain comfort and fluency in writing, teachers should employ a range of strategies. Completing drill and practice exercises alone is unlikely to permit students to master these concepts. Rather, such exercises must be used in conjunction with more context-rich strategies, including the analysis of both literary and popular texts and, of course, the work of the students themselves. Students are often good at recognizing structures in rhetorical models, including sample papers and passages from semesters past, but they are less able to recognize or replicate various structures in their own work. As a result, it is vital to provide students with multiple opportunities to both test and apply their knowledge to their own work and the work of their peers. Ultimately, a combination of demonstration and analysis of adverbial forms and function through sentence-based exercises is a good start, along with identification of elements in specific writing contexts both inside and outside the classroom, and finally, application and replication in students' own writing.

EXERCISES FOR PRACTICE

A. Some of the following sentences contain errors in the use of compound or subordinate structures. Identify the problem sentences, underline the errors, and then revise the sentences to correct the problems.

> **Example:**   I want to buy a new fall wardrobe, however, I'm short on funds right now.
>
> *Corrected:*   I want to buy a new fall wardrobe; however, I'm short on funds right now.

1. Although Bettina won the lottery, she won't see her money for several years.

2. Because Bettina is not satisfied with the waiting period. She will be contacting the Better Business Bureau.

3. I really am not too interested in what happens to people when they win the lottery, I do; however, think it's important for lotteries to be run honestly.

4. My husband is of the opinion that lotteries are a waste of money, moreover, he thinks that people should be putting money in savings, not trying to get rich quick.

5. Still, since the idea of extra money for a larger house, a better car, or a vacation can be tempting. Many folks do spend a few dollars now and then on lottery tickets.

6. College is becoming a real obstacle for many people, in fact few individuals can afford to attend without taking out massive loans.

7. For people who are considering college but who have insufficient funds, winning the lottery could be a dream come true.

8. Travel is also something that many people dream about but can't afford, so it's easy to understand why someone who imagines a trip to Italy might buy a lottery ticket at the local grocery store.

9. Once or twice, when the lottery has been worth millions of dollars. My husband has bought a ticket.

10. However, when he buys a lottery ticket. He doesn't tell me. Because he knows that I'll tease him about it!

B. Combine each of the following pairs of sentences into one sentence in two different ways. First use a subordinating conjunction to create a new sentence; then use a conjunctive adverb to create a new sentence. In some instances you may need to modify resulting (combined) sentences slightly.

> **Example:**   I was feeling ambitious last night. I cooked a gourmet dinner for myself and my husband.
>
> *Combined with subordinating conjunction:* Because I was feeling ambitious last night, I cooked a gourmet dinner for myself and my husband.
>
> *Combined with conjunctive adverb:* I was feeling ambitious last night; therefore, I cooked a gourmet dinner for myself and my husband.

1. Josh graduated with a degree in computer science last May. He moved to Chicago.

2. Dennis was promoted to executive vice president in charge of marketing. He and his wife bought a summer home in Tuscany.

3. I talked to Sheila for several hours on the phone last night. I felt reassured that she was feeling all right.

4. Many people can't tell much different between the two candidates in this election. They will choose not to vote.

5. You will be going to Columbus for lunch and a movie on Saturday. I'll join you at the bookstore.

6. There are two fully stocked bookstores in Toledo. Sometimes I have difficulty deciding which one I like better.

7. We took Sheba to the vet last month for her shots. She is now protected against rabies and other doggie diseases.

8. Woody gets poked and prodded at the veterinarian. He loves the attention everyone gives him there.

9. Woody is a large, confident animal who weighs eighty-six pounds. He is lovable and friendly toward all animals and people.

C. Connect each pair of sentences using a conjunctive adverb to form a single meaningful sentence. Be sure it is punctuated properly.

> **Example:**   Students like to take extended breaks at Thanksgiving. Many classrooms are only half full the Tuesday before the holiday.
>
> Students like to take extended breaks at Thanksgiving; consequently, many classrooms are only half full the Tuesday before the holiday.

1. The sky was clear blue this morning. Now it looks like rain.

2. My cousin won the lottery last year. He has quit his job and moved to Las Vegas.

3. The United States had not been engaged in a war for many years. Many young men and women joined the armed services every year.

4. This is the age of technology. Most people who can afford them own computers.

5. Damon has never learned to read a map. He often finds himself lost and having to ask for directions.

6. The autumn months in the Midwest often have the bluest skies and the mildest weather. They are the most colorful months because of all the leaves that are turning.

7. My dad could never balance a checkbook. He never bounced a check.

8. The pie is not yet done. It's been in the oven for more than an hour.

9. My sister fell in love at first sight. She got married after a very short engagement.

10. Estranged from her family, she had not spoken to her cousin in several years. She recognized his voice immediately on the phone.

D. Read the following paragraph for omitted or inappropriately used conjunctive adverbs. Fix the paragraph by inserting conjunctive adverbs where necessary or changing the ones that have been used inappropriately. When choosing possible conjunctive adverbs, pay close attention to style and meaning.

The day was cold and blustery. Because the sky was clear, we wore no coats and left our hats and mittens at home. However, we got very cold on our walk and had to put our hands in our pockets and keep our heads ducked against the wind to stay warm. We were happy to see a warm fire in the fireplace and hot chocolate on the counter when we returned home as a result. We have learned our lesson, though we'll always check the temperature instead of the sky in the future.

E. In the following examples, find and fix the fragmented adverb clauses. In some cases, revising may include eliminating words and adding punctuation.

    Example: Although he didn't study. Shawn passed the exam.
                    Although he didn't study, Shawn passed the exam.

1. Carol could improve her skills. If she would listen to her older sister's advice.

2. Because she was tired. That's why Kyoko left the party early.

3. They will devote their full attention to the matter. When they get through with the first agenda item.

4. Ken is a great multimedia designer. Although he needs more programming experience.

5. Unless you work harder. You will not succeed.

6. Things don't seem the same anymore. Since you went away.

7. After the class is over. We'll be able to relax.

8. Sonya went ice skating. While Kevin went bowling.

9. Don't forget to phone home. In case you forget something.

10. I went to the baseball game. Even though I'm not a Cubs fan.

F. In the following sentences, find and fix any problems with punctuation. (Not all sentences will require changes.)

    Example: When I retire I'll be so happy.
                    When I retire, I'll be so happy.

    Example: Odile loves chocolate, however she didn't eat much.
                    Odile loves chocolate; however, she didn't eat much.

1. When Scott comes to town we'll be sure to go to the hockey game.

2. Stan loves to cook, however, he never follows the recipe.

3. The dog was quite old; nevertheless he could still chase cars.

4. Even though she hadn't eaten in two days Sheba refused to eat her cat food.

5. The artist was deeply depressed therefore he went to law school.

6. Because of their rising medical bills Tony and Annette must sell their home.

7. No one could lift the boxes Debbie had packed; no one therefore was able to help her move.

8. Bill Gates has been a household name since the early 1980s.

9. June had passed the exam effortlessly, she received the top score moreover.

10. The amateur golfer is not yet ready for the pros. Despite his growing reputation.

G. In the following paragraph, find and fix any fragmented adverb clauses by creating complete sentences.

> Joe is never able to get much sleep. Because he drinks caffeinated colas too late in the day. This makes him cranky and irritable. Whenever he has an early-morning meeting. If he would only switch to caffeine-free cola. He would be much easier to live with. Whether he is at work or at home.

EXERCISES FOR CLASSROOM APPLICATION

A. Select one of the problems discussed in Part Two of this chapter (e.g., adverb clause fragments), and find an explanation of this problem in a handbook or textbook targeted to the student audience you anticipate teaching. Evaluate this explanation. Specifically address the following issues:

Is the explanation sufficiently detailed?

Does the explanation provide enough illustrative examples?

Does the explanation engage the student in appropriate and sufficient exercises or activities so that an understanding of the problem and how to fix it will transfer to his or her writing?

After you have analyzed the explanation, explain how you would expand, amplify, and improve on it.

B. Select another problem discussed in this section (e.g., punctuation with conjunctive adverbs), and describe an activity that would help students avoid this problem in their own writing. Fully develop at least one sample exercise that would be part of this activity to share with your classmates.

C. Based on the problem you selected in Exercise B, find an explanation of this same problem in a handbook or textbook targeted to a student audience you anticipate teaching. Evaluate this explanation for its level of detail, examples, or level of engagement in sufficient activities that will actually transfer to student writing. Explain how you would improve on this exercise or activity.

PART III   STYLE, CHOICE, AND CONVENTION

USING ADVERBIALS

In this chapter we have looked at three types of adverbials—single-word adverbs, phrases, and clauses—and discussed the use of each type in sentences. We have also discussed specific problems novice writers are likely to have when using adverbials. In the course of our discussion, we have suggested that adverbials are perhaps the most flexible of the parts of speech, in that many of them are movable and can be used to provide a wide variety of information in a sentence. Adverbials can also be fun for writers because they can be used for stylistic purposes to provide sentence variety and to emphasize certain parts of the sentence. For example, the following sentences all contain the same words, but the adverbial of frequency, *sometimes,* can be moved in each one in order to provide variety or to change the meaning of the sentence:

1. *Sometimes* I sit on the grass under the trees and think about life.

2. I *sometimes* sit on the grass under the trees and think about life.

3. I sit *sometimes* on the grass under the trees and think about life.

4. I sit on the grass under the trees *sometimes* and think about life.

5. I sit on the grass under the trees and *sometimes* think about life.

6. I sit on the grass under the trees and think *sometimes* about life.

7. I sit on the grass under the trees and think about life *sometimes.*

As you can see, depending on where it is placed in the sentence, *sometimes* can emphasize and modify different parts of the sentence. In sentence 1, the adverbial *sometimes* is located at the beginning of the sentence and modifies the entire sentence. In sentence 2, *sometimes* is placed closer to the verb phrase and subtly stresses the frequency of the action. With respect to the rest of the examples, note that as *sometimes* moves down to different locations in the sentence, it not only adds surface variety to the sentence but also emphasizes different parts of the sentence. For example, in sentence 5, the emphasis is on the frequency of thinking about life, and the reader is left to conjecture with respect to the frequency of sitting on the grass under the trees.

Moving a sentence modifier or subordinating conjunction such as *perhaps* or *consequently* to various parts of a sentence can also change the tone of the sentence according to the information the writer wishes to convey. Compare these four sentences, for example:

1. *Perhaps* the floodwaters will spare Toledo.

2. The floodwaters, *perhaps*, will spare Toledo.

3. The floodwaters will *perhaps* spare Toledo.

4. The floodwaters will spare Toledo, *perhaps*.

In sentence 1, the hope expressed by *perhaps* is straightforwardly expressed by its placement at the beginning of the sentence. However, this emphasis is subtly diminished as the adverbial is moved closer to the end of the sentence. Adverb clauses, too, provide different emphasis according to where they are placed in the sentence. Compare the effect of these sentences:

1. *After John closed the door on the unwelcome guests,* he breathed a sigh of relief.

2. John, *after he closed the door on the unwelcome guests,* breathed a sigh of relief.

3. John breathed a sigh of relief *after he closed the door on the unwelcome guests*.

As with sentence modifiers, placing the adverb clause between the subject and the verb phrase makes it seem as if it is a spoken aside to the reader or obviously optional information. By selecting to place the various types of movable adverbials in different positions in a sentence, a writer can both provide variety and convey messages to readers about the importance of the information.

Writers who are learning the rules of punctuation and how to take control of a sentence may be very familiar with the movability of adverbials but lack the control and understanding of language necessary to use adverbials for creative variety. Therefore, it is important that these writers have opportunities to see how adverbials are used differently in various formats (novels, textbooks, newspapers) in order to make a connection between how other writers use adverbials and the options that are open to them as writers. They must then have the opportunity to "play" and experiment with placing adverbials in different locations in sentences and testing out the effects created by their placement. Adverbials are the writer's friend, and like any friendship, they require time and experience to know each other's potential well.

STYLISTIC FRAGMENTS: ADVERB CLAUSES

As we have explained earlier, some dialects of English are more prestigious than others. Moreover, students are often presented with a double standard in their writing with regard to sentence fragments: While they are often told that the occasional fragment may be considered rhetorically effective in professional models, they themselves are often admonished never to use such fragments because such structures are not only grammatical errors but also reflect poorly on the people who use them. Yet even in what is often referred to as standard English, fragments will naturally occur in speech and in writing, particularly with adverb clauses, for example:

> MARK: *Why did you leave so early?*
>
> SHERI: *Because I was feeling sick.*

Note that Sheri's response, "Because I was feeling sick," is an adverb clause fragment and in the context of the dialogue makes complete sense to the other participant, Mark, and to most readers of the dialogue as well. What this example should also show is that despite the common cautions against using fragments in written discourse, there are numerous contexts and exceptions to this "rule." When writing in more informal contexts or with more personal audiences, it is common to find stylistic fragments in letters, journals, dialogues, e-mail messages, and responses to questions. And yes, even in more formal writing contexts, the use of an adverb clause fragment is occasionally effective for emphasizing a point. Particularly in passages in which a writer may employ series of longer complex sentences, the use of a fragment may help give a sense of closure, drama, and cadence, as here:

> When Joe asked to borrow the family car after wrecking the previous three, his mother scowled and said, "*When hell freezes over.*"

Again, this particular example suggests that fragments are entirely appropriate in fiction or dialogue. But even in other contexts, it is possible to find intentional fragments:

> Karen has made the best of a bad situation. Although she would never have left home if she knew then what she knows now.

In this passage, the writer has chosen to punctuate the adverb clause *Although she would never have left home if she knew then what she knows now* separately for emphasis. Writers may deliberately choose to employ adverb clause fragments because of their natural role in providing relevant explanation, rationale, and establishing general causal and temporal relationships. What makes a fragment more or less acceptable is influenced by factors such as its logical placement, the context in which it is used, and the judgment of the reader as to its effectiveness.

Given that in some contexts fragments can be bad and, as we are suggesting here, in some contexts fragments might be permissible, what's a preservice language arts teacher to do? In encouraging students to experiment with the use of stylistic fragments, we hope to overcome the pejorative association with the word *fragment.* Similarly, in their article "Formal Fragments: English Minor Sentences," Charles Kline and Dean Memering encourage language and linguistic specialists to abandon their association of fragments with error and abandon the term *fragment* in favor of *minor sentence,* a fragment that "expresses a complete idea" or "completes a previously stated idea" (108).

A common practice to help students distinguish their use of fragments is simply to have them underline or bracket the intended fragment and note their reasons for using a fragment in the context of the passage. Such a strategy conforms to Kline and Memering's conclusion that fragments can and do occur in formal written English and that teachers should be more concerned about the conditions under which fragments occur and their frequency of occurrence. By having students examine their own writing with these concerns in mind, they will be able to recognize that using a "fragment" is less about breaking the rules of standard English than it is about understanding the written contexts and social conventions in which stylistic choice can lead to more effective communication.

EXERCISES FOR PRACTICE

A. Find three different types of texts (various magazines, textbooks, novels, etc.), and select a page from each. Describe the intended audience of your selections. Identify the adverbials used in each type of discourse. What kinds of adverbials did the writers use? Do the types of adverbials seem to vary according to the type of discourse? If so, in what ways?

B. Select some short printed texts or parts of longer texts, selecting as many fragments as possible. Make a list of what kinds of texts contain the most fragments, what kinds contain the least, and what accounts for the difference. For at least two of the texts in which you find fragments, explain their effectiveness, that is, why the writer chose to use fragments.

EXERCISES FOR CLASSROOM APPLICATION

A. Describe a lesson that helps students recognize and use adverbials more effectively. For example, you might describe an activity that requires students to examine adverbial use in a particular type of text (e.g., popular magazines or fiction) and then re-create an example of that discourse. Create in detail at least one of the activities or exercises that would be part of this lesson.

B. Assume that you have a student who wants to write effective fragments but uses fragments ineffectively. Explain in detail a strategy that would help give the student control over the use of fragments in his or her writing. How would you help the student eliminate ineffective fragments while helping the student learn to use fragments effectively?

CHAPTER

EIGHT

INTRODUCING ADJECTIVALS

Chapter Preview

Chapter 8 explains how to recognize adjectivals in sentences.

In **Part I** you will learn about

- Adjective phrases, including participial phrases and prepositional phrases
- Adjective clauses, including restrictive versus nonrestrictive clauses, relative pronoun form, and form versus function
- General principles in adjectival modification, particularly as they pertain to single-word adjectives, phrases, clauses, and pronouns

In **Part II** you will learn about the challenges writers can face with

- Form, in particular, comparative and superlative, past participial phrases
- Misplaced modifiers
- Dangling modifiers
- Fragmented adjectival modifiers

In **Part III** you will learn about

- Using adjectivals for purpose
- Selecting and moving adjectivals for variation
- Stylistic fragments

- Usage issues with respect to relative clauses, including decisions writers must make regarding the use of *which*, *who*, or *that* and *who* versus *whom*
- Ambiguous, awkward sentences

_____

PART I   FORMS OF ADJECTIVALS

REVIEW OF SINGLE-WORD ADJECTIVES

In Chapter 3 we described adjectives as words that modify nouns. We also explained that most often when people think of the term *adjective*, they think of single words such as *beautiful*, *ugly*, or *happy*, which are considered adjectives in form. The most common adjectives are indeed single words that are placed before a noun to modify it (e.g., *Edie made some delicious bread*) or after a linking verb as a subject complement (e.g., *That bread was delicious*). As we discussed, we can recognize single-word adjectives by their location in the sentence (before a noun or after a linking verb) and sometimes also by their word form. That is, many single-word adjectives are derived from nouns or verbs and have endings that readily identify them as adjectives, such as *-ful* (e.g., *beauty, beautiful; help, helpful; respect, respectful*), *-y* (e.g., *salt, salty; fault, faulty*), *-en* (e.g., *wood, wooden*), and *-ive* (e.g., *reflex, reflexive, construct, constructive*). However, most common adjectives are not derived from nouns or verbs but are individual words whose meaning is descriptive: *ugly, happy, pretty, nice, mean*, and so forth.

Comparative and Superlative

Earlier in the book we suggested that another way to recognize single-word adjectives is that they can take endings that indicate comparison. The resulting forms are referred to as the *comparative* (comparing two things) and the *superlative* (comparing three or more). As you may recall, the comparative and superlative can be formed by adding the suffixes *-er* and *-est*, respectively, to most one- or two-syllable adjectives (e.g., *nicer, nicest; prettier, prettiest*). Comparatives and superlatives can also be formed by using the words *more* or *most* before adjectives with three or more syllables (and a few shorter ones), as in *more beautiful, most beautiful; more advantageous, most advantageous*.

A final group of single-word adjectives derive from other forms, such as those based on the past and present participles (e.g., *aggravated, aggravating; excited, exciting*). In addition, words that look like adverbs (e.g., *the upstairs bathroom, the outside window*) and nouns (e.g., *window frame, education alliance, family planning*) can function as adjectives. Because single-word forms that aren't, strictly speaking, adjectives, as well as groups of words, can function as adjectives, we refer to all words or word groups that modify nouns as *adjectivals*.

Past and present participles as adjectivals are distinguishable from other
forms used as adjectivals in that they can take the comparative and superlative.
As you can see from the following examples, however, in each instance the comparative and superlative is indicated by *more* or *most*, rather than the endings *-er*
and *-est*.

1. The *more experienced* applicant got the job.

2. The *more revealing dress* costs twice as much as this one.

3. The *most excited* child in the group jumped up and down and started singing.

4. The *most rewarding* experience for Alice was teaching her son to read.

5. Everyone was *more interested* in the gossip column than in the headlines.

6. The Democratic candidate is the *more exciting* of the two.

7. The police were the *most surprised* of anyone by the thief's revelations.

8. Beth is the *most charming* sister of the four.

As we have indicated, past and present participles can be made comparative
or superlative. However, adverbs and nouns that function as adjectivals usually
cannot be, as the following examples show:

1. *Kevin closed the *more upstairs* window before the storm came.

2. *Alice took the *most down* escalator.

3. *A *more foot* doctor is called a podiatrist.

4. *The *most grammar* teacher is a friendly person.

The Position of Adjectivals

As we have mentioned, another distinguishing feature of single-word adjectives
is that they normally precede the noun. For example, we can say *The popular
teacher dismissed the class early* but not *The teacher popular dismissed the class early*
(although we do discuss variations in word order for stylistic effect in Part Three
of this chapter). This particularly distinguishes single-word adjectivals from
phrases and clauses that function as adjectivals, which usually follow the nouns
they modify. For example, we can say *The man running down the street is on fire*
but not *The running down the street man is on fire*. (We discuss phrases and clauses as adjectivals in the subsequent sections of this chapter.)

Adjectives in a Series

A final distinction regarding single-word adjectivals is that they can be written in a series preceding the noun they modify (e.g., *the colorful Easter egg; the
big, bad, ugly, old wolf; the wooden soup bowl*). In English, there is no limit to
the number of adjectivals one can put in a series, but there are some general

rules about the order of the adjectivals when they appear in a series. As you can see in the sentence

> The <u>beautiful</u> but <u>decrepit big round old brown Italian marble coffee</u> table was sold at auction

there is generally a specified order to the placement of adjectivals in a series according to the information they provide. In this sentence, the adjectivals are placed by opinion (*beautiful*), condition (*decrepit*), size (*big*), shape (*round*), age (*old*), color (*brown*), nationality (*Italian*), material (*marble*), and noun qualifier (*coffee*) before the head noun, *table*.

ADJECTIVE PHRASES

Participles

In addition to single-word present and past participles (*tiring, tired*), participles can also appear with modifiers to form participial phrases, one of the most common types of adjective phrases. Although participles and participial phrases take the form of verbs, they are in fact adjectivals that modify nouns in sentences. In the sentence

> *Exhausting all of her resources,* Jenny worried about paying her bills.

the participial phrase *Exhausting all of her resources* modifies the noun subject of the sentence, *Jenny,* providing additional information about Jenny in ways that complete the meaning of the sentence. The actual verb in the sentence is *worried.* Participial phrases can also follow the noun, as in the sentence

> Jenny, *exhausted by the workload,* resigned from her job.

In this example, the participial phrase *exhausted by the workload* also modifies the subject of the sentence, *Jenny,* but is placed for stylistic reasons between the noun and the verb.

There are several things to notice about such examples. First, the participles in participial phrases can be in either the present (*-ing*) or the past (*-ed*) form. The examples in the following lists indicate the forms (present or past) these forms can take:

<u>Present Participles</u>	<u>Past Participles</u>
exhausting	exhausted
tiring	tired
shrinking	shrunk
kissing	kissed
injuring	injured

driving	driven
seeing	seen
singing	sung
freezing	frozen

As you can see from the lists, present participles are regular verb forms that always end in -*ing* and are usually easy to recognize. Past participles, however, do not always take a common -*ed* ending; they sometimes take irregular forms in which a vowel or ending changes (e.g., *shrink, shrunk; see, seen; drive, driven; freeze, frozen*). The following sentences demonstrate present and past participial phrases in various contexts:

Present Participial Phrase

1. *Kissing his mother goodbye,* Seth boarded the train. [Phrase modifies the subject, *Seth.*]

2. Kelly, *driving very cautiously,* avoided an accident on the ice-slick highway. [Phrase modifies the subject, *Kelly.*]

3. The hikers sought shelter, *freezing from the unexpected storm.* [Phrase modifies the subject, *hikers.*]

Past Participial Phrase

4. *Kissed by the sun,* the flowers grew beautifully. [Phrase modifies the subject, *flowers.*]

5. David, *driven crazy by the sounds of the city,* returned to the country. [Phrase modifies the subject, *David.*]

6. Shelter helped warm the hikers, *frozen from the unexpected storm.* [Phrase modifies the subject, *hikers.*]

Another important aspect to notice about participial phrases is their mobility. As we shall explain in the upcoming sections on misplaced and dangling modifiers, it is important to construct sentences in which adjective phrases are located clearly, close to the noun they are intended to modify. However, an advantage of participial phrases is their ability to move around within a sentence and not necessarily detract from the original adjectival function of the phrase:

1. Sonia, *working hard to make ends meet,* took a second job.

2. *Working hard to make ends meet,* Sonia took a second job.

3. Sonia took a second job, *working hard to make ends meet.*

Gerunds and Present Participles

As we explained in Chapter 3, a gerund looks like a verb plus *-ing*, can be modified (as part of a gerund phrase), and functions as a noun:

1. *Walking* is enjoyable. (gerund)

2. *Walking three miles a day* is great exercise. (gerund phrase)

Problems can occur in distinguishing between present participles and gerunds because of their similar *-ing* form. Yet by focusing on the function of the phrase, the distinction between gerunds and present participles becomes clearer:

 1. <u>*Singing*</u> *in the rain* makes me happy. (gerund phrase)

 2. <u>*Singing*</u> *in the rain,* I lost my voice. (present participial phrase)

In sentence 1, the gerund phrase *Singing in the rain* functions as a noun phrase and is the subject of the sentence (*What makes me happy? Singing in the rain*). In sentence 2, *Singing in the rain* functions as an adjectival phrase modifying the subject of the sentence, *I*. In Chapter 3 we explained that one reliable way to identify gerunds or gerund phrases is to substitute the word *it* for the gerund or gerund phrase in question, as in the following example:

> *Talking nonstop* is a bad quality.
>
> *It* is a bad quality. (*It* equals *talking nonstop.*)

If you substitute *it* for a present participial phrase, however, your sentence becomes ungrammatical:

> *Talking nonstop,* Kris told her terrifying story.
>
> **It,* Kris told her terrifying story.

As you can see, the "*it* test" is useful in distinguishing between gerunds and present participles and underscores the importance of determining the function of a form in a sentence.

Prepositional Phrases as Adjectives

As you recall, a prepositional phrase consists of a preposition and a noun or noun phrase, all functioning as a single unit:

1. The woman *in the green uniform* maintained order.

2. We always take a drive *on Sundays.*

As these two sentences indicate, an important thing to note about prepositional phrases is that they can function as either adjectivals or as adverbials. That is, prepositional phrases can modify nouns or verbs. For instance, in sentence 1, the prepositional phrase *in the green uniform* functions as an adjectival in that it modifies the noun, *woman,* which serves as the subject of the sentence. In sentence 2, the prepositional phrase *on Sundays* functions as an adverbial in that it modifies the verb phrase *take a drive* and indicates *when* we like to take a drive.

Distinguishing between prepositional phrases that function as adjectivals and those that function as adverbials can be done through two means. First, if a prepositional phrase can be moved within a sentence, it is likely to be an adverbial. If we return to our example, *We always take a drive on Sundays,* it is possible to recast the sentence so that the prepositional phrase *on Sundays* is at the beginning: *On Sundays we always take a drive.* Again, in this particular example, *on Sundays* functions as an adverbial and indicates *when* the drives are taken. Moving prepositional phrases that function as adjectivals, however, is less possible simply because these structures are linked to the nouns or pronouns they modify. Indeed, in reviewing the first example, *The woman in the green uniform maintained order,* moving the prepositional phrase produces an ungrammatical or illogical sentence, as these examples show:

*In the green uniform, the woman maintained order.

*The woman maintained order *in the green uniform.*

A second way to distinguish between prepositional phrases that function as adjectivals and those that function as adverbials is to substitute a pronoun for the noun and its modifying prepositional phrase. If the substitution makes sense and is grammatical, then the prepositional phrase is most likely an adjectival:

1. *The woman in the green uniform* maintained order.
   She (the woman in the green uniform) maintained order.

2. I wrote *a book about computers.*
   I wrote *it* (a book about computers).

Prepositional phrases show a range of relationships between words in a sentence, indicating space, place or direction, manner, time, or cause. Prepositional phrases that function as adverbials often indicate *where* and *when* relationships in sentences. However, prepositional phrases that function as adjectivals frequently identify qualities or indicate states of being regarding the nouns they modify. They make the nouns they modify more specific:

1. The flowers *on the table* looked beautiful. (*Which* flowers? The flowers *on the table.*)

2. The trees *with the red leaves* are Japanese maples. (*Which* trees are Japanese maples? The trees *with the red leaves.*)

In these sentences, the prepositional phrases specify which flowers or trees are being described.

ADJECTIVE CLAUSES

The Structure of Adjective Clauses

Although phrases and clauses are groups of words that function together as a unit, a clause must, by definition, contain a subject and a verb. In addition, there are two types of clauses: independent and dependent. An adjective clause is a dependent clause. That is, even though it contains a subject and a verb, it cannot stand alone as a sentence because it functions just like an adjective does—as a modifier in a sentence. Adjective clauses can be recognized, then, by their function as noun modifiers. Also, since adjective clauses modify nouns, their placement (usually immediately after the noun they modify) can help you identify them.

Another important means of identifying an adjective clause is by its structure: an adjective clause *always* contains a subject and a verb and *often* contains a word that signifies the beginning of the clause, called a *relative pronoun—who, whom, that, which,* and *whose*. Because adjective clauses begin with *relative pronouns,* they are commonly called *relative clauses.* Throughout our discussion we will use the terms *adjective clause* and *relative clause* interchangeably, although we prefer the term *adjective clause* because it stresses the function of the structure rather than its form. Here are some examples of adjective (relative) clauses in sentences, with the relative pronoun, subject, and verb identified:

1. The man *who won the lottery* was overcome with joy.
   relative pronoun   verb
      (subject)

2. The teacher *whom we all love* retired last week.
      relative   subject   verb
      pronoun

3. I love the old house *that the Jones family restored*.
         relative   subject   verb
         pronoun

4. The new building, *which is bright red*, is an eyesore.
      relative pronoun verb
         (subject)

5. The woman *whose keys we misplaced* was not amused.
      relative   subject   verb
      pronoun

Note that in our description of the parts of an adjective clause, we said that adjective clauses *always* contain subjects and verbs and that they *often* begin with relative pronouns. We described the structure of adjective clauses in this way because there are instances when adjective clauses don't begin with a relative pronoun. Sometimes this happens because users of English have the option to omit the relative pronoun under specific circumstances—and they exercise this option. Consider the following sentences:

1. The movie *that I saw* was really violent.
2. The movie *I saw* was really violent.
3. The man *whom I married* is a wonderful father.
4. The man *I married* is a wonderful father.
5. The book *that has the red cover* is missing.
6. *The book *has the red cover* is missing.

As you can see, the adjective clauses in sentences 2 and 4 don't begin with relative pronouns because these pronouns have been omitted. This is a commonly used variant, which is somewhat less formal than the complete version of the clause (sentences 1 and 3). We included sentence 6 to illustrate the fact that relative pronouns can be omitted only under specific circumstances (e.g., when the relative pronoun is the direct object of the clause). Due to their unconscious knowledge of English structure, native speakers know when it's permissible to reduce the adjective phrase by omitting the relative pronoun. However, the appropriate use of relative pronouns can be a problem area for nonnative speakers.

Although relative pronouns are the most common words that begin adjective clauses, sometimes other words called *relative adverbs—where, when, why—* can occur at the beginning of adjective clauses. Here are some examples of adjective clauses that begin with relative adverbs:

1. Bill found his money at the place *where he lost* it.
    relative adverb   subject   verb
2. Lakeesha studies at a time *when it suits* her.
    relative adverb subject verb
3. You gave me a good reason *why you are* always tired.
    relative adverb subject verb

Note that although the adjective clauses in examples 1, 2, and 3 begin with relative adverbs, they still modify nouns. For example, in sentence 1, the adjective clause describes the noun *place: Which place? (The place) where he lost it.* Often relative adverbs can be omitted and still produce grammatical sentences.

Restrictive Versus Nonrestrictive Adjective Clauses
In our experience, adjective (relative) clauses can be conceptually difficult for a number of reasons, one of which has to do with how they are punctuated when used in written texts. Sometimes relative clauses require punctuation with commas and sometimes they do not, as the following sentences show:

1. The students, *who were getting angrier by the minute,* started shouting slogans the moment the Provost appeared.
2. The students *who didn't purchase their tickets early* weren't able to attend the concert.

There is a relatively straightforward rule that dictates when relative clauses must be set off with commas, but for a writer to follow the rule, he or she must know the context that determines the difference between *restrictive* and *non-restrictive* modification.

Sometimes adjective modification functions solely to provide more information or detail about a noun or nominal. In each of the following sentences, the adjectivals merely provide more information about the nouns they modify; the information being conveyed would be clear even if the modifiers were omitted:

1. My *sweet, gentle* cat is a favorite with our neighbors. [It's nice to know that kitty is *sweet* and *gentle,* but if you omit both words, it's still clear which cat is a favorite with the neighbors.]

2. I have a *terrible, pounding* headache. [How many headaches can a person have at the same time? Only one! *Terrible* and *pounding* offer more information about the nature of the headache, but they're not necessary to identify which headache I have.]

3. For lunch, I ate a *huge* sandwich *with mustard and lettuce.* [OK, the sandwich was *huge,* and it had *mustard* and *lettuce,* but omitting those details wouldn't change the point that I ate a sandwich.]

Modifiers used in this way are *optional.* They do not change the identity of the noun they modify; they merely add detail.

Sometimes, however, adjective modifiers provide information that is essential to the meaning of the noun they modify, restricting or limiting a group of possible referents to the exact item or items the noun represents. (Appositives can also serve this same purpose.) Notice how adjective modifiers in the following sentences limit or restrict the referent, given the context of the sentence.

1. The *neighbor's big, black* dog scared me. [Any of the many dogs in the world could have scared me. So I must give more information to make my statement clear. Which dog scared me? The one that is big and black and belongs to my neighbor.]

2. The teachers *on the second floor* had a party for their students. [There are lots of teachers in the school, but all of them didn't have a party. Only the teachers *on the second floor* had the party.]

3. My son *who has a degree in computer science* moved to Chicago. [I have three sons, so which one am I talking about? The one *who has a degree in computer science.*]

Modifiers that serve to limit or restrict the referent of a noun or nominal are not optional; they are *essential* to the meaning of those words. Adjectives that serve this purpose are called ***restrictive*** modifiers; the others—the optional ones that add information but don't limit the meaning—are called ***nonrestrictive*** modifiers.

So as we have seen, adjective (relative) clauses, like other adjectives, can be either restrictive or nonrestrictive, depending on whether or not they are necessary to limit what the noun or nominal they modify stands for. Unlike most other kinds of adjective modifiers, however, relative clauses require punctuation to indicate whether they are restrictive or nonrestrictive: *nonrestrictive relative clauses require commas* to set them off from the rest of the sentence; *restrictive relative clauses do <u>not</u> require commas.*

> **Nonrestrictive:**   Mrs. Luna, *who had that beautiful garden on Broad Street,* moved to Boston.

[The referent for *Mrs. Luna* is clear—*Mrs. Luna* is a proper noun referring to one particular person. Therefore, *who had that beautiful garden on Broad Street* doesn't provide information that is necessary to restrict or limit the identity of *Mrs. Luna* to distinguish her from other possible referents.]

> **Restrictive:**   The woman who had that beautiful garden on Broad Street moved to Boston.

[Chances are good that more than one woman lived on Broad Street. Which one moved to Boston? The woman with the beautiful garden.]

> **Restrictive:**   Students *who have poor study skills* tend to drop out of school.

[Do all students tend to drop out of school? Of course not. The relative clause *who have poor study skills* provides information that limits or restricts the referent for the word *students* to only those students *who have poor study skills.*]

> **Nonrestrictive:**   Straight-A students, *who have excellent study skills,* tend to graduate with honors.

[The information about these students' study skills is not essential to understanding that *Straight-A students tend to graduate with honors;* it merely provides some supporting detail. The relative clause is therefore nonrestrictive, and so commas set it off.]

> **Restrictive:**   Straight-A students *who have excellent study skills* tend to graduate with honors.

[Notice that the removal of the commas around the relative clause changes the entire point of the sentence. Now it is not *all* straight-A students who graduate with honors but only those *who have excellent study skills.* In this case, the modifier is essential to the meaning of the sentence and so should not be set off with commas.]

Relative Pronoun Form: *Who* Versus *Whom*

Another vexing matter related to adjective (relative) clauses that contain a relative pronoun has to do with the form that the relative pronoun should take. Because adjective clauses frequently modify nouns that are persons, the relative pronoun *who* often begins these structures. Although some current handbooks suggest that the relative pronoun *that* may also be used to refer to human referents (*The man that grabbed my umbrella slipped on the wet pavement*), it makes more logical sense to use *who* in most written contexts, and certain readers therefore consider *that* inappropriate.

Unfortunately, however, unlike other relative pronouns and relative adverbs *(that, which, where, when,* etc.), *who* must sometimes change form—from *who* to *whom*—depending on its function in the clause. Determining the function of the relative pronoun in a clause takes a rather sophisticated knowledge of sentence structure on the part of the speaker or writer. Furthermore, many speakers think that *whom* can sound stuffy and overly formal, even when used properly: *Teachers whom the students like are popular.* For this reason many persons just use *who*, regardless of its function in a clause. Sometimes writers concerned about whether to use *who* or *whom* avoid the problem altogether by using the pronoun *that*, even when it refers to a human referent. As we noted, this is not a good decision since some readers may consider such usage inappropriate.

Despite the sophistication that it takes to choose the proper form of *who*, many authorities of language use feel that the proper selection of this form is important, particularly in written contexts that require semiformal to formal standard English. Following is a procedure that can help simplify the process of determining a relative pronoun's function in a clause. Once the function has been determined, the appropriate form, *who* or *whom*, can be selected.

1. Bracket the relative clause:

   a. The man [(*who, whom*) we saw at the movies] is my teacher.

   b. The child [(*who, whom*) ate too much candy] got sick.

   c. The baby [(*who, whom*) was kissed by her parents] giggled.

   d. The toddler [(*who, whom*)we fed] slept all night.

2. Replace the relative pronoun with the noun or nominal that it stands for. (Remember that the relative pronoun always stands for the noun or nominal that the relative clause modifies.)

   a. The man [*the man* we saw at the movies] is my teacher.

   b. The child [*the child* ate too much candy] got sick.

    c. The baby [*the baby* was kissed by her parents] giggled.

    d. The toddler [*the toddler* we fed] slept all night.

3. Check to see that the words in the relative clause are in the normal order for English sentences (subject-verb, subject-verb-object, subject–verb–subject complement, etc.). If the words are not in the normal order, rearrange them so that they are. (Remember that in passive sentences, the grammatical subject is not the actor; it is the person or thing that receives the action: for example, in the sentence *The baby was kissed by her parents, the baby* is the grammatical subject of the sentence, so the verb, *was kissed,* is singular and agrees with *the baby,* not with *her parents,* even though they are the actors, the ones who did the kissing.)

    a. The man [<u>we saw the man</u> at the movies] is my teacher.
          subject verb   object

    b. The child [*<u>the child</u>* ate too much *<u>candy</u>*] got sick.
          subject verb   object

    c. The baby [*<u>the baby was kissed</u>* by her parents] giggled.
          subject   verb

    d. The toddler [*<u>we fed the toddler</u>*] slept all night.
         subject verb   object

4. If the word the relative pronoun replaces is a subject, use the form *who.* If the word the relative pronoun replaces is any other sentence constituent (direct object, object of a preposition, indirect object, etc.), use *whom.*

    a. The man *whom* we saw at the movies is my teacher.

    b. The child *who* ate too much candy got sick.

    c. The baby *who* was kissed by her parents giggled.

    d. The toddler *whom* we fed slept all night.

Here are some other examples of sentences that have relative clauses containing *who* or *whom.* In each case, the function of the relative pronoun in the relative clause is indicated:

1. The woman *to <u>whom</u> we were referring* won the lottery. (direct object following the preposition *to*)

2. The friend *for <u>whom</u> we bought the roses* is recuperating nicely. (indirect object taking the form of the object of a preposition)

3. My sister, *<u>who</u> brought you fresh bread,* is from Los Angeles. (subject)

4. Oppo, *<u>who</u> was awarded a grant by the government,* left for France. (subject)

5. The office manager ordered sandwiches for the employees *who stayed late.* (subject)

A Final Word About Form Versus Function

Throughout our discussion of English grammar, we have been stressing the importance of the distinction between form and function. We have also argued that function—the *role* words or groups of words play in sentences—is more important for apprentice language users to note than form. We believe, for example, that it is more important to understand that the word *singing* is a nominal and the subject in the sentence *Singing is fun* than to focus on the fact that it resembles a verb or to focus on the term *gerund.* Similarly, in the sentence *We resumed studying Monday,* we think it's more important to note that *Monday* is modifying the verb *resumed,* rather than the fact that *Monday* looks like a noun. For this reason, as we noted earlier, although adjective clauses are commonly identified according to their form, as *relative* clauses, we feel that it is more helpful to identify them as *adjective* clauses. We believe that emphasizing the function of such clauses—to modify nouns or nominals—will help students identify and understand them more readily.

Emphasizing the function of adjective clauses does require a word of caution, however. Although most clauses that begin with relative pronouns modify nouns or nominals and can therefore be called adjective clauses, there are occasions when such clauses do not modify a particular noun or nominal. Sometimes a clause that begins with a relative pronoun can refer to an idea contained in the whole sentence of which it is a part. For example, in the sentence *Last night Laura worked on her school project for several hours, which delighted her parents,* the clause *which delighted her parents* doesn't modify a particular noun or nominal in the sentence. Rather, it seems to modify the circumstances described in the main clause of the sentence—that Laura worked on her school project for several hours. Such clauses are sometimes called *sentence modifiers* or *relative clauses with broad reference.* They are always nonrestrictive and are therefore set off with comma punctuation from the sentence they modify. They usually begin with the relative pronoun *which.*

GENERAL PRINCIPLES IN ADJECTIVAL MODIFICATION

Single-Word Adjectives, Phrases, and Clauses

As we discussed at the beginning of this chapter, single-word adjectives generally precede the nouns they modify, whereas adjective phrases and clauses generally follow the noun:

1. The *big, black* dog bit the burglar. [*Big* and *black* modify *dog,* and as single-word adjectives, they precede the noun.]

2. The policeman *at the station* apprehended the dog. [*At the station* modifies *policeman,* and as a prepositional phrase, it follows the noun.]

3. The burglar *who was bitten* cried loudly. [*Who was bitten* modifies *burglar,* and as a relative clause, it follows the noun.]

There are times, however, when phrases may be moved for stylistic purposes; for example:

1. The *tired, cranky* mother didn't want any supper.

2. The mother, *tired and cranky,* didn't want any supper.

In sentence 1, the single-word adjectives *tired* and *cranky* are combined by using a comma and precede the noun. In sentence 2, they are combined using *and* and follow the noun. In sentence 2, the condition of the *mother* is accentuated by moving the single-word adjectives to follow the noun. When moved from their "normal" positions, adjectivals are usually set off with commas.

Although prepositional phrases and relative clauses usually cannot be moved, nonrestrictive participial phrases can be moved for stylistic effect, as demonstrated in the following sentences:

1. The man, *running down the street,* yelled for help.

2. *Running down the street,* the man yelled for help.

Both of these sentences are grammatical, but moving the participial phrase to the beginning of the sentence changes the focus of the sentence. We discuss moving adjectivals for stylistic effect more fully in Part Three.

Pronouns and Adjectival Modification

As you've seen, nouns can be preceded by modifiers, particularly one-word adjectives, or they can be followed by modifiers, such as prepositional phrases, participial phrases, or adjective clauses. Generally speaking, however, when the noun phrase is replaced by a pronoun, the pronoun cannot be modified by single-word adjectives that precede it. For example, compare the following sentences:

1. *The *tall, lanky* rock star was signing autographs for her fans.

2. She was signing autographs for her fans.

3. *The *tall, lanky* she was signing autographs for her fans.

In sentence 2, the pronoun *she* replaces the entire noun phrase *the tall, lanky rock star.* However, in sentence 3, the attempt to modify the pronoun *she* results in an ungrammatical, confusing sentence.

Pronouns also cannot be modified by clauses or phrases that immediately follow them. However, there is an exception regarding sentences such as the following:

1. We *who are about to die* salute you.

2. He *who lives by the sword* dies by the sword.

3. You *who are causing this trouble* should reconsider your actions.

In these sentences, the pronoun is meant to generalize about a group of people rather than to replace a specific noun phrase. This distinction can clearly be seen by contrasting the following pair of sentences:

1. The man *who was running down the street* tripped on his shoelaces.

2. *He *who was running down the street* tripped on his shoelaces.

The attempt in sentence 2 to replace only the noun being modified and to keep the relative clause as a postmodifier results in an ungrammatical sentence. Nevertheless, as we show later in this chapter, even pronouns can be modified by nonrestrictive adjectivals when they precede a sentence, as in <u>*Standing by the road,*</u> he saw a long funeral procession.

● EXERCISES FOR PRACTICE

A. Underline the adjectivals in the following sentences, and bracket the nouns they modify. (There may be more than one adjectival in a sentence.)

Example: The <u>cranky</u> [baby] <u>in the nursery</u> whined constantly.

1. The laughing children danced enthusiastically in the sparkling rain.

2. Dottie, surprised and delighted, opened the small package as soon as it arrived in the afternoon mail.

3. The golden retriever gently grabbed the bouncing red ball between its massive jaws.

4. Many paths lead from
   The foot of the mountain,
   But at the peak
   We all gaze at the
   Same bright moon. (Ikkyu)

5. The hung jury had deliberated for three grueling weeks before deciding that they could not reach a unanimous agreement on a final verdict.

6. Yesterday's mistakes can be translated into today's joys.

7. The high-density diskette that Kris was using refused to be opened.

8. The store that was going out of business sold all of the merchandise it had in stock at reduced prices.

9. Life is either a daring adventure or nothing. (Helen Keller)

10. The absent-minded professor is sometimes a convenient but humorous stereotype.

B. The following is a passage from *The Confidence Man* by Herman Melville. Underline the adjectivals in the passage, and put brackets around the nouns they modify. This may be a challenge because of the way Melville uses inverted word order for stylistic purposes.

> The stranger was a man of more than winsome aspect. There he stood apart and in repose, and, yet, by his mere look, lured the man in gray from his story, much as, by its graciousness of bearing, some full-leaved elm, alone in a meadow, lures the noon sickleman to throw down his sheaves and come and apply for the alms of its shade.

C. Select a newspaper or magazine, and examine five advertisements in its pages. What adjectivals are commonly used by advertisers to sell products? What types of messages do you think the use of these particular adjectivals conveys to the consumer?

D. In the following sentences, underline each adjectival phrase, and put brackets around the noun it modifies.

Example: Pumping up the crowd, the [boxers] were ready to fight.

1. Smiling broadly, Karen accepted the award.

2. Devastated by the rejection letter, John vowed to try again.

3. The house on the hill is rumored to be haunted.

4. I myself am a question addressed to the world, and I must communicate my answer, for otherwise I am dependent upon the world's answer. (Carl Jung)

5. The minor-league baseball team with over-the-hill players still had an outside chance of winning its division.

6. Everyone in the department is talking about the budget to be voted on next week.

7. Carol, encouraged by the feedback, began practicing the violin more diligently.

8. The documentary about the American eagle was very interesting.

9. No one ever went broke underestimating the taste of the American public. (H. L. Mencken)

10. Jim filed a lawsuit, angered by the promotion decision.

E. In the following sentences, indicate whether the underlined phrases are participial phrases (present or past) or gerund phrases. If the phrases are participials, indicate what is being modified.

> **Example:**   Larry, <u>giving in to temptation</u>, ordered an extra-large pepperoni pizza. (present participial phrase modifying noun *Larry*)

> **Example:**   <u>Concerned about his friend's lack of willpower</u>, Gary gave Larry a lecture. (past participial phrase modifying noun *Gary*)

> **Example:**   <u>Giving in to temptation</u> was Larry's greatest pleasure. (gerund phrase functioning as the subject of the sentence)

1. The team, <u>demoralized by the defeat</u>, walked sadly off the field.

2. <u>Trusting her instincts completely</u>, Janice refused to enter the condemned building.

3. <u>Thinking</u> is more interesting than <u>knowing</u> but less interesting than <u>looking</u>. (Goethe)

4. <u>Exhausted by the week's events</u>, John failed to hear the alarm.

5. The swimmer, <u>breaking the world's record</u>, made the finish line in sixty seconds.

6. <u>Rejecting the will of the people</u> often makes politicians unpopular.

7. <u>Rejecting the outcome of the election</u>, the senator insisted on a recount.

8. Our cat Oscar, <u>drenched by the rain</u>, finally came back inside.

9. <u>Driven by the forces of love</u>, the fragments of the world seek each other so that the world may come into being. This is no metaphor, and it is much more than poetry. (Teilhard de Chardin)

10. <u>Working past retirement</u> keeps a person alive.

F. In each of the following sentences, underline each adjective clause, and put brackets around the noun it modifies.

> **Example:**   The [woman] <u>who won the Ohio lottery</u> told her children that they could not quit their jobs.

> **Example:**   I love the [park] <u>where John proposed to me</u>.

1. We talked to the man who had cleaned the aquarium because we were interested in the filter he used.

2. Who is more foolish, the child [who is] afraid of the dark or the man [who is] afraid of the light? (Maurice Freehill)

3. The reason you are the one whom we all admire is that you always go to dangerous places where most people won't travel.

4. The reason why Eddie missed the rehearsal is that he was involved in an accident that blocked all of the lanes on the highway.

5. The plants in the wetlands provide food for the fish that lay eggs in that swampy environment.

6. Nothing that is worth knowing can be taught. (Oscar Wilde)

7. The chocolate cake, which was sitting on the counter, disappeared mysteriously after the rugby team visited our new house.

8. If you try studying with that new method we learned about, you may get results that will surprise you.

9. Woody bounded into the woods that surround a nearby meadow and harassed a groundhog that was minding its own business.

10. The trees we transplanted have grown steadily since the day we put fertilizer on them.

G. In each of the following sentences, select the appropriate form of the pronoun *who* (*who* or *whom*). Use the procedure described in the chapter to determine which form is appropriate.

> **Example:**   I spoke to the person (*who, whom*) we selected as president.
>
> I spoke to the person [(*who, whom*) we selected as president].
>
> I spoke to the person [*the person* we selected as president].
>
> I spoke to the person [we selected *the person* as president].
>
> (Since *the person* is the direct object in the sentence *we selected the person as president,* the appropriate form is *whom:*)
>
> I spoke to the person *whom* we selected as president.

1. I hate the neighbor (*who, whom*) had our sweet puppy arrested by the dog patrol.

2. We all wondered about the student (*who, whom*) never seemed to study but (*who, whom*) passed every exam.

3. The new members of the Save the Wetlands club, (*who, whom*) you've all met, would like to address our class.

4. Don't you remember your Aunt Tomeka, (*who, whom*) used to baby-sit for you until you were in school?

5. The proceeds of the plant sale will benefit local seniors, (*who, whom*) have been raising funds for a new dock.

6. Ellie and Bob, (*who, whom*) we met because of their association with our son, will be taking us sailing on their boat.

7. Last weekend in Port Clinton, we ran into Oppo and her husband, (*who, whom*) were fishing on the pier with Aaron, (*who, whom*) was born last year.

8. The man for (*who, whom*) we all raised funds will be a hard candidate to defeat.

9. Driving toward Chicago, we discovered a little town in Indiana with many artists (*who, whom*) specialize in painting landscapes.

10. Kris and Kevin were particularly enthralled with one painting and wanted to know (*who, whom*) it was painted by because they thought they might want to buy it.

H. The following paragraph contains both restrictive and nonrestrictive modifiers. Provide appropriate punctuation of the modifiers according to the meaning you wish to convey in the context of the paragraph. Be prepared to defend your decisions.

Yesterday, while I was walking in the park down the street, a young couple who seemed quite hungry were panhandling near a section that is usually quite populated by families enjoying a day's outing. Everyone ignored this needy couple until discouraged and desperate they began to openly beg. Then I was surprised by what I saw: Families who were enjoying picnics began to ask the children to take food to the couple. As the couple sat on a bench with tears in their eyes receiving the food, they began to sing an old gospel tune of thanks. Soon, many families who at first had been distant began to contribute to the needy couple as well. By the time it all had ended, ten different families who thirty minutes earlier had been strangers were sitting all in a circle sharing food and singing.

I. Pick a fiction writer who is a favorite of yours, and select a short passage (roughly half a page long). Examine the passage carefully, and do the following:

1. Underline all adjective phrases and clauses.

2. Comment briefly on the length and types of the adjectivals in the passage. Do they tend to be short or long? Do prepositional phrase adjectivals predominate, or does the writer seem to prefer adjective clauses?

3. Comment briefly on the placement of the adjectivals in the passage. Are many of them moved from their "normal" placement? If so, where has the writer moved them? To the front of the sentence? Elsewhere? Explain why you think the writer selected that placement.

4. Using the information in steps 1–3, write a passage that mimics your author's style in terms of adjective modification. Write a passage at least as long as the one you have examined.

J. In each of the following sentences, underline each prepositional phrase, and indicate whether it is functioning as an adverbial or as a noun modifier (adjectival).

> **Example:**   The man chewing gum <u>in the corner</u> choked. (adverbial; tells where the man is chewing gum)

> **Example:**   The man <u>across the street</u> gave me these flowers to plant. (adjectival modifying *the man;* tells which man)

1. The children standing on the corner waiting for the bus got splashed by mud.

2. All of the cows in the barn must be moved to the pasture before the area can be cleaned.

3. I will not descend among professors and capitalists—I will turn the ends of my trousers around my boots, and my cuffs back from my wrists, and go with drivers and boatmen and men that catch fish or work in the fields. (Walt Whitman)

4. My friend Mary from Pittsburgh found a wonderful dress that really flatters her.

5. All of the people waiting in line to buy tickets groaned loudly when it was announced that the concert had been sold out.

6. The limits of my language are the limits of my thought. (Benjamin Whorf)

7. America is a large friendly dog in a small room. Every time it wags its tail, it knocks over a chair. (Arnold Toynbee)

8. When the mail carrier in his truck stopped to put mail in the mailbox, the dog sitting by the stairs began to bark.

9. The young couple in the photograph are my parents when they were first married.

10. Janet liked the music playing on the radio, so she called up the radio station to find out who the performer was.

PART II   CHALLENGES FOR WRITERS

PROBLEMS WITH FORM

Comparative and Superlative

In Part One you were introduced to various ways to recognize and use adjectivals in a sentence. As we stated, one feature of adjectivals, particularly adjectives and participles, is that they can be used in the comparative and superlative—*tighter, tightest; more interesting, most interesting,* and so on. Because there are two methods for creating comparatives and superlatives—some words take *-er* and *-est* while other words use *more* and *most*—novice writers may get confused about which forms to use.

One area of possible confusion for novice writers when using comparatives and superlatives is the spelling of a word when *-er* or *-est* is added. Generally, the spelling of these words follows the rules for the spelling of plurals or the spelling of past tense forms (change final *y* to *i* and add *-er* or *-est,* etc). One way to help students is by familiarizing them with the basic spelling rules and then giving them ample opportunity for practice, as we explained in "Problems with Verb Inflections" in Part Two of Chapter 4.

Another problem for novice writers may be deciding which words take *-er* and *-est* and which words require *more* and *most.* This confusion may result in combinations such as *more great* (rather than *greater*) or *magnificentest* (rather than *most magnificent*). Once again, one approach to helping students choose the appropriate form is to familiarize them with the basic rules governing the use of *-er, -est, more,* and *most* and then give them opportunities for applying the rules, such as editing sentences that contain errors in form.

It is also important to give students opportunities to work with combinations that may take either form (such as some two-syllable adjectives) in order to develop enough awareness to make stylistic choices. To that end, students can examine writing in different genres (e.g., fairy tales, magazine ads, recipes, laboratory reports) to see if one alternative prevails over the other and to speculate as to the rhetorical effects of that alternative. If students have difficulty assessing the effects of a particular alternative, you can ask them to replace that form with the other option and to read both alternatives aloud. Here's how this might work: Say, for example, that in examining a fairy tale or children's story students notice that the *-er* alternative (*uglier* rather than *more ugly*) is the preferred option. Under these circumstances, they should select a brief passage that contains a comparative or superlative, copy the passage over, substituting the other variant of the adjective, and then read both passages aloud:

Original: Each time Mendel made a mean comment about Benjy's smile, it got fainter and fainter—until it disappeared altogether.

Alternative: Each time Mendel made a mean comment about Benjy's smile, it got more and more faint—until it disappeared altogether.

As your students read both variants, they may need prompts from you to consider important matters such as the audience being addressed, the purpose of the writing, or the context in which the writing occurs. With respect to genres such as children's books and fairy tales, for example, you may need to ask your apprentice writers to visualize the contexts in which these genres often occur (adults reading aloud to children) so that the students can consider and compare the effects of both options on young readers.

A final problem novice writers encounter is in overgeneralizing the rules of creating comparatives and superlatives, which might result in their adding -er or -est in addition to preceding the word with *more* or *most*. Thus the writer might produce such combinations as *more prettier* or *most littlest*. You can help your students overcome this overcorrection by having them edit writing that requires them to make decisions about which form to use. In making such decisions, they will have to both apply the rules of forming comparative and superlative and make stylistic choices.

Form and Past Participles

In addition to forming comparatives and superlatives, another problem area related to the form of adjectivals that novice writers may encounter is in using past participles (verb + -ed). As we discussed in detail in Part Two of Chapter 5, it is not uncommon to see past participles used as adjectivals without the -ed ending that makes them participles (e.g., *I live in a <u>furnish</u> room*; *They sell <u>use</u> books*). In such cases, writers may be confusing their own pronunciation of these words with the written form. To help such students become familiar with the past participle form, another strategy (besides those we offered earlier) is to have students identify and distinguish between the simple form (*use*), the past participle used in a verb phrase (*have used*), and the participle used as an adjectival (*used*) in a variety of written contexts. You can also give students opportunities to use and contrast these forms in written exercises. Students can, for instance, be asked to employ all three forms in magazine ads for imaginary products of their own devising, or they can be asked to compose humorous or silly sentences that contain all three forms (e.g., *I <u>use</u> what I have always <u>used</u> and never feel <u>used</u>* or *I will further <u>furnish</u> my <u>furnished</u> apartment despite the fact that I have <u>furnished</u> it already*).

MISPLACED MODIFIERS

Despite the mobility of some adjectivals, in particular present and past participial phrases, readers usually assume that adjectives and adjectivals modify whichever noun they are closest to:

Teased by the other children, Nan worked even harder on her softball skills.

In this example, the past participial phrase *teased by the other children* modifies the noun *Nan,* and the meaning of the sentence is unambiguous. However, consider this alternative:

X   *Teased by the other children,* her softball skills were a source of embarrassment for Nan.

In this example, it appears that Nan's *softball skills* are being teased by the children rather than Nan herself. When adjective clauses and phrases, particularly particip-ial phrases, are placed next to a noun or noun phrase they are not intended to mod-ify, the modifying phrase is said to be "misplaced." Here is another example:

Walking by the fair grounds, the loud music annoyed the young couple.

Although its proximity would suggest otherwise, the present participial phrase *Walking by the fairgrounds* doesn't modify *the loud music;* it modifies *the young cou-ple.* Logic tells us that music cannot walk by fair grounds (or anywhere else!), so it is clearly the young couple who is doing the walking.

Many times sentences with misplaced modifiers can be easily revised by determining which noun (or noun phrase) in the sentence is being modified and then moving the modifying phrase or clause in closer proximity to that noun. With respect to our last example, the noun being modified can be determined by asking, "*Who* is walking by the fair grounds?" Answering this simple question by restating "The young couple is walking by the fair grounds" helps point out which noun phrase is in fact being modified: *the young couple.* Once the word or phrase being modified has been determined, the modifier is simply moved so that it follows the nominal it modifies:

The loud music annoyed the young couple *walking by the fair grounds.*

Sometimes, however, simply moving an adjective phrase or clause to its nor-mal position (immediately after the noun it modifies) does not produce desirable results. When proper nouns or pronouns are described by a misplaced modifier, the sentence cannot be revised by simply moving the modifier to follow the word it modifies, as the following examples illustrate:

Misplaced: *Walking in the evening,* the sunset pleased Laura.
          *The sunset pleased Laura *walking in the evening.*

Misplaced: *Walking in the evening,* the sunset pleased her.
          *The sunset pleased her *walking in the evening.*

Also, the "slot" immediately following a noun or noun phrase may already be filled with an adjectival; these circumstances may also prevent the simple mov-ing of a misplaced adjectival to follow the noun it modifies:

Misplaced: The man with the two children ran his car into a stop sign *arguing with his sister.*

*The man *arguing with his sister* with the two children ran his car into a stop sign.

Revising sentences with misplaced modifiers, then, may sometimes involve rearranging word order so that the resulting revised sentence makes more sense. For example, the sentence with the misplaced modifier, *Walking in the evening, the sunset pleased Laura,* can be revised by making *Laura* the subject of the main clause and reworking the predicate slightly:

Walking in the evening, Laura found the sunset pleasant.

Walking in the evening, Laura was pleased by the sunset.

As these revisions suggest, if a proper noun or pronoun being modified by a misplaced modifier is already the subject of the main clause, moving the modifier so that it precedes the sentence often does the trick:

Misplaced: We found a lost child *shopping for appliances.*

Revised: *Shopping for appliances,* we found a lost child.

Misplaced: Judy found a lost child *shopping for appliances.*

Revised: *Shopping for appliances,* Judy found a lost child.

This strategy also often works with misplaced modifiers that cannot be moved to follow the noun they describe because there is already an adjectival in that "slot":

Misplaced: The man with the two children ran his car into a stop sign *arguing with his sister.*

Revised: *Arguing with his sister,* the man with the two children ran his car into a stop sign.

DANGLING MODIFIERS

As we have just explained, word order plays an important role in indicating which word an adjectival modifies. Ordinarily, single-word adjectives and adjectivals precede the words they modify, but multiword (phrase and clause) adjectivals follow the words they modify. Of course, adjectives and adjectivals can be moved, but placement still has to conform to rules—it cannot occur haphazardly. That is, even when an adjective modifier is moved, its relationship to the noun or nominal it is modifying should remain clear.

Of course, when crafting sentences, inexperienced writers can lose track of the relationship between an adjective modifier and the noun it describes, particularly when the modifier is a lengthy phrase or clause. Moreover, when such relationships are unclear, problems within sentences can arise. Consider the following examples, each of which illustrates a problem that can result when a writer doesn't carefully attend to the relationship between an adjective modifier and the noun it modifies:

1. My friend Larry found my missing shoe *driving to work last week.*

2. *Driving to work last week,* my missing shoe was found.

As we explained in the preceding section, the sentence in example 1 contains a misplaced modifier—*driving to work last week.* Because the writer hasn't carefully attended to the fact that *driving to work last week* modifies *Larry,* a rather amusing sentence has resulted. The adjectival (*driving to work last week*) immediately follows the noun *shoe;* it therefore appears to be modifying *shoe*—which seems preposterous, since shoes can't drive cars.

Not only can writers misplace adjectival modifiers, they can—and do—lose track of an adjectival's function as a modifier altogether and place adjectivals in sentences that do not contain any noun for them to modify. Example 2 illustrates a sentence with an adjectival modifier—*driving to work last week*—that doesn't have any noun for that adjectival to modify. *Who* is driving to work? The only noun in the sentence is *shoe,* and shoes can't drive cars. A modifier in a sentence that doesn't contain any word for it to logically modify is called a *dangling modifier.* Various adjectival and adverbial structures can inadvertently be left to "dangle," but present and past participial phrases (adjectivals) are the most common offenders, appearing in sentences that have no noun for them to logically modify, as the following examples illustrate:

1. *Sipping espresso at the corner café,* the band sounded too loud.

2. *Walking by the band in our new clothes,* there are usually appreciative looks.

3. Many errors were found *examining the data.*

4. *Distressed by the local gossip,* an unfortunate course of action was chosen.

5. *Reading all of the wonderful essays submitted for consideration,* it was difficult to choose a winner.

The most common place for a dangling participle to appear is at the beginning of a sentence, especially if *it* or *there* is the subject, as in examples 2 and 5. Also, sentences that have dangling participle modifiers are frequently passive, with the agent (the performer of the action stated by the verb) omitted. Notice, for example, that the main clause in the sentence in example 3—*Many errors were found*—is passive; notice also that *whoever* found the errors (the subject of the active sentence *X found many errors*) has been omitted.

There are many ways to rewrite sentences that contain dangling modifiers, but inexperienced writers can benefit from simple, reusable revision strategies as they develop their stylistic repertoire. We present two relatively simple procedures for rewriting sentences that contain dangling participle modifiers. Students who frequently write sentences with dangling modifiers should be encouraged to try both procedures.

Lying on the beach, the sun felt hot.

Method 1: *Change the dangling modifier to an adverb clause.*
Adverb clauses begin with a subordinating conjunction (*although, because, if, since, whether,* etc.); adverb clauses contain subjects and verbs.

1. Add a subordinating conjunction:

    <u>When</u> *lying on the beach,* the sun felt hot.

2. Add a subject, and make the participle into a verb by changing its form or by adding the appropriate form of *be* (*is, am, are, was, were,* etc.):

    When <u>*I lay*</u> *on the beach,* the sun felt hot. (*lying* changed to *lay*)
    When <u>*I was lying*</u> *on the beach,* the sun felt hot. (form of *be* added)

Although this method of revising sentences with dangling modifiers is systematic and simple, it can sometimes yield awkward sentences, as example 4 illustrates.

1. *Sipping espresso at the corner café,* the band sounded too loud.

    Revised: <u>*Whenever Martha sipped*</u> *espresso at the corner café,* the band sounded too loud.

2. *Walking by the band in our new clothes,* there are usually appreciative looks.

    Revised: <u>When we walk</u> *by the band in our new clothes,* there are usually appreciative looks.

3. Many errors were found *examining the data.*

    Revised: Many errors were found <u>*when we examined*</u> *the data.*

4. *Distressed by the local gossip,* an unfortunate course of action was chosen.

    Revised: <u>*Because the committee was distressed*</u> *by the local gossip,* an unfortunate course of action was taken.

5. *Reading all of the wonderful essays submitted for consideration,* it was difficult to choose a winner.

    Revised: <u>*As we read*</u> *all of the wonderful essays submitted for consideration,* it was difficult to chose a winner.

Lying on the beach, the sun felt hot.

Method 2: *Restructure the main clause so that the grammatical subject of the sentence is also the noun being modified by the dangling structure.*

1. Ask: *Who* or *what* is lying on the beach? Make that person or thing the grammatical subject of the main clause:
Who was lying on the beach? Delilah was lying on the beach.

Lying on the beach, <u>Delilah</u> …

2. Restructure the predicate of the sentence so that it has the meaning conveyed by the original sentence:
The original sentence conveys the idea that *the sun felt hot.*

Lying on the beach, <u>Delilah felt the hot sun.</u>

The second method provides the writer with more flexibility in revising than the first method does. However, inexperienced writers may have difficulty restructuring the predicate of the revised sentence so that it conveys the idea expressed in the original sentence. Also, sentences revised using this method may require additional rewriting, as example 3 illustrates.

1. *Sipping espresso at the corner café,* the band sounded too loud.

   Revised: *Sipping espresso at the corner café,* <u>Martha thought</u> the band sounded too loud.

2. *Walking by the band in our new clothes,* there are usually appreciative looks.

   Revised: *Walking by the band in our new clothes,* <u>we</u> usually <u>attract</u> appreciative looks.

3. Many errors were found *examining the data.*

   Revised: *Examining the data,* <u>we found</u> many errors. [We reversed the order of the clauses to correct the misplaced modifier.]

4. *Distressed by the local gossip,* an unfortunate course of action was chosen.

   Revised: *Distressed by the local gossip,* <u>the committee chose</u> an unfortunate course of action.

5. *Reading all of the wonderful essays submitted for consideration,* it was difficult to choose a winner.

   Revised: *Reading all of the wonderful essays submitted for consideration,* <u>we found</u> it difficult to chose a winner.

Of course, the strategies we've explained for revising sentences with misplaced or dangling modifiers don't suggest how students who habitually write these structures can become proficient at finding them in their own writing. To assist with that long-term project, we recommend that you give your students many opportunities to recognize and become familiar with these structures. Students should be given sentence exercises to practice with and should be encouraged to find humorous examples of sentences with dangling and misplaced modifiers in newspapers and magazines and bring them to class.

Also, inexperienced writers who produce these kinds of sentences with any kind of regularity should be encouraged to do a separate reading just to locate dangling and misplaced modifiers during the process of editing their papers. Furthermore, these students can be encouraged to become "experts" at explaining these problems to their peers or editing their peers' papers for these types of modification problems. Finally, each student should be encouraged to note the structures that accompany dangling and misplaced modifiers in his or her writing so that these modification problems can be identified more easily. Do dangling participle phrase modifiers, for example, tend to occur in sentences with *it* as the subject (e.g., *Lying in bed, it was hard to get to sleep*)?

FRAGMENTED ADJECTIVAL MODIFIERS

In Chapter 7, on adverbials, we discussed a commonly occurring sentence fragment, the fragmented adverb clause. As you recall, despite the fact that adverb clauses function in the same way as single-word adverbs (as modifiers), inexperienced writers often mistake these structures for—and punctuate them as—sentences because they contain subjects and verbs. As you may imagine, adverb clause modifiers aren't the only types of modifiers that student writers mistake for sentences. When apprentice writers lose track of the relationship between nouns and their modifiers, an even more serious problem than dangling or misplaced modification can occur; in such instances, the student may punctuate adjectival modifiers as if they were sentences. Examine the following sentences; in each case, the relationship between the modifier and the noun it is supposed to modify has become more tenuous.

1. My friend found a contact lens *walking down Main Street after work.* [The writer has not attended carefully to the relationship between the modifier, *walking down Main Street after work,* and the word it's supposed to modify, *friend;* misplacement has resulted.]

2. *Walking down Main Street after work,* a contact lens was found. [The writer may not realize that *walking down Main Street* is a modifier; the sentence to which it is attached does not contain a noun that it can logically modify.]

3. *Walking down Main Street after work.* My friend found a contact lens. [The writer doesn't recognize *walking down Main Street after work* as a modifier and has punctuated the structure as a sentence.]

As these examples suggest, it is not entirely surprising when students who frequently produce misplaced and dangling adjective modifiers create fragments with these structure as well. The underlying difficulty is that inexperienced writers can easily disassociate lengthy phrase or clause modifiers from the words they modify when they attempt to move these structures. Moreover, since lengthy adjective modifiers can resemble sentences—especially when they contain "verbal"-looking participles—apprentice writers can and do punctuate these structures as if they were sentences. As we have suggested, then, one of the most common types of fragmented adjectival modifiers is the fragmented participial phrase:

1. *Annoyed by my bratty little brother and his friends.* I just couldn't stand the noise any longer.

2. *Leaving home and attending college in New York.* It was my fondest dream throughout high school.

3. Tourists can discover some of the best lakes for waterskiing. *Traveling as far off as California or Florida.*

Another adjective modifier that resembles a sentence—and may therefore be mistaken for one—is the adjective clause. Because an adjective clause usually begins with a relative pronoun or relative adverb (*who, whom, which, that, where, when,* etc.), apprentice writers usually don't punctuate these structures alone as sentences. However, once an adjective clause is attached to a noun, the combined structure—which also resembles a sentence—can be punctuated incorrectly:

1. Imagine yourself losing control of one of the five major sense organs. *The organ that helps the mind visualize a picture.* [The noun *organ*, which is modified by the adjective clause *that helps the mind visualize a picture,* is an appositive. It renames the noun *one* (*of the five major sense organs*) in the preceding clause.]

2. *The genius who developed a new software conception and who figured out a way to market it.* He is now being persecuted by a bunch of frustrated venture capitalists. [The noun *genius,* which is being modified by the adjective clause *who developed a new software conception and who figured out a way to market it,* could be the subject of the following sentence if the pronoun *he* were removed: *The genius who developed a new software conception and who figured out a way to market it is now being persecuted by a bunch of frustrated venture capitalists.*]

As these two examples illustrate, the addition of an adjective clause to modify a noun may cause an inexperienced writer to lose track of that noun's function. When this happens, the noun and the modifying adjective clause that accompanies it may be mistaken for and punctuated as a sentence.

As with any type of error, the best remedy for students who fragment participial phrases or nouns modified by adjective clauses is to become aware of each particular error pattern. Students who frequently write present participial phrase fragments, for example, should be helped to understand that *-ing* words can function as verbs, nominals, and adjectivals. These writers need practice in crafting sentences that incorporate *-ing* word phrases that function in various ways—particularly as adjectivals—and in distinguishing among the functions of different kinds of *-ing* word phrases in sentences. Such writers also need assistance in modifying their editing practices so that they learn to notice suspicious-looking *-ing* word phrases and determine how each is functioning. For example, suppose that a student often writes fragmented participial phrases that precede sentences beginning with *it* (e.g., *Standing on the corner during the festival. It was hot and sticky*). Under these circumstances, this individual should carefully scrutinize any and all *-ing* word groups punctuated as sentences that precede sentences in which the first word is *it*.

Among other activities that can help students who write fragmented adjectivals or fragmented structures that contain adjectivals are sentence-combining exercises that involve these structures. For example, students who write fragmented participial phrases can do combining exercises similar to the following:

Combine the sentences in each pair to create a longer sentence that contains the structure indicated in the examples:

Example: John was standing on the corner. John saw the new mayor and her entourage. [omit]

Standing on the corner, John saw the new mayor and her entourage.

Example: The dogs and cats were fighting over the carcass. [omit] The dogs and cats woke the whole neighborhood.

Fighting over the carcass, the dogs and cats woke the whole neighborhood.

1. The students were eating donuts and talking. The students waited in line for the library to open.

2. The teachers were administering the test. The teachers handed out papers and pencils....

Sentence-combining exercises like these give students practice embedding particular structures properly and help students become more conscious of how phrases and clauses work in sentences. Besides sentence-combining exercises, "uncombining" activities can also help apprentice writers become more aware of how embedded adjectivals (and other embedded structures) work in sentences. In such activities, students "deconstruct" a sentence into its component parts (e.g., *Lying on the floor, the children watched television and ate cookies* can be broken into *The children were lying on the floor; The children watched television;* and *The children ate cookies*).

Although exercises and activities that help students recognize and revise adjective structures—including fragments—are important, teacher intervention is also crucial. This is because students need to modify their editing practices in order to eradicate sentence structure problems, and they need help regarding the accuracy of their assessments, both in identifying problematic structures and in revising them. Besides providing help with basic editing strategies, teachers may also occasionally need to offer specialized editing assistance for students who have special needs or goals. For example, although most teachers advise students who are experiencing difficulty in writing well-formed, grammatical sentences not to attempt appropriate fragments, sometimes students who write occasional inappropriate fragments are also highly motivated to become proficient at writing stylistic fragments. As you can imagine, these students require special attention with respect to their editing processes. To assist students who wish to become skilled at writing stylistic fragments, some teachers require such writers to indicate (by underlining or circling) intentional fragments and to briefly explain in the margin of their papers what effect they intend these fragments to produce. Finally, whether you help students acquire basic or specialized editing skills, all inexperienced writers need to be regularly provided with as many passages to edit as possible because editing their own writing will not afford them sufficient practice.

EXERCISES FOR PRACTICE

A. In the following paragraph, you will find several errors in the form and use of comparatives and superlatives. Identify and correct each error.

> Alice is happyest when she is helping someone. This is most true when it comes to romance. She likes to match couples whom she thinks are most suited for one another. Sometimes the woman is more calmer than the man; sometimes the man is more calm than the woman. She always likes to invite them to dinner, where everyone has a pleasanter time than usual. Her most recentest success was matching her sister with her friend. They are now dating steadily. Who knows what the future may bring?

B. In the following paragraph, find the errors involving past participles used as adjectivals, and correct them.

> There are many ways to live cheaply. You can live in a furnish room and buy use books and clothing. You might feel aggravate sometimes because you don't have anything new or because you are tire of looking for bargains all the time, but it does pay off if you want to save money. You know what they say: a penny save is a penny earn.

C. Find and fix the misplaced modifiers in the following sentences. If a sentence doesn't contain any misplaced modifiers, explain why the sentence is acceptable as is.

> **Example:** Walking home from the store, the ice cream began to melt in the bag Jane was carrying.
>
> **Analysis:** [*Walking home from the store* is misplaced because the ice cream is not doing the walking; Jane is.]
>
> **Revision:** Walking home from the store, Jane felt the ice cream begin to melt in the bag she was carrying.

X 1. The pastor announced that Jack and Jill were getting married smiling.

2. Being the most prestigious of schools, students have made Harvard their number one choice for decades.

3. Hurting financially, the plan to raise salaries had to be abandoned by the company.

X 4. Scattered across the desk, Susan leafed through the files.

5. Succeeding in high school, college was a definite plan for Jennifer.

6. She found a dollar strolling down the sidewalk.

7. Twisting and turning in the wind, I was amazed by the kite.

8. I watched a television show peeling potatoes.

9. Gleaming from the polish, I thought the shoes looked brand new.

X 10. Finicky and temperamental, people avoid owning Siamese cats.

D. Many of the following sentences contain dangling modifiers. Find the dangling modifiers, and rewrite to correct them. Be sure to explain what the problem in the sentence is.

> **Example:** Returning from Europe, North Dakota seemed boring.
>
> **Analysis:** [*Returning from Europe* should not modify *North Dakota.*]
>
> **Revision:** Returning from Europe, Gerald seemed bored by North Dakota.

X 1. Working into the night, the assignment was completed.

X 2. Playing in the snow, her foot got broken.

X 3. The doors were locked, returning home late.

4. Giving it their best shot, the coach was impressed.

5. Hiking the same trail for years, the beauty still amazes me.

6. Disappointed by the outcome, the game was a memorable one.

7. Her words carefully chosen, everyone listened intently to Sharon's speech.

8. Applauding loudly, the singer was pleased with the enthusiastic support.

9. With her parole revoked, jail was the only option.

10. Preparing for their exams, Professor Smith warned against overstudying.

E. In the following paragraph, find and fix any misplaced or dangling modifiers.

Having walked around San Francisco all day, my shoes were killing me. Despite my pain, the city was lovely. Famous for its wide range of restaurants and shops, I especially enjoyed Chinatown. Visiting many of the city's neighborhoods, there was always a hectic but exciting aura. Intrigued and fascinated by its beauty, San Francisco will definitely be a repeat visit for me.

F. Identify three to five dangling or misplaced modifiers in outside reading materials that you find amusing, and explain what makes them funny or ambiguous. You can also make up your own examples in the event that you do not find a sufficient number in your reading materials.

G. In the following paragraph, identify the sentence fragments, and rewrite to correct them.

Running down to the water's edge. We could feel the tow of the waves. As they pulled against our legs. We held onto the rocks jutting out of the sand. To keep our balance. But rather than step backward, we stood where we were. Because we liked the feel of the water as it washed back into the sea. And then as it washed back to try to pull us under.

H. Leaf through a magazine or newspaper, looking for adjective sentence fragments in advertisements. Make a list of the ones you find, and bring the list to class. Be prepared to explain why you think fragments were used instead of complete sentences.

EXERCISES FOR CLASSROOM APPLICATION

A. Create an activity for your students that requires them to identify and correct dangling and misplaced modifiers. Although part of your exercise may involve fixing isolated sentences, part of it should also be contextualized.

B. Devise an activity for your students in which they are required to look in magazines or newspapers (or other sources) to find examples of fragments used for effect in writing.

PART III   STYLE, CHOICE, AND CONVENTION

USING ADJECTIVALS FOR A PURPOSE AND AVOIDING OVERUSE

In Part One we discussed some of the problems students can encounter when they overmodify sentences by trying to cram in too much information. Such cramming can make a sentence awkward, heavy, and hard to read. However, writing teachers do need to encourage their students to use variety in writing by teaching them how to use modification effectively. Indeed, one of the challenges in teaching writing is to help novice writers develop a sense of how to use both short, simple sentences and more elaborate, complex sentences in a variety of ways to create a specific, desired effect in the reader. That is, in language arts classes, students need to learn how to step beyond following conventions; they need strategies for making choices and for developing a sense of style in their own writing.

Many teachers attempt to direct their novice writers toward writing with more sentence variety through sentence-combining exercises. Indeed, sentence combining can be an effective technique for helping students develop their sentence-level writing beyond the limitations of the simple sentence. However, within the context of sentence combining and other style-building pedagogies, the focus for the teacher and the student can be on sentence variety or complexity for its own sake rather than on suiting such variety to a specific text or environment. That is, teaching sentence variety can stop short of teaching how to use variety effectively. Left to their own devices, students get the impression that short sentences are to be avoided and that longer sentences are the sign of mature writing. Students may begin to use figures of speech such as metaphors for their own sake, or they may provide unnecessary amplification or detail that doesn't really convey anything to the reader.

One way to help students develop confidence and skill as stylists is to present the concept of sentence variety as being relative rather than absolute. That is, as students study the ways in which sentences can be varied, they need also to examine the effects of these variations and their suitability with respect to different contexts. In particular, students can develop their awareness of their own choices as writers if they are given an opportunity to look at the writing of others.

Students who have the opportunity to read and discuss writing from a variety of sources—greeting cards, newspaper and magazine articles, fiction and nonfiction prose, and research writing—will begin to develop the skill of making the choices necessary for suiting their own writing to a particular occasion. It is important, however, that novice writers not be instructed to merely mimic a certain style but instead be guided to understanding how the writer has used that style either to reflect a particular convention or to create a specific overall effect.

As novice writers read and discuss examples of writing, they should be invited to engage in writing activities that are personally meaningful. For example, if students read J. D. Salinger's *Catcher in the Rye*, they might be asked to take the perspective of the main character, Holden Caulfield, and respond in writing to an event in their own lives from Holden's point of view, imitating his "style." Such an activity can help students see how style functions within the context of a larger work as well as how writers deploy particular structures to create stylistic effects. Following such an assignment, in which students mimic the style of a particular writer, they can assess the effectiveness of applying that style to retelling an experience of their own. To sum up, novice writers who have the opportunity to examine and experiment with different kinds of writing in a variety of contexts will become more conscious of their own choices as writers and how these choices fit their purposes for writing. They will also be able to avoid variety for variety's sake and begin to use it for stylistic effect.

SELECTING AND MOVING ADJECTIVALS FOR VARIATION

As you will recall from Chapter 7, adverb modifiers can be moved in many instances to provide sentence variety, emphasize particular information, and so forth. Many types of adjective modifiers can also be moved to create various stylistic effects. Although single-word adjective modifiers ordinarily precede the words they modify, sometimes they can be repositioned:

1. The *drunk, disorderly* crowd was ordered to leave the premises.

2. *Drunk and disorderly,* the crowd was ordered to leave the premises.

3. The crowd, *drunk and disorderly,* was ordered to leave the premises.

4. I planted the *tiny, moist* seeds in the garden.

5. I planted the seeds, *tiny and moist,* in the garden.

As these examples illustrate, there are several options for moving adjective modifiers out of their "normal" position. When single-word adjectives are moved, they can precede a sentence if the noun they modify is the subject of the sentence (example 2). They can also often be repositioned to follow the noun they modify, as in examples 3 and 5. Note that when single-word adjectives are moved out of their normal position, they are set off by commas.

Not all single-word adjectives can be moved in the same way as those in the examples, however. In general, coordinate adjectives (which we discussed in Chapter 3) can be moved, but other before-the-noun adjectives cannot be repositioned:

Coordinate Adjectives

1. The *tired, cranky* baby cried piteously.
    Tired and cranky, the baby cried piteously.

2. The *leafy, green* arbor was cool and inviting.
   The arbor, *leafy and green*, was cool and inviting.

Not Coordinate Adjectives

3. The *new brick* house thrilled everyone.

   *The house, *new and brick*, thrilled everyone.
   **New and brick*, the house thrilled everyone.

4. Our *small picket* fence blew over.

   * Our fence, *small and picket*, blew over.
   * *Small and picket*, our fence blew over.

The nature of adjectives (coordinate versus noncoordinate) is not the only thing that can affect their mobility and placement. Qualities of nouns or nominals can also exert an influence on single-word adjective modification. Proper nouns, for example, are modified somewhat differently from most other nouns. They ordinarily require nonrestrictive adjectives or adjectivals set off by commas:

1. <u>Bill</u> returned the iron, *angry and disgruntled.*

2. *Angry and disgruntled,* <u>Bill</u> returned the iron.

3. <u>Bill</u>, *angry and disgruntled,* returned the iron.

4. **Angry, disgruntled* <u>Bill</u> returned the iron.

5. <u>Bill</u> returned the iron, *complaining.*

6. *Complaining,* <u>Bill</u> returned the iron.

7. <u>Bill</u>, *complaining,* returned the iron.

8. **Complaining* <u>Bill</u> returned the iron.

Many of the restrictions regarding adjective modification that apply to proper nouns also govern the modification of pronouns, but note also that placement of the adjective modification immediately after a pronoun results in an awkward sentence:

9. He returned the iron, *angry and disgruntled.*

10. *Angry and disgruntled,* he returned the iron.

11. **He, *angry and disgruntled,* returned the iron.

12. **Angry, disgruntled* he returned the iron.

Single-word adjectivals, of course, aren't the only adjective modifiers that can be moved. Adjective phrases and clauses that modify subject nouns can also be moved to the beginning of a sentence; such adjectivals are called *fronted* modifiers.

Adjectival modifiers of more than one word can also sometimes be moved to the end of a sentence:

1. My <u>cousin</u>, *not knowing when to expect us,* kept dinner hot.
   Not knowing when to expect us, my <u>cousin</u> kept dinner hot.

2. <u>John</u>, *undermined by our criticism,* left the room.
   Undermined by our criticism, <u>John</u> left the room.

3. The <u>house</u>, *between two small hills,* looked inviting and cozy.
   Between two small hills, the <u>house</u> looked inviting and cozy.

4. <u>Kris</u>, *shopping for the best bargain,* surveyed every newspaper ad.
   <u>Kris</u> surveyed every newspaper ad, *shopping for the best bargain.*

5. The <u>toddlers</u>, *enraged by their situation,* howled angrily.
   The <u>toddlers</u> howled angrily, *enraged by their situation.*

In our brief discussion, we have suggested some of the ways in which adjectival modifiers can be moved, yet we have not explained why writers choose one stylistic alternative over another. Sometimes writers front modifiers to vary sentence structure from the normal subject-verb-object order. In other instances, writers manipulate sentences to create a contrast, emphasize a particular detail, or present images in a particular order. Consider these two sentences, for example:

1. Illuminating the stage with thousands of flashlights, the leather-clad fans in the amphitheater milled around restlessly.

2. The leather-clad fans in the amphitheater milled around restlessly, illuminating the stage with thousands of flashlights.

The first option foregrounds the scene of the action (the stage, illuminated by thousands of flashlights); the second option emphasizes the actors (leather-clad fans). Also, the first sentence presents a series of images (lights on a stage, leather-clad fans) in one order; the second sentence presents these images in a different order.

Because students are encouraged to vary the structure of their sentences to avoid monotony and repetition, they often move modifiers just to move them—without considering the appropriateness of the resulting structures or the effect of sentence order on the reader. In our judgment, then, exercises that encourage apprentice writers to change the placement of modifiers in sentences should be accompanied by other activities that invite students to discuss the appropriateness of different stylistic alternatives in various contexts. Students might, for example, discuss the two variants just shown as possible opening sentences for a short essay about a rock concert. Which one would be preferable, and under what circumstances?

Besides many opportunities to experiment with stylistic alternatives and their suitability in different contexts, students need ongoing help in understanding the role of punctuation in clarifying the role of modifying structures. This assistance will enable students to craft these structures effectively and avoid common punctuation errors associated with adjective modification. For example, students who understand the role of commas in separating a modifying structure from the rest of the sentence are less likely to set off such structures with just one comma when two are required, a common error committed by inexperienced writers. As the following illustration suggests, modifiers in sentences that are set off with just one comma can make writing difficult for a reader to process:

1. *The baby, *who wanted more apple juice* whined annoyingly.

2. *Betty and her husband *ashamed by their negligence,* apologized to Fido.

Also, when punctuation is taught in the context of how it works to clarify stylistic alternatives, students can more easily grasp—and have fun producing—closely related alternatives that create subtle nuances in meaning:

1. Joan, *having surveyed all of her alternatives,* decided to leave home.

2. Joan (*having surveyed all of her alternatives*) decided to leave home.

3. Joan—*having surveyed all of her alternatives*—decided to leave home.

In the context of such discussions, even relatively young writers can become excited about discussing the differences in these three sentences and how each punctuation approach (commas, parentheses, or dashes) contributes to those differences.

STYLISTIC FRAGMENTS: ADJECTIVE CLAUSES

Given our own discussion of the tendency for adjective clauses to become fragmented, this section on the stylistic options for fragmenting adjective clauses may seem somewhat contradictory. However, it is important to remember that there are many contexts for writing and speaking, and in some of those contexts, the use of fragmented adjective clauses may be permissible and a matter of stylistic choice.

Fragmented adjective clauses are somewhat less common in spoken and written English than fragmented adverb clauses. This is in part because so many fragmented adverb clauses, as we explained in Chapter 7, are responses to questions. Yet there are still instances in which the use of relative pronouns, particularly *who* and *which*, create fragmented statements. Because adjective clauses serve as modifiers of various nouns in the main clause, how closely connected the adjective clause is may dictate how complete the meaning of the fragment may be, as in some of the following examples:

1. Sally is a devoted jogger. *Who would rather be at the track than in the classroom.*

2. Thomas ate all of the chicken. *Which was very tasty.*

In both examples, there are some common features related to the use of adjective clause fragments that are worth noting. In sentence 1, although the position of the adjective clause *who would rather be at the track than in the classroom* is secondary, it is somewhat clear that the clause is modifying either the noun *Sally* or the subject complement *jogger,* and thus the statement communicates relevant information about Sally's status as a jogger and her devotion to it. Whether or not this particular structure functions effectively is really a matter of sentence variety and stylistic choice, for it would have been equally possible to say *Sally, who would rather be at the track than in the classroom, is a devoted jogger.* Perhaps the writer has chosen to emphasize the clause by punctuating it separately. In sentence 2, the adjective clause *which was very tasty* is clearly meant to modify the direct object *chicken.* And because of the positioning of both the noun *chicken* and the adjective clause *which was very tasty* directly after this noun, there is no ambiguity in meaning, making the fragment a more acceptable stylistic choice. As with sentence 1, however, it would be possible to recast the sentence to eliminate the fragment:

> *Thomas ate all of the chicken, which was very tasty.*

We cannot predict whether a specific English teacher would mark either of our sample fragmented sentences as errors, because, as we explained earlier, the reader ultimately determines whether or not a fragment is effective. However, for some help in determining the "effectiveness" of a fragment, you can refer to Kline and Memering's 1977 study "Formal Fragments: The English Minor Sentence." In their study of both academic and literary texts, Kline and Memering distinguish between acceptable fragments in more professional writing, which they dub "minor sentences," and unacceptable fragments, which they term "broken sentences." And what, you ask, is the difference? For Kline and Memering (and for the authors of this text), an acceptable fragment, or minor sentence, is one that clearly relates to "either the last previous or the next written unit" (109). In other words, the relative acceptability of sentence fragments in written discourse is more a matter of context and clarity than it is about adhering to absolute rules.

We are suggesting, then, that while various types of fragments occur in everyday speech, it is important for writers to consider whether fragments would be considered natural, effective, or appropriate in a particular written context before using them. For instance, as we explained in our section on adverb clauses, when writing dialogue, it is important to apply the natural speech patterns of story characters because in most instances, a dialogue will be more "authentic" if the writer honors the natural speech patterns the text is intended to represent. And not all speech patterns reflect the rules of standard English. However, dialogue is not appropriate in all written genres. In fact, some genres are highly conventional (e.g., laboratory reports) and would be inappropriate (or unlikely) places for dialogue—or sentence fragments—to turn up. As you work with your students, we encourage you to consider their skill level as well as their motivation in gaining proficiency at assessing when fragments are appropriate and when audiences will accept them. As with any unconventional structure, stylistic fragments do pose risks; readers may not consider these structures effective or appropriate. Audience members may also make negative judgments about writers "who can't write complete sentences properly." Students who wish to experiment with fragments in their writing must be willing to read a variety of genres so that they can assess the appropriateness of each fragment that they craft and be sufficiently confident as writers to accept the consequences of their choices.

USAGE ISSUES WITH RESPECT TO RELATIVE CLAUSES

Which, Who, and That

As we explained earlier, relative clauses are often introduced by relative pronouns (*who, whom, which, that*, etc.). We have also already suggested that selection of the proper pronoun can be troublesome to language users for a number of reasons. The selection of *who* or *whom*, for example, depends on the role of the pronoun in the relative clause. Two other conditions that affect the selection of relative pronouns have to do with whether or not they refer to humans and whether they head a restrictive or nonrestrictive relative clause.

Many members of the "older" generation—including English teachers—remember well the often recited rule regarding the selection of *who* or *whom* versus *that* or *which:* "*Who* is for people; *that* is for things." As presented, this time-honored rule dictated that the pronoun *who* (or *whom*) was *always* used to refer to human referents and that the pronoun *that* was *never* used to refer to human referents. However, because it is common usage for many speakers to use the pronoun *that* to refer to human referents, as in the sentence *The man that I saw won the lottery,* this variant often appears in writing. It is likely that audiences have different notions regarding the acceptability of *that* when used to refer to a person. In making students aware of this convention, then, we believe that it is important to explain that it is increasingly preferable to use the forms *who, whom,* and *whose* to refer to people as the formality of a context increases. Students should also be encouraged to consider the preferences of the audiences with whom they are communicating when they make their selection.

Regarding the choice of *which* versus *that*, the rule prescribes that the relative pronoun *that* can only be used with restrictive relative clauses; the pronoun *which*, by contrast, may be used with either **restrictive** or **nonrestrictive clauses** (although in American English, *that* is preferred for restrictive use). Since most language users do not consciously attend to—or understand—the distinction between *restrictive* and *nonrestrictive* modifiers, many are unaware of this rule and therefore don't attempt to apply it in speaking or in writing. It is our sense that because language is never static and is based on changing cultural and social values and mores, the distinction between *which* and *that* in relative clauses has become less of an issue for language arts teachers than other matters, such as sentence fragments or misplaced modifiers.

Who Versus *Whom*

Perhaps the most vexing rule regarding relative pronoun form is the one that governs the selection of *who* or *whom*. Similar to the decision as to whether *that* or *which* should be used in relative clauses, the choice of *who* or *whom* is less of a grammatical issue than it has been in the past, given changing levels of formality in both written and spoken language. Still, because more speakers of English are aware that there is a rule governing the selection of *who* versus *whom*—even if they may not know precisely what it is—people can and do perceive "error" in both speech and writing regarding these forms.

In general, language users who don't know the convention for *who* versus *whom* selection try to determine whether to use one form or the other based on how it sounds. Because *who* is more widely used than *whom* (and may therefore be more "correct-sounding"), *who* is often selected even when it is incorrect, as in the sentence *The man who we elected betrayed us.* (*Whom* is the appropriate form because the relative pronoun is the direct object in the clause.) In most spoken contexts, incorrect use of the pronoun *who* does not attract attention. In written contexts, the importance of the proper selection of *who* or *whom* depends on a number of factors, including formality. The more formal the context, the more important the distinction becomes.

Interestingly, however, even when speakers know how to appropriately select *who* or *whom*, they may elect not to use *whom* because they think it sounds too formal or stuffy. Many language users, hearing the sentence *The man whom we elected betrayed us,* would consider the use of *whom* pretentious even if it is technically correct. Similarly, the more informal option to move a preposition to the end of a relative clause is also preferred by many language users, who consider the alternative excessively formal—especially since the more formal variant can also require the use of *whom*. In the following examples, the first sentence in each pair illustrates the more informal option; the second sentence illustrates the more formal (and technically correct) option:

1. The man *who* I was talking to yesterday has left town.
   The man to *whom* I was talking yesterday has left town.

2. The infant (*who*) I baby-sat for drooled all over me.
   The infant for *whom* I baby-sat drooled all over me.

Even when a relative clause doesn't contain *who* or *whom*, many persons are reluctant to begin a relative clause with a preposition because such variants sound quite formal, especially since they do not permit the relative pronoun to be deleted:

3. The book (*that*) I was referring to was chosen for an award.
   The book to *which* I was referring was chosen for an award.

4. The ideas (*that*) we were talking about excited everyone.
   The ideas about *which* we were talking excited everyone.

Although we don't wish to suggest that there aren't any rules or conventions regarding relative pronoun selection (or the ordering of relative clauses), our point is that language users are far more confident when they understand not only a rule or convention but also the relationship between that rule or convention and the contexts in which it might be used. Under some circumstances, it may be preferable to say *The man who we were talking about* rather than *The man about whom we were talking,* despite the fact that the second option contains the correct form, *whom.* On other occasions, *The man about whom we were talking* (or perhaps *speaking*) would be the more appropriate selection.

AMBIGUOUS, AWKWARD SENTENCES

One of the most frustrating—and exciting—aspects of language study is that there is an exception to just about every rule or generalization, especially in English. In teaching language arts to students, this aspect of language can be ignored, lamented, or celebrated. Obviously, our preference is the last option—celebration. That is to say, since even the most rock-solid generalization about language structure or use can usually be contradicted by some example or situation, we feel it best to express excitement rather than despair regarding this state of affairs.

Ambiguity is a good case in point. Most writing and grammar handbooks stress the importance of communicating clearly and of avoiding ambiguous words and sentences. Earlier in this chapter, for example, we discussed two common problems that can occur with respect to adjective modification: misplaced and dangling modifiers. The inappropriate use or placement of adjective modifiers can cause a number of problems in writing, one of the more serious of which is ambiguity. Still, although ambiguity is not desirable in most contexts, it can be useful—even desirable—in some.

Poets, for example, often deliberately craft sentences that are designed to be ambiguous so that they can be interpreted in multiple ways. Consider the following sentence (from an earlier example), which contains a dangling modifier:

Lying on the beach, the sun felt hot.

Inarguably, in most written contexts, this sentence would be unacceptable; there is no noun in the sentence for the adjectival *lying on the beach* to modify. The sentence also sounds somewhat silly, since it seems to imply that the sun is lying on the beach, which is of course impossible. But what if that same sentence were the opening lines of a poem:

> Lying on the beach
> The sun felt hot.

Under these circumstances, the ambiguity regarding who or what is lying on the beach can be exploited: Is it the writer who is lying on the beach? Or perhaps the writer is so hot that it feels as if the sun is lying on the beach. Or perhaps the writer feels as if he and the sun have merged into one entity and *lying on the beach* describes them both.

Besides poetry, fiction—especially stories written for children—may also contain sentences that deliberately violate the rules that govern how sentences should be crafted in most other contexts. In these specialized contexts, sentences that would ordinarily seem ambiguous, awkward, or odd might be entirely appropriate. One of the delights of the Dr. Seuss children's books, for example, is that they abound with strange and wonderful sentences. As another example, in the context of a fantasy addressed to children, a sentence such as *We found her contact lens walking down Pennsylvania Avenue* might not be ambiguous or odd. (Imagine a story about contact lenses that become animated at night and how a group of children, which includes the writer, discover these contact lenses doing all sorts of odd things—including walking down Pennsylvania Avenue.)

Another type of writing besides fiction and poetry that frequently exploits ambiguity is advertising. Ads in magazines and newspapers can be good sources of examples of creative or unusual language use. For example, advertisements that incorporate brand names in sentences to create two or more interpretations (and thus ambiguity) are quite common.

Our point here is not that students should be encouraged to produce ambiguous, awkward sentences but rather that it is always important to examine the context in which writing occurs. In this way, even seemingly negative qualities such as awkwardness and ambiguity can be evaluated in terms of how they enhance or diminish the effect a writer intends. We also believe that if students are given the opportunity to imagine contexts in which ambiguous, odd, and even silly-sounding sentences are appropriate and to craft writing that contains these types of sentences, they will increase their facility as stylists with respect to all types of writing, including the more typical genres they are assigned to write.

EXERCISES FOR PRACTICE

A. Some of the following sentences are ambiguous; that is, they can be interpreted in two different ways. Explain the two ways in which each sentence could be understood; where appropriate, describe a context in which the more unusual meaning or image would make sense.

Example: She hit the puppy with the stick.

Meaning 1: A girl was using a stick to strike a puppy.

Meaning 2: A girl was hitting a puppy that was holding a stick in its mouth.

Context: Neither of these interpretations creates an unusual image, so no context is necessary.

Example: We fed her cat food.

Meaning 1: We fed her cat the type of food appropriate for cats.

Meaning 2: We fed her food that is ordinarily fed to cats.

Meaning 3: We fed her cat food of some undetermined type.

Context: We played a really nasty prank on her.

1. She kissed the man with the false teeth.

   Meaning 1:

   Meaning 2:

   Context:

2. The children shoved the pirate with the wooden leg.

   Meaning 1:

   Meaning 2:

   Context:

3. The nurse cuddled the puppy with the soft towel.

   Meaning 1:

   Meaning 2:

   Context:

4. The man walking the dog picked up the droppings with a leaf.

   Meaning 1:

   Meaning 2:

   Context:

5. We saw the horse with the binoculars.

   Meaning 1:

   Meaning 2:

   Context:

B. Imagine a context in which dangling or misplaced modifiers would be appropriate—for example, in a children's book. Create some sentences with dangling or misplaced modifiers and then describe a context in which they would be appropriate and explain why. You might wish to write the first few pages of a children's book or create an advertisement that illustrates the suitability of your odd but appropriate selections.

C. Go to the library and find several publications addressed to different audiences (e.g., a children's book, a health magazine, a tax guide). Select passages from each publication, and look at how the authors use modifiers and how they place them. Then comment on how the modification relates to the content and context of the passage or item. How does the modification reflect the writer's sense of readership? (You can choose advertising as well as other types of writing.)

D. Select two different writers with very different styles of writing—for example, Faulkner and Hemingway. Take a passage from each of their books, and underline the adjectivals. Then try to rewrite each passage according to the other writer's style. Put this rewritten passage back into its original context. Now explain why the passage doesn't fit. In what way does the original style fit the context of the story?

E. Find either in writing (in newspapers, magazines, novels, or other types of writing) or spoken English (e.g., from the evening news) some passages that contain relative clauses. Comment on the following:

1. The presence or absence of a relative pronoun
2. The use of *who* and *whom* or *that* to refer to a person
3. Whether the clause is restrictive or nonrestrictive

Bring these examples to class, and be prepared to discuss the contexts in which these relative clauses seem appropriate.

EXERCISES FOR CLASSROOM APPLICATION

A. Select a challenge for novice writers that we have discussed in this chapter. Create one or two possible teaching materials for your future students who might be having this problem. (This can be a group project.)

B. Find a passage in a newspaper or magazine that contains a lot of adjectivals that you feel don't seem to serve a stylistic purpose. Rewrite the passage. What if the passage had been written by your own student? What advice would you give that student?

INTRODUCING NOMINALS

Chapter Preview

Chapter 9 explains the many forms nominals take and how they function in sentences.

In **Part I** you will learn about

- Phrase nominals, especially gerund and infinitive phrases
- Clause nominals, what they look like, and what they do

In **Part II** you will learn about the challenges writers can face with

- *There is/There are* and subject-verb agreement
- Punctuation of appositives
- Fragmented nominals
- Direct versus indirect discourse

In **Part III** you will learn about

- Unusual nominal patterns and when to use them
- Nominal fragments as choices, particularly as they are used in advertising and for effect or emphasis
- When to use dialogue
- How to move appositives

PART I   OVERVIEW OF NOMINALS

As we discussed in Chapter 3, nouns can appear as single words (e.g., *book, disk*) or in phrases (e.g., *the lovely grammar book*). Although we covered the forms and functions of nouns there, we would like to begin our coverage of nominals in this chapter with a brief review of that information, especially in terms of what nouns do and what they look like. Then we will discuss phrases and clauses that function as nouns.

SINGLE-WORD NOUNS

Nouns Versus Nominals

Throughout this book, we have emphasized how difficult it is to identify or classify a word simply by its appearance. For example, it is difficult to classify the word *tomorrow* as only an adverb because this classification does not extend to the use of *tomorrow* in other contexts, such as this:

> *Tomorrow* will be a new day. [*Tomorrow* functions as a noun, the subject of the sentence.]

Because labeling words or giving them restrictive definitions (e.g., "an adverb modifies a verb," "a noun describes a person, place, or thing") can be confusing, throughout our explanations we have focused on what words do; that is, on how they function in sentences. In Chapter 3 we outlined seven functions that nouns can have in an English sentence. To refresh your memory, we repeat them here:

1. *Subject:*   *Potatoes* are delicious.

2. *Direct object:*   Alice likes *potatoes.*

3. *Indirect object:*   We gave the *potatoes* a washing.

4. *Object of a preposition:*   He was hungry for *potatoes.*

5. *Appositive:*   My favorite food, *potatoes,* wasn't on the menu.

6. *Subject complement:*   Those seeds become *potatoes.*

7. *Object complement:*   We declared our favorite food *potatoes.*

You may also recall that although words that "look like" nouns can function in other ways in sentences (e.g., in *the bank director, bank* functions as an adjective; in *we went home, home* functions as an adverb), the functions of subject, direct object, indirect object, object of a preposition, and appositive always require nouns or other words or word groups that act as nouns. And although adjectives may also be subject complements (*This tastes good*) or object complements (*They dyed the eggs purple*), nouns (or other words or word groups that act as nouns) commonly fulfill these functions. We repeat this information here because it is vital to understanding the difference between the concept of "noun" and "nominal." Unlike the word *noun,* which usually refers to a member of a category of words classified on the basis of form or meaning, the word *nominal* refers to all words, phrases, and clauses that function in the seven ways that nouns do.

To distinguish nouns from nominals, let's look at some examples of both nouns and nominals used interchangeably in a variety of functions:

Subject

1. *Candy* is delicious. [noun as subject]

2. *Dancing* is a fun form of exercise. [gerund (nominal) as subject]

3. *To dance the tango* is my goal in life. [infinitive phrase (nominal) as subject]

4. *That he likes to dance* is obvious. [noun clause (nominal) as subject]

Direct Object

5. John loves the *theater.* [noun as direct object]

6. Alice loves *dancing.* [gerund (nominal) as direct object]

7. Virginia likes *to cook lasagna.* [infinitive phrase (nominal) as direct object]

8. Kris knows *what dancing is all about.* [noun clause (nominal) as direct object]

Appositive

9. David's friend, *Jim,* is a poet. [noun as appositive]

10. Virginia's favorite activity, *napping,* requires a couch. [gerund (nominal) as appositive]

11. Kathy's ambition, *to write poetry,* has been realized. [infinitive phrase (nominal) as appositive]

12. Carol's idea *that we all go to her house for supper* is a good one. [noun clause (nominal) as appositive]

As we've discussed in earlier chapters, all the forms that can function in sentences in the ways nouns can are referred to as *nominals.* Because single-word nominals such as gerunds function in the same ways that nouns can, it is sometimes hard to distinguish between the two. We can distinguish single-word nouns from nominals by reviewing the characteristics of noun forms.

DISTINGUISHING NOUNS BY THEIR FORM. As you will recall, one characteristic of nouns is that many of them can be made plural by adding *-s,* (e.g., *book, books; tree, trees; orangutan, orangutans*). However, there is such a thing as the ***mass noun***

(e.g., *food, coffee*), which represents something that cannot be counted, and so mass nouns can't ordinarily be made plural by adding *-s* (except in contexts where they function as countable nouns, referring to individual items, as in *Bill brought three coffees on his tray*). Therefore, because pluralization isn't always a reliable way of identifying nouns, another characteristic is that they can show possession through the addition of *'s* (e.g., *Bob, Bob's; car, car's; food, food's*). Nouns can also have other typical endings, such as *-er* or *-ment* (e.g., *My teacher is kind; The dancer is beautiful; Our government is representative; Your judgment is biased*).

COMMON QUALITIES OF NOUNS.   Besides recognizing nouns by what they look like (form), we can also recognize them by five important qualities that they have in common. First, as just noted, nouns can be divided into categories according to whether they are *countable* (i.e., can be made plural, such as *one dog, two dogs*) or *noncountable* (i.e., cannot be made plural, such as **one discretion, two discretions*). Related to this concept of countability is the fact that nouns can be grouped as *concrete* (e.g., referring to tangible objects, such as *chair, school,* or *teacher*) or *abstract* (e.g., referring to ideas such as *egalitarianism, purity,* or *faith*). As we saw in Chapter 8, nouns can also be preceded by determiners and modified by adjectives, adjective phrases, and adjective clauses:

> The big black bug on your shirt, which is crawling toward your elbow, is definitely not a spider.

In this sentence, the noun *bug* is preceded by the determiner *the* and modified by *big, black* (adjectives), *on your shirt* (adjective phrase), and *which is crawling toward your elbow* (adjective clause). In addition to being modified, nouns can also be joined with other nouns to create compound nouns, such as *bed + bug = bedbug* or *shoe + box = shoebox*.

Nouns Versus Nominals: Summary

We have reviewed nouns and how to recognize them in order to distinguish ways they may differ from the concept of nominals. Generally speaking, nouns constitute a word class, while nominals are other forms (most notably gerunds, gerund phrases, infinitives, infinitive phrases, and noun clauses) that can function in the ways that nouns do. Most nominals are in the forms of phrases or clauses; however, gerunds (e.g., *dancing, kissing, hugging,* etc.) are single words that can share some characteristics that nouns have. Most notably, gerunds can be modified:

1. His incessant *fishing* caused his divorce. [*His incessant* modifies *fishing.*]

2. The phone's constant *ringing* drove me nuts. [*The phone's constant* modifies *ringing.*]

Finally, although in general only nouns or noun phrases can be replaced by a variety of pronouns (e.g., *he, she, his, hers*), both nouns and nominals can be replaced by pronouns such as *it or that:*

1. *Jim* impressed me.
   He impressed me.

2. *Her dancing* captivated me.
   It captivated me.

3. *For Jim to study* was astonishing.
   It was astonishing.
   That was astonishing.

4. *What she did* was wonderful.
   It was wonderful.
   That was wonderful.

PHRASE NOMINALS

As you have already learned, like adjectivals and adverbials, nominals can be single words, phrases, or clauses. There are three forms that phrase nominals can take: *gerund phrases, infinitive phrases,* and *prepositional phrases.* Because phrase nominals function in the same ways as nouns do, they appear often in English sentences. Here are some examples of the three types of phrase nominals (gerund phrases, infinitive phrases, and prepositional phrases) functioning in sentences in the ways nouns do:

Subject

Golf is fun. [noun]

Swimming in the ocean is fun. [gerund phrase]

To win the tournament was Bill's goal. [infinitive phrase]

Under the refrigerator is where it is dirty. [prepositional phrase] ✗ *awkward syntax*

Direct Object

I love *golf*. [noun]

We enjoyed *playing bridge* last night. [gerund phrase]

I love *to golf* at the city park. [infinitive phrase]

Indirect Object

I have given *golf* a good deal of my attention. [noun]

I have given *playing golf* a good deal of my attention. [gerund phrase]

Object of a Preposition

Yesterday we talked about *golf.* [noun]

Last week we argued about *being allowed to play golf.* [gerund phrase]

Appositive

My favorite hobby, *golf,* is quite expensive. [noun]

I benefit from John's favorite pastime, *playing classical guitar.* [gerund phrase]

My goal, *to retire in three years,* is getting closer. [infinitive phrase]

✗ My last refuge, *under the covers,* is safe and warm. [prepositional phrase]

Subject Complement

My hobby is *golf.* [noun]

My hobby is *playing golf.* [gerund phrase]

Our plan was *to leave the party early.* [infinitive phrase]

Object Complement

She considered him a great *golfer.* [noun]

They made their goal *winning the competition.* [gerund phrase]

She declared him *to be a great golfer.* [infinitive phrase]

Although these examples may give the impression that each type of phrase nominal can function in all of the various ways that nouns can, this is not the case. Prepositional phrases occasionally function as nominals, as illustrated in several of the preceding examples, but they usually function as adjectivals and adverbials. Gerund (*-ing* word) nominal phrases and infinitive (*to* + verb) nominal phrases are far more common. However, each is limited with respect to the functions it can serve in a sentence. Infinitive phrases, for example, do not ordinarily function as indirect objects, whereas gerund phrases may. For example, it is acceptable to make the phrase *playing bridge* an indirect object as in the sentence *She gave playing bridge her full attention,* but it would sound odd indeed to say *She gave to play bridge her full attention.* Because gerund and infinitive phrases are the most commonly used phrase nominal structures, let's examine them a bit more closely.

Gerund Phrases

As you will recall from discussions in Chapters 3 and 6, a gerund phrase consists of a gerund plus related words: *I love eating lobster with melted butter* or *Shane's opening the car door was quite a feat.* It is perhaps the gerund phrase's ability to be expanded in multiple ways that accounts for the fact that such phrases are quite common in English. Gerund phrases are structures that can provide a good deal of information and detail, as the following sentences illustrate:

John's singing bothered me.

John's singing in the shower bothered me.

John's singing "Achy Breaky Heart" in the shower bothered me.

John's singing "Achy Breaky Heart" in the shower at midnight bothered me.

Being indifferent bothers me.

People's being indifferent about voting bothers me.

People's being indifferent about voting for president bothers me.

As these examples show, gerund phrases can show details such as time, place, and the nature of the particular action.

Often gerund phrases contain the person or thing that is performing the action—called the *agent*—as in the sentences *John's singing was annoying* or *I was disturbed by the dog's incessant barking*. In the first sentence, *John* is the agent for the gerund *singing*. In the second sentence, *the dog* is the agent for the gerund *barking*. As these examples show, when a gerund takes an agent, the agent is often in the possessive form (*John's, the dog's*) because of the conventions of semiformal written English. Besides being considered "correct" in more formal situations, the possessive form of a gerund's agent can sometimes help distinguish subtle differences in meaning:

1. *The plumber's examining our water heater* made me feel safer. [*The plumber's examining our water heater* is a gerund phrase and the subject of the sentence; it is the *examining of our water heater* that made me feel safer.]

2. The plumber *examining our water heater* made me feel safer. [*The plumber* is the subject of the sentence; it is *the plumber* that made me feel safer. *Examining our water heater* is a participial (adjectival) phrase modifying *plumber*. Which plumber made me feel safer? The one who was *examining our water heater*.]

Besides containing agents, expanded gerund phrases may also include many of the elements commonly found in sentences. Gerund phrases may, for example, contain direct objects that receive the action conveyed by the gerund or adverbials that modify the action conveyed by the gerund. In each of the following examples, note how the gerund phrase closely resembles the sentence with which it is paired:

1. Sentence: John sang. (subject-verb)
   Gerund phrase: *John's singing* was annoying.

2. Sentence: John sang "Achy Breaky Heart." (subject-verb-object)
   Gerund phrase: *John's singing "Achy Breaky Heart"* was annoying.

3. Sentence: John sang "Achy Breaky Heart" off-key. (subject-verb-object-adverbial)
   Gerund phrase: *John's singing "Achy Breaky Heart" off-key* was annoying.

That gerund phrases can sometimes resemble sentences may be a source of difficulty for inexperienced writers, as we will explain later in this chapter.

Infinitive Phrases

The other common phrase nominal in English is the infinitive phrase. As with gerund phrases, infinitive phrases consist of an infinitive plus related words: *For Josh to leave home at sixteen* makes no sense or *My dream is to have built a retirement home in the tropics* by the time I'm sixty. And similar to gerund phrases, infinitive phrases can also convey information and details as they are expanded. Notice the range of information that the infinitive phrase in the following sentence conveys: *For Evey to have offered Josh her apartment for an indefinite stay was wonderful*. The phrase explains *who* committed the action expressed by the infinitive (*Evey*), the object of that action (*her apartment*), the indirect object of the action (*Josh*), and the duration of the action (*for an indefinite stay*). Because infinitives resemble gerunds in many ways, infinitive phrases also often contain elements that are found in sentences. Notice again how the infinitive phrases in the following examples resemble the sentences with which they are paired:

1. Sentence: Mike studies. (subject-verb)
   Infinitive phrase: *For Mike to study* is typical.

2. Sentence: Mike studies computers. (subject-verb-object)
   Infinitive phrase: *For Mike to study computers* is typical.

3. Sentence: Josh lent Mike his laptop computer. (subject–indirect object–direct object)
   Infinitive phrase: *For Josh to have lent Mike his laptop computer* was generous.

4. Sentence: Josh lent Mike his laptop computer regularly. (subject–indirect object–direct object–adverb)
   Infinitive phrase: *For Josh to have lent Mike his laptop computer regularly* was generous.

Although infinitive phrases resemble gerund phrases in many ways, they differ in some respects. For example, as the sample sentences show, agents of infinitives—such as *Josh* in the phrase *For Josh to have lent Mike his laptop computer regularly*—are preceded by the word *for* rather than taking the possessive form, as the agents of gerunds do. Many language users, when comparing similar infinitive and gerund phrases, also consider infinitive phrases to be more formal than gerund phrases. Here are two additional examples that illustrate these differences:

1. *For John to lie* was unthinkable.
   John's lying was unthinkable.

2. <u>*For*</u> *Bill to try that again* would be stupid.
   Bill'<u>s</u> trying that again would be stupid.

Other qualities of infinitives is that they are often inflected (i.e., carry tense), which can cause them to resemble verbs even more than they already do. When infinitives are inflected, they take helping or auxiliary verbs just as verbs do. And just as with verbs, when infinitives are inflected, the helping verb affects the form of the main verb form in the infinitive, as the following examples illustrate:

Infinitives That Have Been Inflected

to study	My fondest hope is <u>*to be studying*</u> *in Florence by next year.*
to complete	<u>*To have completed*</u> *my college education by May 2004* is my goal.
to see	By this time next year, my wife and I want <u>*to have seen*</u> the Grand Canyon.

Besides their ability to be inflected, infinitives can also be made passive. When infinitives are in the passive voice, they can also take additional helping or auxiliary verbs:

Infinitives That Have Been Made Passive

to examine	People want <u>*to be examined*</u> *by a competent doctor.*
to examine	<u>*To have been examined*</u> *by so many doctors* frightened Sue.
to elect	*For Bill* <u>*to have been elected*</u> *chair* shocked everyone.

Like infinitives, gerunds can be inflected or made passive (e.g., *<u>Her having been sad</u> caused us pain* or *We applauded <u>his being elected</u>*). However, such forms are less common than infinitive forms.

Finally, besides their ability to be inflected or made passive, the form of infinitive phrases can be varied in other ways. Although this doesn't happen frequently, under some circumstances the word *to* can be omitted from an infinitive, as shown in these examples:

1. Bettina did all she could for Ralph except <u>*(to) allow him to move into her apartment.*</u>

2. Finally, though, Bettina did let Ralph <u>*(to) share the apartment.*</u>

In these sentences, the structures *allow him to move into her apartment* and *share the apartment* are infinitive phrases, often referred to as "bare" infinitives.

CLAUSE NOMINALS

So far we have reviewed the form and function of single-word nouns and phrasal nominals. In Chapters 7 and 8 we discussed how clauses can function as adverbials and adjectivals. In this section we discuss how clauses can function as nouns.

What Noun Clauses Do

Noun clauses get their name from how they function rather than from how they look. That is, noun clauses function in the same ways as nouns, noun phrases, and phrase nominals do. Primarily, noun clauses function as subjects, direct objects, indirect objects, objects of the preposition, appositives, subject complements, and object complements, as the following examples show:

1. *Subject:*   *That all people are born equal* is a basic principle of the U.S. Constitution.

2. *Direct object:*   The politicians debated *how the campaign should be run.*

3. *Indirect object:*   Shirley gave her plant clippings to *whoever would take them.*

4. *Object of a preposition:* We could see their child-rearing philosophy in *how they raised their children.*

5. *Appositive:*   The idea *that he should be allowed to run for president* is ridiculous.

6. *Subject complement:*   That is *how ice is formed.*

7. *Object complement:*   I will call you *whatever I want.*

What Noun Clauses Look Like

As is evident from the examples just given, noun clauses look a lot like complete sentences. That is, because they are clauses, they contain subjects and verbs (although they cannot stand alone as sentences). Noun clauses are also identifiable because they begin with either a *wh*-word (e.g., *when, who, whom, what, why, where,* or *how*) or with the word *that*:

1. I rejected *what I didn't understand.*

2. *Where she went* is a mystery.

3. *What you want* is reasonable.

4. *That he lied* is evident.

5. Everyone decided *that I should leave.*

WH- CLAUSES.   As their name implies, *wh-* clauses begin with one of the *wh-* words we listed (and their derivatives, such as *whoever* and *whomever*) and function in the same way as nouns do, as subjects, objects, objects of prepositions, and so forth:

1. *Why he'd do that* is beyond me. (subject)

2. We explained *how the safe should be opened.* (direct object)

3. They gave *what he did* a lot of attention. (indirect object)

4. I am proud of *who I am.* (object of a preposition)

Besides beginning noun clauses, *wh-* words function *within* these clauses in various ways:

1. Alice really liked <u>*what John said.*</u> [The noun clause functions as the direct object of the sentence. *What* functions as the direct object within the noun clause.]

2. Kris was impressed by <u>*how*</u> *Kevin figured out the math problem so quickly.* [The noun clause functions as the object of the preposition *by.* *How* functions as an adverbial within the noun clause.]

3. Last October was <u>*when*</u> *they got married.* [The noun clause functions as a subject complement in the sentence. *When* functions as an adverbial within the noun clause.]

4. Susie gave <u>*whoever*</u> *wanted it* some candy. [The noun clause functions as the indirect object in the sentence. *Whoever* functions as the subject of the noun clause.]

5. <u>*Who*</u> *was going to be the next adviser* was open to debate. [The noun clause functions as the subject of the sentence. *Who* functions as the subject of the noun clause.]

6. <u>*Where*</u> *they would spend their vacation* was a topic they happily discussed. [The noun clause functions as the subject of the sentence. *Where* functions as an adverbial within the noun clause.]

To reiterate—and as you can see from the examples—the *wh-* word functions in a variety of ways in the noun clause it begins (as a subject, as an adverbial, as a direct object, as the object of a preposition, etc.).

Sometimes, because *wh-*word clauses resemble other structures, inexperienced writers may confuse these clauses for the other structures. One structure commonly confused with the *wh-*word clause is the adjective clause. However, *wh-*word noun clauses are distinguishable from adjective clauses in several ways. First, *wh-*word clauses can be recognized by their significantly different function in the sentence. That is, whereas a sentence will usually still be complete if an adjective clause is omitted, omitting a noun clause may create a fragment or substantially change the sense and function of the verb—unless the noun clause is an appositive. The following examples illustrate this difference between noun clauses and adjective clauses:

1. That's the place *where we plan to build our new house.* (adjective clause)
That's the place. [The sentence is still complete with the adjective clause omitted.]

2. I rejected *what I didn't understand.* (noun clause)
*I rejected. [The sentence is incomplete when the noun clause is omitted.]

3. I know *what you did last night.* (noun clause)
*I know. [The sense and the function of the verb *know* have changed.]

As demonstrated, omitting a noun clause and analyzing the resulting sentence can be a useful test for distinguishing noun clauses from adjective clauses.

Another way of differentiating between *wh-* clauses and adjective clauses is that the *wh-* word can never be deleted in a noun clause, whereas it is possible to delete a *wh-* word in many adjective clauses:

1. Jaime accidentally broke the lamp *which was sitting on the mantle.* (adjective clause)
Jaime accidentally broke the lamp *sitting on the mantle.*

2. Jaime accidentally broke *whatever was sitting on the mantle.*
*Jaime accidentally broke *sitting on the mantle.*

In sentence 1, the adjective clause can be reduced by eliminating the *wh-* word *which* (as well as the helping verb *was*) and still produce a viable sentence. However, in sentence 2, omitting the *wh-* word that begins the noun clause produces a nonstandard, ungrammatical sentence.

In addition to confusing *wh-* clauses with adjective clauses, writers may confuse *wh-*word noun clauses with information questions (also referred to as *wh-* questions), since the *wh-* word in an information question can seem on the surface to serve a similar function as the *wh-* word in a noun clause. However, as the following examples illustrate, there are significant differences between these two structures:

1. *What* did you do? (information or *wh-* question)
I like *what you did.* (*wh-*word noun clause functioning as direct object)

2. *Where* were you staying? (information or *wh-* question)
Where you were staying was a mystery. (*wh-*word noun clause functioning as subject)

Wh-noun clauses can also be confused with adverb clauses. However, adverb clauses—because they are modifiers—can ordinarily be omitted, whereas *wh*-clauses cannot be, as the following examples illustrate:

1. *When everyone left,* we began to clean up. (adverb clause)
   We began to clean up.

2. *When everyone left* is beyond me. (noun clause)
   *Is beyond me.

When everyone left in sentence 1 is an adverb clause functioning as an adverbial of time; it can be left out, and the result is an independent clause. In sentence 2, *When everyone left* is a noun clause functioning as the subject of the sentence. It cannot be omitted because what results (**Is beyond me*) is not a sentence; it is a fragment. As this explanation suggests, then, to distinguish adverb clauses from noun clauses, you can use the same test as for distinguishing adjective clauses from noun clauses: delete the clause and see if the remainder of the sentence is an independent clause or a fragment.

In addition to the *wh-* words that we've talked about in this discussion, there are some other common *wh-* words used primarily to begin noun clauses: *whenever, wherever, whoever, whomever, whatever, whichever, however.* Noun clauses that begin with these *wh-*words function in many of the same ways as other *wh-*clauses, as these examples illustrate:

1. *Whomever you choose* will be acceptable. (subject)

2. She likes *whatever Bill does.* (direct object)

3. *However you decide to do the job* is all right with us. (subject)

THAT CLAUSES.   Noun clauses that begin with *that* function as *wh-* clauses do—as nominals. They can serve as subjects, direct objects, subject complements, and so forth:

Noun Clause as Subject

1. *Whatever you want to do* is OK with me.

2. *That all people are created equal* is a founding belief of the United States.

Noun Clause as Direct Object

3. I know *where you live.*

4. I believe *that all people are created equal.*

Noun Clause as Appositive

5. The time *when the party should start* is yet to be decided.

6. The belief *that all people are created equal* is not unique to the United States.

As with *wh-* clauses, noun clauses that begin with *that* are also often confused with adjective clauses. However, *that* clauses are also necessary parts of sentences and usually cannot be omitted from a sentence without creating a fragment or changing the meaning of the sentence dramatically. Compare the following sentences:

1. That's the idea *that we wanted to discuss.*

2. The idea is *that we want to discuss buying a home versus renting one.*

In sentence 1, *that we wanted to discuss* is an adjective clause modifying *idea*. In sentence 2, *that we want to discuss …* is a noun clause that functions as a subject complement. If we omit the noun clause in sentence 2, we would produce a sentence fragment (**The idea is.*) However, if we omit the adjective clause in sentence 1, we would still produce a complete sentence (*That's the idea*).

Although they are quite similar to *wh-* clauses, *that* clauses differ from *wh-* clauses in some respects. For example, when a *that* clause functions as a subject complement or a direct object, the word *that* can often be omitted, but *wh-* words cannot be omitted in these circumstances. (The word *that* can never be omitted when the noun clause functions as the subject or as any other sentence constituent.) Compare the following pairs of sentences:

1. The problem is *that we have so little time for ourselves.*
   The problem is *we have so little time for ourselves.* [*That* can be omitted when the *that* clause functions as a subject complement.]

2. The committee decided *that she should go.*
   The committee decided *she should go.* [*That* can be omitted when the *that* clause functions as a direct object.]

3. The question is *where we should eat.*
   *The question is *we should eat.* [The *wh-* word cannot be omitted when the *wh-* clause functions as a subject complement.]

4. The committee decided *what she should say.*
   *The committee decided *she should say.* [The *wh-* word cannot be omitted when the *wh-* clause functions as a direct object.]

In sentences 1 and 2, *that* at the start of the noun clause can be omitted. But in sentences 3 and 4, the *wh-* word at the start of the noun clause cannot be omitted and still produce a grammatical sentence or retain the original meaning of the sentence.

In addition to *that* clauses and *wh-* clauses, noun clauses can begin with the word *if* or *whether:*

1. <u>*Whether* we should close the company</u> was up to debate.

2. They were discussing *whether to close the company.*

3. *If the company should be closed* was the topic of debate.

4. They asked *if the company should be closed.*

However, unlike *that* clauses and *wh-* clauses, which can serve in a variety of functions that nouns, noun phrases, and phrase nominals do, noun clauses headed by *whether* or *if* function primarily as subjects or direct objects. Also, noun clauses that begin with *whether* and *if* usually follow specific verbs that imply a question, such as *ask, discuss,* or *debate;* for example:

1. They <u>asked</u> the conductor *if the train would be on time.*

2. The young couple <u>discussed</u> *whether to get married.*

3. The lost hikers <u>debated</u> *whether to try to return to the base camp.*

Dummy Subjects and Extraposition

As we have indicated in many of our discussions to this point, noun clauses can be used in a variety of functions in a sentence, including as the subject. Here are several examples of noun clauses functioning as the subject of a sentence:

1. *That we are lost* is evident.

2. *What you said* intrigues me.

3. *Whether you will be elected* is open to debate.

4. *Where you went* is where I want to go.

5. *Whomever is elected* must deal with a political mess.

As these examples show, using a noun clause as the subject tends to make a sentence sound formal and somewhat emphatic. For this reason, in most speech and often in writing, a form has evolved that sounds less formal and that people find more comfortable to use. It involves moving the noun clause subject to the end of the sentence:

1. <u>It</u> is evident *that we are lost.*

2. <u>It</u> intrigues me *what you said.*

3. <u>It</u> is open to debate *whether you will be elected.*

Moving the subject to follow the verb phrase leaves the subject position open, which we fill with a *placeholder* (in these sentences, *it*). We say that this placeholder functions as a *dummy subject* and that the noun clause functions as an *extraposed subject.* In such cases of *extraposition,* the word *it* serves only to hold the place of the subject. It does not function as a pronoun or have any referent in the sentence that precedes it.

English uses another placeholder as well, *there*. Although *there* is not generally used to begin sentences with noun clauses as extraposed subjects, it has the identical "**empty**" function as *it* does, as is illustrated in the following sentences:

I cannot deny

1. *It* is undeniable that the actor is a skirt chaser.

2. *There* have been many rumors about his proclivities.

3. *There* is a book out about him.

Sentence 1 begins with the placeholder *it* and is followed by a linking verb and a noun clause. It can be rephrased as *That the actor is a skirt chaser is undeniable.* Sentence 1, then, illustrates an extraposed noun clause (*that the actor is a skirt chaser*), with *it* functioning as a placeholder or dummy subject. Sentences 2 and 3 begin with the placeholder *there* and do not contain extraposed noun clauses, which is why they usually cannot be as easily rephrased as noun clauses can, as these sentences indicate:

Many rumors about his proclivities have existed.

A book is out about him. OK

Because native English speakers use placeholders functioning as dummy subjects naturally in speech, they generally do not have difficulty with them. However, the *there* placeholder can sometimes cause confusion with subject-verb agreement, as we explain in Part Two of this chapter.

Direct Versus Indirect Discourse

A very common structure in both speech and writing is *indirect discourse,* which sounds complicated but is actually only *reported speech,* another name by which it is known. We introduce indirect discourse in this section because it involves a very common usage of noun clauses. Compare the following two sentences, for example:

1. She said, *"I'm going to lunch."*

2. She said *that she was going to lunch.*

Sentence 1 is an example of *direct discourse,* with quotation marks placed around a *direct quote* or *quoted speech* (*"I'm going to lunch"*). Sentence 2 is an example of indirect discourse, with the noun clause (*that she was going to lunch*) replacing the quoted speech. In such noun clauses beginning with *that, that* can be deleted:

She said *she was going to lunch.*

Noun clauses are also used to report questions. In these cases, the noun clause usually begins with *if* or *whether:*

1. She asked, "Are you going to lunch?"

2. She asked <u>whether</u> *I was going to lunch.*

3. She asked *if I was going to lunch.*

As you can see, noun clauses are used in sentences 2 and 3 to replace the quoted speech. In all cases of noun clauses used for reported speech, the noun clause functions as a direct object.

EXERCISES FOR PRACTICE

A. In the following sentences, identify the nouns, noun phrases, or nominals and tell how each one functions in its sentence.

> **Example:** Selena's friend Joe likes running the bakery on the corner of our block.
>
> *Selena's friend* is a noun phrase functioning as the subject.
>
> *Joe* is a noun functioning as an appositive.
>
> *Running the bakery on the corner of our block* is a nominal functioning as a direct object.

1. Man is what he believes. (Chekhov)

2. Everyone was talking about last night's presidential debate.

3. Copernicus was a great scientist whose theories form the basis of modern science.

4. People living in Montana want to keep their state free of littering tourists.

5. David's dog, Spike, is a cute miniature dachshund who enjoys barking at just about anything.

6. Surely joy is the condition of life. (Henry David Thoreau)

7. The best thing about the future is that it comes only one day at a time. (Abraham Lincoln)

8. Despite the commotion in the hallway, Tom was able to get some sleep.

9. Keep away from people who try to belittle your ambitions. Small people always do that, but the really great make you feel that you, too, can become great. (Mark Twain)

10. People put labels on things to help them remember the contents.

B. Some of the following sentences contain nominal phrases. Underline the nominal phrases, identify their specific form, and explain how each one functions in the sentence.

> **Example:** Josh likes <u>to write letters on his computer</u>. Infinitive phrase functioning as the direct object

> **Example:** <u>Running for political office</u> takes a lot of stamina. Gerund phrase functioning as the subject

1. Elton John's singing has become famous around the world.

2. He has been planning to retire for many years.

3. Performing has been his life for more than three decades.

4. His fans would probably be screaming for him to come out of retirement.

5. Most people dream of retiring as soon as they are financially able.

6. But Elton John dreams only of making music until his fans stop attending his concerts or buying his records.

7. Responding to an interviewer, he implied that he would like to slow down but never stop.

8. "Writing music is my life," he was reported as saying.

C. Use each of the following forms in as many different ways as possible. Then identify the function of each of the ways you have used the forms. Use your imagination, and be creative.

> **Example:** prepositional phrase
>
> The man <u>in the living room</u> is not my friend. (prepositional phrase as adjectival)
>
> The children made a mess <u>in the living room</u>. (prepositional phrase as adverbial)

1. prepositional phrase

2. noun phrase

3. infinitive phrase

4. gerund phrase

5. adverbial

6. noun clause

D. Each of the following sentences contains a nominal—an infinitive or a gerund. Expand the nominal to a nominal phrase. Use your imagination.

   Example: Singing was fun.

   Tamoko's singing *La Traviata* over the campfire was fun.

   1. Virginia likes swimming.   *phrases not clauses*

   2. Jesse thinks it is important to talk.

   3. The travelers began to bicker.

   4. Cooking is fun.

   5. Everyone tried to dance.

   6. Eating is necessary.

   7. Stanley enjoys reading.

   8. Kris hates to pack.

   9. Deb attempted to cook.

   10. Terry despises walking.

E. Identify each of the nominal clauses in the following sentences or sets of sentences, and state its function.

   Example: What is before our nose is what we see last. (William Barrett)

   What is before our nose is a *wh-* clause functioning as the subject.

   What we see last is a *wh-* clause functioning as the subject complement.

   1. Resolve to be thyself; and know that he who finds himself loses his misery. (Matthew Arnold)

   2. It is characteristic of the ego that it takes all that is unimportant as important and all that is important as unimportant. (Meher Baba)

   3. Do not seek to follow in the footsteps of the men of old; seek what they sought. (Basho)

   4. Socrates never minded being wrong. He felt that if you disabused him of a notion he had held, he carried that much less baggage around with him. (Stringfield Barr)

   5. Maybe nothing is a tragedy, but I think we can say that to live without appreciating this life is at least a shame. (Charlotte Joko Beck)

6. Satan was being expelled from heaven. As he passed through the Gate, he paused a moment in thought, turned to God, and said, "I hear a new creature called Man is soon to be created" (Ambrose Bierce)

7. As Dostoevsky once said, "The battlefield is the heart of man." The activist knows this and enters the battle where it really happens, inside the heart. (Alan Clements)

8. The trouble with the rat race is that even if you win, you're still a rat. (Lily Tomlin)

9. Just remain in the center, watching. And then forget you are there. (Lao Tzu)

10. I learn by going where I have to go. (Theodore Roethke)

F. Identify the form and function of each of the nominal phrases and clauses in the following sentences. (Some sentences may have more than one nominal.)

> **Example:** In the United States, it is a given that citizens have certain unalienable rights. *That citizens have certain unalienable rights* is a noun clause functioning as the extraposed subject.

> **Example:** To love chocolate is not unusual. *To love chocolate* is an infinitive phrase functioning as the subject.

1. It is the best of all trades to make songs and the second best to sing them. (Hilaire Belloc)

2. To read well, that is, to read true books in a true spirit, is a noble exercise, and one that will task the reader more than any exercise which the customs of the day esteem. (Henry David Thoreau)

3. Vinh's idea that we should protest strip mining got everyone excited.

4. There were a lot of people asking how to use the new computers.

5. It is fun, dancing in the dark.

6. After several explanations, I finally figured out what I'm supposed to do.

7. Hamlet's most famous line—"To be or not to be"—can be quoted by many English speakers.

8. It is the scariest place where the plumber always goes, under the sink.

9. Mr. Rodriguez asked his students to be respectful to one another, especially during disagreements.

10. There was a lot of dancing, flirting, and laughing at the dance on Saturday night.

G. The following sentences contain the words *there* and *it* as meaningful words (adverb and pronoun, respectively) and as placeholders. Underline these words in the sentences, and identify the function of each one. Then tell if the sentence is standard or nonstandard speech.

> **Example:** It was I who told a lie. (placeholder; standard, though somewhat formal).

1. Wayne put the book there on the shelf.

2. When Mary Ann asked her husband if he liked her new hairstyle, he said he hated it.

3. It was a dark night when the invaders came.

4. There are hundreds of volcanoes in the Hawaiian Islands.

5. If you go to the office party on Saturday night, you'll find Alice there dancing.

6. Sarah never liked it when the older kids teased her.

7. It is difficult to decide what to major in.

8. Most people know that there are several major rivers in Montana, including the Missouri and the Yellowstone.

9. Have you been there, to Montana?

10. I went there once. It was beautiful there.

H. Change each of the following sentences from direct to indirect discourse or vice versa.

> **Example:** "I like pizza for breakfast," said Matt.
> Matt said that he likes pizza for breakfast.
> **Example:** Alan wonders if he'll ever retire.
> "Will I ever retire?" Alan wondered.

1. "I have a dream," said Martin Luther King Jr.

2. Carol said she doesn't know how to change the oil in her car.

3. Mrs. Herman told the doctor she didn't like to stay cooped up inside all winter.

4. "Birds of a feather flock together," said Jamie's grandmother when she met Jamie's new boyfriend.

5. "What time will you be home?" Lori asked her roommate.

6. The guide told the students that the museum closes at 6 P.M.

7. Agnes asked the man on the corner if this was the way to the river.

8. "Do you think this will be a cold winter?" we all asked the weatherman.

9. "How can we unplug the sink?" Tom and Diane asked the plumber.

10. Edie wondered if her new boss would require her to travel extensively.

I. Look at the headlines in the daily newspaper. How are direct speech and indirect speech used in these headlines? What effect does their use create? That is, why do you think these forms are used in these particular headlines?

STOP   11/18

PART II: CHALLENGES FOR WRITERS

As we have discussed in Part One, using nominals appropriately and for effect in one's writing can pose a variety of challenges for novice writers. These challenges include subject-verb agreement when using extraposed subjects, punctuating clauses, avoiding fragments, and using nominals effectively in both direct and indirect discourse.

THERE IS OR *THERE ARE* AND SUBJECT–VERB AGREEMENT

As we discussed in the section on noun clauses, *it* and *there* are often used as *placeholders* or *dummy subjects*. Here are some examples of *it* and *there* as dummy subjects:

1. *It* is raining today.

2. Is *it* true that the prince is getting married?

3. *There* was a surprise ending to the movie.

4. *There* were three hundred people on the boat when it sank.

Notice that when *it* and *there* function in this way, they do not refer to anything, in contrast to when they function as part of the sentence meaning (*it* as a pronoun, *there* as an adverb). Here are two sentences in which *it* and *there* function as meaningful words:

1. I like my room. *It* is yellow. [*It* refers to *my room.*]

2. Maria went to Chicago. *There* she met Frank. [*There* refers to where she met Frank.]

When *it* functions as a dummy subject, it can be used in circumstances when there is no subject available—for example, when speaking about the weather, as in *It is raining today. It* can also be a placeholder for gerund phrases, infinitive phrases, and noun clauses. Here are some examples of *it* being used as a placeholder for gerund phrases, infinitive phrases, and noun clauses:

1. It was fun *being in love.* [*Being in love* is a gerund phrase functioning as an extraposed subject.]

2. It is always difficult *to say goodbye.* [*To say goodbye* is an infinitive phrase functioning as an extraposed subject.]

3. It was a good thing *that the pitcher caught the fly ball.* [*That the pitcher caught the fly ball* is a noun clause functioning as an extraposed subject.]

As is evident from these examples, subject-verb agreement is not a challenge when *it* is used as a placeholder because the verb is always in the singular, regardless of the form of the extraposed subject that follows the verb phrase. Here are some more examples to illustrate this point. Notice that in each example, the verb "is" is in the singular form:

1. *It is* undeniable <u>that misery loves company</u>. [*Is* is singular.]
                      extraposed subject

2. *It has* been standard practice <u>that the FBI does not interfere with local authorities</u>. [*Has* is singular.]   extraposed subject

3. *It was* on the fourth of July <u>that the colonies declared independence from England</u>. [*Was* is singular.]   extraposed subject

In all of these cases, the verb agrees with the dummy subject, *it*, in person and number. That is, because *it* resembles the third person pronoun in form and number, the verb following the placeholder *it* also takes the third person singular form.

However, subject-verb agreement can be more of a challenge when *there* is used as a placeholder. One reason for this is that *there* does not have a distinguishable person or number but must instead rely on the extraposed subject to determine whether the verb will be in the third person singular or the third person plural. Here are some examples to illustrate this difference:

1. <u>There are</u> *many family-owned farms in the American Midwest.*

2. <u>There is</u> *a farm down the road owned by my cousin.*

In sentence 1, the extraposed subject, *many family-owned farms in the American Midwest*, is plural. Therefore, the verb, *are*, is used to reflect the third person plural. In sentence 2, by contrast, the extraposed subject, *a farm down the road owned by my cousin*, is singular, and therefore, the verb, *is*, is used to reflect the third person singular. Determining whether to inflect the verb for the third person singular or the third person plural when using *there* as a dummy subject is a challenge for all writers, not just novice writers, and requires awareness of the structure of the sentence. Confusion about the structure of sentences with *there* as a dummy subject often causes inexperienced writers to make the verb agree with *there* in the singular rather than look beyond the verb for the number (singular or plural) of the extraposed subject, as the following example illustrates:

*There is twenty-six letters in the English alphabet.

In this sentence, the writer has inflected the verb in the singular form (*is*) to agree (incorrectly) with the dummy subject, *there*. Instead, the verb should agree with the plural extraposed subject, *twenty-six letters in the English alphabet:*

There are twenty-six letters in the English alphabet.

To help writers determine the number of the verb when using *there* as a dummy subject, an effective strategy is to mentally drop *there* and turn the sentence around. For example, *There are many family-owned farms in the American Midwest* can be transformed into *Many family-owned farms <u>are</u> in the American Midwest*. Similarly, *There is a farm down the road owned by my cousin* can be transformed into *A farm down the road <u>is</u> owned by my cousin*. Inverting the sentence in this way puts the focus of the sentence on the noun, noun phrase, or nominal that functions as the extraposed subject of the sentence, thus making it easier to discern whether to use the singular or plural form of the verb.

PUNCTUATION OF APPOSITIVES

Having read portions of this and other chapters, you already know that an appositive is a noun or nominal that follows another noun or nominal and refers to the same person or thing. Appositives are also commonly described as "structures that rename nouns." Because appositives can be single words, phrases, or clauses and because they can potentially appear wherever a noun might appear, these structures can be quite varied with respect to how they look and how they are placed within sentences. The following examples illustrate some of the possible forms and placements for appositives. The appositives are underlined.

Single-Word Appositive

My husband, <u>John</u>, is a science teacher in Toledo, Ohio. (renames the subject)

Phrase Appositive

I really love *my favorite pastime*, <u>to take long walks in the woods</u>. (renames the direct object)

Endora gave *her new pet*, <u>a short-haired terrier</u>, her complete attention. (renames the indirect object)

John is *a wonderful father*, <u>an outstanding role model for any parent to follow</u>. (renames the subject complement)

John bought me a diamond for *our twenty-fifth anniversary*, <u>an important event in our life</u>. (renames the object of a preposition)

We elected her *treasurer*, <u>a pivotal role in our organization</u>. (renames the object complement)

Clause Appositive

The idea <u>that Marcia would become the next chair of the senate</u> terrified us. (renames the subject)

We considered *Bill's suggestion* <u>that the meetings begin one hour later</u>. (renames the direct object)

In examining the examples of the various appositive structures, you probably noticed that most (but not all) were set off with commas. Because appositives are nonrestrictive, they are usually set off with commas. This means that if an appositive comes at the end of a sentence, it requires a comma in front of it, and if an appositive is placed within a sentence it requires two commas, one before it and one after:

1. Appositive at the end of a sentence: I love my sweet dog, *Woody.*

2. Appositive within a sentence: My sweet dog, *Woody,* loves everyone.

Commas can be particularly helpful in distinguishing object complements from appositives that rename direct objects. Consider the difference in meaning between these two sentences:

1. We called our new puppy, Woody.   *Called his name*
2. We called our new puppy Woody.   *named him*

In sentence 1, the comma that separates the noun *puppy* from the noun *Woody* indicates that *Woody* is an appositive. *We called our new puppy (whose name is) Woody.* ["Come here, Woody!"]. Sentence 2, in contrast, expresses something quite different. The verb *called* is used to mean "named," as in *We named our new puppy (who didn't have a name) Woody.* In this sentence, *Woody* is an object complement. In these two sentences, the existence of the comma changes the entire meaning of the sentence.

As we noted, although most appositives are ordinarily set off with commas, some are not. Appositives—like relative clauses—can be restrictive or nonrestrictive, and restrictive appositives don't require commas. Because most appositives are nonrestrictive, they provide information that is not essential to the meaning of the nouns they rename. In the sentence *My neighbor, Holly, mowed our lawn,* the commas indicate that identifying my neighbor by name (Holly) is not necessary—it's just additional information. Suppose, however, that I have two neighbors and only one of them, Holly, mowed the lawn. Then the appositive would have to be punctuated differently, as a restrictive modifier: *My neighbor Holly mowed our lawn.* Clause appositives in particular are often restrictive, as in these examples:

1. The <u>notion</u> *that retirement leads to poverty* disturbed everyone at the meeting. [Only this particular notion disturbed everyone.]

2. We hated the <u>idea</u> *that she might move to Washington.* [We hated only this particular idea.]

3. We understand your <u>fear</u> *that you will become unemployed.* [Which fear do we understand? Your fear of becoming unemployed.]

Another factor that can affect the placement—and therefore the punctuation—of appositives is whether or not they are moved. Ordinarily, an appositive must directly follow the noun it renames, but occasionally that order can be reversed, especially at the start of a sentence, as in the following examples:

1. *Original placement:*   Our son, *always the helpful computer science major,* fixed our neighbor's aging Macintosh.

   Fronted: *Always the helpful computer science major,* our son fixed our neighbor's aging Macintosh.

2. *Original placement:*   My students, *aspiring language arts teachers,* signed up to tutor children in nearby schools.

   Fronted: *Aspiring language arts teachers,* my students signed up to tutor children in nearby schools.

As the conventions for the punctuating of appositives suggest, the most common type of error that inexperienced writers commit regarding these structures has to do with the omission of commas. The omission of the comma or commas necessary to set off an appositive from the rest of the sentence can result in difficult-to-read structures such as the following:

The two neighbors next door Holly and Brent are always working in their yard.

We baked our favorite meal for Thanksgiving turkey.

After we got home, we engaged in our favorite pastime reading mystery novels; then we went to bed.

Similarly, when apprentice writers use only one comma rather than two to set off an appositive within a sentence, a reader's ability to comprehend the text can be seriously compromised:

*Our twelve-year old parakeet Pickle, flew out the window.

*My husband and I looked frantically for our bird, a pet we had learned to cherish all over the neighborhood.

*Unfortunately, Pickle, our little green friend was nowhere to be found.

Problems in punctuating restrictive versus nonrestrictive appositives effectively also plague inexperienced writers from time to time, although they are less common than errors involving the omission of one or both commas. In general, novice writers who experience difficulties in this area may overgeneralize the rule regarding comma use with appositives and employ commas when they shouldn't to create a sentence such as this: *I hated the idea, that I should come to band practice early*. In this sentence, although the appositive *that I should come to band practice early* is necessary to limit or restrict the noun *idea*, the writer has set off the structure with a comma. However, because appositive structures that are clearly restrictive are far less common than nonrestrictive appositive clauses, students tend to produce more errors involving the omission of one or more commas than errors involving their inappropriate use.

For students who have problems punctuating appositives, it is important to provide assistance in recognizing these structures and the various forms they can take. To help with this endeavor, students need to examine sets of sentences (from a handbook or of your own devising) that illustrate a diversity of single-word, phrase, and clause appositives and identify (by underlining or bracketing) the appositives in these sentences. To be able to recognize appositives in sentences, student writers may also require practice in identifying the important *functions* of nouns and nominals (subject, direct object, etc.) because appositives usually follow these. Sentence pattern practice as described in Part Two of Chapter 2, that focuses students' attention on identifying subjects, direct objects, indirect objects, and subject complements, can be of help here.

As students become proficient at identifying appositives, they should be given opportunities to practice producing—and properly punctuating—appositives in sentences of their own. At the early stages of such practice, students should be given exercises that provide them with models of the appositives they are to produce (e.g., "Underline the appositive in each of the following sentences. For each sentence, craft a similar sentence of your own that contains a properly punctuated appositive of the same structure."). Sentence-combining exercises can also provide apprentice writers with guided assistance in producing sentences that contain properly punctuated appositives:

Combine each of the paired sentences to create a new sentence with an appositive, as the examples illustrate. Underline the appositive in each sentence that you create.

Example: The plants responded to the new fertilizer.
                 The new fertilizer was an organic compound.
                 The plants responded to the new fertilizer, <u>an organic compound</u>.

Example: Seasoned travelers are tolerant of the inconveniences.
                 The inconveniences include standing in line and having their luggage searched.
                 Seasoned travelers are tolerant of the inconveniences, <u>standing in line and having their luggage searched</u>.

Example: My wish has finally been granted.
                 My wish was to see the Grand Canyon.
                 My wish <u>to see the Grand Canyon</u> has finally been granted.

In addition to assigning simple exercises in which students identify appositives, produce sentences of their own with appositives, and combine sentences to produce appositives, it is always helpful to encourage apprentice writers to find examples of these structures in various written genres. As students bring excerpts of writing that contains appositives to class, these examples can be posted or used in class discussions that focus on how appositives are formed, how they affect meaning, how they should be punctuated, and so forth. Such diverse examples can also be used as springboards to help students craft more complex appositive structures that suit particular stylistic purposes in their own writing.

As we have suggested, then, students will acquire a basic understanding of the range of appositive forms and places in sentences in which they might appear if they have opportunities to practice identifying, reproducing, and properly punctuating appositives that follow common noun functions (such as subject, direct object, subject complement, and object of a preposition). In general, with respect to the exercises and activities we have described, it is prudent first to expose students to appositive structures that are easy to identify and reproduce and that are found in relatively short, simple sentences. When students become more proficient in identifying, reproducing, and properly punctuating easily recognized appositives in short sentences, they can be given more challenging exercises. These exercises might require students to identify—or to produce—more unusual appositive structures in lengthy, complex sentences or even short passages. Or they might invite students to revise incorrectly punctuated appositives or to reproduce complex appositives in short pieces of discourse to produce particular stylistic effects. Such "advanced" exercises and assignments are ultimately necessary to help students transfer to their own writing the skill of crafting and properly punctuating appositive structures. Such practice will also enhance students' ability to recognize and revise inappropriately punctuated appositives when they edit their own and others' essays.

FRAGMENTED NOMINALS

Although perhaps less frequently than fragmented adverbials and adjectivals, nominals can be misapprehended for—and punctuated as—sentences from time to time. As we have suggested in Chapter 8, when a noun is modified by an adjective (relative) clause, the resulting structure can be mistaken for a sentence—especially when the noun is functioning as an appositive. In addition, lengthy gerund and infinitive phrases can cause inexperienced writers difficulty, especially when introduced by *for instance* or *for example*.

Fragmented Modified Appositives

Because appositives can follow nouns functioning in a variety of ways (as subjects, direct objects, objects of a preposition, etc.), it is not unusual for an appositive to appear at the end of a sentence and rename a structure such as a direct object. For example, in the sentence *I bought a new fish for my pond, a large yellow koi*, the appositive *a large yellow koi* renames the direct object (*fish*). Whereas inexperienced writers would probably not ordinarily mistake a short phrase such as *a large yellow koi* for a sentence and punctuate it as such, they may be inclined to do so when an appositive appears at the end of a sentence and is modified by an adjective clause:

Fragment:	I bought a new fish for my pond. <u>A large yellow koi</u> <u>*that cost twenty-five dollars*</u>.
Fragment:	Imagine yourself losing control of one of the five major sense organs. <u>The organ</u> <u>*that helps the mind visualize a picture*</u>.
Fragment:	For my engagement ring, I wanted a large diamond in a beautiful setting. <u>A setting</u> <u>*that would match my eventual wedding ring*</u>.

These examples illustrate how very sentencelike modified appositives can appear. To an inexperienced writer, any of the appositives in these sentences (*a large yellow koi, the organ, a setting*) might look a good deal more like a noun subject than the actual subject of each clause (the relative pronoun *that*). In the case of such fragments, then, an inexperienced writer may lose track of an appositive's function and mistake a modified appositive for a sentence.

Fragmented Phrasal Nominals

Phrasal nominals are less likely to appear as fragments than adjectival or adverbial phrases, but they too can cause inexperienced writers difficulty. Besides the fact that phrasal nominals can sometimes resemble sentences—especially when they include infinitives or gerunds—the widespread occurrence of nominal fragments in speech can also contribute to students' production of inappropriate fragments in their writing. Imagine the following brief conversations:

1. What can you do at Cedar Point?
   Lots of things. Go on rides, watch shows, eat, walk around ...

2. Are you sure you want to go swimming in the park?
   Yes, I really want to. Swim in the park for a while.

3. What's bothering you?
   Deciding where to apply to college. It can really stress a person out.

4. What did you buy at the mall?
   A dress.

5. I'd like three donuts, please.
   Which?
   Two glazed and one with those sprinkles.

6. Where did you go?
   The mall.

As these illustrations show, during casual conversations, speakers can elect to omit a good deal of a sentence. In fact, in examples 4, 5, and 6, the speakers have elected to omit everything except a single constituent of the sentence. In example 6, everything in the reply has been omitted except the object of the preposition *to*: *Where did you go?* [*I went to*] *the mall*. Similarly, in example 4, everything has been omitted except the direct object of the reply: *What did you buy at the mall?* [*I bought*] *a dress*. We are suggesting, then, that the ubiquitous presence of fragmented nominal structures in speech may contribute to their misapprehension as sentences.

Furthermore, as we have already explained, the fact that some phrasal nominals resemble sentences may also cause problems for inexperienced writers. The appearance of a gerund or an infinitive in a lengthy phrase may send the signal "verb" and thus cause writers inexperienced with gerund or infinitive phrases to mistake these structures for sentences:

1. To just get by for the next few weeks. That's all I ask.

2. Her driving around in her new Trans Am. It's really annoying everybody.

3. I just have two goals this semester. To pass all of my classes and not to get sick again.

Particularly when gerund or infinitive phrases are somewhat lengthy, they may be confused as sentences in the same way that dependent clauses are misapprehended as sentences.

Sometimes when gerund or infinitive phrases function as appositives, they can be preceded by the expressions *for example* and *for instance.* The presence of either of these expressions can increase the likelihood that an inexperienced writer will punctuate an appositive phrase as if it were a sentence:

1. My high school history teacher created an atmosphere of fear by doing many unfair things. <u>For example, giving tests without warning or calling on people he knew weren't prepared.</u>

2. The Internet can be used for many things. <u>For instance, to find discount air fares, to locate long-lost friends, or to discuss issues and concerns with people who share a similar interest.</u>

Although we can't be certain, the expressions *for example* and *for instance* may prompt students to create fragments because they mistakenly assume that the expressions are functioning as conjunctive adverbs and are signaling the beginning of an independent clause, as indeed these expressions sometimes do.

Fixing Fragmented Nominals

As with other problems in syntax that apprentice writers may experience, the best way for students to remediate fragmented nominals is for them to become familiar with the particular patterns of the fragments they write. Patterns may occur with respect to how fragmented nominals function or the form that they take. If, for example, students produce fragmented appositives, they should become familiar with this particular nominal structure (the appositive) and how it functions. Likewise, students who regularly produce fragmented gerund phrases should carefully scrutinize structures that have an *-ing* form in them. To discover patterns with respect to form or function, recording instances of fragments (and other sentence structure errors) in an error log or notebook is good practice. Keeping such a log can provide students with a predictable and regularized procedure to record individual occurrences of nominal fragments. As the list of nominal fragments lengthens, students may be able to recognize patterns associated with the production of these errors or discover their underlying relationship with other problems the students are experiencing as writers (e.g., using moveable modifiers properly)—especially if you offer assistance.

Once students have become familiar with the patterns of the nominal fragments they produce, they should have the opportunity to identify these kinds of nominal structures (appositives, gerund phrases, etc.) in various kinds of discourse and to practice writing sentences with these structures. As always, students should be encouraged to find passages of writing that contain examples of the structures with which they are working and to bring these passages to class. These excerpts can then be used in class discussion and perhaps included in student logs, as supplementary material to illustrate the proper use and punctuation of the particular nominals that are causing difficulty. At this stage, students should also be instructed in and given practice with different ways of revising fragmented nominals—for example, by joining them to an adjacent sentence or by reworking them altogether:

Fragment:	I want a new computer. <u>One that can scan documents and photographs</u>.
Possible revision:	I want a new computer<u>, one that can scan documents and photographs</u>.
Possible revision:	I want a new computer <u>that can scan documents and photographs</u>.
Possible revision:	<u>The type</u> of new computer I want <u>can scan documents and photographs</u>.

Besides providing students with individual instruction in revising, whenever possible you should offer instruction about and practice with revising in a classroom setting. You can, for example, provide individual groups with the same fragment to revise and ask each group to write the revised option on the board. Once these revised alternatives are in front of the class, students can discuss and compare them with respect to different criteria (e.g., ease of revision for each alternative, focus of each resulting sentence, how each resulting sentence sounds). During class revision sessions, groups can also be provided with the same excerpt or passage of writing that contains a nominal fragment. After all of the groups have found and fixed the fragment, they can discuss which revised variant is the best one for its context. Finally, so that students can transfer their skills in identifying and reworking fragmented nominals to their own writing, they need practice, both individually and in groups, in editing progressively longer passages that contain these kinds of errors.

DIRECT VERSUS INDIRECT DISCOURSE

Toward the end of Part One, we described the difference in forms between direct and indirect discourse:

Direct discourse:	"I want to go to the circus," said Amiyalli.
Indirect discourse:	Amiyalli said that she wanted to go to the circus.
Direct discourse:	"Do you like fried rice?" asked Mary.
Indirect discourse:	Mary asked whether I like fried rice.

As is evident from these examples, in terms of form, direct discourse and indirect discourse have specific sets of conventions. Direct discourse requires the use of quotation marks (e.g., *"How wonderful!" exclaimed Agnes*), whereas indirect discourse appears as a noun clause (e.g., *Agnes exclaimed* that it was wonderful) and does not require any special punctuation.

In the case of direct versus indirect discourse, the forms generally reflect the functions. That is, direct discourse is a record of the *exact* words someone said, either in speech or in writing. It is repeating words *verbatim,* and for this reason it is sometimes called a *direct quote.* Indirect discourse, by contrast, is a report of what someone has said or written. In indirect discourse, many of the same words are repeated, but not all of the words are repeated exactly. In fact, if the very same words are repeated in indirect discourse, the result may be confusing. Compare the indirect discourse (also called *reported speech*) in the following examples to see how the reported sentence must vary from the direct quote:

George said, *"I like baseball."* (direct discourse; records George's exact words)

George said *that he likes baseball.* (indirect discourse; reports the gist of what George said)

*George said *that I like baseball.* (inaccurate statement; George said nothing about *me*)

As is obvious from this example, in addition to being in the form of a noun clause, indirect speech requires a shift in pronouns; for example, in the example, *I* in *I like baseball,* George's statement about himself, was shifted to *he* in *that he likes baseball,* our report of what George said. Besides a shift in pronouns, converting direct to indirect discourse sometimes requires a shift in tense—for example:

Direct discourse:	*"Can* I leave now?" Mary asked.
Indirect discourse:	Mary wondered whether she *could* leave.

In the first sentence, the question is in the present tense (*can*). When put into indirect discourse, however, it shifts to the past tense form (*could*). Although the rules vary with respect to when to shift tenses, experts generally agree that shifting from present to past tense occurs when the speech is in the past:

Present tense:	Suat *asks,* "*Can* I have more soup?"
	Suat *asks* if she *can* have more soup.
Past tense:	Suat *asked,* "*Can* have more soup?"
	Suat *asked* if she *could* have more soup.

However, in common usage, the need for the tense shift is not always clear (witness our initial example: *George said, "I like baseball"* was changed to *George said that he likes baseball*). This construction sounds perfectly natural (and grammatical), and so in oral discourse especially, we often mix tenses. (Note that it would also be perfectly acceptable for us to have written *George said that he liked baseball.*)

Because of the different conventions we have discussed, student writers often have difficulty punctuating direct and indirect discourse, distinguishing quotes from nonquotes, and knowing how to capitalize words in a quotation. Because students are uncertain of these aspects of direct versus indirect discourse, they often use them inappropriately. Here is an example from a student essay:

> At first I thought it was a shadow on my wall. But then I heard him say the fateful words. "Baby, Baby, he whispered. I thought how ridiculous."

As this excerpt illustrates, this inexperienced writer wants to use a direct quotation to add vividness to her narration, but she isn't quite sure how to do so.

Rather than discouraging students who have difficulty using direct or indirect discourse effectively, there are several things teachers can do, both to help students produce the accurate forms of direct and indirect discourse and to use these forms appropriately. First, students need to be given rhetorical models of direct and indirect discourse to familiarize them with how each looks in context and how each is used effectively in those contexts. Fiction (either short stories or novels) and feature articles in magazines and newspapers are good sources for both kinds of discourse. You can easily find such examples or encourage your students to find and bring to class their own excerpts, passages, and short pieces that contain examples of both direct speech and indirect speech.

Besides examining writing that contains direct and indirect speech, students also need opportunities to read direct and indirect discourse aloud. This can be accomplished in class by letting students give or read speeches that contain examples of each, by acting out dialogues, or by doing dramatic readings of excerpts that are brought to class. You can also have students practice recording what a classmate has said and reading it back to the class, in direct or indirect form (as you specify).

Finally, to become proficient at using direct and indirect discourse, students need practice in applying the rules related to both types of recorded speech in actual writing. To help students apply such rules in fairly simple contexts, you can give them sentences that are written in direct discourse and ask students to transform these to indirect discourse, and vice versa. Students can also compose (and possibly perform) short pieces of writing that contain direct discourse, indirect discourse, or both. For example, students—either in groups or individually—can be given cartoon strips in which all language has been removed and told to create their own interpretation of the events by providing under each frame (rather than in balloons) their own narration, including direct speech. You can make such an assignment more challenging by requiring students to include examples of both direct and indirect speech in their interpretations.

Once students have become proficient at using direct and indirect speech properly in simple contexts, they can attempt more ambitious projects, such as writing a feature news story into which they must incorporate correctly punctuated instances of both direct and indirect discourse. Finally, we believe that in conjunction with these and other teaching strategies and assignments, it is important for students to be given opportunities to find, interpret, and properly apply the rules regarding direct and indirect discourse as presented in handbooks. Vital to that end is class instruction in which you explain and illustrate how to punctuate examples of direct and indirect discourse in a variety of text passages. In conjunction with or following these explanations and examples, students also need classroom practice punctuating actual examples of writing, both individually and in groups.

● EXERCISES FOR PRACTICE

A. In the following sentences, underline the extraposed structures, and identify their form and function.

> **Example:**   There was a dark stain on our clothes <u>where we had carried the blackberries in our aprons.</u> (noun clause used as the extraposed subject)

1. There was great celebration when the soldiers returned from World War II.
2. It troubled Iris that she couldn't find her high school diploma.
3. The idea that people could fly was appealing to the Wright brothers.
4. It was ridiculous to expect a child to do quantum physics.
5. Highly preposterous was what critics called Galileo's theory.
6. There was a great sigh of relief when the president announced his resignation.
7. It was in 1990 that the Berlin Wall came down.
8. It goes without saying that the dental hygienist has an important job.
9. It was fun taking care of the litter of puppies for a week.
10. There are times when parents are not responsible for their children's actions.

B. Extraposition is often a stylistic choice. The following sets of quotations all contain extraposed structures. Rewrite the sentences to omit the extraposition. Why do you think the author chose to use extraposition? Consider such aspects of writing as focus and formality. (There may be more than one way to rewrite the sentence.)

> **Example:**   Man can live his truth, his deepest truth, but he cannot speak it. It is for this reason that love becomes the ultimate human

answer to the ultimate human question. (Archibald MacLeish)

Man can live his truth, his deepest truth, but he cannot speak it. For this reason, love becomes the ultimate human answer to the ultimate human question.

Example: We have learned the answers, all the answers. It is the questions that we do not know. (Archibald MacLeish)

We have learned the answers, all the answers. We do not know the questions.

1. There is no virtue in an abundant life if it does not lead to a more noble man. (Walt Whitman)

2. It is not the answer that enlightens, but the question. (Eugene Ionesco)

3. It is the best of all trades to make songs and the second best to sing them. (Hilaire Belloc)

4. It is more important to find out what you are giving to society than to ask what is the right means of livelihood. (Jiddu Krishnamurti)

5. There is nothing with which every man is so afraid as getting to know how enormously much he is capable of doing and becoming. (Søren Kierkegaard)

C. Determine which of the following sentences have problems with subject-verb agreement, and correct the mistakes.

1. There was more people at the wedding reception than at the wedding.

2. There is a feeling of freedom when standing at the top of a mountain.

3. There has been a lot of rumors about Esther's true identity.

4. There is many things we could say about this new park, but "beautiful" is not one of them.

5. There was discussion and disagreement, but no one came to blows.

6. There is going to be a new motel built where the old one was destroyed by the tornado.

7. There is the problem, that we have to use gas to fuel our cars.

8. There have been several bills on the floor of Congress regarding this issue, but none have passed.

9. There is someone for everyone.

10. There are going to be a lot of pie eaten at the pie-eating contest at the fair.

D. Correct the punctuation of the appositives in the following sentences as needed. If no change is necessary, explain why.

Example: Virginia has three sisters. Her sister, Ethel, lives in Minnesota.

Revised: Virginia has three sisters. Her sister Ethel lives in Minnesota.

1. Montana, a western state has a small population for its size.

2. Montana a state known for its many rivers and parks, is ironically quite arid.

3. We visited Montana, a place of great beauty last summer.

4. What we liked best was the snow on the Big Belt Mountains, a range that stretches for hundreds of miles.

5. As expected, the switchbacks on another beautiful set of mountains, the Beartooths, were quite frightening.

6. One funny incident when a waitress told us to go home still makes us chuckle.

7. The idea that "foreigners" people who come to populate their state, are increasing in number bothers many Montanans.

8. Unfortunately, Montana, the Big Sky Country is attracting many developers.

9. It is doubtful whether their aims, to cut down trees and mine for minerals, will benefit the state.

10. Nevertheless, the great beauty and wilderness the pride of Montana will be hard to destroy.

E. Find the fragments in the following paragraph and correct them. If you think a fragment should not be changed, explain why.

Last winter was very cold and snowy. A hard one for everyone. Still, there were optimists who enjoyed the weather. Despite the high fuel bills and the slippery roads. They saw the weather as an opportunity to engage in outdoor sports. For example, skiing, ice skating, and sledding. Not to mention, ice fishing and building snowmen. The beauty of the freshly fallen snow and getting warm again are two incentives for getting out in the bad weather. Bad weather that gives other people the flu. I like to hear stories about winter sports, but most of all I like to watch them from a distance. Sipping hot chocolate, which is my favorite pastime.

F. Mark Twain was famous for recording slang and nonstandard English in dialogue to re-create authentic-sounding speech. Read the following passage from *Huckleberry Finn*. Rewrite the direct speech as indirect speech. Then compare the original passage and your rewritten passage by reading them both aloud. How has the effect of the passage changed by using indirect speech? (This can be a group or whole-class activity.)

> We stopped talking and got to thinking. By and by Tom says:
> "Looky here, Huck, what fools we are to not think of it before! I bet I know where Jim is."
> "No! Where?"
> "In that hut down by the ash hopper. Why, looky here. When we was at dinner, didn't you see a man go in there with some vittles?"
> "Yes."
> "What did you think the vittles was for?"
> "For a dog."
> "So'd I. Well, it wasn't for a dog."
> "Why?"
> "Because part of it was watermelon."
> "So it was—I noticed it. Well, it does beat all that I never thought about a dog not eating watermelon. It shows how a body can see and don't see at the same time."

EXERCISES FOR CLASSROOM APPLICATION

A. Devise an exercise or activity for students who frequently use nominal fragments in their writing.

B. Develop an activity in which you use drama to help students distinguish between written direct and indirect speech.

PART III   STYLE, CHOICE, AND CONVENTION

For writers, choosing how to use nominals is often a stylistic choice. It can even be a choice that goes against some writing conventions. In Part Three we discuss how students can expand and create variety in their writing by using unusual nominal patterns such as extraposition or prepositional phrases as nominals. We will also discuss how to use fragments for stylistic effect, when and how to move appositives, and how to use dialogue effectively within a narrative.

UNUSUAL NOMINAL PATTERNS AND WHEN TO USE THEM

In Chapters 5 and 7, we discussed how writers can rearrange structures within a sentence to emphasize a part of the sentence or to produce an effect, as is illustrated by the following examples of adverbial movement:

1. A burglar can *often* evade police for a very long time.

2. *Often* a burglar can evade police for a very long time.

3. *Because he was tired*, the little boy yawned loudly.

4. The little boy yawned loudly *because he was tired*.

In the first two sentences, placing *often* either after the modal *can* or at the beginning of the sentence changes the stress and rhythm of the sentence. In sentences 3 and 4, moving the adverb clause, *because he was tired*, also changes the rhythm of the sentence as well as the stress.

In Chapter 5 and in this chapter, we have also discussed the movement of the subject to follow the verb phrase in sentences where *it* or *there* is used as a placeholder subject, (e.g., *It was surprising that Zelma retired so late in life* or *There were more men on the scaffold than it could hold*). There is another type of extraposition of the subject, however, that does not entail the substitution of *it* or *there*, as in the following sentence:

Seldom can a burglar evade the police for very long.

As you can see from this sentence, sometimes for emphasis a writer may also choose to move part of the verb phrase to the front of the sentence. This type of extraposition is especially common in exclamatory sentences, such as *Boy, can he really jump!* In fact, extraposition is a common stylistic device in English, so common that we seldom notice it unless we are asked to find the subject of the sentence.

Extraposed Phrases and Clauses

As we discussed in Part Two, writers commonly choose to use extraposition to sound less formal, as in these examples:

Formal: That every vote counts is common knowledge.
Less formal: It is common knowledge that every vote counts.

In these sentences, using the *that* clause as the subject of the sentence (*That every vote counts*) gives the sentence a distinct formality. It also emphasizes the content of the clause. Moving the *that* clause to an extraposed position (*It is common knowledge that* ...) both makes the sentence less formal and emphasizes a different part; in this case, *common knowledge* is stressed. This effect is especially obvious when comparing the following two sentences:

1. Where I'm going is none of your business.

2. It's none of your business where I'm going.

Although the content of both of these sentences conveys anger and resentment, the choice of where to place the *wh-* clause indicates which is more aggravating, to be asked where one is going (sentence 1) or to be asked at all (sentence 2).

Experienced writers often use extraposition for both the effect of the formality it can convey and the stress it can put on specific parts of the sentence. Here are some examples to illustrate this point:

1. It is a terrible, an inexorable law that one cannot deny the humanity of another without diminishing one's own. (James Baldwin)

2. There is nothing more difficult than to become critically aware of the presuppositions of one's thoughts. (E. F. Schumacher)

3. 'Twas the night before Christmas, when all through the house / Not a creature was stirring, not even a mouse. (Clement C. Moore)

In these examples, the writers have chosen extraposition for several reasons. To illustrate, let's rephrase each of the quotes to eliminate extraposition:

1. That one cannot deny the humanity of another without diminishing one's own is a terrible, an inexorable law.

2. Nothing more difficult exists than to become critically aware of the presuppositions of one's thoughts.

3. The night before Christmas it was, when all through the house / Not a creature was stirring, not even a mouse.

As you can see, reversing the extraposition and rearranging the components of the sentence changes each sentence in different ways. These examples also illustrate that sometimes some rewording is required when noun phrases are extraposed, as in sentences 2 and 3.

Many inexperienced writers use extraposition or unusual placement in an attempt to craft sentences that sound more formal or more "proper," only to have them stand out as stilted or too jarring in style. In other words, inappropriate extraposition can have the same effect that the overuse of the passive voice can have. To help novice writers avoid these and other problems with extraposition, sentence combining is a useful strategy because it can help writers become aware of the stylistic choices they have. For example, students could examine the two sentences *There was a storm* and *The house was destroyed* and combine them in a variety of ways:

1. A storm destroyed the house.

2. It was a storm that destroyed the house.

3. There was a storm that destroyed the house.

Following the generation of such alternatives, students can compare the resulting variants to the original sentences. Besides sentence-combining practice, novice writers can also look for examples of the stylistic use of extraposition in essays, stories, and novels and then attempt to rewrite specific sentences from these sources to see how the rewording changes the effect of each sentence in its context.

Prepositional Phrases and Extraposition

Use of extraposition is not restricted to nominals. There are occasions when the writer or speaker uses *it* as a dummy subject in sentences that have predicates that describe a location. Usually this description is in the form of an adjective-and-prepositional-phrase combination. Here are some examples of that combination:

1. It is <u>dirty under the refrigerator</u>.
   adjective   prepositional phrase

2. It is <u>hot in the boiler room</u>.
   adjective   prepositional phrase

3. It is <u>loud outside the classroom</u>.
   adjective   prepositional phrase

In sentences such as these, the prepositional phrase functions as an adverbial. However, to be creative or to stress the importance of the location, a writer can choose to place the prepositional phrase before the verb phrase to create the following sentences:

1. *Under the refrigerator* is dirty.

2. *In the boiler room* is hot.

3. *Outside the classroom* is loud.

When students are given the opportunity to try moving parts of sentences to different locations, they can begin to see ways in which they themselves can be creative with language and use it to greater effect in their writing.

NOMINAL FRAGMENTS AS CHOICES

As we have suggested, although many inexperienced writers produce inappropriate fragments, when students become aware of sentence boundaries and develop the ability to recognize fragments as incomplete sentences, they may then be able to use fragments skillfully to create various stylistic effects or to add variety and flavor to their writing. As with the other types of fragments that we have already discussed, there are some circumstances, depending on the audience and purpose of the writing, in which nominal fragments may be effective.

The most common use of nominal fragments is in dialogue:

1. "What are you doing?"
   "Driving." (single-word nominal, not a complete sentence)

2. "Where are you going?"
   "To Toledo." (prepositional phrase, not a complete sentence)

3. "Why are you going?"
   "To get a haircut." (infinitive phrase, not a complete sentence)

4. "What did you say?"
   "That I'm going to get a haircut." (noun clause, not a complete sentence)

Because nominal fragments like those in the examples are so common in speech, they can be used in certain types of writing to give it a natural feel or rhythm, especially when a writer wants to represent dialogue between two or more persons—or even an interior dialogue. Notice how fragments are used in the following paragraph.

> Chocolate. My thoughts kept racing toward chocolate. Just what I needed. Of course, not just any chocolate. I needed something special. Chocolate fudge oozing over chocolate ice cream? Nah. Chocolate cheesecake, rich and creamy? Not to eat now. No, what I needed was chocolate in its simplest and purest form: a candy bar.

This passage contains three complete sentences and seven fragments designed to imitate an interior dialogue, the author's train of thought. Such a passage might be part of a narrative detailing the author's search for the perfect candy bar or an essay describing the joys of chocolate. However the paragraph is used, it is obvious that the writer has control of the fragments and has chosen to use them to create the dynamic effect of dialogue.

Fragments in Advertising

Nominal fragments are very common in advertising. In written advertisements, such fragments are intended to catch the eye and the interest of readers quickly, inviting them to continue reading in order to learn more. Nominal fragments can also provide a concise summary of the appeal or qualities of the product. Here are some examples of uses of nominal fragments in advertising:

> What you've been waiting for. To own a new luxury sedan.
>
> The best deal ever. Total coverage plus a 10-year warranty.
>
> Results in 30 days, 100% guaranteed.

It is obvious that the writers of these advertisements have control of sentence structure and have chosen to use nominal fragments to appeal to their audience fast.

Fragments for Emphasis or Effect

As with other less conventional structures, student writers can learn to use nominal fragments for effect in a variety of ways. As we've described, they can choose to use words, phrases, or clauses to emphasize specific points or to focus on a result, as the following paragraphs illustrate:

In a Narrative

The judge read the jury's verdict to the packed courtroom. Guilty. No chance of parole. 47 years. These words went buzzing through Alex's ears. They became high-pitched and screaming.

In an Expository Essay

Dorothy Day was a well-known political and social activist for half a century, from the 1920s to the 1970s. Her most famous legacy is the soup kitchens and homeless shelters she established in the Great Depression to feed the dispossessed. Houses of Hospitality. That's what they were called, and that's what they've been to millions who come to their doors seeking a hot bowl of soup and a warm bed. Anarchist. Pacifist. Nut. Saint. All are names that were applied to Dorothy Day, one of the most inspiring figures of the twentieth century.

As we have suggested in earlier chapters, although crafting fragments that will be perceived as appropriate and effective may be challenging—even risky—for novice writers, it is important that students who have control of sentence structure have the opportunity to experiment using fragments in a variety of ways. Students can be encouraged to use fragments for specific effects in classroom assignments, in exercises requiring creative writing, or even in working for the school newspaper.

WHEN TO USE DIALOGUE

It is our experience that teachers are often reluctant to encourage their students to use dialogue or quoted speech in a piece of writing because students may experience problems with these options. It is also the case that confusion with dialogue or quoted speech can sometimes cause writers to produce sentence fragments. However, there are a number of contexts in which the use of dialogue can contribute to the effectiveness of a piece of writing, and there are some genres in which dialogue is arguably indispensable. Depending on the aims of the course or the scope of an assignment, the use of dialogue can be entirely appropriate in expository or persuasive writing as well as in fiction. And imagine a screenplay in which no character uttered a word!

Just as varied sentences are necessary to create particular stylistic effects, dialogue or quoted speech also has its place as a way of making people's ideas or thoughts concrete. As we have suggested, even within an expository writing assignment, dialogue can play a role by giving explanations and descriptions a sense of clarity and crispness. For instance, while all too many writing assignments tend to treat narrative, exposition, and argument as discrete genres, it is more realistic to help student writers understand the ways in which these strategies can occur in one assignment to create a sense of development and detail. Consider the following example:

> Tina's grandmother was one of those women who always encouraged her kin to be positive, forward thinkers. In times of conflict and change, Grandma Josie was known to say "When one door closes, another soon opens."

As this passage suggests, the quotation *"When one door closes, another soon opens"* provides concrete support for the statement about Tina's grandmother's having an encouraging and optimistic outlook on life. Although this is a short example, it is equally possible to have more extended dialogue in an essay to give the same sort of realistic and concrete expression of the context or situation being described, whether it be an argument between two persons on opposite sides of a social issue such as gun control or as an opening dialogue that is meant to serve as a springboard for the text as a whole.

A related issue when using dialogue and realistic speech is whether such speech has to maintain grammatical correctness. Although standard English is the medium of most television and radio broadcasters regardless of their region, the use of flawless English in scripted dialogue would be unrealistic because few people who are not professional speakers speak flawless standard English in everyday life. There is a world of difference between the Rolling Stones' famous line "I can't get no satisfaction" and the grammatically flawless "I cannot get any satisfaction." For expressing oneself in the context of a popular song, the choice is clear: the Stones' "vernacular" version is more appropriate than the "perfect" version. Similarly, if a quotation is attributed to a Kentucky grandmother who never attended school or to an inner-city child, the language should reflect the speaker's actual speech and usage regardless of grammatical correctness. Some of the works of John Steinbeck or Studs Terkel contain excellent examples of authentic dialogue and quoted speech.

A final issue regarding the use of dialogue or quoted speech in the context of more formal written discourse is the question of whether or not to use it. That is, what is gained or lost by using dialogue? Dialogue or quoted speech is a stylistic choice that may add a sense of persona and even humor to a student's written work, so that the reader can actually "hear" a human voice behind the words. Whatever the choice, there should ideally be a balance between dialogue and narration. Relying on dialogue to provide description, detail, and flavor should not preclude analysis and clarity of purpose and focus. Part of the choice can and should be dependent on the audience and purpose of the writing. Let us take a procedures manual, for example. Procedures manuals could conceivably benefit from dialogue, but the purpose of such manuals calls for stating concise, clear steps on how to complete a task. The use of dialogue would not further that end and might even make the communication less precise and hence less effective.

Novice writers are already quite familiar with using dialogue or quoted speech in oral discourse. This is because in everyday speech we readily quote others and even repeat whole dialogues or parts of them almost verbatim. Look at the following sample of quoted speech in a communication:

SALLY: And then I said, "How long have you been working here?" And she said, "Two months." And then I said, "Didn't they train you to make change?"

RENATA: And what did she say?

SALLY: Nothing. She just stood there.

RENATA: Well, I would have said, "Give me back my money."

Because students use dialogue or quoted speech in their daily lives, this familiarity can help them transfer their skill in using oral language to their writing. However, when teaching student writers to make choices regarding the use of dialogue or quoted speech in expository writing, they need to be aware of and make choices regarding two issues. First, because as native speakers we speak in fragments and in our various dialects, reporting this conversation in written form requires that the writer decide to what extent to reproduce "errors" from speech in a piece of writing. The extent to which such forms, natural in speech, can appear in written contexts is, as we have suggested elsewhere, a matter of audience and formality. The second issue regarding dialogue or quoted speech has to do with how often and in what contexts to use these stylistic options. As with any other stylistic decisions, however, students cannot become proficient at making such choices unless they are given opportunities to read, discuss, and experiment.

Finally, note that the fact that dialogue is written does not mean that it will not be spoken. That is, a written speech can be delivered orally, with the speaker deliberately emphasizing certain words above others; a play can be acted on a stage before a live audience; and poetry and fiction can be read aloud at coffeehouses and other venues. Thus it is clear that practice in crafting dialogue has the potential to contribute to students' development as speakers as well as writers.

MOVING APPOSITIVES

Although appositive structures are not as movable as adverbials, their placement can be varied. In some instances, the movement of an appositive can create a smaller, more "local" effect by shifting the emphasis in a sentence. As the following examples illustrate, shifting an appositive from its normal place following the noun to which it refers to the beginning of a sentence, immediately preceding the noun, can emphasize particular information or detail:

1. Our next-door neighbor's son, *a veteran car mechanic,* helped us start our aging automobile. (emphasizes *next-door neighbor's son*)
   A veteran car mechanic, our next-door neighbor's son helped us start our aging automobile. (emphasizes that the neighbor's son is *a veteran car mechanic*)

2. The yellow tabby cat, *a grizzled and mangy fellow,* sat on the fence hissing at our dog. (emphasizes the cat's color, *yellow,* and type, *tabby*)
   A grizzled and mangy fellow, the yellow tabby cat sat on the fence hissing at our dog. (emphasizes that the cat was *grizzled* and *mangy* and the cat's male gender)

3. The students in Tom's class, *a majority of the school's political science majors,* drove to Kentucky to watch the presidential debate. (emphasizes that the students are *in Tom's class*)
   A majority of the school's political science majors, the students in Tom's class drove to Kentucky to watch the presidential debate. (emphasizes that the students are *political science majors*)

Besides shifting the emphasis, fronting an appositive modifier may have other effects. With respect to the sample sentences just given, for example, it can be argued that fronting the appositive has in each instance altered the cause-and-effect relationship implied in each of the sentences. In sentence 1, for example, fronting the appositive *a veteran car mechanic* suggests that it is the son's expertise as a car mechanic, not his relationship to us (*the neighbor's son*), that may have prompted him to fix our car. In sentence 2, the fronting of *a grizzled and mangy fellow* strengthens the inference that the hissing occurred because of the nature of the cat rather than the simple presence of the dog. That is, the cat was hissing because he's a tomcat (*fellow*) who has seen quite a bit of combat and hard times (*grizzled and mangy*) in his life. Finally, in the third sentence, moving the appositive *a majority of the school's political science majors* to the beginning strengthens the inference that it was the fact that the students were mostly political science majors, and not the fact that they were in Tom's class, that motivated them to drive to Kentucky to see the presidential debate.

The other major reason for moving appositional structures is to affect the formality of a piece of writing. Unlike shifts in emphasis within a particular sentence, formality is usually seen as a text-level concern. A change in the formality of a particular sentence, then, ordinarily is an attempt by the writer to modulate the overall formality of his or her discourse. It may be, for example, that a sentence "sticks out" because it seems too formal or too informal compared to the sentences surrounding it. Sometimes writers may "fiddle" with an individual sentence not because it calls attention to itself but rather because they have a sense that making the particular sentence more or less formal will help them maintain the level of formality they have been constructing. Although it can be debated as to which of the appositive variants (fronted or regular placement) is more formal, in general, moving—or extraposing—nonrestrictive clause appositives creates sentences that sound slightly less formal. Finally, as with any other structures whose placement can be varied, appositives can be repositioned to create sentence variety. However, because appositives are less easily moved than other structures such as adverbials, it is wise to caution apprentice writers to consider other factors besides *simply* variety—such as formality and the changes that a shift in emphasis might cause to meaning—when considering options for placement. Students who wish to experiment with the stylistic options afforded by the placement of appositives should be encouraged to identify these structures in different genres of writing and to note matters such as the frequency, type, and placement of appositives. Also, either in small groups or in large class discussions, students should be engaged in activities that require them to craft pairs of sentences with regularly placed and moved appositives and to discuss the differences in meaning and formality these options create.

Stop

EXERCISES FOR PRACTICE

A. Find some examples of writing featuring unusual nominal patterns. Describe the effect of these patterns.

EXERCISES FOR CLASSROOM APPLICATION

A. Develop an exercise in which you have your students investigate sentence variety by using clauses, extraposition, appositives, and other nominals. Have them focus on what structures are used most commonly and what options they discover.

B. Design an activity in which your students employ advertisements to show how nominal fragments are used in writing. This activity should require them to demonstrate their knowledge of what these fragments look like and the various effects they can produce. For example, you might have your students select a product and design an ad using nominal fragments.

C. Devise an activity that requires students to write dialogues and punctuate them appropriately.

D. Design an activity that requires your students to report something that they observe and to use dialogue in the report.

COMPOUNDING IN
AND WITH SENTENCES

Chapter Preview

Chapter 10 explores sentence complexity.

In **Part I** you will learn about

- Punctuation, parallelism, and correlative conjunctions
- Logical relationships within and between sentences
- Punctuation of compound structures

In **Part II** you will learn about the challenges
writers can face with

- Correlative conjunctions
- Commas in conjoined structures and sentences
- Faulty parallelism
- Fragmented compound structures

In **Part III** you will learn about

- Distinguishing between mature and immature style
- Making choices about stylistic options, including using
  short sentences for emphasis, using parallel structures
  effectively, and using connecting words appropriately

PART I   CONJOINING BETWEEN AND WITHIN SENTENCES

In this chapter we will continue to discuss ways that structures in sentences can be compounded, as well as how sentences themselves can be joined to create longer sentences. Throughout this discussion we will use the terms *compound* and *conjoin* interchangeably to refer to the same principle of putting smaller pieces together to create a larger compound structure.

As you may recall, in Chapter 5 we discussed how various words and constituents in simple sentences can be combined to create compound structures such as compound subjects, as in *Bob and Tom asked for more porridge*. A diagram of the compound structure of this sentence might look like this:

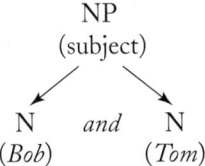

The diagram shows that the noun phrase that functions as the subject of the sentence *Bob and Tom asked for more porridge* is made up of two nouns, *Bob* and *Tom*, that are combined using the conjunction *and* to produce the compound subject *Bob and Tom*.

Because kernel (simple) sentences can be combined to create larger structures, in Chapter 6 we explained the two major techniques that can be used to join simple sentences to create larger structures: *conjoining* and *embedding*. As we explained, two sentences can be joined equally to create a *conjoined* sentence, or they can be combined in such a way that one sentence becomes a subsidiary part *embedded* in the other. Conjoined sentences are commonly referred to as *compound* sentences, and embedded sentences are commonly referred to as *complex* sentences. (Sentences that involve both types of combining are often referred to as *compound-complex* sentences.) The sentence *We went to the water, but we didn't jump in* is a compound sentence and can be diagrammed in this way:

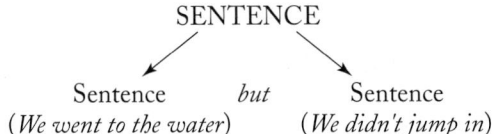

This diagram shows that the conjoined (compound) sentence *We went to the water, but we didn't jump in* is really made up of two sentences (*We went to the water* and *We didn't jump in*) that are combined using the conjunction *but*. The diagram also shows that the two simple sentences are joined equally; neither is a part of the other.

In contrast, the sentence *The potatoes that grow in our yard always taste deli-cious* contains an embedded structure. This sentence can be diagramed as follows:

SENTENCE

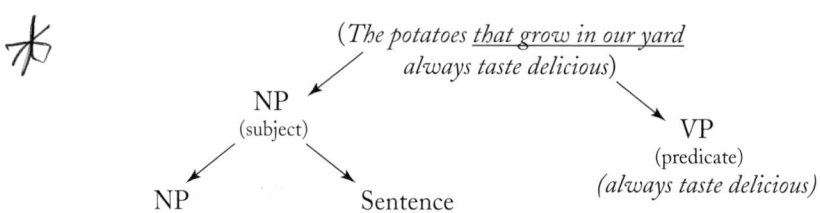

This diagram shows that the subject of the sentence, *The potatoes that grow in our yard*, is made up of a noun phrase (*The potatoes*) and a relative clause (*that grow in our yard*). Notice how the relative clause *that grow in our yard* is made a part of another sentence through embedding. In the diagram, the clause *that grow in our yard* is a constituent of the subject noun phrase *The potatoes that grow in our yard*.

So that you can more easily contrast sentences combined by conjoining with sentences combined by embedding, here is a diagram that contrasts the two forms based on our examples:

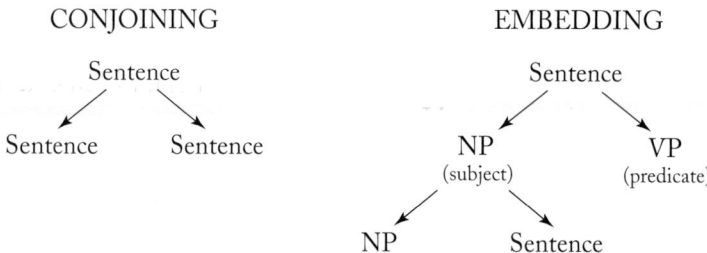

In Chapters 6, 7, 8, and 9 we discussed three major clauses that can occur in Eng-lish: adverb clauses, adjective clauses, and noun clauses. In the remainder of this chapter we will complete our exploration of the ways of combining English sen-tences by examining compound sentences more closely.

COMPOUNDING IN SENTENCES: A REVIEW

As we explained in Chapter 5, different structures in sentences can be com-pounded, as these examples illustrate:

1. *Tennis and swimming* are my favorite activities. (compound subject)

2. Nathan likes *the big red ball* but not *the little blue car*. (compound direct object)

3. Carol sent *Sara and Laura* each a big package. (compound indirect object)

4. Jim saw the wild horses run _out of the forest_ and _across the plains_. (compound prepositional phrases)

5. The sparrow _spread_ and _flapped_ its wings. (compound verb)

6. Mary hung the _large_ and _detailed_ map across the wall of her study. (compound adjective)

Nouns, noun phrases, nominals, adverbs, adverb phrases, adverbials, adjectives, adjective phrases, and adjectivals can all be compounded for all of their many functions.

When nouns, noun phrases, or nominals are compounded, they can be replaced entirely by pronouns or used in conjunction with pronouns, as in these examples:

1. Carol sent _Sara and Laura_ each a big package. (compound indirect object)
   Carol sent _them_ each a big package. [The compound indirect object _Sara and Laura_ is replaced by one pronoun, _them_.]

2. We like _Tom and his wife_. (compound direct object)
   We like him and his wife. [One noun in the phrase _Tom and his wife_ is replaced by the pronoun _him_.]
   We like _them_. [The entire compound direct object is replaced by one pronoun, _them_.]

Frequently, when speaking in the first person, it is natural to combine a noun with a pronoun, as in _Betty and I went on a shopping spree_, because it is usually considered odd to refer to oneself by one's own name. The flexible nature of compounding allows this mixing of forms within structures.

Punctuating Compound Structures

In Chapter 3 we discussed how to punctuate compound adjectives (also called _coordinate adjectives_). As we explained, when two adjectives are used to give two independent descriptions of the same thing, they can be separated by a conjunction such as _and, or, but,_ or _yet,_ as in

The chicken breast was _tender_ _and_ _large_.

In such sentences, the two adjectives (_tender, large_) have been conjoined using the conjunction _and_ to produce a compound structure (_tender and large_). However, in some instances the conjunction _and_ can be dropped and a comma inserted, as in

The chicken breast was _tender, large_.

This use of a comma as a substitute for _and_ is especially common when using compound adjectives before a noun, as in The _large, tender_ chicken breast made our *mouths water.* This type of substitution is commonly used with compound adjectives but only rarely with other compound structures. For example, a sentence with the compound structure <u>*Bob, Cassie came to the reception*</u> rather than <u>*Bob and Cassie came to the reception*</u> would be ambiguous and confusing. So would a compound structure such as *The girls <u>ran, skipped</u> across the yard.* Such ambiguity rarely occurs when coordinate adjectives separated by a comma are used appropriately.

However, when compound structures of any sort consist of three or more items in succession, commas should ordinarily be used to separate them, as the following examples illustrate:

1. The *big, hairy, and scary* dog turned out to be gentle and cuddly.

2. *Alan, Ott, and Joe* worked together on their cars.

3. The children *played, laughed, and ate* all day long.

4. The aim of most people is *to live, laugh, and love* the best they can.

The general rule of punctuation in English for three or more items in succession is to place a comma after each item except the final one. The comma may, as a stylistic option in such a series, be omitted before the conjunction (as in *Alan, Ott and Joe* instead of *Alan, Ott, and Joe*). But omitting the comma may lead to ambiguity, as in *The breakfast menu offered cereal or toast, ham and eggs.* Is *ham and eggs* one item or two? If someone doesn't want cereal, is the alternative just *toast* or *toast, ham and eggs*? Consequently, it is wise always to use a comma where one is needed.

Punctuation, Parallelism, and Correlative Conjunctions

In Chapter 5 we explained that structures can be conjoined using phrases as well as single words such as *and, or,* or *but.* There is a small set of phrases that perform a joining function: *both ... and, either ... or, neither ... nor, not only ... but also,* and *whether ... or.* Such phrases are called *correlative conjunctions* because they show an equal relationship, as these examples indicate:

1. Donna likes <u>both</u> *chocolate* <u>and</u> *vanilla* ice cream. [*Chocolate* and *vanilla* are adjectives describing flavors of ice cream. Using *both ... and* indicates that the items are given equal importance.]

2. Students can choose <u>either</u> *to live in a dorm* <u>or</u> *to live off campus.* [*To live in a dorm* and *to live off campus* are both infinitive phrases providing alternative housing options for students to choose from. Using *either ... or* indicates that the two options are equal.]

3. <u>Neither</u> *my mother* <u>nor</u> *I* have blue eyes. [*My mother* and *I* are both noun phrases or nouns. Like *either ... or, neither ... nor* presents two equal options. They differ only in that *either ... or* presents *positive* options and *neither ... nor* presents *negative* ones.]

4. The horses ran <u>not only</u> *out of the stable* <u>but also</u> *across the busy roadway.* [*Out of the stable* and *across the busy roadway* are both prepositional phrases. Using *not only … but also* requires this symmetry of both form (prepositional phrases) and type of information (where they ran). It serves the same purpose as *both … and,* but use of this correlative conjunction implies that the information that follows *but also* is somewhat more unexpected or alarming than the information that follows *not only.*]

5. Julia didn't know <u>whether</u> *to laugh* <u>or</u> *to cry.* [*To laugh* and *to cry* are both infinitives in form. Using *whether … or* indicates that a choice must be made between two equal options.]

As these examples show, commas are not used to separate correlative constructions when only two structures are involved. But the rule for comma use with compound structures of more than two items is true for some correlatives as well, and so sentences such as the following are common:

1. This book will be of interest <u>not only</u> *to scholars, researchers, and teachers* <u>but also</u> *to the general reader.*

2. We didn't know <u>whether</u> *to shout, stamp our feet, and wave our arms* <u>or</u> *to sit quietly and be happy.*

(Note that no examples are given for *both … and, either … or, neither … nor,* and *not only … but also* because these conjunctions should not be used with more than two items or options.)

Although novice writers may not make consistent errors in punctuating parallel structures, correlative structures can be a problem for them because correlative structures *do* indicate an equal relationship and for that reason require equal forms (parallel structures). Novice writers may produce faulty parallelism, as in *She likes <u>both</u> running <u>and</u> to enjoy herself.* Because *running* and *to enjoy* are structured in an equal relationship, the form they each take should be the same: *She likes <u>both</u> to run <u>and</u> to enjoy herself* or *She likes <u>both</u> running <u>and</u> enjoying herself.* We will discuss faulty parallelism and other problems in conjoining sentences in Part Two of this chapter.

COMPOUNDING SENTENCES: A REVIEW

We have already explained in earlier chapters some of the important principles that dictate how compound or conjoined sentences are structured. As you may recall, one major issue with respect to compounding sentences has to do with the logical relationship created between (or among) such sentences when they are joined. The other has to do with the proper punctuation of compound structures, which is more a matter of conventions associated with written standard English.

Logical Relationships

In combining two kernel (simple) sentences to create a compound structure, the English language user has essentially two options: to join the sentences with no connecting word or to join them with a connecting word (conjunction). The two types of connecting words that are used to join simple sentences into compound sentences are called *coordinating conjunctions* and *conjunctive adverbs:*

Two simple sentences: John got tired. He went home.

Option 1:   John got tired; he went home. (no connecting word)

Option 2:   John got tired, *so* he went home. (coordinating conjunction)
John got tired; *therefore,* he went home. (conjunctive adverb)

[handwritten margin note: note punctuation (semi-color)]

As the examples indicate, a compound sentence in which the simple sentences are linked merely by proximity can't reveal the nature of the relationship between these sentences as precisely as a compound sentence that employs a connecting word or expression.

Still, whenever simple sentences are joined together, they either directly state or indirectly imply some kind of relationship with each other. Although the compound sentence *John got tired; he went home* does not contain a conjunction that specifies the relationship between the parts, it does suggest a sequence of events (that John got tired *before* he went home) and implies as well a cause-and-effect relationship (that John may have gone home *because* he was tired). By contrast, the compound sentences *John got tired, so he went home* and *John got tired; therefore, he went home* unambiguously characterize the relationship between John's getting tired and his going home as being one of cause and effect: John went home as a consequence of being tired.

Although linguists and grammarians have categorized the relationships between clauses in compounded (and embedded) sentences in different ways, most identify at least four major types of meaning relationships: *additive, contrastive, cause-and-effect,* and *temporal.* In general, *additive* relationships express some sort of equivalency or similarity between the compound structures. *Contrastive* relationships suggest a connection between the compound structures that is contrary to expectation. *Cause-and-effect* relationships convey a sequence between the compound structures: an act and then its consequences. And *temporal* relationships express various time sequences that relate the compound structures to one another. (We discussed the first three of these four relationships in Part Two of Chapter 7.) Following are examples of compound sentences that illustrate the four commonly identified logical relationships, with the connecting words and expressions set in italics:

Additive

1. John laughed, *and* Belle cried.

2. John mowed the lawn; *in addition,* he trimmed the hedges.

3. *Not only* did Beasley study, *but* he *also* helped his roommate.

4. I'm not leaving here; *moreover,* Betty's not going either.

5. All of the citizens helped; *for example,* the Moores cleaned up the park.

6. Ed is going to complain; *furthermore,* he will demand his money back.

Contrastive (Adversative)

1. John laughed, *but* Belle cried.

2. John refused to mow the lawn; *however,* he did trim the hedges.

3. John thought Bette had never been a good student; *nevertheless,* she graduated from college with honors.

4. None of the students studied for the exam, *yet* they all passed.

5. We all thought that no one would help us; *in fact,* we had more volunteers than we needed.

Cause-and-Effect

1. John laughed, *so* Belle laughed too.

2. All of the citizens offered to help; *for this reason,* the Moores got involved too.

3. John refused to mow the lawn; *therefore,* the grass soon stood three feet high.

4. None of the students studied for the exam; *consequently,* they all failed.

Temporal

1. John laughed; *then* Belle cried.

2. John refused to mow the lawn; *simultaneously,* he announced his intention to sell his lawn mower.

3. Beasley studied; *at the same time,* he listened to Mozart.

4. Many of the students ordered hot dogs at the game; *afterward,* they all got sick.

As these sentences illustrate, the meaning relationships that connecting words in particular categories create between the simple sentences they join can be quite similar or quite different. The words *but* and *however*, for example, create virtually identical contrastive relationships and can be used interchangeably; the only difference in meaning that the two words suggest has to do with formality:

> I was looking forward to eating at the new restaurant, *but* the experience disappointed me. [*But* is less formal.]
>
> I was looking forward to eating at the new restaurant; *however,* the experience disappointed me. [*However* is more formal.]

In contrast, the additive relationships created by *for example* and *moreover* are not similar; these expressions cannot be used interchangeably. *For example* suggests that the second simple sentence will exemplify or contain a more specific instance of a larger, more general category mentioned in the first simple sentence. *Moreover* merely suggests that the second sentence is going to provide additional related information.

> I am looking for a plant that can stand a good deal of shade; *for example,* a hosta would be suitable. [*Plant* is the larger category; … *hosta* is a type of plant.]
>
> I am looking for a plant that can stand a good deal of shade; *moreover,* it should be tolerant of sandy soil and dry conditions. [The text following *moreover* gives additional information.]

The point here is that although these four categories of meaning relationships are useful tools in helping writers see broad similarities and differences among the logical relationships that coordinating conjunctions and conjunctive adverbs can create within compound sentences, they do not provide a precise classification system. In fact, some connecting words such as *or* don't fit easily into any category. On the one hand, it can be argued that *or* creates an *additive* relationship between or among the clauses it connects because it sets up two (or more) equivalent possibilities, as in *I'm going to drive to Chicago this weekend, or I will fly there from Detroit.* On the other hand, it can be argued that each of the possibilities in the clauses that *or* connects *contrast* with one another.

Punctuating Compound Structures

In spoken English, the major challenge for the language user in creating compound sentences (assuming that each simple sentence is properly formed) is to express the logical relationship between or among the clauses appropriately. However, as we explained in Part Two of Chapter 7, semiformal or formal written contexts present an additional challenge because of punctuation conventions. If we look again at the options for combining sentences discussed earlier, it's clear that several different punctuation conventions apply:

Two simple sentences:	John got tired. He went home.
Option 1:	John got tired; he went home. (no connecting word)

Option 2:	John got tired, *so* he went home. (coordinating conjunction)
	John got tired; *therefore,* he went home. (conjunctive adverb)

As Option 1 shows, sentences joined without a connecting word ordinarily require a semicolon (;). However, when three or more sentences are combined, commas plus the word *and* are acceptable—even preferable—since they unify the events in the newly combined sentence:

1. Woody pulled out of his leash; he ran through a flower bed; he sent our neighbor's cat running up a tree.

2. Woody pulled out of his leash, he ran through a flower bed, and he sent our neighbor's cat running up a tree.

Unfortunately, despite the fact that both coordinating conjunctions and conjunctive adverbs join sentences (independent clauses) to create compound sentences, they do not employ the same punctuation to accomplish this. Coordinating conjunctions are quite flexible and can accompany several different punctuation options. When connecting short sentences with a coordinating conjunction, it is usual to use a comma before the conjunction, although in very short sentences the comma may be omitted. Sentences joined with a coordinating conjunction can also take a semicolon if one of the clauses already contains a comma.

1. No punctuation:	John cried and Mary laughed.
	Eva got over her cold but now Marv has it.
2. Semicolon:	Indigo studied her calculus; *yet* she didn't do well on her exam, despite taking extra time to finish.
	Andy's mother urged him repeatedly to get the oil changed in his car, a brand-new, bright-red Hyundai; *so* he made an appointment for the Thursday after Christmas.
3. Comma:	The results of the proficiency test were disappointing, *so* the teachers met to determine a plan of action.
	The managers decided to have a sale of the damaged merchandise, *but* they reduced the prices of their best-selling products too.

Unlike compounded sentences joined by coordinating conjunctions, which permit a range of punctuation options, sentences that employ conjunctive adverbs _always_ require semicolons. Also, depending on the placement of the conjunctive adverb, one or two commas are required:

1. Fuji hid under the bed; _nevertheless,_ she got taken to the vet.

2. Fuji hid under the bed; she got taken, _nevertheless,_ to the vet.

3. Fuji hid under the bed; she got taken to the vet, _nevertheless._

As the examples illustrate, besides requiring a semicolon, conjunctive adverbs must also be set off with commas when they join sentences. Despite the seeming "simplicity" of compound sentences, these structures often cause problems even for experienced writers because of the various punctuation conventions and because of the additional complications created by the mobility of conjunctive adverbs.

EXERCISES FOR PRACTICE

A. Each of the following sentences or sets of sentences contains compound structures. Underline each of the compound structures, identify the forms within each structure, and state how each structure functions in the sentence (nouns as compound subject, gerunds as compound direct object, etc.).

> **Example:**   The impatient man regretted calling the policeman
> underline{incompetent and stupid}. (compound adjective phrase as
> object complement)
>
> underline{Running and jumping} are two of my dog's favorite activities.
> (gerunds as compound subject)

1. The weather today is sunny but cold.

2. I am not anxious to give you the truth. But I am very anxious to have you understand that all truth and power are feeble to you except your own. (Walt Whitman)

3. Sally was mad at her teacher for being unfair and grading too hard.

4. The mail carrier either dropped the letter or lost it.

5. There are three kinds of people in the world: those who can count and those who can't.

6. The black, fuzzy cat mewed and purred yet did not move as Kris but not Kevin stroked its shiny fur.

7. Across the river and through the woods to Grandmother's house we go!

8. We sit together, the mountain and I, until only the mountain remains. (Li Po)

9. Do you know whether Mary Jo gave Jessica or Joanne this plant I'm holding?

10. Nothing is ever lost by courtesy. It is the cheapest of the pleasures; it costs nothing and conveys much. (Erastus Wiman)

B. The following is the final verse of "The Twelve Days of Christmas." We have written out the text with all twelve days included but without punctuation. How would you punctuate it?

> On the twelfth day of Christmas my true love gave to me twelve drummers drumming eleven pipers piping ten lords a-leaping nine ladies dancing eight maids a-milking seven swans a-swimming six geese a-laying five gold rings four calling birds three French hens two turtledoves and a partridge in a pear tree

C. Most of the following sentences contain unpunctuated compound structures. Insert punctuation where appropriate. Be prepared to support your answers.

Example: The ice-cream truck carries ice pops ice-cream sandwiches and frozen yogurt.

The ice-cream truck carries ice pops, ice-cream sandwiches, and frozen yogurt.

1. Angela has a lot of animals: two dogs three birds a rabbit twelve cats and a goat.

2. The birds but not the rabbit are in a cage.

3. Terry would like to go to Hawaii Florida or California for vacation.

4. Most people want only to earn a living to live happily and to die peacefully.

5. Francis Ford Coppola Peter Bogdanovich and William Friedkin were popular film directors in the 1970s.

6. Charles Dickens wrote *David Copperfield* and *Great Expectations* but not *Sense and Sensibility.*

7. Which do you like to do most read cook eat or take naps?

8. Carol gave Dick and Joanne tickets to the opera.

9. If you go to the train station, you can catch a train wait for a train or watch trains arrive but you can't stay there all night and sleep on the benches.

10. Many people believe it is not what you know but whom you know that matters.

D. Select five of the following compound structures, and create sentences that contain them. As an alternative, you could find examples of sentences containing them in written material, including this text. If your sentences are not original, be sure to cite their sources.

> **Example:** Noun phrases as compound direct object
>
> The queen announced a noteworthy change in her cabinet and a new decree outlawing chewing gum.

1. Nouns as compound subject

2. Compound verb phrases

3. Noun phrases as compound direct object

4. Nominals as compound subject

5. Gerund phrases as compound appositive

6. Adjectives as compound subject complement

7. Adjectives as compound object complement

8. Nouns as compound indirect object

9. Noun phrases as compound objects of a preposition

10. Prepositional phrases as compound adverbials

E. The following paragraph contains errors in punctuating compound structures. Find the errors and correct them.

> It is a common practice in the United States but perhaps not in other countries to put wedding, and engagement announcements in the local newspaper. Many interested people, and family members wait eagerly to find out who is getting engaged and who is getting married. Sometimes they even look for who is getting divorced! The wedding announcements often detail the members of the wedding party, who presided over the wedding, the location of the honeymoon and, the bride's wedding dress. The bride, her mother or, the couple, places the announcement in the paper. I don't know who pays for it!

F. All of the following sentences are compound sentences. For every sentence, bracket each simple (or complex) sentence, and underline the means of connection (e.g., semicolon, coordinating conjunction plus punctuation, conjunctive adverb plus punctuation).

> **Example:** [The ponies grazed peacefully]; [they weren't aware of the coyotes].

Example: [After the award show, everyone went out for dinner]; [no one was very hungry, <u>however</u>].

1. We do not stop playing because we are old; we grow old because we stop playing.

2. Grammar conventions are often vexing for people; in fact, even many otherwise confident adults feel insecure about their usage of "correct" forms.

3. We love quiet; we suffer the mouse to play; when the woods are rustled by the wind, we fear not. (Native American chief to the governor of Pennsylvania, 1796)

4. Doubt is an uncomfortable condition, but certainty is a ridiculous one. (Voltaire)

G. As in poetry, song lyrics often play with sentence structure to create a rhythmic effect. The following traditional song, "Wabash Cannonball," contains several compound structures. Try to identify them, and explain the effect the writer was trying to create by combining various structures.

> From the great Atlantic Ocean to the wide Pacific shore,
> From the queen of flowing mountains to the southland by the
>   shore,
> She's mighty tall and handsome and quite well known by all,
> She's the combination of the Wabash Cannonball.
> Listen to the jingle, the rumble, and the roar
> As she glides along the woodland through the hills and by the
>   shore.
> Hear the mighty rush of the engine, hear that lonesome hobo
>   squall,
> You're traveling through the jungles on the Wabash Cannonball.
> She come down from Birmingham one cold December day
> As she rolled into the station, you could hear the people say,
> "There's a girl from Birmingham, she's long and she is tall,
> She come down from Birmingham on the Wabash Cannonball."

H. Some of the following compound sentences are illogical because an inappropriate connecting word has been used. Revise each problem sentence by replacing the connecting word with an appropriate one or by rewriting one of the clauses.

Example: I hate Beethoven, so I listen to his music all of the time.

I hate Beethoven, so I never listen to his music. (sentence rewritten)

Example: The theoretical arguments were persuasive; for example, the accompanying illustrations were bright and colorful.

The theoretical arguments were persuasive; moreover, the accompanying illustrations were bright and colorful. (connecting word replaced)

1. It was getting later all the time, so I decided to keep on working.

2. The arguments in favor of legalizing alcohol for eighteen-year-olds aren't very persuasive; therefore, it is quite likely that many states will adopt this type of legislation.

3. Following the very difficult election, many citizens became cynical; yet these same individuals vowed they would never vote again.

4. In response to public outrage, several committees were charged with conducting an investigation; as can be imagined, many people were reluctant to serve on these committees.

5. No one wanted the difficult job of contending with possible political fallout, and yet, remarkably, few people applied for the positions.

6. Journalists interviewed quite a few of those who volunteered to be on the investigating committees and asked them to account for their willingness to serve; most really didn't have an answer.

7. Several volunteers did give their reasons; they explained their commitment to service as an obligation of citizenship, however.

8. Watching the proceedings made me proud and humble, yet I wasn't ready to volunteer for a similar task.

9. Citizenship is hard to define, so social theorists continue to construct theories about what it entails.

10. Sometimes the most difficult tasks must be the most enjoyable, yet how does one explain people's willingness to take them on?

I. Some of the following compound sentences are punctuated inappropriately. Identify these, and correct the punctuation.

Example: The begonias looked healthy, however they all wilted and died.

The begonias looked healthy; however, they all wilted and died.

1. To construct a picket fence, you need to measure the perimeter of your yard, then you need to calculate the amount of wood you need.

2. These days many people are opting for plastic fencing material rather than wood, wood requires too much maintenance.

3. Heat, sunlight, rain, and humidity all damage painted surfaces, for example, painted wood shingles show their age rather quickly.

4. Still, plastic fencing, despite its artificial (and undesirable) appearance is very costly; in fact, a plastic fence costs about twice what a wood fence costs.

5. In making a decision about how to spend resources, many factors are important, for instance available disposable income is a vital consideration.

6. Sometimes limited resources can force people into unwise financial decisions, in addition, such limitations can prompt persons to purchase faulty, unsafe products.

7. Despite the availability of consumer protection agencies, many persons get taken advantage of by unscrupulous vendors, these vendors may be more common than ever, in fact.

8. Citizens need to become familiar with resources that exist to assist them, however, this isn't always as simple as it may seem.

9. Nonprofit organizations often don't have the funds to advertise the availability of their services, so consumers often aren't aware of these.

10. Volunteerism also may have diminished, consequently, many community outreach efforts may have been discontinued. *stop wed 12/3*

PART II   CHALLENGES FOR WRITERS

In addition to problems related to subordination and to connecting sentences with conjunctive adverbs, which we discussed in Chapter 7, there are several other vexing problems writers may encounter when conjoining sentences. Among the ones we discuss in this section are problems with using correlative conjunctions (also known as *paired coordinators*), problems when using commas in a series, problems with awkward and ambiguous parallel structures, and problems with fragmented predicates.

PROBLEMS WITH CORRELATIVE CONJUNCTIONS

As we have suggested, novice writers sometimes have problems when using correlative conjunctions (*both ... and, either ... or, neither ... nor, not only ... but also,* and *whether ... or*). These problems may involve using *both ... and* and *whether ... or* incorrectly, ambiguous sentences caused by the misplacement of the correlative, using *not only ... but also* incorrectly, or having difficulty with subject-verb agreement.

Using *both ... and* and *whether ... or*

One of the problems apprentice writers may experience when using correlative conjunctions is overgeneralizing the use of *both ... and* and *whether ... or,* using them to connect both complete sentences and parts of sentences. When this happens, awkward or ungrammatical structures may result because *both ... and* and *whether ... or* cannot be used to connect full sentences.

Unlike *both ... and* and *whether ... or,* most correlative conjunctions can connect both parts of sentences and complete sentences, as these examples indicate:

Parts of Sentences Conjoined

1. Dick *neither* skis *nor* sleds. [*Neither ... nor* connects the verbs *skis* and *sleds.*]

2. The mail carrier left *either* a big box *or* a large bag of mail for you next door. [*Either ... or* connects the noun phrases functioning as direct objects, *a big box* and *a large bag of mail.*]

3. Alice likes *not only* cooking *but also* eating what she cooks. [*Not only ... but also* connects the gerund *cooking* and the gerund phrase *eating what she cooks,* which are functioning as direct objects.]

Complete Sentences Conjoined

4. *Either* the mail carrier will deliver your mail *or* you will have to pick it up at the post office. [*Either ... or* connects the sentences *The mail carrier will deliver your mail* and *You will have to pick it up at the post office.*]

5. *Neither* does he have a computer *nor* does he intend to get one. [*Neither ... nor* connects the sentences *He does not have a computer* and *He does not intend to get one.* When using *neither ... nor* to connect sentences, deletion, rearrangement, and addition may be necessary, as this example shows.]

6. *Not only* did the mice eat food from the cupboard, *but* the rats *also* had their share. [*Not only ... but also* connects the sentences *The mice ate food from the cupboard* and *The rats had their share.* When using *not only ... but also* to connect sentences, movement and addition may be necessary, as here.]

However, *both ... and* and *whether ... or* can be used *only* to conjoin parts of sentences, as in the following examples:

Parts of Sentences Conjoined

1. Amiyalli likes *both* chocolate ice cream *and* chocolate cake.

2. Di couldn't decide *whether* to join in the game *or* to watch from the sidelines.

Complete Sentences Conjoined

3. **Both* <u>Amiyalli kept her cake,</u> *and* <u>she ate it too.</u> [ambiguous]

4. **Whether* <u>Josh had sent the flowers</u> *or* <u>someone else had sent them.</u> [fragment]

Native speakers of English rarely have difficulties with these structures. However, nonnative speakers of English may be confused when trying to use these correlative conjunctions and thus produce problematic sentences like those shown here.

Correlatives and Ambiguity

Another problem novice writers may have in using correlative conjunctions is that they may not pay attention to where the conjunction should be placed and thus create an ambiguous or confusing sentence. Here are some examples of the types of sentences that can result when inexperienced writers don't attend carefully to the placement of correlative conjunctions:

1. **He *both* <u>went to the museum</u> *and* <u>to the zoo.</u> [What follows each part of the correlative must be parallel—in the same grammatical form. *Went to the museum* is a complete predicate; *to the zoo* is a prepositional phrase. The structure is therefore not parallel, and so the meaning is not clear. To express what the writer probably meant to say, this sentence should be corrected to read *He went <u>both</u> to the museum <u>and</u> to the zoo.*]

2. **Shirley will go *either* <u>to the conference</u> *or* <u>work on her paper.</u> [*To the conference* is a prepositional phrase; *work on her paper* is a complete predicate. The structure is not parallel and is therefore unclear. This sentence should probably be corrected to read *Shirley will <u>either</u> go to the conference <u>or</u> work on her paper.*]

The rule when using correlatives is to place each conjunction immediately before the word or phrase that expresses the alternatives or items being offered or compared:

1. George likes *both* <u>pizza</u> *and* <u>spaghetti.</u> [*Pizza* and *spaghetti* are nouns functioning as direct objects; thus *both* and *and* should directly precede each noun.]

2. Shirley promised *either* <u>her daughter</u> *or* <u>her sister</u> a copy of her book. [*Her daughter* and *her sister* are noun phrases functioning as indirect objects; thus *either* and *or* should directly precede each noun phrase.]

To help students use correlative conjunctions appropriately, it is important to be sure that they are aware that correlative conjunctions are *pairs* of coordinators that work together, and so one shouldn't ordinarily be used without the other. To underscore the fact that these conjunctions work together as a set, it may be helpful to give students practice in underlining correlative conjunctions in sentences and circling the phrases or sentences that the correlative conjunctions are combining. If, for example, apprentice writers are creating ambiguous sentences because they tend to misplace the first conjunction in a pair of correlatives, they need to learn the rule that the first correlative conjunction in the pair always directly precedes the part of the sentence that it combines with another part. Students can learn this by making and carefully examining two separate sentences containing the phrases being combined. For example, suppose a student produces a sentence such as *Both Cassie likes to eat dumplings and cornbread.* The first step would be for the students to underline the conjunctions and circle or bracket the words or phrases being combined, which would produce

<u>Both</u> Cassie likes to eat [dumplings] <u>and</u> [cornbread].

With the teacher's help, the students can create two separate sentences:

Cassie likes to eat <u>dumplings</u>.
Cassie likes to eat <u>cornbread</u>.

By creating two separate sentences, students can see what needs to be combined. In our example, *dumplings* and *cornbread* are intended to be combined, since *Cassie likes to eat* is the same in both sentences. When asked what Cassie likes to eat, the students can easily reply *dumplings and cornbread.* This can be diagrammed as

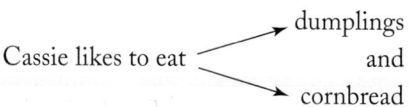

The teacher can then tell the students to apply the rule of putting each of the correlative conjunctions directly before the part of the sentence being combined, to produce *Cassie likes to eat <u>both</u> dumplings <u>and</u> cornbread.*

Problems with *not only ... but also*

Perhaps the most common problems that writers have with correlatives involve the expression *not only ... but also.* There are two types of difficulties writers can have with this connective expression. One problem involves omitting *but ... also* or *also* from the conjoined second sentence or phrase, as in

1. *Not only did I go to bed early, I slept until noon the next day. [*But ... also* is missing from the second sentence, which has been conjoined to the first in what is now a comma splice.]

2. *Not only big Jim but little Molly went. [*Also* is missing from the second phrase to conjoin it to the first phrase, *big Jim.*]

Another common problem novice writers may have in using *not only ... but also* relates to the fact that *also* can be replaced with the substitutes *too* or *as well.*

As these examples show, *too* or *as well* can be used to replace *also* without changing the meaning of the sentence:

1. Not only was Jane tired, *but* she was *also* sick.

2. Not only was Jane tired, *but* she was sick, *too*. [*Too* substitutes for *also*.]

3. Not only was Jane tired, *but* she was sick *as well*. [*As well* substitutes for *also*.]

Novice writers may be aware of the interchangeability of *also, too,* and *as well* but
can become confused when using these correlatives and produce wordy and
redundant sentences such as these:

1. *Not only did Mary go to Columbia, but Joy also went there, too. [Use either
   also or *too* but not both.]

2. *Not only does Molly work for Montana State University, but she also volunteers at the hospital as well. [Use either *also* or *as well* but not both.]

3. *Not only does Kathy know famous people, but she knows some ordinary
   people as well, too. [Use either *as well* or *too* but not both.]

Once again, to help students who are having problems using *but also* or *also*
properly, we suggest that the teacher emphasize the fact that the correlatives work
together as a pair. Students should also be given opportunities to find and underline *not only … but also* in sentences and to connect sentences using *not only … but
also*. This type of practice will also help them avoid wordy, redundant structures.

Correlative Conjunctions and Subject-Verb Agreement

Apprentice writers experience a range of problems with subject-verb agreement,
some of which can occur when correlative conjunctions are used to combine words
or phrases in a compound subject. One common problem involves subject-verb
agreement when the subject is a mix of plural and singular nouns joined by a word
other than *and*, as in *Either Jane or the students are confused*. The general rule for
determining subject-verb agreement when the connector is not *and* is *proximity*;
that is, that the verb should agree in number with the subject that is closest to it in
the sentence. Therefore, a sentence such as *Either Jane or the students is confused*
would not be grammatically correct. If we separate the combined structures in this
sentence into individual structures, we can see the source of the problem:

1. Jane *is* confused. [The singular noun *Jane* takes the third person singular
   form of the verb, *is*.]

2. The students *are* confused. [The plural noun *students* takes the third person
   plural form of the verb, *are*.]

Separating these two sentences shows that *students* is a plural noun; in order for
a verb to agree with the noun *students*, it must take the third person plural form

(in this case, *are*). Because *students* is the closer subject to the verb, the verb must agree with it: *Either Jane or the students <u>are</u> confused.*

Another challenge for writers using correlatives to join compound subjects is that sometimes even when a subject and verb do agree properly, the sentence may still sound awkward. For example, the sentence *Either Jane or the students are confused*—although correct—may sound odd to many speakers of English. Their natural sense of language tells them that if they took out the conjunctions and uncombined the subject/nouns, they would end up with the sentence *Jane are confused*, which is ungrammatical. A common strategy for avoiding the awkwardness that can arise when combining singular and plural subject nouns or noun phrases is to combine them as sentences rather than as phrases:

> *Either* <u>Joan is confused</u> *or* <u>the students are</u>.

In this way, each verb can agree in number with its subject.

To develop skill in crafting well-formed sentences with compound subjects joined with correlatives such as *either … or*, students need to be given an opportunity not only to practice applying the rules for subject-verb agreement but also to practice reacting to whether the resulting sentences sound good. That is, since students need to develop a sense of style and an ear for how sentences sound as well as to learn how to apply rules properly, they need practice in rewriting grammatically correct sentences that may "still sound funny." As with most issues of subject-verb agreement, it is especially important to make the rules clear when working with nonnative speakers of English and to give such writers extra practice in determining subject-verb agreement in sentences.

COMMAS IN CONJOINED STRUCTURES AND SENTENCES

In earlier chapters we have discussed some of the punctuation challenges writers face when they combine sentences using conjunctive adverbs (*however, therefore,* etc.). Here we will discuss some of the challenges writers may face in punctuating sentences that contain coordinating conjunctions (*and, but, for,* etc.), which combine sentences or elements within sentences. Using commas in sentences combined with coordinating conjunctions can be confusing for students, mostly because rules vary according to the situation and because writers can choose to a certain degree when to use commas according to the effect they wish to create. When conjoining sentences with coordinating conjunctions, then, there are times when a comma is necessary and times when it isn't. The difficulty students have is in figuring out when those appropriate times are.

One challenge for students in punctuating sentences combined with coordinating conjunctions is in knowing the rules and conventions. Although handbooks may vary with respect to the rules they give, it is conventional to use a comma with coordinating conjunctions when they combine two independent sentences, for example:

1. Jakimba went to class, *yet* she didn't study. [*Yet* combines the two sentences *Jakimba went to class* and *She didn't study*. A comma before the conjunction *yet* marks the boundary between these two sentences.]

2. Ethel left on vacation, *but* she stopped at the bank first. [*But* combines the two sentences *Ethel left on vacation* and *She stopped at the bank first*. A comma before the conjunction *but* marks the boundary between these two sentences.]

Using a comma before the conjunction is especially appropriate when the sentences have different subjects (e.g., *Woody barked at the passing cars, and Alice reprimanded him*). However, despite the convention that a comma should precede the coordinating conjunction when it joins two independent clauses, writers often choose to omit this comma when combining short sentences (e.g., *The dogs barked and the horses whinnied*).

Regardless of the fact that novice writers may be aware of the convention for using a comma with a coordinating conjunction that joins two sentences, they may become confused in applying that rule because they may not always be able to distinguish between two complete sentences and two structures that are actually part of one sentence. Thus they may add commas where they are not needed, such as between structures that are not independent sentences, as these examples illustrate:

1. *The policeman said that Joely ran a red light, and that she was speeding. [*That Joely ran a red light* and *that she was speeding* are nominals functioning as a compound direct object and thus should not be separated by a comma.]

2. *The traffic cop gave her a ticket, and lectured her on driving carefully. [*Gave her a ticket and lectured her on driving carefully* is a compound verb phrase and thus should not be separated by a comma.]

3. *Spike jumped, and barked when David opened the door. [The comma is erroneously placed between the two verbs in the verb phrase.]

In each of these examples, the writer has mistaken compounded structures within a sentence for complete sentences and has consequently used commas inappropriately with coordinating conjunctions.

A second problem novice writers may have when punctuating combined sentences has to do with comma placement. That is, they may know that a comma is necessary but become confused about where to put it. One result of this confusion is that they may place the comma after the conjunction, as in

1. *Either you like it *or,* you don't. [comma after *or* instead of before it]

2. *This food was expensive *yet,* it didn't taste very good. [comma after *yet* instead of before it]

These problems of knowing when to use a comma and where to place it may become even more confusing for students when a series of sentences or parts of sentences are combined. In general, the problems students experience when combining a series of sentences are similar to the problems they can have when combining two sentences, as these sentences illustrate:

1. *On Saturday, Nicco wrote a letter Peter delivered it and Mary Helene read it. [This is a series of three short sentences, so a comma is needed after each item in the series except the last. It should therefore read *On Saturday, Nicco wrote a letter, Peter delivered it, and Mary Helene read it.*]

2. *The doorbell rang, the pizza arrived and, we started the meeting. [The final comma has mistakenly been placed after the conjunction *and* instead of before it.]

Sometimes confusion with commas can be intensified when novice writers try to combine a series of parts of sentences. In such instances, writers may erroneously put the comma before the first item or after the last item in the series:

1. *The speeding car turned, to the right, to the left, and around the corner. [The first comma is incorrectly inserted *before the first item* in a series of prepositional phrases.]

2. *Jacy bought chips, soda, and ice cream, for the party. [A comma has been incorrectly inserted *after the last item* in a series of nouns.]

To help students know when and where to use commas when combining sentences and parts of sentences with coordinating conjunctions, they need practice in reviewing and properly applying conventions for comma use. Once they understand the appropriate rules and how to use them, students should be given opportunities to edit sentences and passages of writing for errors in comma usage as well as opportunities to properly punctuate unpunctuated sentences, especially if the sentences are in excerpts of writing.

Once students are familiar with the conventions of punctuating sentences combined with coordinating conjunctions, they are ready to learn how to make stylistic choices with respect to such sentences. One option with regard to sentences that might ordinarily be connected with a coordinating conjunction is to write (and punctuate) the sentences separately. In such instances, the second sentence begins with the coordinating conjunction (*but, and, so, for, yet, or*). The rule in such cases is that a comma is normally not needed, just as if the sentences were combined:

1. John studied hard. *So* he passed the exam.

2. John doesn't like spaghetti. *But* I do.

However, students often want to place a comma after the conjunction at the beginning of the sentence:

1. *John studied hard. *So*, he passed the exam.

2. *John doesn't like spaghetti. *But*, I do.

It is perfectly grammatical to begin a sentence with a conjunction, but it is not conventional for that conjunction to be followed by a comma. Putting a comma after the conjunction in such sentences is overpunctuating.

In becoming confident and effective stylists, the challenge for students is to understand how to effectively use the choice of beginning a sentence with a conjunction. That is, students need to learn that the strategy of beginning a sentence with a coordinating conjunction is primarily used for emphasis. For instance, compare these two examples:

1. She was always soft-spoken, *but* she didn't take any guff.

2. She was always soft-spoken. *But* she didn't take any guff.

The meaning of the two examples is essentially the same, but the second sentence in example 2 is more emphatic because it is punctuated separately and begins with a conjunction. As we discuss in Part Three of this chapter, using conjunctions at the beginning of a sentence is a writer's choice—but it is a choice that should not be overused. To help novice writers learn to make such choices, they should have practice in finding examples of how professional writers use conjunctions at the beginning of sentences. After students have found such examples, they need to have the opportunity of reading the examples out loud in order to develop a sense of how starting sentences with conjunctions creates emphasis. Finally, students need to have the opportunity to experiment with punctuation on their own and to test the effect of this experimentation by reading each punctuated example aloud themselves or having a classmate read it aloud.

FAULTY PARALLELISM

Another rather common challenge that compound structures pose for writers is faulty parallelism. Ordinarily, when two or more structures are conjoined, the act of structuring them in this way suggests an equal relationship between or among them. In stylistically fluent writing, therefore, it is expected that conjoined structures take the same form. If, for example, three nominals form a compound direct object, all three should be gerunds or all three should be infinitive phrases or all three should be *wh-* noun clauses, and so on:

1. I enjoy *hiking, swimming,* and *skiing.* (gerunds)

2. I love *to hike in the woods, to swim in rivers,* and *to ski down mountains.* (infinitive phrases)

3. I wondered *what Mary did, where she went,* and *why she left.* (noun clauses)

Here are a few other examples of conjoined structures. In each case, both the nature of the structure (compound subject, compound direct object, compound object of a preposition, etc.) and the form of the compounded elements within the structure (gerunds, infinitives, adjective clauses, etc.) is identified.

1. *To swim without a life jacket or to climb rocks without a safety line* is dangerous. (infinitive phrases as compound subject)

2. To get away from us, Woody tried *barking and dodging.* (gerunds as compound direct object)

3. Evan wasn't *what people expected or what they wanted.* (*wh-* noun clauses as compound subject complement)

Because apprentice writers often do not notice when two or more structures are conjoined, they are liable to create sentences that exhibit *faulty parallelism.* Most handbooks define faulty parallelism as a problem that arises when words or groups of words linked by coordinating conjunctions are parallel in content but not parallel in form:

1. I went <u>hiking</u>, <u>swimming</u>, and <u>to ski</u>. [*To ski* isn't parallel in form.]
         gerund   gerund   infinitive

2. We both bought cars that <u>get good mileage</u>, <u>didn't cost too much</u>, and <u>the cars</u>
                        verb phrase   verb phrase
   <u>were made in Detroit</u>. [*The cars were made in Detroit* isn't parallel in form.]
     independent clause

These two sentences exhibit the most common kind of fault in parallelism: one (or more) of a series of conjoined structures is not parallel in form with the others, and the resulting sentence is awkward. That is, in most sentences, faulty parallelism does not radically diminish readability; it does not make a sentence unclear or ambiguous. There are exceptions, however. In some instances, faulty parallelism can seriously undermine a reader's ability to interpret the meaning of a sentence by making it ambiguous, as in the following example:

Both entertainers make their audiences excited and enjoy themselves.

The problem that faulty parallelism creates in this sentence is that the reader isn't sure which structures are being conjoined. Does the sentence contain a compound predicate:

Both entertainers   *make their audiences excited.*

                          enjoy themselves.

[The entertainers make their audiences excited; the entertainers enjoy themselves.]

Or does the sentence contain a compound objective complement:

Both entertainers make their audiences   *excited.*

enjoy themselves.

[The audiences are made excited and are made to enjoy themselves.]

The first step in revising for faulty parallelism is to recognize the problem in the sentence. As we have suggested in other discussions of sentence structure issues, encouraging students to read their writing out loud is a good practice. Students should also be encouraged to examine writing from a variety of sources (and genres) for conjoined structures and should also be given the opportunity to discuss the form of these structures.

Once students become aware of unbalanced conjoined structures in their own writing, they can be assisted with revision strategies. For sentences with two conjoined structures that create ambiguity (e.g., *Both the entertainers make their audiences excited and enjoy themselves*), students may need practice in recognizing and revising all kinds of sentences that can be interpreted in more than one way because of structural ambiguity:

1. We fed her dog biscuits.

2. Shooting men can be dangerous.

3. Tickling babies can be fun.

4. Both entertainers make their audiences excited and enjoy themselves.

In revising such sentences, students need practice in determining what, exactly, they mean to say, as well as in reshaping the sentence accordingly:

Original: We fed her dog biscuits.
Revision: We fed her dog its favorite treat, biscuits.

Original: Both entertainers make their audiences excited and enjoy themselves.
Revision: Both entertainers make their audiences excited. They also enjoy themselves while they're on stage.

For most other sentences that exhibit faulty parallelism, apprentice writers need practice in identifying conjoined structures and in recognizing the element that is not parallel in form. They also need assistance in developing an array of strategies for reworking sentences that aren't parallel. As a start in this project, teaching revision steps such as the following often prove useful.

Every night, John practices guitar, reads the newspaper, and he also falls asleep in his chair.

(1) Underline the main portion of the sentence—the part that applies to all the conjoined structures; then bracket and number each conjoined structure.

> <u>Every night, John</u> [practices guitar],[1] [reads the newspaper,][2] and [he also falls asleep in his chair].[3]

(2) Identify the form that is not parallel. Sometimes students may see this easily. Or they can try reading the main structure with each conjoined structure to help them identify the structure that is not parallel in form.

> Every night, John *practices guitar.*
>
> Every night, John *reads the newspaper.*
>
> *Every night, John *he also falls asleep in his chair.*

(3) Revise the nonparallel form so that it matches the others.

> Every night, John <u>practices guitar</u>, <u>reads the newspaper</u>, and <u>falls asleep in</u>
>   verb phrase   verb phrase   verb phrase
> <u>his chair</u>.

Note that although revising the form of one nonparallel structure to match the ones that are already parallel is more efficient, some writers may prefer to revise the already parallel forms to match the one that isn't parallel:

Original: Marla is <u>loud</u>, <u>self-centered</u>, and <u>an annoying</u>
                  adjective   adjective   noun phrase
<u>busybody</u>.

Revision: Marla is <u>a loud talker</u>, <u>a self-centered oaf</u>, and
                       noun phrase   noun phrase
<u>an annoying busybody</u>.
        noun phrase

In this example, instead of converting the noun phrase *an annoying busybody* to the adjective *annoying*, the writer chose to convert the other two adjectives to noun phrases so that all three elements would be parallel in form. Either solution is acceptable; stylistic considerations will ordinarily determine which to use.

An alternative to making the nonconforming structure parallel in form is to make it into a separate sentence, as in these examples:

> Every night, John practices guitar *and* reads the newspaper. *Then* he falls asleep in his chair.
>
> Every night, John practices guitar *and* reads the newspaper. *After that,* he falls asleep in his chair.

This option requires some attention to connecting words or expressions both within the original sentences and at the beginning of the new one.

Faulty parallelism is a problem that often persists, even in the writing of more experienced stylists, because conjoined structures can be quite complex and therefore difficult to replicate. It is hard to advise when, exactly, apprentice writers should be made aware of faulty parallelism since they may already be challenged to recognize and revise structures that are considered ungrammatical, such as inappropriate fragments and fused sentences. However, as students become more concerned with crafting sentences that are not only grammatically correct but also graceful and elegant, they may become motivated to revise structures that exhibit faulty parallelism.

FRAGMENTED COMPOUND STRUCTURES

Inexperienced writers do occasionally end a sentence with a series of compound structures and then lose track of the final conjoined structure's relationship with the rest of the sentence. This can result in a sentence fragment—although not as common a type as many other inappropriate fragments we have discussed. Most often fragments involving conjoined structures take the form of isolated compound predicates that are punctuated as if they were sentences:

1. He begins talking like he knows about a topic. *And makes a fool of himself every time.*

2. I was upset, disappointed. *And wondered what I'd gotten myself into.*

3. If I were offered $50,000 tax free, I would save $25,000 of it for emergencies. *And spend the remainder on useful things for my apartment.*

Sometimes, however, because sentences can end with other types of conjoined structures besides compound predicates, these too can cause inexperienced writers difficulty:

1. I considered my commanding officer a tough, no-nonsense person. *But also someone who cared about the "little guy."* (fragmented compound object complement)

2. The next day everyone was bugging me because I didn't turn the man in for unlawful entry. *And for coming into my room uninvited.* (fragmented compound modifying prepositional phrase)

As with any other type of inappropriate fragment, the key to helping the writer is to help her discover a pattern. Students who like to use—and who have difficulty with—conjoined structures should be encouraged to become familiar with these types of sentence constituents by identifying them in their own writing and in writing in a variety of genres. Students should also be encouraged to analyze the forms that conjoined structures take and to make note of the types of form and structure patterns that most often give them trouble. If, for example, a particular writer creates inappropriately fragmented predicates, he should carefully scrutinize every "sentence" that begins with the word *And, But,* or *Or* to see if it contains a verb without a subject. Finally, although sentence exercises that invite students to identify and fix fragmented compound structures are helpful, students also need practice in editing essays or lengthy passages that contain these types of errors.

EXERCISES FOR PRACTICE

A. Some of the following sentences contain errors involving correlative conjunctions. Identify the errors and correct them.

> **Example:**   Both he liked to sing and to listen to music.
> He liked both to sing and to listen to music.

> **Example:**   Tom not only typed up the paper, but he signed it.
> Tom not only typed up the paper, but he also signed it.

1. Whether it will snow or the weather will be pretty.
2. James Taylor has not only been performing since the 1970s, he is still popular.
3. Neither Michael or Damon likes children.
4. Jim went either to White Springs or Sulphur Springs.
5. Andrea not only likes chocolate, Nicholas likes it too.
6. Do you know whether the television works or whether this blank screen is a sign that it is broken?
7. Either Bradley and Ben went to the petting zoo or to the amphitheater.
8. Lee persuaded the cook neither that he likes eggs in his salad or nuts.
9. Marsh liked both to smoke and to play the lottery.
10. Randall both wrote the love letters, and he mailed them to his beloved.

B. Some of the following compound sentences contain faulty parallelism. Identify the errors and correct them.

> **Example:**   Rosamund likes both to play in the park and swimming in the lake.
> Rosamund likes both to play in the park and to swim in the lake. [*Swimming* is changed to *to swim* to make it parallel with *to play.*]

1. Sheri will either call you tomorrow or it will be the next day.

2. Kris likes both to bowl and walking for exercise.

3. Not only does Jennifer speak Spanish, but also French.

4. Do you know whether it would be better to work at home, or should I go to the office?

5. Neither this computer nor my radio can give me the information I want.

6. It snowed either yesterday or the day before.

7. Toni Morrison has won both the Pulitzer Prize and received the Nobel Prize for literature.

8. Alice doesn't know whether she'll move to Ann Arbor or if she'll stay in Bowling Green.

9. Exercise is not only good for you but also fun.

10. The couple will either have chocolate fudge sundaes at their wedding reception, or the guests will eat cake.

C. The following sentences contain errors in punctuation. Underline each error, correct it, and explain why it is an error.

> **Example:**   The happy children, clapped their hands, stomped their feet, and sang for joy.
>
> The happy children clapped their hands, stomped their feet, and sang for joy. [No comma is needed before the first item in a series.]

1. The children carried their sled up the hill with anticipation yet they decided at the top not to use it and built snowmen instead.

2. Mae likes children. But, she only likes other people's children.

3. Jeanie sent Thelma, Sheri, and Julia, sweaters for Christmas.

4. The dogs, and cats played surprisingly well together.

5. Neither the teacher, nor the students like tests.

6. Henry David Thoreau was famous for writing essays but he wasn't known for writing novels.

7. Bette called Marlin, and told him the news.

8. Ethel has been going to graduate school so she is very busy.

9. David and John stay up late grading papers for, that is what teachers do.

10. Chanti babbled, but didn't talk.

D. Revise the following sentences to correct faulty parallelism.

> **Example:**   Everyone admires Barbara because of her courage and she is a kind person.
>
> Everyone admires Barbara because of her courage and her kindness.

1. My favorite film stars make their viewers happy and enjoy themselves.

2. For me, weekends are enjoyable, carefree, and my love life picks up tremendously.

3. Usually, on Saturday we go shopping, or else we stay in our rooms and play cards, watch television, listen to our stereo or whatever strikes our fancy.

4. My roommate is dull, wishy-washy, and always saying boring things.

5. For giving a child a male influence, the alternatives to fathers are grandfathers, uncles, neighbors, and one really successful organization for this purpose is Big Brothers of America.

6. The legalization of drugs would protect people from black market pressures and purity of those drugs.

7. When I was a teenager, you could ask people for dates, drive to away games at other schools, and could just cruise around town to see what was happening.

8. People who drive these automobiles say that they get cheap repairs, good gas mileage, and they can fit in small parking spaces.

9. Traveling off to far-off places is fun, exciting, and a lot of planning is required.

10. Scientists are to this very day still wondering whether they should use genetics to make people smarter or should they just forget the whole idea.

E. Select a piece of your own writing that you produced in response to an assignment in the past year or so. Identify parallel structures. How frequently did you use these? Can you find any examples of problems with faulty parallelism? What do you think caused these problems?

F. Some of the following sentences are punctuated improperly and contain inappropriate fragmented conjoined structures. Identify and revise the flawed sentences.

> **Example:**   I wondered whether Mark would study for the exam. And whether he would pass it.
>
> I wondered whether Mark would study for the exam and whether he would pass it.

1. As I sat in the dark with the joystick in my hand, I began to experience the excitement of stalking a zombie. And shooting it down in cold blood.

2. The article I chose seemed like a good one to evaluate because it contained both good and bad points. And was fairly easy to follow because of the examples it provided.

3. Even though the poem the student wrote ended in a positive way, school officials were concerned that he was headed for trouble. So they expelled him.

4. Encouraging husbands to be more sympathetic to their working wives would have many benefits both for the wives. And for their husbands as well.

5. The essay we selected was well organized, informative. And accompanied by full-page illustrations that broke down the process.

6. In fact, the article was so entertaining, it didn't seem like a history lesson at all. Or like boring, academic writing.

7. When an author puts too much information in an article, it can make the article hard to follow. And difficult to understand.

8. Fraternities and sororities are important organizations on a college campus because they show students how to form communities. And how to engage in philanthropy.

9. Still, I understand that "going Greek" is not for everyone because some folks prefer not to be tied down to one group. Or to be responsible to a single group of friends and housemates.

10. The magazine's treatment of the issue was ultimately fair because it presented both sides of the argument. And it showed how very difficult and ambiguous the problem was.

EXERCISES FOR CLASSROOM APPLICATION

A. Imagine that your students are experiencing difficulty with one of the problems we've discussed in Part Two of the chapter (e.g., faulty parallelism). Describe a lesson or a series of activities that would address the problem. Complete one sample exercise from this lesson.

B. Devise an activity that requires your future students to become aware of patterns of use for one of the structures we've covered in this chapter (e.g., fragmented compound structures). As you design the activity, be sure to describe the age and skill level of your students as well as your aim or purpose in familiarizing them with this structure.

PART III   STYLE, CHOICE, AND CONVENTION

ASSUMPTIONS ABOUT MATURE AND IMMATURE STYLE

Although it may be difficult to define "mature" style precisely, if asked to compare the following three passages in terms of maturity, most adult language users would find the first passage to be more sophisticated or mature than the second or third:

1. Today we visited the art museum, where we looked at and discussed paintings by a variety of artists. After walking through the galleries for two hours, we ate lunch in the cafeteria and then returned to school happy.

2. Today we visited the art museum. We looked at and talked about paintings. They were by many artists. We walked through the galleries for two hours. Then we ate lunch in the cafeteria. Then we returned to school. We were happy.

3. Today we visited the art museum and we looked at and talked about paintings and they were by many artists. We walked through the galleries for two hours and then we ate lunch in the cafeteria and after that we returned to school but we were happy.

Passage 2 would probably be considered immature-sounding because it contains many short, choppy sentences. Passage 3 would also be judged as immature because of the way in which the sentences are combined, using compounding only and no embedding.

These intuitive feelings about the three passages have in fact been confirmed in a number of research studies that found that children's sentences increase in length and complexity as they progress through school. Moreover, although researchers have debated what, exactly, constitutes a "mature" or "complex" style, few dispute that the incidence of main clause coordination diminishes and that of subordination increases as children advance through the grade levels.

The intuitions of most adult language users, along with the research studies that confirm them, hold important implications about style for the apprentice writer. First of all, they suggest that noticeable accumulations of short, choppy sentences in a piece of writing make that writing seem immature, unsophisticated, and unskilled—unless there is a particular reason for such sentences *that is apparent to the reader.* Inexperienced writers should therefore carefully examine sentence length and complexity when they are revising drafts and combine short, choppy sentences into longer, embedded ones, unless they have deliberately crafted short sentences to create a particular effect.

Besides attitudes toward short, choppy sentences, the widespread sense that compound structures are immature structures also contributes to the common notion that embedded sentences indicate greater sophistication of thought or are more cognitively complex than conjoined sentences. In fact, the association of compounding with simplicity of thought and embedding with complexity of thought is so widespread that historically it has informed theories about the language use and, by extension, the thought processes of particular social groups. Compound structures (and less abstract thought) have been attributed to women and to people who inhabit preindustrial, "oral" cultures; embedded structures (and more abstract, complex thought) have been attributed to men and to persons who live in industrialized, "literate" cultures.

Regardless of the validity of any theory about whether or to what extent particular groups tend to prefer compounding over embedding, the association of embedding with complexity of thought is widespread, particularly among the educated. Indeed, the assumption that subordination reflects sophisticated, complex thought may account for the tendency of students to create dense, excessively embedded sentences. Such sentences are in turn marked as being "awkward" or "run-on" by writing teachers, giving rise to confusion and frustration on the part of the students, who are only trying to supply what they think the teacher wants.

As with other matters related to the development of style, in order to develop a sense of when short, uncombined sentences are appropriate or when compounded structures are more effective than embedded ones, students need opportunities to read and discuss a variety of texts so that they can develop a sense of how sentence length and complexity contribute to the overall effect of a piece of writing. Students also need to be provided with opportunities to compare stylistic alternatives that employ simple, compounded, and embedded structures and to discuss whether and why particular audiences would consider these alternatives simple, sophisticated, overly complex, or unintelligible.

MAKING CHOICES ABOUT STYLISTIC OPTIONS

Although short, choppy sentences can create problems for novice writers, there are occasions when such sentences are necessary to create particular stylistic effects. Furthermore, various conjoined structures—even those that may present problems for apprentice writers—can be powerful stylistic tools.

Using Short Sentences for Emphasis

In Chapter 5 we noted that novice writers may overuse or misuse the passive voice in the belief that it sounds more "educated." That type of thinking can also influence a novice writer's choice of sentence length. That is, sometimes novice writers believe that only the longest sentences sound the "smartest," regardless of how these sentences are combined. Ideally, of course, writers should use a mix of sentence lengths and structures to convey their intended meaning most effectively. One choice, then, is to use short sentences. When short sentences are used sparingly and in contrast to longer sentences that contain a variety of structures, such structures can cause the meaning being conveyed to stand out or be emphasized. The following short passage illustrates how a short sentence can be used to catch the reader's attention:

> Among the sounds of the churning and chugging of the engine and the beeps and squawks of the feathered passengers, the captain of the steamboat could barely hear himself think. After weeks of hard days of working on the river, he had allowed himself the freedom of a celebration, and now he was paying for it with an unclear head and a queasy stomach. Suddenly, his mind cleared. Up ahead he saw rolls of white—the boat was approaching rapids—and he would have to gather all the strength he had left if he was to save his crew, his cargo, his boat, and himself.

This passage contains four sentences. Three of the sentences vary in length from thirty to thirty-seven words, but one sentence contains only four words: *Suddenly, his mind cleared.* Juxtaposed against the longer sentences, the short sentence catches the reader's attention. It functions as a turning point in the paragraph, which begins by describing a rather gloomy and groggy situation that quickly changes to a dangerous one. Had the writer used only long sentences, it would not have been possible to create this effect as emphatically.

Besides pointing out important shifts or turns, short sentences can also be used effectively to create rhythm in a piece of writing. For example, in the following short paragraph, the use of short sentences creates a feeling of energy that would not be there had the sentences been combined.

> George saw his prey. It was there in the dark. Quietly, he took a step closer. "My luck is getting better," he thought. His rifle came up. The noise of the fire rang in his ears. Too late did he see the child running out of the brush.

As this passage illustrates, a series of short sentences can create an intensity that can build momentum, especially in a story.

When and How to Use Parallel Structures

Parallelism in any piece of writing means that particular structures are repeated in consistent manner. When used effectively, parallel structures can bring cadence, balance, or emphasis to a piece of writing, as these passages illustrate:

1. Rather than love, than money, than fame, give me truth. (Henry David Thoreau)

2. Where id was let there ego be. (D. H. Lawrence)

3. To every reproach I know but one answer, namely, to go again to my work. "But you neglect your relations." Too true, then I will work the harder. "But you have no genius." Yes, then I will work the harder. "But you have detached yourself from people: you must regain some positive relation." Yes, I will work the harder. (Ralph Waldo Emerson)

In passage 1, Thoreau develops an emphatic rhythm by repeatedly using *than* before "strong" nouns (*than love, than money, than fame*). Had Thoreau expressed the same thought without repeating the word *than,* the sentence would have packed a weaker punch:

Rather than love, money, or fame, give me truth.

Lawrence, in passage 2, uses parallel structure to create a sense of balance. He uses two words that contrast in a specific context (*id* and *ego*) and joins them with a form of *be* (*was* and *be*) in each clause, like a seesaw. Compare his use of parallel structure with some alternative ways he could have chosen to express the same meaning:

Let ego be where id was.

Replace id with ego.

Substitute ego for id.

Ego is better than id.

Each of these grammatical sentences represents choices a writer can make to express essentially the same idea. Lawrence's choice to use parallel structures in an almost poetic construction helps him create more rhythm and balance in his sentence and thus make the sentence more memorable.

Emerson's use of parallel structure is more on the sentence level. Like Thoreau, he uses repetition, which creates a similarly strong emphatic cadence, but Emerson juxtaposes sentences to create that cadence, which has the effect of a dialogue. To create this effect, he uses the same sentence structure to express the different points of view to which he has only one stubborn answer: *I will work the harder.*

Although most novice writers do not aspire to become great literary figures, they can learn to use parallel structure as a means of bringing rhythm, balance, and emphasis to their writing. In so doing, they can make their writing not only more grammatical but also more appealing and readable. To learn how to use parallel structures creatively, students should become familiar with writing that they can use as models. The Declaration of Independence and the Gettysburg Address are classic examples of parallel structure used effectively; however, students may find examples in the advertisements and popular literature of the modern world more relevant and appealing. After becoming familiar with the effective use of parallel structures, students should also be given opportunities to focus on creating parallel structures in their own writing as a way of increasing their ability to express themselves effectively, to catch their readers' attention, and perhaps even to add strength, beauty, and grace to their writing.

Choosing Connecting Words Appropriately

Another stylistic option open to writers is word choice. One aspect of word choice is the careful selection of vocabulary; we discuss it here in the context of combining sentences. When writers decide to combine short sentences into longer ones, they must make stylistic choices about how to make those connections. Two common ways to combine shorter sentences into longer structures is by using coordinating conjunctions (*and, but, yet,* etc.) and by using conjunctive adverbs (*however, therefore, furthermore,* etc.). Some of these words have similar meanings (*for example, but, yet,* and *however* all express contrast), but when a writer tries to use them interchangeably, she may discover that each connector conveys a subtle difference in meaning. For example, compare the ways in which the two sentences *Bill was tired* and *He wanted to finish the task at hand* can be combined:

1. Bill was tired, *but* he wanted to finish the task at hand.

2. Bill was tired; *however,* he wanted to finish the task at hand.

3. Bill was tired, *yet* he wanted to finish the task at hand.

Although each sentence basically provides the same information, there are small, subtle differences in how the information is presented. In sentence 2, replacing *but* with *however* raises the level of formality of the sentence and puts greater emphasis on what follows the conjunction. In the third sentence, replacing *but* with *yet* increases the sense of contrast between the content of the two sentences being conjoined but doesn't increase the level of formality.

As these sentences illustrate, many of the words used to combine sentences have several counterparts (e.g., *and, in addition, furthermore, moreover, so, therefore, consequently*). Their meanings may be similar, but their ability to create the desired effect on a reader depends on how the writer uses them. The first step for novice writers in making the choice of which connector to use is in becoming aware of the choices themselves. After they become familiar with connectors and how to conjoin sentences using them, it is important for writers to develop a sense of the nuances in meaning such connectors can convey. To do this, exercises alone are insufficient. Rather, it is important for students to have practice in comparing connectors used in a variety of contexts and in discussing the effects created by that use. For example, students should have the opportunity to practice using *so, therefore,* and *consequently* in a paragraph or an essay as well as to discuss why each word was chosen.

EXERCISES FOR PRACTICE

A. Find an example of writing with a substantial number of short, simple sentences and short sentences that have been compounded. You might examine genres such as children's literature, recipes, and health tips in popular magazines. Describe the effect these sentences have and how they relate to the purpose of the writing and to the audience being addressed.

B. The following passages from fiction, nonfiction, poetry, and speech contain examples of effective use of various forms of parallel structures (compound structures, word choice, inverted sentence structure, etc.). Identify the parallel structures, and explain the effect the writer creates by using these structures.

1. A week passed, and no news arrived of Mr. Rochester; ten days, and still he did not come. Mrs. Fairfax said she should not be surprised if he were to go straight from the Leas to London, and thence to the Continent, and not show his face again at Thornfield for a year to come; he had not unfrequently quitted it in a manner quite as abrupt and unexpected. When I heard this I was beginning to feel a strange chill and failing at the heart. I was actually permitting myself to experience a sickening sense of disappointment, but rallying my wits, and recollecting my principles, I at once called my sensations to order; and it was wonderful how I got over the temporary blunder—how I cleared up the mistake of supposing Mr. Rochester's movements a matter in which I had any cause to take a vital interest. (Charlotte Brontë, *Jane Eyre*)

2. I had three chairs in my house; one for solitude, two for friendship, and three for society. When visitors came in larger and unexpected numbers there was but the third chair for them all, but they generally economized the room by standing up. It is surprising how many great men and women a small room will contain. I have had twenty-five or thirty souls, with their bodies, at once under my roof, and yet we often parted without being aware that we had come very near to one another. Many of our homes, both public and private, with their almost innumerable apartments, their huge halls and their cellars for the storage of wines and other munitions of peace, appear to me extravagantly large for their inhabitants. They seem so vast and magnificent that the latter seem to be only vermin which infest them. I am surprised when the herald blows his summons before some Tremont or Astor or Middlesex House, to see come creeping over the piazza for all inhabitants a ridiculous mouse, which soon again slinks into some hole in the pavement. (Henry David Thoreau, *Walden*)

3. 'Twas the night before Christmas, when all through the house
   Not a creature was stirring, not even a mouse.
   The stockings were hung by the chimney with care
   In hopes that St. Nicholas soon would be there.
   The children were nestled all snug in their beds,
   While visions of sugar-plums danced in their heads.
   And Mamma in her kerchief and I in my cap
   Had just settled our brains for a long winter's nap.
   When out on the lawn there arose such a clatter
   I arose from my bed to see what was the matter.
   Away to the window I flew like a flash,
   Tore open the shutters, and threw up the sash.
   The moon on the breast of the new-fallen snow
   gave the luster of mid-day to objects below. (Clement C. Moore, *A Visit from St. Nicholas*)

4. Four score and seven years ago our fathers brought forth on this continent a new nation, conceived in liberty and dedicated to the proposition that all men are created equal. Now we are engaged in a great civil war, testing whether that nation, or any nation so conceived and so dedicated, can long endure. We are met on a great battlefield of that war. We have come to dedicate a portion of that field as a final resting-place for those who here gave their lives that that nation might live. It is altogether fitting and proper that we should do this. But, in a larger sense, we cannot dedicate—we cannot consecrate—we cannot hallow—this ground. The brave men, living and dead, who struggled here have consecrated it, far above our poor power to add or detract. The world will little note nor long remember what we say here, but it can never forget what they did here. (Abraham Lincoln, Gettysburg Address)

C. Reexamine the passages in Exercise B. How would you describe the style used by each author? What would you say are the indicators of a mature style evident in each author's piece?

D. Examine written materials from at least two different sources (e.g., fiction, textbooks, magazines, scholarly journals) for examples of parallel structures. Do you see any patterns? What purposes do the structures serve? (Do they enhance readability? Do they make the writing more musical? Do they make the writing more forceful?)

E. Select a short piece of your own writing (two to three pages) that you have already handed in for a class. Rewrite some of the sentences, converting the passive voice to the active voice or substituting various connecting words for others.

Read the two drafts out loud to a friend or roommate. Then ask your listener to contrast the effect of the second draft with that of the first.

F. Examine magazine and newspaper ads for sentences that contain parallel or compounded structures. Speculate as to why the advertiser may have chosen to use these structures. What alternative structures can you think of for your examples?

EXERCISES FOR CLASSROOM APPLICATION

A. Design an activity that would give your students the opportunity to examine and practice writing using parallel structures. (You might, for example, have them read and analyze speeches and then create a short speech themselves.)

B. Design a unit that would require your students to examine compound and parallel structures in storybooks addressed to young children aged five to eight or so. As part of the unit, have them compose and illustrate a storybook of their own (either as individuals or as a group) that would use these structures. (For illustrations, they might draw, use computer graphics, or cut out or trace pictures from books. Obviously, because our focus is on language skills, the illustrations are not as important as the content.)

GRAMMAR AND
THE WRITING PROCESS

Chapter Preview

Chapter 11 discusses the relationship between grammar and the
writing process.

In this chapter you will learn about

- Revising and editing
- Resources for teaching
- Revision and word choice
- Revising for fluency

REVISING AND EDITING

Although the writing process involves many stages, this chapter will concentrate on revising and editing, distinguishing between the two. Often students, whether working independently or in teams or groups, mistake editing for revising. Generally, the revision process is thorough and deep, focusing on both text-level and sentence-level changes to the writing one has produced. Editing is a much more superficial review of a text. Although editing can be considered a form of revision, we will define *revision* as the substantial text- and sentence-level refinement of structure and ideas and *editing* as the correction of grammar and punctuation errors.

Text-level, or content-level, revision often includes attention to the way in which content and form can make ideas more cohesive, coherent, and focused. For instance, it is common to find that novice student writers may engage in what has been termed "writer-based prose," in which ideas that are completely clear to them are clear to no one else. In such circumstances, the revision process, which is inherently social in nature, enables these students to make their writing more "reader-based" by paying attention to the level of detail and example within paragraphs, the logical connections between ideas through the use of content-level transitions. and the general construction of a point of significance. These are called *global* revisions.

Although grammatical correctness and general appropriate usage can be an important part of larger global revisions, the emphasis on sentence-level issues falls under the domain of local revision. Yet when students revise locally, there is a continued distinction between revision of sentence structure and the editing of mechanics and punctuation. Regardless of whether revision is global or local, a continuing problem that remains is the writer's misunderstanding of what constitutes revision of either the global or local category, particularly as students work in a peer review setting.

Despite their instructors' best efforts at teaching writing as a process of communication, apprentice writers sometimes attend too much to mechanics and punctuation, silently circling grammar and punctuation errors on peers' texts without commenting on the ideas themselves. Because the writing students we teach are not trained in writing process theory, this is somewhat understandable, given the social assumptions that English class is about grammar and not about writing. Indeed, consider the statement many of us have heard upon revealing our occupation: "Oh, you're an English teacher. I'd better watch my grammar."

As we have suggested, then, while careful attention to correct grammar and punctuation may help clarify relationships or establish connections between ideas, ultimately it is the emphasis on more global, rhetorical concepts of audience, purpose, focus, development, and organization that contributes to the success of student writing. Although many language arts teachers will customize global and local revision activities around specific questions relating to the particular assignment, other questions to address in a global revision session will include the identification of the audience and its knowledge about and interest in the topic, the clarity of focus and commitment to that focus throughout the document, the development and support of important ideas through appropriate examples and an explanation of their significance with respect to the ideas they are meant to illustrate, and the logical organization of the paper through a pattern of ideas that contribute to the main or controlling idea.

Another distinction between revising and editing is the points in the writing process when they are likely to occur. For instance, although as language arts teachers we have adopted the characterization of prewriting (invention), drafting, and revising as sequential stages in the writing process, research and experience have made it clear that these activities are in fact recursive. Thus within the writing process, revision will occur numerous times during versions and drafts as a writer expands textual details and refines focus and organization. Editing can also occur throughout the process, but to attend to such issues as spelling, grammar, and punctuation while the process is under way is often fruitless, since global revisions may involve the discarding and rewriting of entire paragraphs and sometimes entire drafts. In fact, focusing on editing early in the process of writing may lead to a false presumption that the final version is grammatically and mechanically correct. For that reason, experienced writers know that it is best to wait until the end of the process for final editing. Editing can be aided through activities such as electronic spelling and grammar checkers—although, as we caution later in this chapter, sole reliance on these options is unwise because of their contextual and technological limitations. In general, then, regardless of the technology options available, the process of editing involves "conventional" activities such as proofreading, reading aloud to listen for errors, and so forth.

Although every writer develops a personally distinct drafting, revising, and editing process, there are some strategies that will make the final editing stages more focused and ultimately more successful. First, students should be prepared to address the issue of correctness. While there are many exceptions and alternatives to a range of grammar and spelling rules, some rules nonetheless apply. Thus the purpose of an editing session is to catch both major and minor errors that may impede communication or damage a writer's credibility. A second major issue involves fluency and **coherence** within and between sentences and paragraphs. Ideally, these connections should be clear from the ideas themselves. However, there are certain options—many of which have been discussed throughout *Grammar for Language Arts Teachers*—to help in the process, including the use of transitions between sentences and paragraphs and compound and complex sentences to express logical and coherent relationships among ideas.

Another issue to address is consistency. Despite the recognition of options, such as the choice to spell the word *canceled* with one *l* or two (as in *cancelled*), it is vital to create a sense of grammatical consistency. Other issues of consistency involve time and tense; for instance, a common error noted by teachers involves shifting tense between past and present, ultimately creating a lack of clarity and cohesion between events and a reader's understanding of when they occurred. Finally, it is vital to consider style and word choice within the particular writing context, for although context often governs these choices as we draft, it is important to consider the impact on our readers of the connotations of various words and the tone with which we say them. Consider, for example, the simplicity of sentence length and style in newspaper articles, determined in part by research on the reading levels of the general public but also by the need to save space for other equally important news of the day. Other considerations include the use of gender-neutral pronouns in order not to alienate segments of the audience as well as determining the extent to which readers will understand various terms, synonyms, or jargon. Overall, good editing involves a system of checks and balances. Although the use of spell-checking and grammar-checking software may be a first step in the editing process, it cannot, as we have stressed, replace careful proofreading of the hard copy by the individual writer as well as one or several external readers.

Indeed, peer review can also aid the editing process, as long as such review doesn't replace global revision for content and structure. Given this concern, it is important for teachers to contextualize grammar instruction in a language arts course and in written comments on student work or in student conferences about that work. Without such contextualization, students may assume that grammatical correctness is the most important feature of a piece of writing. This view may as well be exacerbated by the fact that there seems to be a widespread fear of speaking—or writing—incorrectly in front of an "English teacher." Thus it goes without saying that students in language arts or writing courses often suffer from a sort of grammar anxiety that may detract from their ability to invent, draft, and revise fluently. Indeed, much research on "basic" or "developmental" writers has noted the tendency of these students to focus on getting individual sentences "right" too early in the writing process without attending to the actual development of a solid draft to work from.

A related issue is determining the point in the writing process at which it is necessary for teachers to focus on grammar instruction. Some teachers begin teaching grammar much too early, stressing correctness of form over fluidity and clarity of expression. In such instances, attention to grammar may even discourage apprentice writers from adequately inventing and generating ideas that may or may not make their way to a final draft. In a language arts classroom, then, too great a focus on correctness can send the wrong message to students—that writing and grammar are the same. With this phenomenon in mind, we recommend that early phases of the writing process concentrate on exactly that: writing. What this entails is focusing on the students' ability to originate ideas in a range of forms—verbal and written—and to generate as much text as possible for potential use in a later, more refined assignment. This highly creative phase of the writing process, commonly known as prewriting, is actually the most important one.

Because both teachers and students should avoid an emphasis on grammar in the prewriting stage, any type of writing that constitutes prewriting warrants a delay of grammatical correction on the part of teachers. For instance, in many writing classes, it is common for teachers to ask students to keep a journal. Even if the journal is earmarked for a specific purpose (e.g., a reading journal that allows students to respond to and dialogue with assigned texts), the prewriting assignments that go into it help students learn to generate the more focused, formalized, and synthesized responses that they will later incorporate into expository or persuasive writing.

Besides the matter of when in the writing process grammar instruction should occur, the type of writing students do is also a factor in determining the extent to which strict attention to grammatical correctness is warranted. Genres such as the journal that encourage inventing and exploration on the part of the students should deemphasize grammar. Other, more creative types of genres, such as short stories and poetry, where the use of dialogue in the former case and of personification of inanimate objects in the latter help give writing an authenticity and sense of style, may also warrant more latitude with respect to grammatical correctness. Forcing a strict adherence to standard English usage when students experiment with such genres may limit students' experimentation with language and may cause the resulting writing to be stilted and decontextualized.

Inevitably, then, context is a key factor in determining where grammar instruction fits into the writing process. Indeed, the fact that a journal entry, intended for the eyes of the student alone or of student and teacher, may contain some errors is of little significance for a writer's ultimate academic or professional success. Contrast this context, however, with that of a résumé and cover letter accompanying an application for one's first job after graduation. In this context, a grammatical error might be the equivalent of a stain on one's tie or a tear in one's scarf, noticeable and subject to judgment by others. And with the advent of more public genres and modes of delivery, such as electronic documents for the World Wide Web, the context in which grammar errors are or are not significant has changed dramatically. Appropriately, students themselves often seem very aware that online writing has a wider audience than the face-to-face writing they may share with peers, and in our experience, they often take more care with online genres.

Certainly, genre, context, and audience are very important issues in deciding how much emphasis to place on grammar. Yet regardless of these issues, it is also important to recognize that as novice writers develop their skill and fluency, they must experiment with forms and structures of the English language. That is, the mastery of a broad range of forms and styles requires practice, and teachers must therefore recognize that as syntactic fluency is evolving, students will make mistakes along the way. In various studies of basic writers, for example, the predominance of simple sentences over other types has been tied to students' fears of making mistakes on more complex sentences that involve both conjoining and embedding. Often this type of writing anxiety is the result of overcorrection on the part of teachers. Such overcorrection commonly manifests itself in a student paper returned with every error marked, regardless of the seriousness of the error. In fact, novice teachers often spend more time circling errors than they do commenting on student papers or explaining at student conferences why the errors in question are significant enough to warrant attention. The impression students get is that they are not really writing or conveying ideas but are simply making mistakes. As a result, the relationship between writer and reader becomes an adversarial one. Yet the use of compound and complex sentences reflects an attempt on the part of students to connect ideas and establish cause-and-effect relationships between those ideas.

Our own position is that students should have the opportunity to experiment with sentence complexity without fear of punishment for not punctuating correctly or for creating ill-formed sentences. Although major errors such as comma splices, fused sentences, or inappropriate fragments are causes for concern, the fact that students are making these errors may reflect syntactic growth that should be fostered in a nonthreatening way. For that reason, it is important for students to learn and for teachers to understand that developing a mature style and learning how to edit skillfully will take time and patience.

Although general guidelines regarding the time and place for grammar instruction are helpful, it is still necessary to contextualize such instruction and activities around the needs of actual student writers and with respect to specific writing assignments. In determining the extent and nature of grammar instruction, it is always good practice to consider the skill level of the students themselves. Just as a math teacher presumes a knowledge of algebra before moving on to calculus or trigonometry, a language arts teacher should consider the current grammatical knowledge of her students. For instance, expecting students to correctly use a semicolon to punctuate sentences with conjunctive adverbs may be unreasonable if students have not had any instruction in the options for creating and punctuating compound sentences.

When teaching grammar, it is also important to focus on the local context. By this we mean that if in the process of reviewing students' work, it becomes clear that many students are having a problem with adverb clause fragments—*Because I was tired* and the like—then the teacher needs to construct lessons that deal with this problem at the time when it is occurring in student writing. Conversely, the teacher should question teaching the difference between restrictive and nonrestrictive clauses if no students are having problems recognizing the distinction and when there may be more serious errors to deal with.

Finally, teachers should consider the severity of the errors students are actually making when determining what grammatical concepts to teach. An inappropriate fragment is a more serious problem than being unable to distinguish between *who* and *whom* in a relative clause, and verb tense errors are more serious than omitting commas after introductory sentence modifiers. Although every teacher will have a pet peeve (e.g., "Never end a sentence with a preposition"), perhaps one way to view the distinction between a major and a minor error is to consider the extent to which any error impedes communication or may be seen as a marker of diminished educational attainment or social status. Of course, even these distinctions can be based on various cultural contexts; yet as Maxine Hairston's survey of English teachers across the country suggests, there are some errors that seem to get and perhaps warrant more serious attention than others. Errors in subject-verb agreement and the use of double negatives, for example, attract more notice than errors relating to the misuse of a colon do.

As we have suggested, then, the process of teaching grammar and usage is one of contextualization and prioritization. For that reason, we encourage the use of texts both inside and outside the school culture, including advertisements, memoranda, passages from classical and modern literature, newspaper articles, brochure copy, the Internet, and above all, student writing. As we've mentioned before, sentence fragments are ordinarily more acceptable in advertisements than in business correspondence. Having students compare various examples of writing and examine the differing rhetorical and cultural contexts in which this writing occurs will help them understand that the "rules" of grammar are not absolute.

RESOURCES FOR TEACHING

As students progress through school, their exposure to various academic communities can challenge them as writers because of unfamiliar styles, genres, and specialized terminology that academic disciplines and various professions employ in their written discourse. Experienced writers use a variety of tools to help them adapt their writing appropriately to different audiences and contexts, including reference works such as a dictionary or **thesaurus**. Of course, experienced writers know how to use these reference works appropriately. But often the ability to use a dictionary or thesaurus is a skill that teachers presume their students have when that is simply not the case. And writing textbooks and grammar handbooks rarely offer detailed instruction in how to use these tools. Thus the question becomes how students should use the dictionary in ways that genuinely help them develop knowledge of language choice in context.

Because dictionary definitions incorporate both denotative and connotative meanings of a word, it is important for the writer to consider not only the general meaning of a word but also its appropriateness in the particular writing context. Also, dictionaries provide a listing not just of possible meanings for a word but also of possible functions (noun, verb, adjective, etc.). Unfortunately, apprentice writers don't always know strategies for making use of this information, such as examining both the sentence and the passage in which a word is to be used to determine how the word is functioning in its larger and more immediate context. Similarly, it is often easier for writers to identify a more appropriate meaning among the alternatives listed for a particular word if they consider the grammatical function of the alternatives. In this way, the use of the dictionary becomes more interactive, confirming understandings of function and context that the writer may have a clear sense about but required some external validation.

Thesauri can also cause difficulties for inexperienced writers who don't know how to use them with respect to word choice and ultimately style and tone. Consider, for example, the word *hate* as it would be used in the sentence *Tom hates peas and carrots.* Other options, according to the thesaurus include *abhor, abominate, despise, detest,* and *loathe,* as in the following examples:

Tom *abhors* peas and carrots.

Tom *abominates* peas and carrots.

Tom *despises* peas and carrots.

Tom *detests* peas and carrots.

Tom *loathes* peas and carrots.

Note the differences in nuance and style when the synonyms are used as alternatives to *hate.* The options for the word *hate* do not change the meaning of the sentence in any significant way. However, the shift in style and tone between the original sentence *Tom hates peas and carrots* and the alternative *Tom loathes peas and carrots* may or may not be appropriate for the particular context in which it is to be used. If Tom happens to be a six-year-old, perhaps a more simplistic choice may be in order, although that would also depend on the overall style of the writing and its level of formality. Such choices also tie in to the concept of authorial voice or persona and the need to rely on words that not only fit the rhetorical context but also fit the writer. Finally, part of this context includes the readers and their knowledge of such definitions themselves. So should it be *Tom hates peas and carrots* or *Tom abominates peas and carrots*?

Another problem with respect to choosing synonyms from a thesaurus relates to differences in how a word and its various derivatives can function in a sentence. For example, whereas it may be appropriate to use options such as *abhor* or *loathe* as substitutes for the word *hate,* the use of the verb *abominate* seems awkward in this sentence, with its overtones of great horror or injustice. It may therefore be inappropriate to employ a word that takes a child's distaste for peas and carrots to an extreme that compares it to great injustices, such as racism and poverty. For that reason, students need to understand that a thesaurus merely provides possible word choice options from which the writer must choose the one that fosters clear communication and fits the overall rhetorical context. Ultimately, the thesaurus and the dictionary should be used in tandem in order for students to confirm denotative and connotative meanings of words and to understand their appropriateness in the context, with the audience, and for the purpose of their writing.

Although the dictionary and the thesaurus have long found a useful place on the writer's shelf, technological advances in word processing have encouraged more and more students to compose online without referring to books. Such composing often entails the use of software packages that edit writing as it is produced on the screen. Indeed, as we composed these paragraphs in Microsoft Word 2000, red lines appeared underneath misspellings and typographical errors, and green lines appeared under sentences that contained possible grammatical or contextual errors or struck the computer as too long or too wordy. Such electronic tools can be helpful in eliminating errors that might crop up during the drafting stage. For example, the computer might automatically fix the misspellings of particular words. Yet as experienced writers, we know that overreliance on spelling and grammar checkers can have significantly negative consequences if student writers fail to proofread for more contextual errors. This is particularly important because electronic tools often fail to catch misused homonyms, words that sound the same but are spelled differently and mean different things and function differently in sentences, such as *their, they're,* and *there* or *two, too,* and *to.*

In addition, sentence variety and complexity can be the target of a grammar checker that objectively and arbitrarily decides that a sentence is too long when in the writing context it may be perfectly acceptable as is. Therefore, rather than relying solely on such technological tools as grammar and spell checkers, students need to engage in a range of commonsense activities to ensure careful proofreading and editing. First, writers should always print out hard copies of papers and assignments and read them in this format because to rely on online review alone can be difficult given screen size and general readability issues in an electronic setting. Second, as we have recommended elsewhere throughout the book, students should read their work aloud in order to catch errors or to determine whether the length of a sentence reduces clarity and readability. Finally, peer review in both revision and editing is of paramount importance. Ultimately, texts are written for readers. Thus the importance of this part of the writing process in confirming the options available through such tools as the dictionary, the thesaurus, and spelling and grammar checkers cannot be underestimated by students or by teachers.

REVISION AND WORD CHOICE

As we have repeatedly stressed, issues of revision and word choice are based on levels of social and linguistic convention. It goes without saying that such conventions are situational. The process of adapting word choice and other aspects of language use to various situations is often referred to as *register.* On one level, register implies degrees of formality in a given rhetorical context. For instance, the letter a student might write to a friend back home is quite different from the cover letter the student would write when applying for a job. Often our level of social connection to our readers and listeners makes determining levels of formality a very instinctive process. We know we can get away with grammatical errors with our friends, whereas in more professional relationships, writers and speakers tend not to take chances for fear that such errors provoke a negative social judgment. Such distinctions between formal and informal register have their roots in the work of the Roman orator Cicero, who developed a concept for speakers and writers that can be loosely translated as "what is fitting." Cicero also delineated three levels of style: plain, medium, and ornate.

A common problem for novice writers, then, is their use of a style that they may think fits the occasion but in fact doesn't. One manifestation of this is the novice writer's overreliance on the thesaurus as a way of making word choices seem more sophisticated and of enhancing the overall tone of the writing. The result may attempt to mimic academic discourse conventions, with students using big words that they think enhance credibility. However, inappropriate word choice and convoluted syntax can actually hinder overall fluency and expose the writer's novice status. For that reason, teachers should caution students not to rely so heavily on the thesaurus. Rather, apprentice writers should use the thesaurus as a reference tool to identify synonyms that fit not only the rhetorical situation but also the authentic voice of the writer.

Another aspect of register involves the use of specialized language or jargon and also the use of slang or **colloquialisms**. "Legalese," for example, applied to the terminology of lawyers and the court system, relies on words with very specific and sometimes obscure meanings (e.g., *testator, writ, usufruct, jointly and severally*). Other examples of specialized register or jargon may include "computerese," or language pertaining to technology systems (e.g., *hard drive, floppy disk, random access memory, cookie, download*). And even though the use of such terms may become more widespread as more and more users gain experience with computers, such terms are still alien and intimidating for a large segment of the population. The point here is that jargon presumes a knowledge base that the general public or nonspecialists often do not possess; thus writers need to be aware of their audience for a given piece of writing and sensitive about whether to use jargon when speaking to that audience.

Still other problems, in terms of clarity, comprehension, and general formality, can occur when apprentice writers use slang or colloquialisms. *Slang* refers to the vast array of made-up or altered words and phrases that are not part of the standard vocabulary and—much like specialized terminology and jargon—are known primarily to members of an in-group or subculture. Besides being associated with a particular group or subgroup, slang is often short-lived, its terminology replaced by new terms by members of the next generation. For example, some Americans alive today remember that in their youth, expressions like *far out, rad,* and *bitchin* conveyed a sense of something good, but many more Americans will not be familiar with such *colloquialisms* (extremely informal expressions). Of course, in writing, particularly in the use of interior monologue or quoted dialogue, the use of these terms preserves the authenticity of persona and voice. But in the same way that more general usage errors are being considered major or minor, depending on context, it is equally difficult to escape the judgment of others who may see the use of slang and colloquialisms as status markers. For example, as an alternative to the verb *die,* which expression should a writer or speaker use: *pass on, expire, croak,* or *kick the bucket?* The term *expire* may be the preferred term in a medical context, where the language user wishes to sound informed yet objective and emotionally detached. Conversely, neither *croak* nor *kick the bucket* would be appropriate in this context because each is too informal and would denote a lack of professionalism on the part of the user. *Pass on* would come across as gentle and appropriate in a social context but would sound too dainty in medical circles. To reiterate, then, slang is often inappropriate in writing because of both its transitoriness and its lack of formality.

To help students understand why slang expressions are inappropriate for most audiences, teachers can list slang expressions and colloquialisms from some time in the past and ask students to interpret them. Because, as we mentioned earlier, slang is short-lived and often generational, terms and phrases used by earlier generations may not be understood by students, and students themselves probably use language that is alien to most adults. Such a discussion between students and teachers about appropriate style and usage in various rhetorical situations can be highly informative for novice writers.

Despite these general cautions against using slang and colloquialisms in written discourse, it is important for students to learn that they should exercise judgment, but not to the point of stripping a piece of writing of all its flavor, style, and voice. Of course, learning how to make choices about words and sentences is a long and arduous process. Therefore, many students prefer to learn and rely on a small set of rules, myths about writing told to them by colleagues, instructors, parents, and other authority figures. To help students begin the process of understanding that these rules aren't applicable to all situations (and that they are often inaccurate), as a first-day activity, teachers can ask students to list all the things they believe they should or shouldn't do grammatically. Here are some of the items that will almost certainly turn up on the list:

Never use *I.*

Never use *you.*

Never use the passive voice.

Never begin a sentence with a conjunction.

In the case of the first two items, the use of *I* and *you* has to do with the fact that the first and second person points of view are often considered too informal for written discourse. Although it is important to maintain a consistent point of view (e.g., avoid shifting from the second person *you* to the third person *he, she,* or *they*), there is no absolute rule that would exclude the use of *you* (or *I*) in all circumstances. In fact, the more informal reference may in many rhetorical contexts create a bond between writer and reader, particularly if there is a persuasive case to be made. To help students visualize in what contexts the first or second person can be powerful and persuasive, teachers can have students review popular texts such as advertisements or any other genre in which it is clear that "not all 'rules' are really rules."

Regarding the use of the passive voice, it is somewhat understandable that advertising language relies on the active voice, fragmented sentences, and a plethora of adjectives to get concise messages across. Yet despite the role of the active voice in adding clarity and conciseness to written discourse, there is room for the use of the passive, particularly in ceremonial contexts (e.g., *Sara was awarded the prestigious Fiddler fellowship*). In this sense, the actual person and action become more significant. But regardless of the appropriateness of some passive constructions, context, as always, dictates this and many other editing and stylistic choices.

Similarly, as we discussed in Chapter 10, whether or not to begin a sentence with a conjunction is also a stylistic choice. Starting a sentence with a conjunction usually makes the sentence more emphatic (*But I decided to stay home*).

Again, it is always useful to create activities and assignments that help students see when various stylistic alternatives are—or are not—appropriate.

REVISING FOR FLUENCY

As we discussed in Chapter 5, embedding and conjoining are useful ways to enhance the overall fluency and coherence of written discourse. Conjoining is the more basic approach of combining two words, phrases, or sentences to create a more detailed and more concise text overall; embedding is the more sophisticated approach, allowing for the inclusion of clauses that convey a range of relationships.

One type of compounding allows the writer to combine nouns, verbs, adjectives, and adverbs in such a way as to make sentences more detailed and fluent. For example, look at these two sentences:

John rode his bike to school.

Jane rode her bike to school.

They sound choppy and immature when written separately. But look what happens when they are combined:

John and Jane rode their bikes to school.

The resulting sentence is more concise and fluent. Such compounding makes sense with verb phrases as well. The sentences *Kris hiked in the mountains* and

Kris swam in the ocean can be combined to create *Kris hiked in the mountains and swam in the ocean.*

Note that although this revision results in a compounded predicate, the sentence is still what is referred to as a *simple sentence* because it has only one independent clause. What would make it a *compound sentence,* consisting of two or more main independent clauses? *Kris hiked in the mountains, and she swam in the ocean* would be a compound sentence conveying the same information. Given the simplicity of the two original sentences, it is a matter of style which of the revised versions is more acceptable. Very little information is conveyed other than the acts of hiking and swimming and where they took place. Additional detail might attribute cause or effect to these actions, and such a relationship could be expressed in a *complex sentence,* one that contains both a main independent clause and a subordinate dependent clause: *Because she loved to exercise, Kris hiked in the mountains and swam in the ocean.* Both the subordinate relationship of the clause *Because she loved to exercise* and the conjunction *because* provide more information (e.g., *Kris hiked in the mountains and swam in the ocean* is now the main or most important part of the sentence, as *because* creates a cause-and-effect relationship; we now know why Kris hiked and swam—because she loved to exercise).

Often in teaching sentence combining, teachers encourage students to write compound and complex sentences to help them attain sentence variety and syntactic fluency. Our example lends credence to the claim that more complex sentences help in achieving that goal. Simple sentences, especially one after the other, begin to sound like children's prose or the once popular reading primers ("See Spot run"). Yet it is wise to review the relative merits of the advice to increase sentence complexity in each particular writing context. If every sentence were a complex sentence, with structures embedded in such a way that the rhythm of the writing and the overall tone became predictable and winded, the result would be just as awkward as if every sentence were a simple sentence. The bottom line is that in the final stages of the revising process, students should be encouraged to examine their drafts, noting the length, complexity, and placement of their sentences. This task is particularly important in the revision process, for it is there that novice writers have the opportunity to review the connections between ideas and may see opportunities for embedding and conjoining that were not apparent before. Novice writers can also examine overly long, highly embedded sentences to see if they can be simplified. Through peer revising and editing workshops, students may begin to consider options for making connections between sentences through both compounding and embedding. For example, if a passage in a draft reads something like *Kris went home. She was tired,* students may discuss a number of options for revision:

Compound sentence: Kris was tired; therefore, she went home.

Compound sentence: Kris was tired, so she went home.

Complex sentence:	Kris went home because she was tired.
Complex sentence:	Because she was tired, Kris went home.
	(*and so on*)

Although there are numerous ways to help writers develop syntactic fluency, as students consider these options, they need to remember that revision not only helps clarify relationships between ideas but also helps establish coherence within and between paragraphs. This coherence is vital to more natural, content-based transitions. As our examples suggest, options for revision include the selection of a conjunctive adverb (*however, furthermore, for instance, indeed, moreover,* etc.) or a coordinating conjunction (*and, or, but, for, so, yet, nor*) or a subordinating conjunction (*although, because, since,* etc.). Furthermore, words that create similar logical relationships (e.g., *therefore, so, because, since*) have nuances of meaning; for example, *so* tends to be less formal than *therefore.* Also, the choice of a particular connective may allow options in placement. The use of a subordinator (*although, because,* etc.) allows the main and dependent clause to be reversed (e.g., *Because Fido was hungry, he devoured his food from the can* versus *Fido devoured his food from the can because he was hungry*).

Like the use of any combining, embedding, or coherence strategy, the use of transitions requires careful review. Students know instinctively that transitions such as *therefore, however,* and *consequently* are common to more academic discourse conventions. As a result, they can misuse or overuse such transitions, creating contrastive or cause-and-effect relationships between ideas and sentences that actually don't exist. Other problems occur when such transitions (especially *for example*) occur at the beginnings of sentences in so frequent a fashion that a piece writing can seem formulaic and lacking in variety. It is therefore important for students to assess common transition word choices to create variety in their work.

The ancient Greek rhetoricians have spoken of a concept called *kairos,* or the right moment in time to make the most persuasive case in the most persuasive way. Like many of life's choices, the use of various grammatical constructions must be moderated in ways that always acknowledge the concept of *kairos,* which for many of today's rhetoric and writing specialists signifies a keen awareness of rhetorical context: audience, purpose, and genre. It is this awareness on the part of teachers and students that makes the study, the teaching, and the application of grammar a lifelong process of literacy and language arts.

EXERCISES FOR PRACTICE

A. Look up a common word in the thesaurus, and find a range of synonyms. Use each of the synonyms in a sentence of similar structure, and compare the style and tone of each sentence. Bring your results to your group for discussion and comparison of results.

B. Look up one of your synonyms from Exercise A in a dictionary. What typical functions does this word serve: noun, verb, adjective? Based on your understanding of the definition, in what rhetorical context would the word best be used, and in what function? Again, bring your results to your group for discussion and comparison.

C. Conduct an experiment in which you generate a range of colloquialisms that you use with colleagues, family, and friends of various generations and nationalities. How well do people in your experiment understand the terms? What might this say about the appropriateness of these terms in certain rhetorical contexts?

D. Working with your group partners, select a piece of writing of at least two pages that is a first draft; that is, it should require significant global revision. Explain in detail what revisions are needed on the text level (audience awareness, organization, development, etc.). Next, find a piece of writing that is nearly finished but needs to be edited. Together with your group partners, do the required editing. Finally, compare your revising and editing processes. Articulate the differences in a report that you will deliver to the class.

EXERCISES FOR CLASSROOM APPLICATION

A. Devise an activity that would require your students to use and report on how a spelling checker affected a piece of their writing. What types of errors did the program find? What types of errors did it overlook (e.g., synonyms)? Based on their findings, students (in groups) should compose a set of recommendations regarding the most efficient use of such devices.

B. Design an activity that requires your students to use a grammar checker on a portion of a piece of writing, and have them bring that portion to class for peer review. In each group, students should formulate answers to the following questions: Did students catch the same errors as the grammar checker? What items did the checker overlook? What items did the checker find with which the students disagreed (e.g., overly long sentence)? Overall, what might the results say about the relationship between technology and editing?

ANSWER KEY

ANSWERS TO SELECTED EXERCISE QUESTIONS

Answers are provided here for the first half of all Exercises for Practice questions.

CHAPTER 2, PART I

Exercise A, p. 40

1. The borful hugglebumps / smitted a dort dragoo.
2. Pobocity / crawmed the sizzleswitch ambetly.
3. A mendokit /drims each zooey.
4. Cartolilly / has fritchened mubbily.
5. These fappy ammosaws / frowzed a zort.

Exercise B, p. 41

1. John / gave Alice a nice present.
2. The light in the refrigerator / went out.
3. The trapeze artist / dated the mustached woman.
4. The young lover / ran up his phone bill.
5. Writing letters / is an enjoyable pastime.

Exercise C, p. 41

1. No snowflake / ever falls in the wrong place. (Zen saying)
2. Surely joy / is the condition of life. (Henry David Thoreau)
3. Ninety-eight percent of the adults in this country / are decent, hardworking, honest Americans. (Lily Tomlin)
4. Comedy / is simply a funny way of being serious. (Peter Ustinov)
5. All truths / wait in all things. (Walt Whitman)

Exercise D, p. 42

Revised versions of incomplete sentences will vary.

1. Giant power plant to be built near Livingstone   F
   Revised: A giant power plant is to be built near Livingstone.
2. Investigators to consider withholding evidence   F
   Revised: Investigators are to consider withholding evidence.
3. Local reaction to weather mixed   F
   Revised: Local reaction to weather is mixed.
4. Home team / rallies for win.   C
5. Setting things into perspective   F
   Revised: City is setting things into perspective.

411

Exercise E, p. 43

1. The ghost suddenly <u>appeared</u> in front of them. (intransitive)
2. The seamstress <u>felt</u> the softness of the material. (transitive)
3. She <u>felt</u> sad at the news. (linking)
4. The police <u>looked</u> everywhere for the criminal. (intransitive)
5. You <u>look</u> lovely tonight. (linking)
6. The students in the classroom <u>seemed</u> serious. (linking)
7. The florist <u>smelled</u> the flowers. (transitive)
8. The flowers <u>smelled</u> sweet. (linking)
9. The car <u>sounds</u> funny. (linking)
10. The bank teller <u>sounded</u> the alarm. (transitive)
11. Did you <u>taste</u> the fudge? (transitive)
12. Yes, it <u>tasted</u> delicious. (linking)
13. The wounded soldiers <u>lay</u> on stretchers. (intransitive)
14. He <u>lied</u> to me! (intransitive)
15. They <u>remain</u> friends to this very day. (linking)

Exercise F, p. 44

1. subject + *be* + subject complement
2. subject + transitive verb + direct object
3. subject + transitive verb + direct object
4. subject + transitive verb + indirect object + direct object
5. subject + transitive verb + direct object + object complement

Exercise G, p. 44
Answers will vary.

Exercise H, p. 45
Answers will vary.

CHAPTER 2, PART II

Exercise A, p. 55

1. Bill / shouldn't mess with that electrical outlet.
   Potential problem: Mess appears to be a noun but is in fact functioning as a verb.
2. Sometimes sorrow / dogs my steps.
   Potential problem: Dogs appears to be a noun but is in fact functioning as a verb.
3. Running / is a common way to stay fit.
   Potential problem: Running appears to be a verb but is in fact functioning as a subject.
4. The jump / was too dangerous for the children.
   Potential problem: Jump appears to be a verb but is in fact functioning as a subject.
5. Attending concerts / is costly.
   Potential problem: Attending appears to be a verb but is in fact functioning as a subject.
6. In the hallway / is where Fluffy sleeps.
   Potential problem: In the hallway is a prepositional phrase, but it is in fact functioning as a subject.

7. Wonderful / is the word for it.
   Potential problem: Wonderful appears to be an adjective but is in fact functioning as a subject.
8. Maybe they / 'll bus the children to another school.
   Potential problem: Bus appears to be a noun but is in fact functioning as a verb.

Exercise B, p. 56

1. The door [to the hallway] / was ajar.
2. The speaker [for the stereo] / wouldn't work.
3. The people [in the living room] / are strangers to me.
4. The price [of oranges] / is high all year round.
5. The dirt [around the potted plant] / is very dry.

Exercise C, p. 56

Answers will vary.

Exercise D, p. 56

One of the controversial issues regarding public education these days is the public funding of charter schools. Proponents of charter schools argue that they are more adaptable to the needs of students in particular communities. [fused sentence] They claim as well that charter schools are more responsive to students with special needs or talents. Those who argue against public funding of charter schools express concern that such funding may undermine public education. [comma splice] They also cite data that suggest that students in charter schools do not demonstrate improved academic performance. It is unfortunate that persons who have opposing opinions regarding this issue and who have students' best interests at heart have not as yet been able to work out opportunities for compromise. [comma splice] Politicians, in particular, need to show leadership in creating compromise for the benefit of all their constituents.

Exercise E, p. 57

Last night I watched a popular game show on TV. These types of programs [delete this comma] have become more popular in recent years. It is interesting to speculate as to what the appeal of these shows tells us about our culture. Do they suggest that we are a nation of gamblers? I suspect the answer to that question [delete this comma] is "probably not." Everyone likes a contest. Everyone likes to win. The day I win a contest, I will buy [delete this comma] a new car and a larger house.

Exercise F, p. 57

Answers will vary; we provide one as an example.

1. From "The *Titanic*"

   Oh, they built the ship *Titanic* to sail the ocean blue,
   and they thought they had a ship that the sea would not leak through.
   But the Lord's almighty hand knew this ship would never stand.
   It was sad when that great ship went down.

> Oh, it was sad, Lord, sad. Oh, it was sad, Lord, sad.
> Husbands and wives, little children lost their lives.
> It was sad when that great ship went down.

2. Adapted from *Roughing It* by Mark Twain

> On some of those mountains to the southwest, it had been raining every day
> for two weeks, but not a drop had fallen in the city. On hot days in late
> spring and early autumn, the citizens could quit fanning themselves and
> growling. They could go out and cool off by looking at the luxury of a
> glorious snowstorm going on in the mountains. They could enjoy it at a
> distance in those seasons every day. But no snow would fall in their streets or
> anywhere near them.

Exercise G, p. 58
Answers will vary.

CHAPTER 3, PART I

Exercise A, p. 84

1. Alice (subject); Italy (object)
2. John (subject); bus (object of preposition); Chicago (object of preposition); New York (object of preposition)
3. He (subject); Kris (indirect object); book (direct object)
4. Idea (subject); me (object of preposition)
5. Bill Clinton (subject); president (appositive); Democrat (subject complement)

Exercise B, p. 85
Answers will vary.

Exercise C, p. 85
Answers will vary.

Exercise D, p. 86

1. She drove <u>a</u> Ferrari to <u>the</u> party. Indefinite article; definite article
2. <u>An</u> aardvark can also be called <u>an</u> anteater. Indefinite articles
3. <u>This</u> book is very good. Demonstrative
4. I brought <u>these</u> cookies for Sarah. Demonstrative
5. His name was one in <u>a</u> series. Indefinite article

Exercise E, p. 86
Answers will vary; we provide a model.

> Nonnative speakers of English can experience many difficulties when learning English grammar. First, they may have trouble learning to use the -*s* plural inflection accurately. Especially at this stage of learning, they may add -*s* to nouns that aren't plural. Second, they may have many difficulties with learning irregular plural forms.

Exercise F, p. 86

1. The <u>women's</u> clinic is on Main Street. Plural possessive

2. Her <u>teeth</u> were causing great pain. Irregular plural
3. Our <u>students'</u> grades improved significantly. Plural possessive
4. <u>Kris's</u> family is from New York. Singular possessive
5. After the cart tipped over, <u>loaves</u> of bread were scattered in the aisle. Plural

Exercise G, p. 87

1. As I left that <u>awful</u> party, Bartilda gave me a <u>nasty</u> look.
2. Those <u>little brown</u> bats in our basement gave me a <u>terrible</u> scare.
3. Won't anyone in our class tell me why I failed that <u>preposterous</u> test?
4. Before you come to my <u>new</u> house, our <u>wonderful</u> friend, Bob, is going to fix our <u>leaky</u> roof.
5. The plants in the kitchen wilted after John gave them that <u>cheap</u> fertilizer.

Exercise H, p. 88

1. Please help! There's a mangy stray cat in my yard. OK
2. Last summer our friends bought a red brick house. OK
3. Plants with dark green foliage are my favorite. OK
4. All of the students cried when their <u>warm</u>, <u>energetic</u> teacher retired.
5. Don't you think that is a <u>sad</u>, <u>depressing</u> story?

Exercise I, p. 88
Answers will vary.

Exercise J, p. 88
Answers will vary.

Exercise K, p. 89
Answers may vary; we provide an example.

Yesterday, I went for a long walk in the woods because I wanted to enjoy the beauty of the spring weather. *The weather* [the referent for the pronoun *it* was unclear] was very nice. While walking, I saw many children riding their bikes and playing games with each other. *Watching the children* [the referent for the pronoun *this* was not clear] was fun. Everyone was enjoying *himself* [*theirself* is not a word; *himself* agrees with its referent, *everyone,* in number, but it seems to imply that all the children were boys; it would be preferable to make the sentence gender-inclusive by writing *All of the children were enjoying themselves*] in the pretty weather. *The spectacle* [the referent for the pronoun *it* was unclear] was enjoyable to watch. After a while, I got tired. While I was sitting on a bench resting, a bird came and sat next to me [*myself* is inappropriate; the pronoun is not reflexive or intensive; it is merely the object of the preposition *next to*]. Overall, *everyone* [the referent of *we* was unclear] had a pleasant afternoon.

Exercise L, p. 89

1. <u>To walk three miles a day</u> is impressive. Infinitive phrase as subject
2. <u>Swimming the shark-infested waters</u> is dangerous. Gerund phrase as subject
3. Her mother's hobby, <u>collecting Beanie Babies</u>, was becoming an obsession. Gerund phrase as appositive

    4. Terry loves <u>washing his new car</u>. Gerund phrase as direct object

    5. Kris likes <u>to eat Japanese food</u>. Infinitive phrase as direct object

Exercise M, p. 90

Answers will vary.

CHAPTER 3, PART II

Exercise A, p. 104

1. Terry's house is on a small lot. On this lot there are many trees—maples, <u>birches</u> [*-es* plural], and oaks—with just as many <u>leaves</u> [irregular plural]. When <u>it's</u> [contraction, not a possessive] windy, the <u>leaves</u> [irregular plural] blow into the <u>neighbors'</u> [plural possessive] yards. Because there are so many trees, <u>branches</u> [*-es* plural] also sometimes fly onto their roofs. The neighbors get upset with Terry for not trimming her trees. They have strong <u>beliefs</u> [regular plural] in being good citizens. They think Terry is a bad neighbor. <u>Echoes</u> [*-es* plural] of this turn up every week in the local police <u>chief's</u> [singular possessive] reports.

Exercise B, p. 105

    1. Ms. Smith asked Julie and <u>me</u> to stay after school. Objective case

    2. <u>We</u> guys are going to the movies on Saturday. Subjective case

    3. They gave the award to him and me. Correct as is, objective case

    4. Just between you and <u>me,</u> I don't like opera. Objective case

    5. Hardworking students always impress <u>us</u> teachers. Objective case

Exercise C, p. 105

    1. The guests looked <u>grateful</u> for the break in the boring conversation. Subject complement completes linking verb *looked.*

    2. The students complained consistently. Correct adverb form to explain manner in which students complained.

    3. Sally feels <u>bad</u> about the misunderstanding. Subject complement completes linking verb *feels.*

    4. Joe sings so <u>awfully</u> that it drives us crazy. Adverb form required to indicate how Joe sings.

    5. She gave the book to her sister <u>quickly</u> before anyone else noticed. Adverb form needed to modify the verb *gave.*

Exercise D, p. 106

Answers may vary; we provide an example.

Students always have to work hard to improve their grades. One priority is to have them turn in their assignments on time. Students may ignore their deadlines, but they can eliminate their weaknesses by careful planning and attention to their schedules. Taking such actions will help tremendously. Students should be responsible to themselves. Putting personal responsibility first is always the sign of a successful undergraduate. She might even graduate first in her class.

Exercise E, p. 106

1. To walk up a hill backward is the way to get a really good workout. Infinitive phrase as fragmented subject
2. Giving her all every day makes her a great worker. Gerund phrase as fragmented subject
3. Scrooge wouldn't have liked taking a vacation at Christmas. Gerund phrase as fragmented object
4. Karen's fundraising idea, to have a raffle, was a good one. Infinitive phrase as fragmented appositive
5. Eating pizza every day for lunch is not a recipe for good health. Gerund phrase as fragmented subject

CHAPTER 4, PART I

Exercise A, p. 134

1. I <u>have seen</u> the truth, and it <u>makes</u> no sense. (Anonymous)
2. A combustion engine <u>can use</u> gasoline as fuel.
3. Margaret <u>elbowed</u> her way onto the crowded bus.
4. I <u>was looking</u> at the stars.
5. I <u>am giving up</u> procrastination. <u>I'll start</u> tomorrow.

Exercise B, p. 134

1. The president [will (arrive) at the airport at noon].
2. A physicist [can (extrapolate) the origins of the universe].
3. Pavlov [had (trained) his dogs to associate the ringing of a bell with the presence of food].
4. Walking the dog [(is) Barb's favorite form of exercise].
5. Many people [don't (understand) the president's explanations].

Exercise C, p. 135

1. Miguel <u>has</u> lived in Spain all of his life. [*Has* combined with *lived* creates a present perfect. It tells us that an action began in the past and continues in the present.]
2. You <u>ought to</u> wear a coat in this cold weather. [*Ought to* carries the meaning of necessity or strong suggestion. It is advisable to wear a coat to protect oneself from the cold.]
3. <u>Would</u> you help me with this zipper? [*Would* is being used to form a polite question.]
4. The majority of people <u>are</u> willing to help others. [*Be* (*are*) is in the present tense. It tells us that the stated action is a general truth.]
5. Kevin <u>will</u> paint the house next year. [*Will* marks the future tense and implies near certainty about what is being stated.]

Exercise D, p. 135
Answers will vary.

Exercise E, p. 135
Explanations will vary. We provide some as models.

1. That car *stopped* right in front of me. [Change *stoped* to *stopped* because you must double the consonant when -*ed* is added to a one-syllable word that ends in a vowel and consonant.]
2. The elevator had *passed* my floor before I *realized* it. [Change *pass* to *passed* because it is being used as a past participle, and thus requires the -*ed* ending (as a regular verb).]
3. I *ran* down the road yesterday. [Change *runned* to *ran* because *run* is an irregular verb and the past tense form is *ran*.]
4. She *has* called home several times today. [Change *have* to *has* because *she* requires the third person singular.]
5. Everybody could *understand* the problem. [Change *understood* to *understand* because the past tense is being carried by the auxiliary, *could*. In addition, when a modal is used, the verb following it is in the bare form (*understand*).]

Exercise F, p. 136

Answers will vary. We have provided some examples.

1. Past progressive; represents an activity in progress in the past that was occurring before another activity
2. Present perfect; represents a past action
3. Present; states a general truth
4. Past; describes an action that was completed in the past
5. Past perfect; represents an action that was completed before another completed past action

Exercise G, p. 136

Explanations of the time frames will vary. We have underlined and numbered the verb phrases and given simple explanations as a model.

It is¹ for us the living, rather, to be dedicated here to the unfinished work which they who fought² here have³ thus far so nobly advanced. It is⁴ rather for us to be here dedicated to the great task remaining before us—that from these honored dead we take⁵ increased devotion to that cause for which they gave⁶ the last full measure of devotion; that we here highly resolved⁷ that these dead shall not have died⁸ in vain; that this nation, under God, shall have⁹ a new birth of freedom; and that government of the people, by the people, for the people, shall not perish¹⁰ from the earth.

Lincoln begins by stating current conditions (at the time of the writing) and from that perspective describes an action completed (*they who fought here*) and actions that began before the speech but are still taking place at the time of the speech (*have thus far so nobly advanced*). That perspective remains in verb phrases 5–7 (*take, gave, resolved*) as Lincoln refers to the past event. He then shifts to refer to the effect of the past actions on the future throughout the rest of the speech (*shall not have died, shall have, shall not perish*).

Exercise H, p. 137

1. Charlie doesn't live in Florida.
2. Mary Helene had hardly opened the door.
3. Nobody likes applesauce on his mashed potatoes.
4. Miyuki was unhappy after her retirement.
5. I have heard nothing from the college about admissions.

Exercise I, p. 137

1. Some class members (is, <u>are</u>) leaving early today.
2. The <u>members</u> of Congress (votes, <u>vote</u>) on the agriculture bill today.
3. One of my friends (<u>is</u>, are) traveling to a reunion this summer.
4. Either the president or his wife and daughter (has, <u>have</u>) to meet with the press.
5. Some of these apples (is, <u>are</u>) going into a pie.

Exercise J, p. 138

1. Marty's cat is <u>very</u> quiet. [*Very* tells to what extent Mary's cat is quiet.]
2. Put the sofa <u>down</u>. [*Down* tells where to put the sofa.]
3. The giraffe wants its supper <u>now</u>. [*Now* tells when the giraffe wants its supper.]
4. <u>Never</u> enter a dark alley <u>alone</u>. [*Never* tells when not to enter a dark alley alone; *alone* tells in what condition not to enter a dark alley.]
5. The baby seems <u>surprisingly</u> contented. [*Surprisingly* tells how contented the baby seems.]

Exercise K, p. 138
Answers will vary.

CHAPTER 4, PART II
Exercise A, p. 152

I am writing to you today to ask for your assistance with our annual neighborhood park cleanup. Last year the city *received*[1] over a hundred volunteers for this important activity. We were *touched*[2] by the overwhelming response, and our mayor *hopes*[3] to receive a similar one this year. You may wonder, What did the folks who *volunteered*[4] last year do? They did a variety of things. Some picked up *used*[5] containers and *packed*[6] them into large receptacles that the park *provided*[7] for this purpose. Others *raked*[8] up dead leaves. Still others repaired and painted some of the shelters in the park. This year we have *prepared*[9] lots of snacks and exciting activities to keep you *motivated*[10] while you work! So come one, come all, and make this year's the best park cleanup day ever. As always, the city *counts* (or *is counting*)[11] on you for your support.

Descriptions will vary; the following are suggestions.

1. *Last year* marks the sentence as past tense; *receive* is a regular verb and so needs an *-ed* ending.
2. *Touched* is a past participle used as an adjective and therefore needs the addition of *-ed* because it is a regular verb.
3. *Mayor* is third person singular, and so the verb needs the addition of the third person singular *-s*.
4. *Last year* marks the sentence as past tense; *volunteer* is a regular verb and so needs an *-ed* ending.
5. *Used* is a past participle used as an adjective and therefore needs the addition of *-ed* because it is a regular verb.
6. The discussion is about what people did at last year's picnic, and the remainder of the sentence is in the past tense. Consequently, *pack*, a regular verb, needs to add *-ed* to be in the same past tense form as the other verbs in the sentence.

7. Because the sentence discusses what happened last year, we have put the regular verb *provide* in the past tense by adding *-ed.* If the park puts or keeps these receptacles out all the time, it would also be correct to put the verb in the third person singular (*provides*) to indicate continuing action.

8. The discussion is still in the past tense, so *-ed* must be added to the regular verb *rake.*

9. The sentence is in the present perfect, which is formed by using *have* and the past participle form of the main verb. *Prepare* is the main verb in the verb phrase and therefore needs to be in the past participle form, *prepared.*

10. *Motivated* is a past participle used as an adjective and therefore needs the addition of *-ed* because it is a regular verb.

11. *City* is third person singular, and so the verb needs the addition of the third person singular *-s.*

Exercise B, pp. 153

My friend, Mary, has *done*[1] many interesting things in her life. You *could*[2] say she's a world traveler. She has lived with her family in Indonesia, Malaysia, South Africa, Burundi, and Korea. When I visited her home, I *saw*[3] pictures of her that she had *taken*[4] while living in those countries. They seem so foreign to me! I haven't *traveled*[5] much in the world. I haven't *gone*[6] anywhere as adventurous as Mary has.

Descriptions will vary; the following are suggestions.

1. The sentence is in the present perfect, which is formed by using *have* and the past participle form of the main verb. The irregular verb *do* is the main verb in the verb phrase and therefore should be in the past participle form, *done.* The writer has mistakenly used the past tense form, *did,* in place of the participle.

2. In written standard English, double modals are unacceptable because the meaning can be just as well expressed using only one word—in this case, *could.*

3. The sentence is in the past tense and so needs the past tense form of the irregular verb *see,* which is *saw.* The writer has mistakenly used the past participle form, *seen.*

4. The sentence is in the present perfect, which is formed by using *have* and the past participle form of the main verb. The irregular verb *take* is the main verb in the verb phrase and therefore should be in the past participle form, *taken.* The writer has mistakenly used the past tense form, *took,* in place of the participle.

5. The sentence is in the present perfect, which is formed by using *have* and the past participle form of the main verb. The regular verb *travel* is the main verb in the verb phrase and therefore should be in the past participle form, *traveled.* The writer has mistakenly omitted the *-ed* ending from *travel.*

6. The sentence is in the present perfect, which is formed by using *have* and the past participle form of the main verb. The irregular verb *go* is the main verb in the verb phrase and therefore should be in the past participle form, *gone.* The writer has mistakenly used the past tense form, *went,* in place of the participle.

Exercise C, pp. 153

Answers will vary; the following are suggestions.

1. The cost of those glittery socks *makes* me angry. [Even if a modifying phrase comes between subject and verb, the verb must agree with the subject, which in this case is *cost.*]

2. John and his friend from college *want* lower taxes. [Two singular nouns joined by *and* form a plural, so the verb must be plural.]

3. Bettina, Marketta, and Zoolita play tennis together every Saturday. [Sentence is correct as written.]

4. Nandy or her sisters *shop* for the family's groceries every Wednesday. [When the subject is formed of two or more nouns or noun phrases connected by *or*, the verb must agree with the closest noun or noun phrase. In this sentence, the closest noun phrase is *sisters*, which is plural; so the verb should be in the third person plural, *shop*.]

5. The high price of fossil fuels *is* disturbing many consumers. [If a modifying phrase comes between subject and verb, the verb must agree with the subject, which in this case is *price*.]

Exercise D, pp. 153
Answers will vary.

Exercise E, pp. 154

If anyone asks me what's exciting about my life right now, *I'd* say that *it's* my *son's* engagement. My husband and I are both ecstatic about it even though *there's* not much time until the wedding. As the wedding approaches, *we're* landscaping our front yard in anticipation of the reception. Some people ask us, "*Aren't* you worried about whether you'll get along with your daughter-in-law?" But we just shake our heads and smile because we know that our son has chosen wisely. As our friend Clarissa says, "*You've* planted the seed; now enjoy the shade of the tree!"

Exercise F, p. 154
Negations are underlined; rewrites and explanations will vary.

You <u>don't know</u> about me without you have read a book by the name of *The Adventures of Tom Sawyer;* but that <u>ain't no</u> matter. That book was made by Mr. Mark Twain, and he told the truth, mainly. There was things which he stretched, but mainly he told the truth. That is <u>nothing</u>. I <u>never seen anybody</u> but lied one time or another, without it was Aunt Polly, or the widow, or maybe Mary. Aunt Polly—Tom's Aunt Polly, she is—and Mary, and the Widow Douglas is all told about in that book, which is mostly a true book, with some stretches as I said before.

… The Widow Douglas, she took me for her son, and allowed she would sivilize me; but it was rough living in the house all the time, considering how dismal regular and decent the widow was in all her ways; and so when I <u>couldn't stand it no longer</u> I lit out.

Exercise G, p. 155
Explanations will vary; the following are suggestions.

1. I felt *good* when the teacher complimented my handwriting. [*Well* is an adverb, or when used as an adjective, it means "in good health." In this sentence, *good* is most appropriate because it describes how the person felt after being complimented.]

2. I've been sick, but I feel *well* today. [Here *well* is an adjective meaning "in good health."]

3. She thinks really *quickly* on her feet. [*Quick* is the adjective form, *quickly* the adverb form. In this sentence, the word is used to describe the speed of the action (how fast she thinks) and so modifies the verb, which means that the adverb form is required.]

4. Katie talks more *loudly* than Courtney. [There are two problems in this sentence. First, the comparative *more* is used together with the comparative *-er* added onto the following word (to create *louder*), whereas the phrase needs only *more* or *-er*, not

both. Second, *loud* is the adjective form; in this sentence, the writer is describing the verb *talk,* so the adverb form (*loud* + *-ly*) should be used.]

5. What is the *worst* thing you've ever done? [The adjective is irregular and requires a change in word when in the superlative form. Instead of the nonword *baddest,* the writer should use *worst.*]

Exercise H, p. 155

1. *Only* modifies *I.* No one else has five dollars.
2. *Only* modifies *have.* I have no money beyond five dollars (and perhaps no access to any other money).
3. *Only* modifies *five dollars.* It implies that five dollars is a small sum.
4. *Only* modifies *five dollars.* The effect is similar to the construction in sentence 3 but perhaps a bit more emphatic.

Exercise I, p. 155

1. *Even* modifies *I.* The cha-cha is so simple to do that even someone like me, who isn't a great dancer, can do it.
2. *Even* modifies the verb phrase *can dance.* I dance so well that I have mastered the difficult cha-cha.
3. *Even* modifies *cha-cha.* The cha-cha is more challenging than the other dances I have mastered.
4. *Even* modifies *cha-cha.* The effect is similar to the construction in sentence 3 but perhaps a bit more emphatic.

CHAPTER 5, PART I

Exercise A, p. 175

1. statement
2. information question
3. exclamation
4. yes-no question
5. statement

Exercise B, p. 176

Answers may vary.

1. Would you tie that sail down?
2. Was Maria's running out of hall screaming caused by her fear of crowds?
3. Matt spilled the vanilla shake all over Debby's black dress.
4. What did many of the voters decide to do after the election?
5. What a marvelous fiction writer Carlos is!

Exercise C, p. 176

Answers may vary.

1. Statement. The sentence is in "normal" word order, so it is not a question, and it does not imply sufficient excitement to be an exclamation.
2. Yes-no question. The sentence is in inverted word order and does not begin with an information word such as *when* or *what.*

3. Information question. The sentence is in inverted word order and begins with an information word, *what*.

Exercise D, p. 177

1. JAIME: Have you seen my new baby? Yes-no question used as a request for a compliment.

   BRIAN: He's such a big boy. Statement used as a compliment.

2. MOM: This room is a mess. Statement used as a request for cleaning the room.

   SON: I don't have time to clean it. Statement used as an explanation for not cleaning or denial of the request.

3. JULIE: Are you really going to eat that whole pie? Yes-no question used as an exclamation or as a request to save some of the pie for her.

   TIM: Why shouldn't I? Information question used either for information or as a statement of intention to eat the pie.

Exercise E, p. 177

1. George is doing very well in <u>history and math</u> at this new school. Compound object of a preposition
2. Barb <u>is washing dishes and talking on the phone</u> right now. Compound verb phrase
3. Jacky dyed her hair <u>blue and orange</u>. Compound object complement
4. You are the <u>most stubborn and most difficult</u> person I've ever met! Compound adjective modifying a subject complement
5. <u>Either Deb or Sue</u> is going to the movies this weekend. Compound subject

Exercise F, p. 178
Answers will vary.

Exercise G, p. 178
Answers will vary.

Exercise H, p. 179

1. Nancy ran and skipped all the way on her first day at school.
2. The soup is hot and creamy.
3. Josh loves his mom and dad.
4. They went to the zoo and the park.
5. Stanley, Angie's older and good-looking brother, lives in Florida.

Exercise I, p. 179
Answers will vary.

Exercise J, p. 180
Answers may vary.

1. The class voted on the notebook format. (passive to active)
2. The porch on our neighbors' house was renovated last summer. (active to passive)
3. A tiny little chipmunk was cornered by Tabby near the garage. (active to passive)

4. Since last summer, external evaluators have assessed the essays. (passive to active)
5. A comprehensive solution was proposed by several concerned citizens. (active to passive)

Exercise K, p. 181
Answers may vary.

1. All of the invitations have been lost. [*By* + *my supervisor* has been deleted to avoid angering or embarrassing the supervisor.]
2. The small coastal village was devastated by the tidal wave.
3. First, the dry ingredients are added to the mixture. Then, the marinated vegetables are added. Finally, everything is tossed in a large pasta bowl. [*By* + *you* has been deleted to avoid repetition.]
4. The subjects of the experiment were observed on two different occasions. [*By* + *me* has been deleted to put the focus on the the subjects and conform to a more academic style.]
5. The handcrafted dolls were bought by the tourists from Belgium.

Exercise L, p. 181
Answers will vary.

CHAPTER 5, PART II

Exercise A, p. 194
Answers will vary. We have identified some errors that relate to the content of this chapter. There will be other problems with the paragraph, such as word choice and use of verb tense, that we have not identified.

1. On the other hand, a lot of plants have installed in some industrialized areas for the purpose of exporting goods. [The writer has tried to use the passive. Not only is the passive not fully formed (it should read *have been installed*), but using the passive makes the sentence awkward. The sentence would be better if it read *Some industrialized countries have installed plants for the purpose of exporting goods.*]
2. As a result, the manufactured goods are a variety of models, shades, colors, and so on. [The sentence is OK.]
3. Those materials have influenced the spirit of Korea. They have influenced the daily life of Korea. [These two sentences might be more focused and less repetitive if they were joined and put in the passive voice: *The spirit and daily life of Korea have been influenced by those materials.*]
4. The youth now have no respect for old people. Old people now try to enjoy themselves outside of their homes. [These sentences are OK grammatically, although joining them would make them less repetitious: ... *no respect for old people, who now try....* We discuss adjectival modifiers in Chapter 8.]
5. As a result, there a significant gap appears between the old and the young. [The writer has unsuccessrully tried to use a moved (extraposed) subject. The sentence should read either *there is a significant gap* or *a significant gap appears.*]
6. So visitors to Korea are easy to get a bad impression about Korea. They are easy to find bad clichés about Korean people. [The writer needs to use a moved (extraposed) sub-

ject and combine the repetitive structures in the sentences: *So it is easy for visitors to Korea to get a bad impression about Korea and encounter neagtive clichés about Korean people.*]

Exercise B, p. 194

1. <u>Erma Jean</u> was going somewhere yesterday.
2. <u>The children</u> will attend the special memorial service after dinner.
3. <u>The owner</u> prepared our pasta.
4. <u>Livia</u> is playing a new trick on us now.
5. <u>The fox</u> ran over the hills and through the woods.

Exercise C, p. 195

1. has
2. do
3. have
4. was
5. are

Exercise D, p. 195

Answers will vary. We have revised some sentences as models.

This week marks the kickoff of Master State University's annual fundraising campaign. *We need a few minutes of your time to explain the goals of this campaign to you.* As you are all aware, MSU already does many great things for its students and staff, but more can and should be done! Currently, all of our resources are used by the many programs and opportunities offered by MSU. Yet we need to do more. *Our various departments and programs need to offer more scholarships. Our students need to receive more support as they conduct research, travel to conferences, and pursue their studies.*

Not only do personnel costs deplete MSU resources, but maintenance costs for buildings and facilities also consume huge sums of money. But we have entered a new century and are challenged by this new era. We are challenged to provide new technology for our students, faculty, and staff—new technology that will be used to spur new ideas and build new hopes.

Please take a moment out of your busy schedule to think about what program or initiative might benefit from your generous gift. Your contribution will, of course, be tax-deductible. But most important, *your kindness will enhance the education of generations of future students.*

Exercise E, p. 196

Answers will vary.

Exercise F, p. 196

Answers may vary.

1. The owner should shampoo and groom that dog if she expects anyone to pet it.
2. Sid watched as Fluffy attacked the mouse.
3. Someone should eat that last taco or I'll throw it away.

4. The dentist told Joe that he needed to cap some of his teeth.

5. The cost of the procedure astonished Joe.

Exercise G, p. 197

Answers may vary.

1. Last week I volunteered to help out with a new fundraising initiative.

2. Dean Whorf encouraged all alumni to express their opinions regarding the new program.

3. The leaves were swept off every lawn on the street.

4. Amazingly, someone finished that cold coffee.

5. The fact that Ginny Lou didn't finish the exam amazed us.

CHAPTER 5, PART III

Exercise A, p. 205
Answers will vary.

Exercise B, p. 205
Answers will vary.

Exercise C, p. 206
Answers will vary.

Exercise D, p. 206
Answers will vary.

Exercise E, p. 206
Answers will vary.

Exercise F, p. 206
Answers will vary.

Exercise G, p. 206
Answers will vary.

Exercise H, p. 206
Answers will vary.

CHAPTER 6, PART I

Exercise A, p. 214

1. Simple
2. Complex
3. Simple
4. Complex
5. Complex

Exercise B, p. 214

1. That the sun sets in the west is indisputable.

2. Do you know <u>where my keys are</u>?
3. We carry with us the wonders <u>we seek without us</u>.
4. My favorite piece of music is the one <u>we hear all of the time if we are quiet</u>.

Exercise C, p. 215

1. The waitress <u>hastily</u> put out the fire. (single-word adverb; modifies *put out*)
2. What is life? It is a flash of a firefly in the night. It is a breath of a buffalo in the winter time. It is as the little shadow that runs <u>across the grass</u> and loses itself <u>in the sunset</u>. (phrase, modifies *runs;* phrase, modifies *loses*)
3. Did you buy this book <u>to give it as a present</u>? (phrase, modifies *buy*)
4. <u>So long as little children are allowed to suffer</u>, there is no true love <u>in this world</u>. (clause, modifies *is no true love;* phrase, adverb complement modifying *no true love* following linking verb *is*)
5. The past would be startled <u>if it could see itself on the pages of the historian</u>. (clause, modifies *would be startled*)

Exercise D, p. 215

1. We seldom see anybody <u>who is not uneasy and afraid to live</u>. (clause, modifies *anybody*)
2. Cary Grant was a <u>popular Hollywood</u> actor in the1930s, 1940s, and 1950s. (both are single-word adjectives that modify *actor*)
3. The <u>many-colored</u> photographs <u>on her desk and walls</u> were pictures <u>of dearly loved friends and relatives</u>. (compound adjective, modifies *photographs;* phrase, modifies *photographs;* phrase, modifies *pictures*)
4. The street <u>where I live</u> is being repaved. (clause, modifies *street*)

Exercise E, p. 216

1. The invariable <u>mark</u> of wisdom is <u>to see the miraculous in the common</u>. (single-word noun [part of noun phrase *the mark*] functioning as the subject; infinitive phrase functioning as the subject complement)
2. <u>What Jesse doesn't know</u> is <u>that his wife is planning a party for him</u>. (noun clause functioning as the subject; noun clause functioning as the subject complement)
3. If <u>you</u> don't know <u>where you are going</u>, <u>you</u> can't get lost. (pronoun functioning as the subject of a dependent clause; noun clause functioning as the direct object of a dependent clause; pronoun functioning as the subject of the main clause)
4. <u>Giving fair grades</u> can be challenging for <u>teachers</u>. (gerund phrase functioning as the subject; noun functioning as the object of a preposition)

Exercise F, p. 217
Answers will vary.

CHAPTER 6, PART II
Exercise A, p. 223

1. *Nearing the large parking lot* is a sentence fragment; it is attempting to modify the noun *cars*.
2. *As far as I can tell* is a sentence fragment; it is attempting to modify the predicate by qualifying my judgment that John isn't too upset.

3. *Because of her attitude toward Bill* is a sentence fragment; it is modifying the verb phrase *will not be attending* by explaining why.
4. No fragment

Exercise B, p. 224

1. Misplaced modifier. *Walking down Pennsylvania Avenue* seems to be modifying *litter*.
2. Misplaced modifier. *To get admitted to a good college* seems to be modifying *Mr. Jones*.
3. Misplaced modifier. *The audience* seems to be *striding boldly down the catwalk*.
4. Sentence is OK.
5. Dangling modifier. *Examining the data from the investigation* has nothing to modify. Who was examining the data from the investigation?

Exercise C, p. 224

1. Fused sentence. *I have only two sisters* and *their names are Laura and Evey* are both complete sentences. They should not be punctuated as if they were one sentence.
2. Comma splice. *Evey lives in Los Angeles* and *she is an executive at an insurance company* are both complete sentences. They cannot be combined with a comma only.
3. Sentences are OK.
4. Comma splice. A semicolon is required to separate the sentence beginning with *however* from *Everyone laughed*.
5. Sentences are OK.

Exercise D, p. 225
Answers will vary.

Exercise E, p. 225
Answers will vary.

CHAPTER 7, PART I
Exercise A, p. 239

1. <u>When you are finished eating</u>, you should drive to Toledo. *When you are finished eating* modifies the verb phrase *should drive* and describes when you should drive to Toledo.
2. Those cameras are hard to find <u>in the United States</u>. The prepositional phrase *in the United States* modifies the verb phrase *are hard to find*, telling where the cameras are hard to find.
3. <u>After class</u>, Anita and Juan walked <u>hand-in-hand to the House of Brats</u>. *After class* modifies the verb *walked* by telling when they walked; *hand-in-hand* modifies the verb *walked* by indicating how they walked; *to the House of Brats* is a prepositional phrase modifying the verb *walked*, indicating where they walked.
4. <u>Because she was angry with her sister</u>, Laura cleaned her room <u>agonizingly slowly</u>. *Because she was angry with her sister* modifies the verb phrase *cleaned her room; agonizingly* and *slowly* are both adverbs modifying the verb phrase. They indicate how Laura cleaned.
5. <u>Over the mountains</u> and <u>through the woods</u> trotted the three glorious brown stags. Both underlined phrases are adverbial prepositional phrases modifying the verb *trotted*, indicating where the stags trotted.

Exercise B, p. 240

1. Noun
2. Adverbial; modifies *studied*
3. Adverbial; modifies verb phrase *tripped over*
4. Noun
5. Noun

Exercise C, p. 241

Answers will vary.

Exercise D, p. 241

1. <u>To free herself from guilt</u> (infinitive phrase; tells why Grace confessed), Grace confessed her sins to a stranger <u>at the bus stop</u> (prepositional phrase; tells where Grace confessed).
2. The wayward bus broke <u>through the guard rail</u> (prepositional phrase; tells where the bus broke through) and plunged <u>over a steep cliff</u> (prepositional phrase; tells where the bus plunged).
3. The picture was hanging <u>at an angle</u> (prepositional phrase; tells how the picture was hanging); <u>against the back wall</u> (prepositional phrase; tells where the picture was hanging).
4. The magician <u>always</u> (adverb; tells the frequency with which he performed) performed <u>in the shadows</u> (prepositional phrase; tells where he performed).
5. Kris sang <u>happily</u> (adverb; tells how Kris sang) <u>as she prepared a simple meal</u> (adverbial clause; indicates when Kris was singing).

Exercise E, p. 242

Answers will vary.

Exercise F, p. 242

1. <u>Because I was feeling depressed</u>, I didn't go to the party. Indicates the reason or cause for not attending the party
2. He made a large charitable donation <u>after he visited the homeless shelter</u>. Indicates when he made the charitable donation; implies why.
3. <u>If the market maintains its stability</u>, the stockbrokers will keep their jobs. Indicates the conditions under which stockbrokers may keep their jobs
4. She lent him the money, <u>though she doubted she would ever be repaid</u>. Contrastive relationship between the act of lending money and the doubts she has about doing so
5. George devoted a lifetime to stamp collecting, <u>even though it is an expensive hobby</u>. Contrastive relationship between the choice of hobby and the expense

Exercise G, p. 242

Answers may vary.

1. Jennifer cried with sorrow because her puppy died.
2. Because the test was very difficult, very few people passed it.
3. If they study more, this would ensure a higher pass rate.
4. As the soup was very hot, Tom sipped it slowly.
5. He misses his grandmother very much since she moved away in October.

Exercise H, p. 243
Answers will vary.

CHAPTER 7, PART II

Exercise A, p. 254

1. (Correct as written)
2. Because Bettina is not satisfied with the waiting period, she will be contacting the Better Business Bureau.
3. I really am not too interested in what happens to people when they win the lottery; I do, however, think it's important for lotteries to be run honestly.
4. My husband is of the opinion that lotteries are a waste of money; moreover, he thinks that people should be putting money in savings, not trying to get rich quick.
5. Still, since the idea of extra money for a larger house, a better car, or a vacation can be tempting, many folks do spend a few dollars now and then on lottery tickets.

Exercise B, p. 255
Answers will vary. We provide some as models.

1. After Josh graduated with a degree in computer science last May, he moved to Chicago.
   Revised: Josh graduated with a degree in computer science last May; then he moved to Chicago.
2. When Dennis was promoted to executive vice president in charge of marketing, he and his wife bought a summer home in Tuscany.
   Revised: Dennis was promoted to executive vice president in charge of marketing; consequently, he and his wife bought a summer home in Tuscany.
3. Because I talked to Sheila for several hours on the phone last night, I felt reassured that she was feeling all right.
   Revised: I talked to Sheila for several hours on the phone last night; thereafter, I felt reassured that she was feeling all right.
4. Because many people can't tell much difference between the two candidates in this election, they will choose not to vote.
   Revised: Many people can't tell much difference between the two candidates in this election; consequently, they will choose not to vote.
5. Although you will be going to Columbus for lunch and a movie on Saturday, I'll join you at the bookstore.
   Revised: You will be going to Columbus for lunch and a movie on Saturday; however, I'll join you at the bookstore.

Exercise C, p. 256
Answers will vary. We provide some as models.

1. The sky was clear blue this morning; however, now it looks like rain.
2. My cousin won the lottery last year; consequently, he has quit his job and moved to Las Vegas.
3. The United States had not been engaged in a war for many years; nevertheless, many young men and women joined the armed services every year.

4. This is the age of technology; therefore, most people who can afford them own computers.

5. Damon has never learned to read a map; therefore, he often finds himself lost and having to ask for directions.

Exercise D, p. 256
Answers will vary; we provide a model.

> The day was cold and blustery. *However,* because the sky was clear, we wore no coats and left our hats and mittens at home. *As a result,* we got very cold on our walk and had to put our hands in our pockets and keep our heads ducked against the wind to stay warm. *Consequently,* we were happy to see a warm fire in the fireplace and hot chocolate on the counter when we returned home as a result. We have learned our lesson, *and so* we'll always check the temperature instead of the sky in the future.

Exercise E, p. 257
Answers may vary.

1. Carol could improve her skills if she would listen to her older sister's advice.
2. Because she was tired, Kyoko left the party early.
3. They will devote their full attention to the matter when they get through with the first agenda item.
4. Ken is a great multimedia designer, although he needs more programming experience.
5. Unless you work harder, you will not succeed.

Exercise F, p. 257

1. When Scott comes to town, we'll be sure to go to the hockey game.
2. Stan loves to cook; however, he never follows the recipe.
3. The dog was quite old; nevertheless, he could still chase cars.
4. Sheba refused to eat her cat food even though she hadn't eaten in two days.
5. The artist was deeply depressed; therefore, he went to law school.

Exercise G, p. 258

Joe is never able to get much sleep because he drinks caffeinated colas too late in the day. This makes him cranky and irritable whenever he has an early-morning meeting. If he would only switch to caffeine-free cola, he would be much easier to live with, whether he is at work or at home.

CHAPTER 7, PART III
Exercise A, p. 262
Answers will vary.

Exercise C, p. 262
Answers will vary.

CHAPTER 8, PART I

Exercise A, p 278

1. The <u>laughing</u> [children] danced enthusiastically in the <u>sparkling</u> [rain].
2. [Dottie], <u>surprised</u> and <u>delighted</u>, opened the <u>small</u> [package] as soon as it arrived in the <u>afternoon</u> [mail].
3. The <u>golden</u> [retriever] gently grabbed the <u>bouncing red</u> [ball] between its <u>massive</u> [jaws].
4.   <u>Many</u> [paths] lead from
     The [foot] <u>of the mountain</u>
     But at the peak
     We all gaze at the
     <u>Same bright</u> [moon].
5. The <u>hung</u> [jury] had deliberated for <u>three grueling</u> [weeks] before deciding that they could not reach a <u>unanimous</u> [agreement] on a <u>final</u> [verdict].

Exercise B, p. 279

The stranger was a [man] <u>of more than winsome [aspect]</u>. There he stood apart and in repose, and, yet, by his <u>mere</u> [look], lured the [man] <u>in gray</u> from his story, much as, by its [graciousness] <u>of bearing</u>, some <u>full-leaved</u> [elm], <u>alone in a meadow</u>,* lures the <u>noon</u> [sickleman] to throw down his sheaves and come and apply for the [alms] <u>of its shade</u>.

   *You might argue that *in a meadow* is an adverbial. Why would it seem to be one?

Exercise C, p. 279

Answers will vary.

Exercise D, p. 279

1. <u>Smiling broadly</u>, [Karen] accepted the award.
2. <u>Devastated by the rejection letter</u>, [John] vowed to try again.
3. The [house] <u>on the hill</u> is rumored to be haunted.
4. I myself am a [question] <u>addressed to the world</u>, and I must communicate my answer, for otherwise I am dependent upon the world's answer.
5. The minor-league baseball [team] <u>with over-the-hill players</u> still had an outside [chance] <u>of winning</u> its division.

Exercise E, p. 280

1. Past participial phrase modifying *team*
2. Present participial phrase modifying *Janice*
3. All gerunds
4. Past participial phrase modifying *John*
5. Present participial phrase modifying *swimmer*

Exercise F, p. 280

1. We talked to the [man] <u>who had cleaned the aquarium</u> because we were interested in the [filter] <u>[that] he used</u>.
2. Who is more foolish, the [child] <u>[who is] afraid of the dark</u> or the [man] <u>[who is] afraid of the light</u>?

3. The reason you are the [one] <u>whom we all admire</u> is that you always go to dangerous [places] <u>where most people won't travel.</u>
4. The reason why Eddie missed the rehearsal is that he was involved in an [accident] <u>that blocked all of the lanes on the highway.</u>
5. The plants in the wetlands provide food for the [fish] <u>that lay eggs in that swampy environment.</u>

Exercise G, p. 281

1. I hate the neighbor *who* had our sweet puppy arrested by the dog patrol [*Who* is the subject of the relative clause.]
2. We all wondered about the student *who* never seemed to study but *who* passed every exam. [Both times, *who* is the subject of the relative clause.]
3. The new members of the Save the Wetlands club, *whom* you've all met, would like to address our class. [*Whom* is the direct object of the clause.]
4. Don't you remember your Aunt Tomeka, *who* used to baby-sit for you until you were in school? [*Who* is the subject of the clause.]
5. The proceeds of the plant sale will benefit local seniors, *who* have been raising funds for a new dock. [*Who* is the subject of the clause.]

Exercise H, p. 282
Answers will vary.

Exercise I, p. 282
Answers will vary.

Exercise J, p. 283

1. The children standing <u>on the corner</u> waiting <u>for the bus</u> got splashed <u>by mud.</u> [All are adverbials; the first two modify adjectivals (Standing where? Waiting for what?); the last one modifies the verb <u>got splashed.</u>]
2. All <u>of the cows in the barn</u> must be moved <u>to the pasture</u> before the area can be cleaned. [The first two are adjectivals; *of the cows* modifies *all*, and *in the barn* modifies *cows*. *To the pasture* is an adverbial modifying the verb *moved.*]
3. I will not descend <u>among professors and capitalists</u>—I will turn the ends <u>of my trousers around my boots</u>, and my cuffs back <u>from my wrists</u>, and go <u>with drivers and boatmen and men that catch fish or work in the fields.</u> [Five of the six prepositional phrases are adverbials; one, *of my trousers*, is an adjectival. All the adverbials tell where.]
4. My friend Mary <u>from Pittsburgh</u> found a wonderful dress that really flatters her. [adjectival; modifies *friend*]
5. All <u>of the people waiting in line</u> to buy tickets groaned loudly when it was announced that the concert had been sold out. [*Of the people* is an adjectival; it modifies *all*. *Waiting in line* is an adverbial; it modifies the adjectival *waiting*, telling where.]

CHAPTER 8, PART II
Exercise A, p. 294

Alice is <u>happiest</u> when she is helping someone. This is <u>truest</u> when it comes to romance. She likes to match couples whom she thinks are the most suited for one another. Sometimes the woman is <u>calmer</u> than the man; sometimes the man is <u>calmer</u> than the woman. She always likes to invite them to dinner, where everyone has a <u>more pleasant</u> time than usual. Her <u>most recent</u> success was matching her sister with her friend. They are now dating steadily. Who knows what the future may bring?

Exercise B, p. 294

There are many ways to live cheaply. You can live in a <u>furnished</u> room and buy <u>used</u> books and clothing. You might feel <u>aggravated</u> sometimes because you don't have anything new or because you are <u>tired</u> of looking for bargains all the time, but it does pay off if you want to save money. You know what they say: a penny <u>saved</u> is a penny <u>earned</u>.

Exercise C, p. 295

1. The pastor announced that Jack and Jill were getting married smiling.

Analysis: [*Smiling* seems to be telling how Jack and Jill were getting married.]
Revision: Smiling, the pastor announced that Jack and Jill were getting married.

2. Being the most prestigious of schools, students have made Harvard their number one choice for decades.

Analysis: [*Being the most prestigious of schools* seems to be modifying *students.*]
Revision: Students have made Harvard, [being] the most prestigious of schools, their number one choice for decades.

3. Hurting financially, the plan to raise salaries had to be abandoned by the company.

Analysis: [*Hurting financially* seems to be modifying *the plan.*]
Revision: The plan to raise salaries had to be abandoned by the company [because it was] hurting financially.

4. Scattered across the desk, Susan leafed through the files.

Analysis: [*Scattered across the desk* seems to be modifying *Susan.*]
Revision: Susan leafed through the files [that were] scattered across the desk.

5. Succeeding in high school, college was a definite plan for Jennifer.

Analysis: [*Succeeding in high school* seems to be modifying *college.*]
Revision: Succeeding in high school, Jennifer made definite plans for college.

Exercise D, p. 295

1. Working into the night, the assignment was completed.

Analysis: [*Working into the night* cannot modify *assignment.*]
Revision: Working into the night, Ahmed completed the assignment.

2. Playing in the snow, her foot got broken.

Analysis: [*Playing in the snow* should not modify *foot.*]
Revision: Playing in the snow, Leslie broke her foot.

3. The doors were locked, returning home late.

Analysis: [*Returning home late* cannot modify *doors.*]
Revision: The doors were locked because Tony got home late.

4. Giving it their best shot, the coach was impressed.

Analysis: [*Giving it their best shot* should not modify *coach.*]
Revision: Because the team gave winning their best shot, the coach was impressed.

5. Hiking the same trail for years, the beauty still amazes me.

Analysis: [*Hiking the same trail for years* cannot modify *beauty.*]
Revision: Despite the fact that I have been hiking the same trail for years, the beauty still amazes me.

Exercise E, p. 296

Answers will vary. We provide one as a model.

After I walked around San Francisco all day, my shoes were killing me. Despite my pain, I found the city to be lovely. Famous for its wide range of restaurants and shops, Chinatown was especially enjoyable. Visiting many of the city's neighborhoods, I experienced a hectic but exciting aura. Intrigued and fascinated by its beauty, I decided that San Francisco would definitely be a repeat visit for me.

Exercise F, p. 296

Answers will vary.

Exercise G, p. 296

Answers may vary. We provide one as a model.

Running down to the water's edge, we could feel the tow of the waves as they pulled against our legs. We held onto the rocks jutting out of the sand to keep our balance. But rather than step backwards, we stood where we were because we liked the feel of the water as it washed back into the sea and then as it washed back to try to pull us under.

Exercise H, p. 296

Answers will vary.

CHAPTER 8, PART III

Exercise A, p. 306

1. She kissed the man with the false teeth.

Meaning 1:   She kissed the man who was wearing false teeth.
Meaning 2:   She held the false teeth up to the man's face and used them to give the man a "kiss."
Context: In sentence 2, she was trying to be humorous (or perhaps cruel).

2. The children shoved the pirate with the wooden leg.

Meaning 1:   The children pushed a pirate who had a leg made of wood.
Meaning 2:   The children used a wooden leg to poke at a pirate.

Context: Meaning 2 may be a bit far-fetched because pirates are often depicted as having one leg made of wood, whereas children are unlikely to have access to a wooden leg to use as a weapon and are even less likely to encounter a pirate!

    3. The nurse cuddled the puppy with the soft towel.

Meaning 1:   The nurse cuddled a puppy who was holding a towel in its teeth.
Meaning 2:   The nurse cuddled a puppy by wrapping it in a towel.
Context: The action conveyed in sentence 2 is more conventional, but the action conveyed in sentence 1 is also feasible.

Exercise B, p. 307
Answers will vary.

Exercise C, p. 308
Answers will vary.

Exercise D, p. 308
Answers will vary.

Exercise E, p. 308
Answers will vary.

CHAPTER 9, PART I
Exercise A, p. 325

1. *Man* is a noun functioning as the subject; *what he believes* is a nominal functioning as the subject complement.
2. *Everyone* is a pronoun functioning as the subject; *last night's presidential debate* is a noun phrase functioning as the direct object.
3. *Copernicus* is a noun functioning as the subject; *a great scientist* is a noun phrase functioning as the subject complement; *whose theories* is a noun phrase functioning as the subject of a dependent clause; *the basis of modern science* is a noun phrase functioning as the subject complement in a dependent clause.
4. *People living in Montana* is a noun phrase functioning as the subject; *to keep their state free of littering tourists* is a nominal functioning as the direct object.
5. *David's dog* is a noun phrase functioning as the subject; *Spike* is a noun functioning as an appositive; *a cute miniature dachshund* is a noun phrase functioning as the subject complement; *who* is a pronoun functioning as the subject of a dependent clause; *barking at just about anything* is a nominal functioning as the direct object of a depedent clause.

Exercise B, p. 326

1. <u>Elton John's singing</u> has become famous around the world. Gerund phrase functioning as the subject

2. He has been planning <u>to retire</u> for many years. Infinitive phrase functioning as the direct object

3. <u>Performing</u> has been his life for more than three decades. Gerund functioning as the subject.

4. His fans would probably be screaming for him to come out of retirement. No nominal phrases (noun phrases only)

Exercise C, p. 326
Answers will vary.

Exercise D, p. 327
Answers will vary.

Exercise E, p. 327

1. *That he who finds himself loses his misery* is a *that* clause functioning as the direct object.

2. *That it takes all that is unimportant as important and all that is important as unimportant* is a *that* clause functioning as an extraposed subject.

3. *What they sought* is a *wh-* clause functioning as the direct object.

4. *That if you disabused him of a notion he had held, he carried that much less baggage around with him* is a *that* clause functioning as the direct object.

5. *[That] we can say* is a *that* clause functioning as a direct object. *That to live without appreciating this life is at least a shame* is a *that* clause functioning as a direct object within a noun clause.

Exercise F, p. 328

1. *To make songs* is an infinitive phrase functioning as the extraposed subject; *to sing them* is an infinitive phrase functioning as the subject complement following an implied *is*.

2. *To read well* is an infinitive phrase functioning as the subject; *to read true books in a true spirit* is an infinitive phrase functioning as an appositive.

3. *That we should protest strip mining* is a *that* clause functioning as an appositive.

4. *How to use the new computers* is an infinitive phrase functioning as the direct object.

5. *Dancing in the dark* is a gerund phrase functioning as an extraposed subject.

Exercise G, p. 329

1. Wayne put the book <u>there</u> on the shelf. (adverb; standard)

2. When Mary Ann asked her husband if he liked her new hairstyle, he said he hated <u>it</u>. (pronoun; standard)

3. <u>It</u> was a dark night when the invaders came. (placeholder; standard)

4. <u>There</u> are hundreds of volcanoes in the Hawaiian Islands. (placeholder; standard)

5. If you go to the office party on Saturday night, you'll find Alice <u>there</u> dancing. (adverb; standard)

Exercise H, p. 329

Answers may vary slightly.

1. Martin Luther King said he had a dream.
2. Carol said, "I don't know how to change the oil in my car."
3. Mrs. Herman told the doctor, "I don't like to stay cooped up inside all winter." [Acceptable alternative: "Mrs. Herman told the doctor she didn't like, "Stay cooped up all winter."]
4. When she met Jamie's new boyfriend, Jamie's grandmother said that birds of a feather flock together.
5. Lori asked her roommate what time she'd be home.

Exercise I, p. 330

Answers will vary.

CHAPTER 9, PART II

Exercise A, p. 343

1. There was great celebration <u>when the soldiers returned from World War II</u>. (noun clause used as the subject)
2. It troubled Iris <u>that she couldn't find her high school diploma</u>. (noun clause used as the subject)
3. The idea <u>that people could fly</u> was appealing to the Wright brothers. (noun clause used as an appositive)
4. It was ridiculous <u>to expect a child to do quantum physics</u>. (infinitive phrase used as the extraposed subject)
5. Highly preposterous was <u>what critics called Galileo's theory</u>. (noun clause used as the extraposed subject)

Exercise B, p. 343

Answers will vary.

Exercise C, p. 344

1. There <u>were</u> more people at the wedding reception than at the wedding.
2. (Sentence is OK.)
3. There <u>have</u> been a lot of rumors about Esther's true identity.
4. There <u>are</u> many things we could say about this new park, but "beautiful" is not one of them.
5. There <u>were</u> discussion and disagreement, but no one came to blows.

Exercise D, p. 345

1. Montana, a western state, has a small population for its size.
2. Montana, a state known for its many rivers and parks, is ironically quite arid.
3. We visited Montana, a place of great beauty, last summer.
4. (No change; the appositive is preceded by a comma and ends with a period at the end of the sentence.)
5. (No change; the appositive is preceded and followed by a comma.)

Exercise E, p. 345

Answers may vary; here is one possible response.

Last winter was very cold and snowy, a hard one for everyone. Still, there were optimists who enjoyed the weather, despite the high fuel bills and the slippery roads. They saw the weather as an opportunity to engage in outdoor sports, for example, skiing, ice skating, and sledding, not to mention ice fishing and building snowmen. The beauty of the freshly fallen snow and getting warm again are two incentives for getting out in the bad weather, bad weather that gives other people the flu. I like to hear stories about winter sports, but most of all I like to watch them from a distance, sipping hot chocolate, which is my favorite pastime.

Exercise F, p. 345

Answers will vary.

CHAPTER 9, PART III

Exercise A, p. 355

Answers will vary.

CHAPTER 10, PART I

Exercise A, p. 366

1. The weather today is <u>sunny but cold</u>. (adjectives as compound subject complement)
2. I am not anxious to give you the truth. But I am very anxious to have you understand that all <u>truth and power</u> are feeble to you except your own. (nouns as compound subject of dependent clause)
3. Sally was mad at her teacher for <u>being unfair and grading too hard</u>. (gerunds as compound object of a preposition)
4. The mail carrier <u>either dropped the letter or lost it</u>. (compound predicate)
5. There are three kinds of people in the world: <u>those who can count and those who can't</u>. (pronouns, each modified by a relative clause, as compound appositive)

Exercise B, p. 367

On the twelfth day of Christmas, my true love gave to me twelve drummers drumming, eleven pipers piping, ten lords a-leaping, nine ladies dancing, eight maids a-milking, seven swans a-swimming, six geese a-laying, five gold rings, four calling birds, three French hens, two turtledoves, and a partridge in a pear tree.

Exercise C, p. 367

1. Angela has a lot of animals: two dogs, three birds, a rabbit, twelve cats, and a goat.
2. The birds, but not the rabbit, are in a cage. [*These commas are optional.*]
3. Terry would like to go to Hawaii, Florida, or California for vacation.
4. Most people want only to earn a living, to live happily, and to die peacefully.
5. Francis Ford Coppola, Peter Bogdanovich, and William Friedkin were popular film directors in the 1970s.

Exercise D, p. 368
Answers will vary.

Exercise E, p. 368

[*The first two commas are optional.*] It is a common practice in the United States, but perhaps not in other countries, to put wedding and engagement announcements in the local newspaper. Many interested people and family members wait eagerly to find out who is getting engaged and who is getting married. Sometimes they even look for who is getting divorced! The wedding announcements often detail the members of the wedding party, who presided over the wedding, the location of the honeymoon, and the bride's wedding dress. The bride, her mother, or the couple places the announcement in the paper. I don't know who pays for it!

Exercise F, p. 368

1. [We do not stop playing because we are old]; [we grow old because we stop playing].
2. [Grammar conventions are often vexing for people]; in fact, [even many otherwise confident adults feel insecure about their usage of "correct" forms].

Exercise G, p. 369
Answers will vary.

Exercise H, p. 369
Answers may vary. We provide some as models.

1. It was getting later all the time, *but* I decided to keep on working. (connecting word replaced)
2. The arguments in favor of legalizing alcohol for eighteen-year-olds aren't very persuasive; therefore, it is *not* likely that many states will adopt this type of legislation. (sentence rewritten)
3. Following the very difficult election, many citizens became cynical; *moreover,* these same individuals vowed they would never vote again. (connecting word replaced)
4. (no revision necessary)
5. No one wanted the difficult job of contending with possible political fallout, and yet, remarkably, some people did apply for the positions. (sentence rewritten)

Exercise I, p. 370

1. To construct a picket fence, you need to measure the perimeter of your yard; then you need to calculate the amount of wood you need.
2. These days many people are opting for plastic fencing material rather than wood; wood requires too much maintenance.
3. Heat, sunlight, rain, and humidity all damage painted surfaces; for example, painted wood shingles show their age rather quickly.
4. Still, plastic fencing, despite its artificial (and undesirable) appearance, is very costly; in fact, a plastic fence costs about twice what a wood fence costs.
5. In making a decision about how to spend resources, many factors are important; for instance, available disposable income is a vital consideration.

CHAPTER 10, PART II
Exercise A, p. 384
Answers will vary. We provide some as models.
1. Either it will snow or the weather will be pretty.
2. Not only has James Taylor been performing since the 1970s, but he is also still popular.
3. Neither Michael nor Damon likes children.
4. Jim went to either White Springs or Sulphur Springs.
5. Not only does Andrea like chocolate, but Nicholas likes it too.

Exercise B, p. 384
Answers will vary. We provide some as models.
1. Sheri will call you either tomorrow or the next day.
2. Kris likes both bowling and walking for exercise.
3. Not only does Jennifer speak Spanish, but she also speaks French.
4. Do you know whether it would be better for me to work at home or to go to the office?
5. (No changes are necessary.)

Exercise C, p. 385
1. The children carried their sled up the hill with anticipation, yet they decided at the top not to use it and built snowmen instead. [A comma is needed before the conjunction to separate two independent clauses.]
2. Mae likes children. But she only likes other people's children. [A comma should not follow a coordinating conjunction.]
3. Jeanie sent Thelma, Sheri, and Julia sweaters for Christmas. [A comma should not follow the final item in a series.]
4. The dogs and cats played surprisingly well together. [No comma is needed in a compound subject consisting of only two items.]
5. Neither the teacher nor the students like tests. [No comma is needed in a compound subject consisting of only two items.]

Exercise D, p. 386
Answers will vary. We provide some as models.
1. My favorite film stars make their viewers happy, and they enjoy themselves whenever they perform.
2. For me, weekends are enjoyable and carefree, and my love life picks up tremendously.
3. Usually, on Saturday we go shopping, or else we stay in our rooms and play cards, watch television, listen to our stereo, or do whatever strikes our fancy.
4. My roommate is dull, wishy-washy, and boring.
5. For giving a child a male influence, the alternatives to fathers are grandfathers, uncles, and neighbors. Also, one really successful organization for this purpose is Big Brothers of America.

Exercise E, p. 386
Answers will vary.

Exercise F, p. 386
Answers will vary. We provide some as models.

1. As I sat in the dark with the joystick in my hand, I began to experience the excitement of stalking a zombie <u>and</u> shooting it down in cold blood.
2. The article I chose seemed like a good one to evaluate because it contained both good and bad points <u>and</u> was fairly easy to follow because of the examples it provided.
3. (No changes are necessary.)
4. Encouraging husbands to be more sympathetic to their working wives would have many benefits both for the wives <u>and</u> for their husbands as well.
5. The essay we selected was well organized, informative, <u>and</u> accompanied by full-page illustrations that broke down the process.

CHAPTER 10, PART III
Exercise A, p. 393
Answers will vary.

Exercise B, p. 393
Answers will vary.

Exercise C, p. 394
Answers will vary.

Exercise D, p. 394
Answers will vary.

Exercise E, p. 394
Answers will vary.

Exercise F, p. 395
Answers will vary.

CHAPTER 11
Exercise A, p. 409
Answers will vary.

Exercise B, p. 410
Answers will vary.

Exercise C, p. 410
Answers will vary.

Exercise D, p. 410
Answers will vary.

RECOMMENDED AND SELECTED REFERENCES

ESL Texts

Azar, Donald, and Betty Schrampfer-Azar. *Understanding and Using English Grammar: Workbook.* 2nd ed. Englewood Cliffs: Prentice, 1992.

Celce-Murcia, Marianne, and Diane Larson-Freeman. *The Grammar Book.* Boston: Heinle, 1999.

Raimes, Ann. *Grammar Troublespots: An Editing Guide for Students.* New York: St. Martin's, 1992.

Schrampfer-Azar, Betty. *Chartbook: A Reference Grammar.* 2nd ed. Englewood Cliffs: Prentice, 1993.

Grammar and Writing

Barry, Anita. *English Grammar: Language as Human Behavior.* Upper Saddle River: Prentice, 1998.

Batholomae, David. "The Study of Error." *College Composition and Communication* 31 (1980): 253–69.

Beason, Larry. "Ethos and Error: How Business People React to Errors." *College Composition and Communication* 53 (2001): 33–64.

Biber, Douglas, Stig Johansson, Geoffrey Leech, Susan Conrad, and Edward Finegan. *Longman Grammar of Spoken and Written English.* New York: Longman, 1999.

Bizzell, Patricia. *Academic Discourse and Critical Consciousness.* Pittsburgh: U of Pittsburgh, 1992.

Christensen, Francis. *The Christensen Rhetoric Program: The Sentence and the Paragraph.* New York: Harper, 1968.

Conference on College Composition and Communication. *The National Language Policy.* Urbana: NCTE, 1988.

Connors, Robert J., and Andrea A. Lunsford. "Frequency of Formal Errors in Current College Writing, or Ma and Pa Kettle Do Research." *College Composition and Communication* 39 (1988): 395–409.

Cooper, Charles R. "An Outline for Writing Sentence-Combining Problems." *English Journal* 62 (1973): 96–102, 108.

Daiker, Donald A., Andrew Kerek, Max Morenberg, and Jeffrey Sommers, eds. *The Writer's Options: Combining to Composing.* 5th ed. Reading: Addison, 1994.

D'Eloia, Sarah. "The Uses—and Limits—of Grammar." *Journal of Basic Writing* 1 (1977): 1–20.

Dillard, J. L. *Black English: Its History and Usage in the United States.* New York: Random, 1972.

Elley, W. B., I. H. Barham, H. Lamb, and M. Wyllie. "The Role of Grammar in a Secondary English Curriculum." *Research in the Teaching of English* 10 (1975): 5–21.

Faigley, Lester. "Names in Search of a Concept: Maturity, Fluency, Complexity, and Growth in Written Syntax." *College Composition and Communication* 31 (1980): 291–300.

Flower, Linda. "Writer-Based Prose: A Cognitive Basis for Problems in Writing." *College English* 41 (1979): 19–37.

Goodman, Kenneth. "A Linguistic Study of Cues and Miscues in Reading." *Elementary English* 42 (1965): 639–43.

Hairston, Maxine. "Not All Errors Are Created Equal: Nonacademic Readers in the Professions Respond to Lapses in Usage." *College English* 43 (1981): 794–806.

Halliday, M. A. K., and Ruqaiya Hasan. *Cohesion in English.* New York: Longman, 1976.

Harris, Muriel. "Mending the Fragmented Free Modifier." *College Composition and Communication* 32 (1981): 175–82.

Harris, Muriel, and Katherine E. Rowan. "Explaining Grammatical Concepts." *Journal of Basic Writing* 6 (1989): 21–41.

Hartwell, Patrick. "Grammar, Grammars, and the Teaching of Grammar." *College English* 47 (1985): 105–27.

Haswell, Richard. "Minimal Marking." *College English* 45 (1983): 600–04.

Hopper, Paul. *A Short Course in Grammar.* New York: Norton, 1999.

Horner, Bruce. "Rethinking the 'Sociality' of Error: Teaching Editing as Negotiation." *Rhetoric Review* 11 (1992): 172–99.

Hunt, Kellogg. *Grammatical Structures Written at Three Grade Levels.* Urbana: NCTE, 1965.

Hunt, Kellogg. "Early Blooming and Late Blooming Syntactic Structures." In *Evaluating Writing.* Ed. Charles Cooper and Lee Odell. Urbana: NCTE, 1977.

Hunter, Susan, and Ray Wallace, eds. *The Place of Grammar in Writing Instruction.* Portsmouth: Boynton/Cook, 1995.

Joos, Martin. *The Five Clocks.* New York: Harcourt, 1961.

Kagan, Donna. "Run-On and Fragment Sentences: An Error Analysis." *Research in the Teaching of English* 14 (1980): 127–38.

Kline, Charles R., Jr., and W. Dean Memering. "Formal Fragments: The English Minor Sentence." *Research in the Teaching of English* 11 (1977): 97–110.

Kollin, Martha. *Understanding English Grammar* and *Exercises for Understanding English Grammar.* 4th ed. New York: Macmillan, 1994.

———. *Rhetorical Grammar: Grammatical Choices, Rhetorical Effects.* 2nd ed. Needham Heights: Allyn, 1996.

Kroll, Barry M., and John Schafer. "Error Analysis and the Teaching of Composition." *College Composition and Communication* 29 (1978): 242–48.

Labov, William. *The Study of Nonstandard English.* Urbana: NCTE, 1970.

Lanham, Richard. *Style: An Anti-Textbook.* New Haven: Yale UP, 1974.

Liles, Bruce L. *A Basic Grammar of Modern English.* 2nd ed. Englewood Cliffs: Prentice, 1987.

Loban, Walter. *Language Development: Kindergarten through Grade Twelve.* Urbana: NCTE, 1976.

Noguchi, Rei. *Grammar and the Teaching of Writing: Limits and Possibilities.* Urbana: NCTE, 1991.

O'Hare, Frank. *Sentence Combining: Improving Student Writing Without Formal Grammar Instruction.* Urbana: NCTE, 1973.

Romano, Tom. "Breaking the Rules in Style." *English Journal* 77 (1988): 58–62.

Shaughnessy, Mina. *Errors and Expectations: A Guide for the Teaching of Basic Writing.* New York: Oxford UP, 1977.

Strong, William. *Sentence Combining: A Composing Book.* 3rd ed. New York: McGraw, 1993.

Van de Kopple, William J. "Something Old, Something New: New Functional Sentence Perspective." *Research in the Teaching of English* 17 (1983): 85–99.

Weathers, Winston. *An Alternate Style: Options in Composition.* Rochelle Park: Hayden, 1980.

———. "Grammars of Style: New Options in Composition." *Freshman English News* 4 (1976): 1–4, 12–18. Rpt. in *Rhetoric and Composition: A Sourcebook for Teachers and Writers.* Ed. Richard Graves. 2nd ed. Upper Montclair: Boynton/Cook, 1983.

Weaver, Constance. *Grammar for Teachers: Perspectives and Definitions.* Urbana: NCTE, 1979.

———. *Teaching Grammar in Context.* Portsmouth: Boynton/Cook, 1996.

Williams, Joseph M. "The Phenomenology of Error." *College Composition and Communication* 32 (1981): 152–68.

———. *Style: Ten Lessons in Clarity and Grace.* 6th ed. Boston: Addison, 1999.

Witte, Steven, and Lester Faigley. "Coherence, Cohesion, and Writing Quality." *College Composition and Communication* 32 (1981): 189–204.

Wolfram, Walt, Carolyn Temple Adger, and Donna Christian. *Dialects in Schools and Communities.* Mahwah: Erlbaum, 1999.

Electronic Resources

English Grammar 101: http://englishgrammar101.com

GrammarNOW! A Grammar, Editing, Proofreading Resource: http://www.grammarnow.com

HyperGrammar, produced by the Writing Centre at the University of Ottawa: http://www.uottawa.ca/academic/arts/writcent/hypergrammar/

National Council of Teachers of English: http://www.ncte.org

Online English Grammar: http://www.edufind.com/english/grammar/

Online Writery at the University of Missouri: http://web.missouri.edu/~writery/

Online Writing Center at the University of Texas at Austin: http://uwc-server.fac.utexas.edu/

Purdue University Online Writing Center: http://owl.english.purdue.edu/

WORKS CITED

Braddock, Richard, Richard Lloyd-Jones, and Lowell Schoer. *Research in Written Composition*. Urbana: NCTE, 1963.

Dillard, J. L. *Black English: Its History and Usage in the United States*. New York: Random, 1972.

Elley, W. B., I. H. Barham, H. Lamb, and M. Wyllie. "The Role of Grammar in a Secondary English Curriculum." *Research in the Teaching of English* 10 (1975): 5–21.

Goodman, Kenneth. "A Linguistic Study of Cues and Miscues in Reading." *Elementary English* 42 (1965): 639–43.

Hairston, Maxine. "Not All Errors Are Created Equal: Nonacademic Readers in the Professions Respond to Lapses in Usage." *College English* 43 (1981): 794–806.

Halliday, M. A. K., and Ruqaiya Hasan. *Cohesion in English*. New York: Longman, 1976.

Kline, Charles R., Jr., and W. Dean Memering. "Formal Fragments: The English Minor Sentence." *Research in the Teaching of English* 11 (1977): 97–110.

Shaughnessy, Mina. *Errors and Expectations: A Guide for the Teaching of Basic Writing*. New York: Oxford UP, 1977.

Weaver, Constance. *Teaching Grammar in Context*. Portsmouth: Boynton/Cook, 1996.

GLOSSARY
OF IMPORTANT TERMS

ACCEPTABILITY   Appropriateness in a given context. A usage that is *acceptable* may be suitable in a given context even though it may not conform completely to the rules of standard English. Compare *grammaticality*.

ACTIVE VOICE   Mode of expression in which the subject is the agent or performer of the action in a sentence and the direct object is the receiver of that action. For example, in the sentence *He hit the ball, he* is the subject (agent) and *ball* is the direct object (receiver of the action). Compare *passive voice*.

ADJECTIVAL   A word function category that includes all words, phrases, and clauses that modify nouns. In the sentence *The pretty little baby in the living room screamed for her mother, who had stepped into the kitchen,* the words *pretty* and *little* and the word groups *in the living room* and *who had stepped into the kitchen* are all adjectivals.

ADJECTIVE   A word form category consisting of single words that are usually used to modify nouns, such as *big, blue,* and *handsome.* Adjectives can be compared (e.g., *big, bigger, biggest*) and can be qualified (e.g., *very big, too tight*).

ADJECTIVE CLAUSE   A dependent clause that functions as an adjectival and usually begins with a relative pronoun such as *who, which,* or *that.* It follows the noun or noun phrase it modifies and can be restrictive or nonrestrictive. For example, in the sentence *I know the man whom she will marry, whom she will marry* is a restrictive adjective clause. In the sentence *That man, whom she will marry next week, is a dentist, whom she will marry next week* is a nonrestrictive adjective clause. A nonrestrictive clause must be set off with commas. Also known as a *relative clause.*

ADJECTIVE PHRASE   A group of words headed by an adjective. For example, in the sentence *She is quite pretty,* the word group *quite pretty* is an adjective phrase. Adjective phrases function as adjectivals.

ADVERB   A word form category consisting of single words that are used to modify verbs, adjectives, and other adverbs. Adverbs answer such questions as Where? When? How? and With what intensity? Similar to adjectives, some adverbs can be compared (e.g., *most hastily, most slowly*) and qualified or intensified (e.g., *very happily, somewhat peevishly*). In addition, some adverbs can be placed in a variety of positions in a sentence without changing the fundamental meaning (*Soon we'll be there; We'll soon be there; We'll be there soon*).

ADVERB CLAUSE   A dependent clause that functions as an adverbial and is headed by a conjunction such as *because, so, unless, although,* or *if.* In the sentence *We eat olives at every meal because we like them, because we like them* is an adverb clause.

ADVERB PHRASE   A group of words headed by an adverb. For example, in the sentence *He works very hard,* the word group *very hard* is an adverb phrase. Adverb phrases function as adverbials.

ADVERBIAL   A word function category that includes all words, phrases, and clauses that modify verbs. In the sentence *Consequently, John always brushed his teeth quite fervently because he was in a hurry, consequently, always, quite fervently,* and *because he was in a hurry* are all adverbials.

ADVERBIAL COMPLEMENT An adverbial that follows *be* used as a linking verb. For example, in the sentence *We are downtown, downtown* is the adverbial complement.

AFFIX A prefix or suffix.

AGENT The performer of an action indicated by a verb. In active sentences, the agent is usually the subject. In passive sentences, the agent usually follows the verb phrase and is preceded by the word *by*. For example, in the sentence *The window was shut by the janitor, the janitor* is the agent. Agent phrases introduced with *by* are prepositional phrases functioning as adverbials.

ANTECEDENT The noun that a pronoun substitutes for.

ANTECEDENT AGREEMENT Correspondence in person (first, second, or third), number (singular or plural), and possibly gender (masculine or feminine) between a pronoun and its antecedent. For example, in the sentences *Everybody likes Thomas. He's very popular, He,* in the second sentence, agrees in person (third), number (singular), and gender (masculine) with its antecedent, *Thomas,* in the first sentence.

APPOSITIVE A word function category consisting of nouns, noun phrases, and nominals that rename other nominal structures. In the sentence *Mike, my friend's husband, is over six feet tall, my friend's husband* (a noun phrase) renames *Mike* (a noun) and thus functions as an appositive.

APPRENTICE WRITER Someone who is developing skills in writing.

ARTICLE A determiner (*a, an,* or *the*).

ASPECT The nature of the action of the verb, expressing relationships such as duration and completion. *Progressive aspect* conveys the relationship of an event to actions occurring in the present. *Perfect aspect* conveys the relationship of present actions to the past. *Future aspect* conveys the relationship of present actions to the future.

AUDIENCE The expected reader or readers of any form of writing.

AUXILIARY VERB A verb used before the main verb in a verb phrase to form structures that reflect aspect or conditions or attitudes toward the action (e.g., the phrase *can dance* expresses ability) and provide support when constructing questions and negatives. *Do, have, be,* and modals (*can, will,* etc.) function as auxiliary verbs. Also called *helping verbs* or simply *auxiliaries.*

BLACK ENGLISH VERNACULAR (BEV) A dialect of English used by some African Americans in the United States that features rule-governed variations in grammar, lexicon, and usage from standard English. Also known as *Ebonics* or *African American English Variety* (*AAEV*). See also *dialect* and *language variety.*

CLAUSE Any structure containing a subject and a verb. Clauses can be independent or dependent. The sentence *Marjorie sings every morning* is a simple sentence and an independent clause. In the sentence *Marjorie sings every morning before she eats breakfast, Marjorie sings every morning* is an independent clause and *before she eats breakfast* is a dependent clause. Compare *phrase.*

COHERENCE The overall relationship of ideas within a piece of writing.

COHESION The connections within and between sentences. Cohesion can be provided through grammatical relationships (e.g., *because* used to connect one idea to another, antecedent agreement) and semantic relationships (e.g., the words and meanings conveyed to relate one idea to another). Cohesion is also provided by knowledge the writer expects of the reader and knowledge the reader brings to the reading. Compare *coherence.*

COLLOQUIALISM Language used in informal speech. For example, *What's up?* is a colloquialism.

COMMA SPLICE An error caused by joining two complete sentences with a comma instead of a semicolon or a period. *Mike loves rice, it's his favorite food* is an example of a comma splice.

COMMAND   See *imperative.*

COMMON NOUN   Any noun that is not a proper noun. Common nouns fall into four categories: count nouns (e.g., *pencil, scissors*), noncount nouns (e.g., *sugar, flour*), concrete nouns (e.g., *table, ocean*), and abstract nouns (e.g., *punctuality, democracy*).

COMPARATIVE   The form of adjectives and adverbs that shows comparison between two objects, aspects, or qualities. The comparative is formed by adding *-er* to the end of the adjective or adverb or by preceding the word with *more* (e.g., *higher, more beautiful*). Some irregular adjectives or adverbs require a change in the form itself (e.g., *good, better*).

COMPLEMENT   A word function category consisting of words that appear in the predicate and "complete" the meaning of the sentence or phrase. Complements may be in the form of adjectives, adjective phrases, nouns, noun phrases, or nominals. When *be* is used as a linking verb, the complement may also be an adverbial, as in *The dog is outside.* See also *subject complement, object complement,* and *adverbial complement.*

COMPLEX SENTENCE   A sentence consisting of one independent clause combined with a dependent clause in the form of an adjective clause, an adverb clause, or a noun clause. Some examples of complex sentences are *That song you are listening to is one of my favorites; Although it's still snowing, I'm going to start shoveling;* and *I know what you are thinking.*

COMPOUND SENTENCE   Two independent sentences combined using a conjunction. *Tom went to the market, but Penny went home* is a compound sentence. Also called a *conjoined sentence.*

COMPOUND STRUCTURE   Two forms joined together using a conjunction. Some examples of compound structures are *Batman and Robin, bark but not bite, run or jump,* and *Colorado as well as Wyoming.* Also called a *conjoined structure.*

CONJOINED SENTENCE   See *compound sentence.*

CONJOINED STRUCTURE   See *compound structure.*

CONJUNCTION   A word or phrase used to combine words, phrases, and sentences. Two common types of conjunctions are coordinating conjunctions (e.g.. *and, but, so, yet, for*), which are used to combine structures and complete sentences, and subordinating conjunctions (e.g., *because, while, unless, when, after, although*), which are used to combine a dependent clause with an independent clause. See also *conjunctive adverb* and *correlative conjunction.*

CONJUNCTIVE ADVERB   A word or phrase, often movable, used to combine sentences and independent clauses (e.g., *however, nevertheless, therefore, as a consequence*).

CONSTITUENT   A part of a larger whole. For example, all of the forms in a sentence are constituents of the sentence, a noun is a constituent of a noun phrase, and so on.

CONTEXT   The situation in which language is used. For example, words are used in the context of a sentence; a sentence is used in the context of a paragraph, dialogue, or story; and so on. *Context* can also refer to aspects of the setting, such as audience.

CONTRACTION   A word formed by omitting letters from a word (*can't* for *cannot*) or from two combined words (*you're* for *you are*). Certain contractions involve other spelling changes (*won't* for *will not*), but all can be recognized by the apostrophe, which marks the place where letters were omitted.

COORDINATING CONJUNCTION   Words used to combine structures and complete sentences (e.g. *and, so, but, yet, for,* etc.).

CORRELATIVE CONJUNCTION   A coordinating conjunction made up of two parts that show an equal relationship between the structures they connect. *Neither … nor, either … or, both … and*, and *not only … but also* are all correlative conjunctions. See also *conjunction*.

COUNT NOUN   A noun that can show number. A count noun can be preceded by an article (*a, an*, or *the*) and can be made plural and be preceded by numbers (e.g., *five rocks*). Compare *noncount noun*.

DANGLING MODIFIER   In a sentence, an adjective phrase or clause that lacks a noun that it can logically modify. For example, in the sentence *Lying on the beach, the sun beat down with intensity, Lying on the beach* is a dangling modifier because grammatically, it modifies the noun that immediately follows it, *sun*, but that makes no logical sense.

DECLARATIVE SENTENCE   A sentence that makes a statement (e.g., *It's a nice day*). Also called a *statement*.

DEFINITE ARTICLE   The determiner *the*. It is often used to mark a previously identified noun.

DEMONSTRATIVE PRONOUN   A pronoun that indicates the location of its antecedent in relation to the speaker. There are four demonstrative pronouns: *this, that* (singular), *these, those* (plural). The same words can also function as determiners; compare, for example, *This is dumb!* with *This ball has lost all its air. This* is a demonstrative pronoun in the first example and a determiner in the second.

DEPENDENT CLAUSE   A clause, usually in the form of an adverb clause, an adjective clause, or a noun clause, that cannot stand alone without creating a sentence fragment. Some examples of dependent clauses are *because it's there, which was on the floor,* and *where you lived*. Also called a *subordinate clause*.

DESCRIPTIVE GRAMMAR   The approach that holds that the rules of grammar are determined by how language is used. Compare *prescriptive grammar*.

DETERMINER   A word that precedes a noun or a noun and its modifiers and provides information about the specificity of that noun. Articles and possessive adjectives are two types of determiners.

DIALECT   A specific set of variations in pronunciation, grammar, and word choice of speakers of one language, usually associated with a location (regional dialect) or a community of speakers (social dialect). See also *Black English Vernacular* and *language variety*.

DIRECT DISCOURSE   Information quoted in its exact original form. *"It's hot in the sun," said Penelope* is an example of direct discourse. Also known as *direct speech* or *direct quotation*.

DIRECT OBJECT   A word function category consisting of a noun, noun phrase, or other nominal that follows the verb phrase in a sentence with a transitive verb and receives the action of that verb. For example, in the sentence *Sam threw the bat, the bat* is the direct object.

DISCOURSE   Any form of communication. The two main types of discourse are oral discourse and written discourse.

DISCOURSE COMMUNITY   The community within which one writes. A discourse community normally has specific expectations of and requirements for the use of language within the community. Law, medical, and academic journals all contain writing produced within and for specific discourse communities. See also *speech community*.

DOUBLE NEGATIVE   Two or more words denoting negation in one sentence. *I don't have no idea* is an example of a double negative. See also *negation*.

EDITING   Reading a piece of writing for the purpose of finding errors and mistakes and correcting them. Compare *revision*.

EMBEDDING   Incorporating a dependent clause into an independent (main) clause to form a sentence. Adjective clauses and noun clauses are examples of clauses that can be embedded. In the sentence *Marvin didn't know whether to laugh or cry*, *whether to laugh or cry* is an embedded noun clause.

EMPTY PHRASE   Writing that conveys no real meaning in the context in which it is written.

ERROR   Evidence of a patterned lack of knowledge on the part of the writer with respect to an appropriate convention. For example, if a writer repeatedly misspells *their* as *they're* throughout a piece of writing, it is an error. Compare *mistake*.

EXCLAMATORY SENTENCE   A sentence that functions as an exclamation. In written form, it ends with an exclamation point: *Look at that plane! What a beautiful day! Don't move! Are you crazy!*

EXPLETIVE   A placeholder (*there* or *it*) in the noun position.

EXTRAPOSITION   The movement of one structure out of the expected subject-verb-object (SVO) word order of English sentences. The moved structure is referred to as *extraposed*. For example, the sentence *Ice cream is what Deb wanted* has an extraposed direct object, *ice cream*. In the sentence *There are ants on the ceiling*, *ants* is the extraposed subject.

FAULTY PARALLELISM   An error typified by a phrase, clause, or sentence that contains two structures that should be similar in form due to their placement in the sentence (parallel) but are not. For example, the sentence *Levi likes swimming and to back-pack* evidences faulty parallelism in the direct object because *swimming* and *to back-pack* are different forms. To be parallel, the sentences should read *Levi likes swimming and back-packing* or *Levi likes to swim and to back-pack*. See also *parallel structure*.

FLUENCY   Production of a flow of words that is easy to read or understand.

FORM   The label applied to the appearance of words, such as *noun, verb, adjective*, or *infinitive*. Compare *function*.

FORMAL LANGUAGE   Language that adheres strictly to the rules of standard written English. Compare *informal language*.

FRAGMENT   A part of a sentence that is punctuated as if it were a complete sentence (e.g., *Potatoes. To be home again. Because I was overjoyed.*).

FUNCTION   How a word form is used in the context of a sentence—for example, as a subject, direct object, nominal, or adjectival. Compare *form*.

FUSED SENTENCE   An error consisting of two independent sentences combined without an appropriate conjunction or punctuation marker at the sentence boundary. *He gave me a puppy I love it so much* is a fused sentence.

GENRE   A specific type of writing, such as a novel, a magazine article, a newspaper article, a children's book, or a scientific journal article.

GERUND   The base form of a verb + *-ing* used as a nominal in sentences. In the sentence *Barking is my dog's favorite nocturnal activity*, *barking* is a gerund that functions as the subject.

GERUND PHRASE   A gerund and its modifiers or complements. In the sentence *My dog loves barking at the moon*, *barking at the moon* is a gerund phrase.

***GET* PASSIVE**   A sentence in the passive voice in which *get* substitutes for *be* or *have* in the verb phrase. *That team got clobbered by its rival* and *I got my hair cut* are examples of *get* passives. See also *passive voice*.

GLOBAL ERROR   An error that prevents the listener or reader from understanding the intended meaning of a statement or passage. Compare *local error*. See also *error* and *mistake*.

GRAMMATICALITY   Strict adherence to the rules of standard written English. Compare *acceptability*.

HEAD   The word that functions as the main part of a phrase or clause. In *the pretty kitty, kitty* is the head of the noun phrase; in *may have been joking, joking* is the head of the verb phrase; in *the man who came to dinner, who* is the head of the adjective clause.

HELPING VERB   See *auxiliary verb.*

HYPERCORRECTION   Making "corrections" to one's language where they are not needed out of concern about making a mistake. For example, in the sentence *Let's keep this between you and I*, the speaker has eliminated the correct pronoun, *me*, and "corrected" it to *I*. Also known as *overcorrection*. See also *error* and *mistake*.

IMPERATIVE   A sentence in the form of a command. The subject in the imperative is often not expressed but is always understood to be *you*. *Fix this sentence* is an example of an imperative.

INDEFINITE ARTICLE   *A* or *an*. See *article* and *determiner*.

INDEFINITE PRONOUN   Any pronoun used as a quantifier (*many, all, any, either, each*, etc.). Many indefinite pronouns can also be used as determiners. Compare, for example, *Either of you will have to stop for gas* and *Either way, you'll have to stop for gas. Either* in the first sentence is an indefinite pronoun; in the second, it's a determiner.

INDEPENDENT CLAUSE   Any construction containing a subject and a verb (and possibly other words) that can function as a complete sentence. In the sentence *I love Spike because he's cute, I love Spike* is the independent clause. Also known as a *main clause*. Compare *dependent clause*. See also *complex sentence*.

INDIRECT DISCOURSE   A report of what a person said without using that person's exact words, usually in the form of a noun clause or an infinitive phrase. For example, if Mom said, "Come for dinner at seven o'clock," a report of this in indirect discourse might be *Mom told us that we should come at seven o'clock* using a noun clause or *Mom told us when to come for supper* using an infinitive phrase. Also known as *indirect speech* or *indirect quotation*. Compare *direct discourse*.

INDIRECT OBJECT   A word function category consisting of a noun, noun phrase, or other nominal that follows the verb phrase in a sentence with a transitive verb but does not receive the action of that verb. The indirect object generally answers the question *to whom* or *for whom*. In the sentence *Bob gave Cassie a ring, Cassie* is the indirect object (*a ring* is the direct object). Many sentences allow the indirect object to be moved to the end of the sentence, preceded by *to* or *for*, as in *Bob gave a ring to Cassie*.

INFINITIVE   A word form created by combining *to* with the base form of a verb, as in *to walk* or *to eat*, and functioning as a nominal, adjectival, or adverbial. The verb in an infinitive is never changed to show person or number, but it can be changed to show aspect, as in *I ought to have done that*.

INFINITIVE PHRASE   A phrase consisting of an infinitive plus all its modifiers and complements. In the sentence *Dwayne wanted to feed the dogs, to feed the dogs* is an infinitive phrase.

INFLECTION   An ending (affix) added to a word that conveys grammatical meaning. There are seven regular inflections in English: (1) *-s* to show plural (e.g., *monkey, monkeys*); (2) *'s* to show possession (e.g., *Mike, Mike's*); (3) third person singular *-s* (*She walks*); (4) *-er* for the comparative; (5) *-est* for the superlative; (6) *-ed* for the past tense and past participle; and (7) *-ing* for the present participle. Because verbs (as well as some adjectives and adverbs) can have irregular forms, inflection may also take the form of a change in spelling and pronunciation (e.g., *swim, swam, swum*).

INFORMAL LANGUAGE   Language that reflects everyday or conversational usages and may therefore not always follow the rules of standard written English. Compare *formal language*.

INFORMATION QUESTION   Any question that begins with words such as *who, what, how, when,* or *why*. Such questions seek to elicit pieces of information as responses rather than a simple *yes* or *no*.

INTENSIFIER   An adverb that provides information regarding degree. Intensifiers such as *too, quite, somewhat, very,* or *extremely* can appear before adjectives (e.g., *too pretty, very diligent*) or adverbs (e.g., *quite slowly, so diligently*).

INTERROGATIVE PRONOUN   Any of the so-called *wh-* words (*who, what, when, where, why,* and *how*) used at the beginning of information questions. Each interrogative pronoun substitutes for a function. For example, *who* and *what* are substitutes for all the forms that can function as subjects or direct objects. *When, where, how,* and *why* are substitutes for all the forms that can function as adverbials.

INTRANSITIVE VERB   A verb that does not require a direct object or subject complement to complete the predicate. *The children play* and *The faucet leaked* are examples of sentences with intransitive verbs. Compare *transitive verb*.

IRREGULAR VERB   A verb that does not form the past tense or past participle by adding *-ed*. *Run (ran, run)* and *eat (ate, eaten)* are examples of irregular verbs. Compare *regular verb*.

JARGON   See *specialized terminology*.

KERNEL SENTENCE   A simple sentence, main clause, or independent clause.

LANGUAGE VARIETY   Language use specific to one's region, gender, social group, or other group that varies from standard written English. See also *dialect* and *Black English Vernacular*.

LEXICON   A list of words, as in a dictionary, in a language or dialect, or in a language user's vocabulary.

LINKING VERB   A verb that "links" the subject with a complement, as in *This smells delicious* or *They grew tired*.

LOCAL ERROR   A mistake in grammar or mechanics that does not prevent the listener or reader from understanding the intended meaning of a statement or passage. Compare *global error*. See also *error* and *mistake*.

MAIN CLAUSE   See *independent clause*.

MAIN VERB   The verb that carries meaning in a verb phrase that also contains auxiliaries. For example, in the verb phrase *may have been kissing, kissing* is the main verb.

MASS NOUN   See *noncount noun*.

MISTAKE   Evidence of a momentary lapse in attention. For example, if a writer spells *their* correctly fifteen times in a paper but misspells it *they're* once, that is a mistake. Compare *error*.

MODAL   Any of a class of auxiliary verbs that serve to provide information such as ability, probability, or permission. *Can, might,* and *should* are common modals. In a verb phrase containing a modal, the modal comes at the start of the verb phrase.

MODIFIER   Any word that describes or applies to something else in the sentence. Adjectivals and adverbials are the most common modifiers.

NEGATION   The use of words (e.g., *not, no one, never*) to show an absence of activity or substance.

NOMINAL   Any word that functions in the way that nouns do, regardless of its apparent form. Infinitives, infinitive phrases, gerunds, gerund phrases, and noun clauses are the most common nominals.

NOMINAL CLAUSE   See *noun clause.*

NOMINATIVE CASE   See *subjective case.*

NONCOUNT NOUN   A noun that refers to something that cannot be counted or itemized, such as *honesty.* All abstract nouns (e.g., *justice, prejudice, charity*) are noncount nouns, but not all noncount nouns are abstract (e.g., *water, sugar*). An indefinite article cannot normally be used with a noncount noun (e.g., **an optimism*). Also known as a *mass noun.*

NONRESTRICTIVE CLAUSE   An adjective clause that provides information about the noun it modifies but is not essential to defining the noun. Because the clause is not essential, it is set off with commas. For example, in the sentence *John, about whom I've told you so much, is my older brother, about whom I've told you so much* is a nonrestrictive clause. Compare *restrictive clause.* See also *adjective clause.*

NONRESTRICTIVE MODIFIER   A modifier that provides information that is not essential to the definition of the noun it modifies. Nonrestrictive modifiers may consist of adjective clauses as well as single words or phrases and often function as appositives. In the sentence *Julia, my mom, was born in 1963, my mom* is a nonrestrictive modifier. Compare *restrictive modifier.*

NOUN   A word form category consisting of words that name persons, places, concepts, and ideas. A noun can be the head of a noun phrase; be inflected to show possession; and be modified by determiners, adjectives, infinitive phrases, participial phrases, and adjective clauses. Nouns can be abstract or concrete, count or noncount. Count nouns can be inflected to show plural number. Nouns can function as subjects, direct objects, indirect objects, appositives, objects of a preposition, subject complements, and object complements. See also *count noun* and *noncount noun.*

NOUN CLAUSE   A clause that functions in the ways a noun can (subject, direct object, etc.). Noun clauses often begin with *that, whether, if, when, how,* or *what.* In the sentence *I know that you are happy, that you are happy* is the noun clause. In the sentence *Matt knows when the play starts, when the play starts* is the noun clause. Also called a *nominal clause.*

NOUN PHRASE   A noun and its modifiers. *The long black gown* and *each and every one of them* are both noun phrases.

NOVICE WRITER   See *apprentice writer.*

NUMBER   Aspect of word form indicating whether a noun, pronoun, or verb is singular or plural.

OBJECT COMPLEMENT   The word or words that follow a direct object and describe it. For example, in *Jacy dyed her hair red, red* is the object complement of the direct object *her hair* and tells what color her hair was dyed. Some transitive verbs require an object complement to complete the predicate.

OBJECT OF A PREPOSITION   The noun or noun phrase that follows a preposition. In the phrase *in a jiffy, a jiffy* is the object of the preposition *in.*

OBJECTIVE CASE   The form of pronouns functioning as direct objects, objects of prepositions, or indirect objects. The pronouns *me, you, him, her, it, us,* and *them* are all in the objective case.

ORAL MEDIUM   The spoken word as a means of transferring information in a culture or social group. Compare *written medium.* See also *discourse.*

PARALLEL STRUCTURE   The requirement that when any constituent of a sentence contains two or more coordinated or equivalent structures, those structures must be in the same grammatical form. For example, in *My sister sings, dances, and is skillful at the piano*, the final verb phrase is not parallel and should be corrected to *plays piano skillfully*. See also *faulty parallelism*.

PARTICIPIAL PHRASE   A participle and its modifiers and complements. Participial phrases are usually used as adjectivals (e.g., *The angels hovering overhead sang hymns of praise; Walking by the bakery, David suddenly developed a hankering for cinnamon rolls*).

PARTICIPLE   Either of the two forms of a verb that are used to express the progressive aspect and perfect aspect, respectively. The *present participle* is formed by adding -*ing* to the base form of the verb (e.g., *I am walking to the beach*). The *past participle* of a regular verb is formed by adding -*ed* to the base form (e.g., *I have walked to the beach*). Participles can also be used as adjectivals (*That's an interesting picture; The workers didn't seem disgruntled*). See also *participial phrase*.

PARTICLE   The nonverb part of a phrasal verb. Particles look like prepositions but function as part of a verb. In the phrasal verb *get out of*, *out* and *of* are the particles. See also *phrasal verb*.

PASSIVE VOICE   Mode of expression in which the receiver of the action is the focus of a sentence and the agent or performer of the action is indicated in a prepositional phrase starting with *by*, as in *The ball was hit by the boy*. Only sentences with transitive verbs can be expressed in the passive voice. Compare *active voice*.

PAST PARTICIPLE   See *participle*.

PAST TENSE   See *tense*.

PERFECT ASPECT   See *aspect*.

PERSON   The distinction between the speaker (first person, *I*), the person spoken to (second person, *you*), and the person or thing spoken about (third person, *he, she, it, they*).

PERSONAL PRONOUN   Any of the pronouns that substitute for nouns, noun phrases and nominals (e.g., *I, you, they*). Personal pronouns have three cases: subjective (*he, she*, etc.), objective (*him, her*, etc.), and possessive (*his, hers*, etc.).

PHRASE   A group of words that does not contain both subject and verb but acts together as a meaningful unit; a specific form plus its modifiers and complements. The nine most common types of phrases in English are the noun phrase (e.g., *the little puppy*), verb phrase (e.g., *might have been*), prepositional phrase (e.g., *in a little while*), adjective phrase (e.g., *very little*), adverb phrase (e.g., *quite poorly*), present participial phrase (e.g., *lurking in the shadows*), past participial phrase (e.g., *caught in the act*), infinitive phrase (e.g., *to be young again*), and gerund phrase (e.g., *running for president*). Compare *clause*.

PHRASAL VERB   A multiword combination of a verb and one or more particles that work together to convey one meaning. Most phrasal verbs have one-word synonyms, for example, *ask out* (*invite*), *look over* (*review*), *get out of* (*exit, leave*).

PLACEHOLDER   *It* or *there* used in a sentence with an extraposed (moved) subject or one that does not have an obvious subject. In *It might rain today*, *it* is the placeholder. In *There are fifty buffalo in the backyard*, *there* is the placeholder.

PLURAL   Involving more than one item or individual. Nouns, pronouns, and verbs differentiate the plural from the singular. Most English nouns can be changed to the plural by adding -*s*. However, a small group of nouns have irregular forms (e.g., *child, children; moose, moose*). See also *number*.

POSSESSIVE   The form of nouns and pronouns that indicates ownership or belonging. The possessive case is formed by adding '*s* to the noun (e.g., *Mike's*) or by using specific pronoun forms (e.g., *mine, yours*). Possession can also be shown in English by converting the noun in the possessive case to a prepositional phrase using *of* (e.g., *the door of the barn* becomes *the barn's door*).

POSSESSIVE ADJECTIVE   The possessive form of a pronoun that can be combined with a noun (e.g., *my dog, your watch, his atlas, her shoes, its leash, our house, their lunch*).

POSSESSIVE PRONOUN   The pronouns *mine, yours, his, hers, its, ours,* and *theirs* used to show possession or belonging.

PREDICATE   The part of a sentence that contains the verb phrase and all of its modifiers and complements. In *The dictionary is a reliable source of information, is a reliable source of information* is the predicate.

PREFIX   One or more letters added to the beginning of a word that alter its meaning. For example, *un-* in the word *uninterrupted* is a prefix.

PREPOSITION   A word form category consisting of words that convey relationships, usually in combination with a noun or noun phrase in the form of a prepositional phrase, such as *on the way.* Prepositions can be single words (e.g., *on, at, in, by, beyond*) or phrases (*instead of, according to, insofar as*).

PREPOSITIONAL PHRASE   A preposition combined with a noun or noun phrase. Some examples of prepositional phrases are *to the zoo, at Mom's house, by the way,* and *over the trees.*

PRESCRIPTIVE GRAMMAR   The approach to grammar that holds that rules determine how language is used. Compare *descriptive grammar.*

PRESENT PARTICIPLE   See *participle.*

PROGRESSIVE ASPECT   See *aspect.*

PRONOUN   Any word that can substitute for a noun or noun phrase in a sentence. English has several types of pronouns, including personal pronouns (*I, you, he, she, it, we, they*), possessive pronouns (*mine, yours, his, hers, ours, its, theirs*), and reflexive pronouns (*myself, yourself, himself, herself, itself, ourselves, yourselves, themselves*).

PROPER NOUN   Any noun that refers to a person, place, or entity by its name. All proper nouns are capitalized. *Sandra, President Lincoln, the Empire State Building, Oklahoma,* and the *Russians* are all proper nouns. Compare *common noun.*

QUANTIFIER   A word or phrase before a noun that specifies its amount. For example, *many, a few of,* and *ten pounds of* are all quantifiers. Quantifiers can be used with both count and noncount nouns.

QUESTION   A sentence asking for information. In a question, subject and verb are transposed from their normal positions, and in writing, the sentence ends with a question mark, as in *Are you tired?*

REDUNDANCY   Repetition in speech or writing. Redundancy can be in form (*more better*) or in meaning (e.g., *My little sister is younger than I am*).

REFERENT   The noun or noun phrase that a pronoun refers to. See also *antecedent.*

REGISTER   Structural language use, including the level of speech appropriate for a particular context, which involves the social situation and the relationship between speaker and audience. Two common registers are *formal* and *informal.* Other specialized registers include *legal* and *medical.*

REGULAR VERB   A verb that forms its past tense and past participle forms by adding *-ed* (e.g., *walked, baked*).

REFLEXIVE PRONOUN   A form of pronoun used primarily when the direct or indirect object refers to the subject of the sentence, formed by adding *-self* or *-selves* to a form of the relevant pronoun. For example, in the sentence *I gave myself a manicure, myself* is a reflexive pronoun. See also *pronoun.*

RELATIVE CLAUSE   See *adjective clause.*

RELATIVE PRONOUN   Any of the words (*who, which,* or *that*) that can begin an adjective clause. In the sentence *The blouse that Myrtle bought is the prettiest, that* is the relative pronoun.

RESTRICTIVE CLAUSE   An adjective clause that limits or restricts the noun it modifies. Because it is essential to the meaning of the associated noun, a restrictive clause is not set off with commas. In *The man whom you should vote for just entered the room, whom you should vote for* is a restrictive clause. Compare *nonrestrictive clause.* See also *adjective clause.*

RESTRICTIVE MODIFIER   A modifier that limits or restricts the noun it modifies. Restrictive modifiers may consist of adjective clauses as well as single words or phrases and often function as appositives. In the sentence *Joan's sister Leslie lives in Nova Scotia, Leslie* is a restrictive modifier that identifies which of Joan's sisters is being described. Compare *nonrestrictive modifier.*

REVISION   The process of rewriting a piece of writing on both the sentence level and the rhetorical level. Compare *editing.*

RULE-GOVERNED   Following specific linguistic rules and patterns.

RUN-ON SENTENCE   A lengthy sentence that is grammatical but contains an excessive amount of embedding or compounding. The term is also sometimes used to refer to a fused sentence. Compare *comma splice* and *fused sentence.*

SENTENCE   An independent clause (subject and predicate) and possibly other constituents punctuated as a complete grammatical entity. There are four types of sentences: (1) statements (declarative sentences), such as *I saw you yesterday;* (2) questions (interrogative sentences), such as *What are you doing?* (3) commands (imperative sentences), such as *Go to the store;* and (4) exclamations (exclamatory sentences), such as *What a ride!* Sentences can consist of one independent clause (simple sentences), a combination of independent clauses (compound sentences), or a combination of independent and dependent clauses (complex sentences).

SENTENCE BOUNDARY   The beginning or end of a complete sentence. The sentence boundary is marked by initial capitalization and by terminal punctuation with a period (.), question mark (?), semicolon (;), or exclamation point (!).

SENTENCE FRAGMENT   See *fragment.*

SENTENCE VARIETY   Avoiding repetition by using differing forms and sentences of different lengths in a piece of writing.

SIMPLE SENTENCE   A sentence made up of only one independent clause. See also *sentence.*

SINGULAR   Involving only one item or person. Nouns, pronouns, and verbs differentiate the singular from the plural. See also *number.*

SLANG   Informal terms for objects and actions that come into use at a particular time period or among a particular social group. Most slang terms lose currency rapidly; only a few gain such widespread acceptance that they become part of the standard language.

SPECIALIZED TERMINOLOGY   Language used by specific groups of people to refer to activities particular to that specific group. Such fields as medicine, law, grammar, education, banking, and farming all have their respective specialized terminology. Also known as *jargon.*

SPEECH COMMUNITY   A social or regional group whose members use language in the same distinctive way. See also *discourse community*.

STANDARD AMERICAN ENGLISH   The variety of English accepted as the norm expected of an educated, informed user of the language. Standard American English is the level of language used in textbooks, newspapers, and many other widely disseminated materials.

STATEMENT   See *declarative sentence*.

STUDENT WRITER   See *apprentice writer*.

STYLE   See *register*.

SUBJECT   A word function category designating the performer of the action in a sentence (the remainder of the sentence is known as the predicate). Nouns, noun phrases, and nominals function as subjects.

SUBJECT COMPLEMENT   A word function category consisting of words that complete sentences with linking verbs and describe or rename the subject. Adjectives, adjectivals, nouns, noun phrases, and nominals can function as subject complements. In the sentence *This banana is ripe*, *ripe* is the subject complement.

SUBJECTIVE CASE   The form of pronouns functioning as subjects or subject complements. The pronouns *I, you, he, she, it, we*, and *they* are all in the subjective case. Also known as *nominative case*.

SUBJECT–VERB AGREEMENT   Correspondence in person and number between the subject and the verb. In English, such agreement is problematic only in the present tense, where it requires the addition of *-s* to the verb when the subject is in the third person singular (e.g., *she laughs*). At all other times in the present tense, the base form of the verb is used (e.g., *we play*).

SUBORDINATE CLAUSE   See *dependent clause*.

SUBORDINATING CONJUNCTION   Any word such as *before, after, when, because, unless*, or *although* that shows the relationship between the subordinate (dependent) clause and the main (independent) clause. See also *conjunction*.

SUFFIX   One or more letters added to the end of a word that change its meaning or its part of speech. For example, in the words *unobtainable, destructive*, and *operation*, *-able, -ive*, and *-tion* are suffixes.

SUPERLATIVE   The form of a single-word adjective or adverb that contrasts it with two or more competitors. The superlative is formed either by adding *-est* to the word (e.g., *biggest, loveliest*) or preceding the contrasted word with the word *most* (e.g., *most desirable, most convenient*). A very small number of words have irregular superlative forms (e.g., *good, best*).

SYNTAX   Sentence structure and grammar.

TENSE   Either of two inflected forms of the verb—present and past. Compare *time*. See also *aspect*.

THESAURUS   A dictionary of synonyms and antonyms.

TIME   The moment when an action occurs, expressed by the tense and aspect of the verb.

TRANSITIVE VERB   A verb that requires a direct object. Many transitive verbs can also take indirect objects. With rare exception, only sentences with transitive verbs can be expressed in the passive voice. In *Jesse ate the ice cream*, *ate* is the transitive verb and *ice cream* is the direct object.

USAGE   The way words are actually used in a particular discourse community.

VERB   The word or group of words that express the action in a sentence. Verbs are usually divided into two types, action and linking. Action verbs are then subdivided into two main types, transitive and intransitive.

VERB PHRASE   The verb and all its auxiliaries. *Have gotten, may have been biting,* and *was getting* are all verb phrases.

VOICE   See *active voice* and *passive voice.*

WH- QUESTION   See *information question.*

WRITTEN MEDIUM   All the literature and other writing serving as a means of transferring information in a culture or social group. Compare *oral medium.* See also *discourse.*

YES-NO QUESTION   A question that is phrased in such a way as to elicit an answer of only *yes* or *no,* as in *Are you happy?* Compare *information question.*

INDEX